AGAINST
THE
PEOPLE

AGAINST THE PEOPLE

How Ford Nation Is Dismantling Ontario

edited by
Bryan Evans & Carlo Fanelli

Fernwood Publishing
Halifax & Winnipeg

Copyright 2025 © Bryan Evans and Carlo Fanelli

All rights reserved. No part of this book may be reproduced or transmitted in any form by any means without permission in writing from the publisher, except by a reviewer, who may quote brief passages in a review.

Copyediting: Karen May Clark
Development editing: Wayne Antony
Cover design: John van der Woode
Text design: Brenda Conroy
Printed and bound in Canada

Published by Fernwood Publishing
Halifax and Winnipeg
2970 Oxford Street, Halifax, Nova Scotia, B3L 2W4
www.fernwoodpublishing.ca

Fernwood Publishing Company Limited gratefully acknowledges the financial support of the Government of Canada through the Canada Book Fund and the Canada Council for the Arts. We acknowledge the Province of Manitoba for support through the Manitoba Publishers Marketing Assistance Program and the Book Publishing Tax Credit. We acknowledge the Nova Scotia Department of Communities, Culture and Heritage for support through the Publishers Assistance Fund.

Library and Archives Canada Cataloguing in Publication
Title: Against the people : how Ford nation is dismantling Ontario / edited by Bryan Evans & Carlo Fanelli.
Names: Evans, Bryan, 1960- editor. | Fanelli, Carlo, 1984- editor.
Description: Includes bibliographical references and index.
Identifiers: Canadiana 20240534484 | ISBN 9781773637242 (softcover)
Subjects: LCSH: Ford, Doug, 1964- | LCSH: Progressive Conservative Party of Ontario. | LCSH:
Ontario—Politics and government. | LCSH: Ontario—Economic policy. | CSH: Ontario—Politics and government—2003-
Classification: LCC FC3080.2 .A43 2025 | DDC 971.3/05—dc23

CONTENTS

Acknowledgements viii
About the Contributors ix

1 **The Class Politics of Conservative Rule** *Bryan Evans & Carlo Fanelli* ... 1
   From Family Compact to Ford Nation 2
   Ford Nation Populism 8
   Revealing Ford, Resisting Ford 10

2 **Manufacturing a Fiscal Crisis** *Venai Raniga* 13
   Economic Performance 13
   Ford's Fiscal Situation 20
   Austerity and Privatization, Not Adequate Funding 26

3 **Arts and Culture on Life Support** *Aylan Couchie* 28
   (Un)Welcome to Ford Nation 29
   Initial Cuts and Community Responses 30
   WTF?!: A Year of Significant Reductions 32
   Remix 2019: The Pandemic and Beyond 34
   OCAD University: A Microcosm of Wider Policy Impacts 36
   A Society Without Art? 39

4 **Schools for Sale** *Chris Chandler* 41
   Setting Up Public Education for Privatization 42
   Financial (Il)Literacy 46
   Funding Shortfalls 48
   Betraying Children's Futures 51

5 **Privatizing Ontario's Universities** *David Leadbeater* 53
   Phase One: Destabilizing Cuts and Privatization 54
   Phase Two: Laurentian–CCAA Debacle and Anti-Democratic Education Politics 58
   Phase Three: Hardened Neoliberalism and Blue-Ribbon Delusions 64
   A Truly Public Education 68

6 **Everyday Justice in Ford's Ontario** *Kathy Laird* 70
   Jeopardized Human Rights Enforcement 71
   Justice Delayed and Denied to Tenants and Landlords 71
   Understanding Tribunals 72
   The Human Rights Tribunal 76
   The Landlord Tenant Board 80
   Making Justice Inaccessible 83

7 Health Care SOS *Michael Hurley & Doug Allan* 85
Funding 86
Hospital Staffing 86
Hospital Bed Capacity 87
The Current Situation and Future Plans of the PCs 88
Health Care Privatization 92
Make Health Public 100

8 Unequal Ontario *Carlo Fanelli & Katherine Nastovski* 102
Legislating Worker Precarity 102
Rich Get Richer, Rest Get Poorer 108
Workers' Struggles Ahead 111
What's Left? 113

9 Why Are People in Ontario Hungry? *Maria Rio* 117
Before Ford 118
The Ford Era 121
Challenges for the Non-Profit Sector 125
From Palliative Care to Hunger Cure 129

10 Bulldozing Indigenous Lands *Dayna Nadine Scott & Dania Ahmed* ... 132
The Breathing Lands 132
Legal and Historical Context of Indigenous–Provincial Relationships 133
Structural Changes in the Ford Government 135
Fast Tracking Critical Mineral Extraction 136
The Integrated EV-Supply-Chain Dream 137
Indigenous Resistance and Assertions of Jurisdiction 138
Indigenous Sovereignty and the Future of Lands and Resources in Ontario's Far North 141

11 Child Care When Convenient
Rachel Vickerson, Carolyn Ferns & Brooke Richardson 143
Child Care in Ontario 143
Ontario Child Care Pre-Ford 144
CARE Tax Credit: 2018–2020 145
Municipal Cost Sharing 146
2020–2022: COVID-19 147
Canada-Wide Early Learning and Child Care Agreement: 2022–2024 148
Advocacy in the Ford Era 152
Blame and Credit-Taking 154
Uncovering Ford's Real Agenda and Protecting Hard-Won Gains 156

12 Riding the "Gravy Train" *William Paul* 157
    Early Start 157
    Highway 413 and the Bradford Bypass 159
    Greenbelt Follies 160
    Boundary Issues 164
    Whose Health? 165
    Buying Influence 167
    For the People 169

13 Locking in Unsustainable Development *Mark Winfield* 171
    The First Ford Government: 2018–2022 172
    The Second Ford Government: 2022+ 175
    Megaprojects Trump the Environment 179

14 De-Democratizing Ontario *Tom McDowell* 182
    Parliamentary Democracy 182
    Ford Government and Parliamentary Procedure 183
    Dismantling Public Health Care 185
    Constitutional Authority and the Restructuring of Local Government 186
    Marginalizing the Legislature 188
    Reaching for Authoritarianism 191

15 Strong Mayors, Weak Cities *Carlo Fanelli & Ryan Kelpin* 194
    Upending Local Democracy 195
    Mayor of Ontario, Premier of Toronto 199
    Municipal Futures 202

16 Building Tenant Power *Lily Xia* 207
    Ford's Policies 207
    Tenants Fighting Back 213
    Supporting Tenants' Rights 218

17 Fighting Ford *John Clarke* 219
    Harris and Ford: Common Sense? 219
    Fighting Back 222
    Class Compromise 226
    The Struggle Ahead 228

Endnotes 231
Index 271

ACKNOWLEDGEMENTS

The editors wish to gratefully acknowledge the Herculean efforts of the authors, as well as the staff at Fernwood Publishing, who moved mountains to expedite the production of this book under extreme time constraints. Specifically, we thank Art Bouman, Anumeha Gokhale, Karen May Clark and Wayne Antony. We would be remiss not to further acknowledge Wayne Antony, who, as acquisitions editor, not only met our proposal for this book with great enthusiasm but whose comments and suggestions greatly strengthened its rigour. We wish to also thank Julie Wilson for her research assistance. The authors also thank the Dean's Office, Faculty of Arts, Toronto Metropolitan University, for their contribution to the production of this book. Finally, Carlo would like to thank Agostino, Leonardo, Luna and Samantha for their patience and support of this work.

We would like to dedicate this book to all struggling for a more equal, just and better future in Ontario and beyond.

ABOUT THE CONTRIBUTORS

Dania Ahmed is a Juris Doctor candidate at Osgoode Hall Law School with a strong interest in human rights and environmental justice. Her academic and professional endeavours are marked by contributions that explore the intersections of social equity, environmental policies, access to justice and community mobilization. Dania is interested in the many ways in which legal frameworks can be used for societal betterment.

Doug Allan has been a union researcher for the past thirty-two years, much of it specializing in Ontario health care public policy and collective bargaining.

Chris Chandler is a vice-president of the Toronto local of the Ontario Secondary School Teachers' Federation and has worked in public education as a teacher and union activist for almost thirty years, witnessing first-hand the changes to Ontario's schools wrought by five different provincial governments. Chris's professional interests as a trade unionist have focused on occupational health and safety within the education sector and other industries; the intersection of political action by unions with community organizing; and leveraging the collective power of unions to pressure employers to reduce greenhouse gas emissions and electricity use in their business operations.

John Clarke became involved with anti-poverty organizing when he helped to form a union of the unemployed in London, Ontario, in 1983. In 1990, he became an organizer with the Ontario Coalition Against Poverty (OCAP) and held this position for twenty-eight years. He has since been the Packer Visitor in Social Justice at York University.

Aylan Couchie (she/her) is a Nishnaabekwe interdisciplinary artist, curator and writer hailing from Nipissing First Nation in Northern Ontario. She is in her fourth year of pursuing a PhD in cultural studies at Queen's University. She splits her time living and working between her home community and Toronto, where she is employed as assistant professor of Indigenous Digital Art, Culture and Media at the University of Toronto.

Bryan Evans is a professor in the department of politics and public administration at Toronto Metropolitan University and is a member of the steering committee for the Ontario office of the Canadian Centre for Policy

Alternatives. His research is concerned with business lobbying, public interest advocacy, democratic administration and political economy.

Carlo Fanelli is an associate professor of work and labour studies at York University. He is the author of *Megacity Malaise: Neoliberalism, Labour and Public Services in Toronto*; co-author of *From Consent to Coercion: The Continuing Assault Against Labour*; and editor of *Alternate Routes: A Journal of Critical Social Research*.

Carolyn Ferns is the policy coordinator at the Ontario Coalition for Better Child Care. Carolyn worked for over ten years at the Childcare Resource and Research Unit, where she co-authored the series, *Early Childhood Education and Care in Canada*. Carolyn has a bachelor's degree in early childhood education and a master's degree in early childhood studies. She is a member of the Board of Directors of both Child Care Now and the Childcare Resource and Research Unit.

Michael Hurley is president of the 40,000-member Ontario Council of Hospital Unions–CUPE. He is a co-author of four studies published in *New Solutions* on the Ontario Health Care System and its workforce.

Ryan Kelpin has a PhD in political science from York University. Focused on the relationship between Ontario and Toronto from 1996 to 2023, his dissertation examined how the province routinely utilized its constitutional powers to restructure Toronto's democratic decision-making institutions and processes in the name of neoliberalism. Ryan teaches at York University and Seneca Polytechnic, contributes to *Canadian Dimension* and *The Grind* and has published in the *Canadian Journal of Urban Research*, *Alternate Routes* and the *Journal of Australian Political Economy*.

Kathy Laird is a member of Tribunal Watch Ontario, a public interest organization that monitors accessibility and fairness at Ontario's adjudicative tribunals. She has served as counsel to the Chair of the Human Rights Tribunal of Ontario and as an adjudicator at the Human Rights Board of Inquiry, the Pay Equity Hearings Tribunal and the Child and Family Services Review Board. She was executive director of the Ontario Human Rights Legal Support Centre and litigated as a legal clinic lawyer before numerous tribunals and courts at all levels.

David Leadbeater was an associate professor of economics before being one of over two hundred faculty and staff terminated in 2021 by Laurentian University. His teaching and research interests are in the economic development of Canada, urban and regional economics, labour economics, colonialism and economic theory. He was active in Laurentian's faculty association and in Sudbury's labour movement, and co-authored, with Caitlin K. Kiernan, the report, "Decline and Crisis in Ontario's Northern Universities and Arts Education," for the Canadian Centre for Policy Alternatives.

Tom McDowell is a lecturer in the department of politics and public administration at Toronto Metropolitan University. His research critically examines the policy and institutional impacts of neoliberalism. He is the author of *Neoliberal Parliamentarism: The Decline of Parliament at the Ontario Legislature*, and has recently published peer-reviewed articles in the *Journal of Social Policy*, *Critical Policy Studies*, *The Canadian Journal of Political Science*, *Studies in Political Economy* and the *Canadian Review of Sociology*.

Katherine Nastovski is an assistant professor in work and labour studies in the Department of Social Science at York University. Her research focuses on struggles for workers' justice, labour transnationalism and the relevance of colonialism, imperialism and racism for thinking about workers' organizing.

William Paul is the editor of *School Magazine*, a publication devoted to improving school funding, critical pedagogy and community engagement. He was once a teacher and special education consultant with the Board of Education for the city of York and a principal with the Toronto District School Board. From these positions, he has watched the decline of public goods with keen interest.

Venai Raniga is a political researcher with the Canadian Union of Public Employees (CUPE), Canada's largest union. Based in Toronto, he is committed to being in struggle with the working class and un/learning through political resistance. With over a decade of experience advocating for economic and social justice, he has been involved in community and labour movements using research to inform policy and drive positive change.

Brooke Richardson is a care activist, scholar and mother motivated by the belief that good care is foundational to meaningful lives and a democratic society. She is an assistant professor in child and youth studies at Mount Saint Vincent University and adjunct faculty in the Department of Sociology at Brock University. Her research and scholarly work focus on the privatization of child care in Canada, political representations of the child care policy "problem," reconceptualization and reassertion of care in early childhood education and reimagination of child welfare systems through an ethics of care lens.

Maria Rio, the CEO of Further Together, is a passionate advocate for social and economic justice. Having come to Canada as a refugee at an early age, Maria accessed charitable services and experienced poverty; this inspired her to dedicate her career to helping others. Over a decade of experience in fundraising has shaped Maria into a prominent voice in the sector, with a focus on social justice, dismantling oppression and community-centric fundraising.

Dayna Nadine Scott is a professor at Osgoode Hall Law School and the Faculty of Environmental and Urban Change at York University. She held the York Research Chair in Environmental Law and Justice in the Green Economy from 2018 to 2023. As director of Osgoode's Environmental Justice and Sustainability Clinic, Dayna has been working alongside the leadership of Neskantaga First Nation since 2017.

Rachel Vickerson is the policy and project manager at Child Care Now, Canada's national child care advocacy association, and has been involved in the fight for universal child care and decent work for educators for several years. She has held previous positions with the Association of Early Childhood Educators Ontario, the Ontario Coalition for Better Child Care and the Childcare Resource and Research Unit. She has a master's degree in public policy from the University of Toronto.

Mark Winfield is a professor of environmental and urban change at York University. He is also co-chair of the faculty's Sustainable Energy Initiative and co-ordinator of the joint Master of Environmental Studies/Juris Doctor program offered in conjunction with Osgoode Hall Law School. He has published articles, book chapters and reports on a wide range of topics, including climate change, environment and energy law and policy. He is co-editor of *Sustainable Energy Transitions in Canada*.

Lily Xia has been a tenant organizer since 2018, fighting against mass evictions in Ottawa with the Herongate Tenant Coalition. Now organizing in Toronto, she continues to support working-class tenant solidarity and struggles against landlords and bosses.

1

THE CLASS POLITICS OF CONSERVATIVE RULE

Bryan Evans and Carlo Fanelli

LED BY DOUG FORD SINCE 2018, Ontario's Conservative government is the latest iteration of the province's decades-long trajectory of neoliberal restructuring. The underlying principles of neoliberalism are: tax cuts for the wealthy and corporations (so they'll invest in more machinery and workers); less government (because the market knows better); less unionized labour (so workers cost less); fewer regulations (for efficiency reasons); and more private-sector service delivery (because public services are costly). With it in place, inflation-targeting by the central bank, regressive tax reform, privatization and contracting out, weakened protective legislation and new restrictions on the rights of workers have flourished. In the time since the neoliberal revolution of the 1970s, income and wealth inequality have spiked, economic volatility has worsened and life has become ever more insecure. This is as much the case in Ontario as around the world.[1] Claims that a rising tide lifts all boats have proven to be entirely misleading.

In the elections of 2018 and 2022, the Progressive Conservative campaign slogans were "For the People" and "Get It Done." The question is: "Just what was getting done and for which people?" This book grapples with answers to these questions. The Ford Nation Conservatives are a departure from Ontario's long-held, self-regarding view as being a place of propriety, moderation and tempered progressivism — a polity where, in the decades following the Second World War, publicness, a public sphere and public interest were broadly understood across society as the necessary elements for a well-functioning society and economy. In this respect, the Ford Conservatives are a departure unlike any in modern Ontario politics.

From Family Compact to Ford Nation

The economic and ideological moorings of mid- to late-twentieth-century Ontario are now largely forgotten. The contemporary Ontario Progressive Conservatives, the party of Ford Nation, is a vehicle to move Ontario toward a deep market fundamentalism and thereby remake how citizens relate to their government. The effect is to ultimately accept that there is no such thing as a social contract binding different components of society to one another. It is, in many ways, an Ontario version of Margaret Thatcher's proclamation, "There is no such thing as society," but there is always business. Consequently, the Ford Conservatives benefit from a dimming of the relevance of politics to the lived lives of large parts of the population and particularly to the working class. While the power of business has been expanding for decades, the experience of politics and democracy for ordinary citizens is one of "reduced power, influence and effectiveness" in the context of limited economic regulation, public services and programs.[2] The expansion of a broad-based apolitics and anti-politics — general disinterest to outright avoidance — is the result. For many, those who remain engaged seek only to advance their specific interests.

It is interesting to think of the Ford Conservatives from a historical perspective by reaching back to the time of the "Family Compact" of the late eighteenth century. The Family Compact was a hand-picked political and economic ruling class. Upper Canada's first Lieutenant-Governor, John Graves Simcoe, fully exploited his powers to appoint persons to office and allocate benefits in an effort to create a "regional oligarchy."[3] Members of Simcoe's inner circle were awarded land grants of 3,000 to 5,000 acres.[4] The main popular grievance was the abuse of public administration as expressed through a "narrow and selfish" distribution of patronage.[5] A substantial range of positions attached to the Upper Canadian state were dispensed as patronage: executive and legislative councils, "judges, heads of executive departments ... district sheriffs, justices of the peace, coroners, county registrars, customs commissioners, district immigration officers, 1,500 militia officers."[6] The patronage, even corruption, of the nineteenth and early-twentieth centuries embedded within the Upper Canadian state and its culture endured into the present.

So while the Ford Conservatives did not invent patronage by any stretch of the imagination, it appears that well-connected insiders are benefiting materially from these networks of the wealthy.[7] Moreover, the rather opaque decisions which led to the opening of parcels of land in the Greenbelt, the effective privatization of Ontario Place to a for-profit corporation, and the closure and proposed move of the Ontario Science Centre certainly reinforce such an impression.[8] Ford's own open musings about curating judicial appointments to ensure only conservative-thinking persons are appointed is a case in point of explicit politicization.[9]

The Ford Nation Conservatives owe the traction of their political and ideological orientation to the economic crisis of the 1970s and the de-industrialization of Ontario which followed through the 1990s, including the decline of assumed economic growth and some degree of economic inclusion. Today, Ontario is, of course, a vastly different place than it was during the post-WWII "golden years," where an ethos of redistributive politics largely prevailed. It is in this historical context that we must situate the current Ford government as part and parcel of the remaking of Ontario's political economy and consequently the re-making of Ontario's Progressive Conservative party.

At various points in Ontario's history, but particularly in the decades following 1945 to the mid-1980s, the capacities of the Ontario government, often reluctantly and through various class and other struggles and contestations, electoral and otherwise, were directed toward building public education (universities, colleges), public health care (hospitals, social assistance), an array of cultural and popular public assets, and even roads, highways and other vital infrastructure. In short, it was an Ontario where social and economic development policies were directed at modernizing an industrial economy. And that development required ensuring some mobility for working-class Ontarians. While this was always uneven and unequally distributed, the elements were put in place to allow for an unprecedented degree of social and economic inclusivity and progress. Not all social groups had a seat at the table, but there was a provincial state able to apply its legal and fiscal powers to reshape what had been a remarkably staid and unequal society. That project officially ended in 1995, with the election of Progressive Conservative Premier Mike Harris and the "Common Sense Revolution" (CSR) that followed.[10]

Of course, the antecedents of what came to be called neoliberalism emerged in the 1970s, as governments across Canada and around the world, struggling to respond to both high inflation and high unemployment, shaped the economic and political history of the decade and beyond. It was in this cauldron of economic crisis, the most serious since the Great Depression of the 1930s, that the material and political foundations of new conservative movements solidified and gained traction. Like elsewhere, Ontario governments engaged in severe public sector austerity and fiscal constraint, even as workers were bearing the brunt through wage freezes and rising costs of living. All of this reflected the shifting balance of class power in the advanced capitalist economies. The so-called Golden Age of Capitalism was fading, but fading only as business organized in unprecedented ways to roll back the gains of this period.

Yet that early variant of neoliberalism was constrained. In Ontario, for instance, a Progressive Conservative government led by Bill Davis proposed, in response to the rise in petroleum prices, that the government purchase 25 percent of Suncor Ltd. shares for $650 million. It was an attempt to recreate a provincial version of the then-popular federal crown corporation Petro-Canada. But things soon changed. By 1984, treasurer Larry Grossman emphasized a greater role for the market in the production and delivery of public goods and services: "We must invite more private sector sharing of what has come to be considered as public sector responsibilities.... Given finite taxpayers' dollars, we must provide greater latitude."[11] Although the ideological turn within the party was well underway, Ontario's Progressive Conservatives remained broadly pragmatic, right-of-centre, unwilling or unable to make a break from the pragmatic, capitalist centrism that characterized the party's time in government from 1943 to 1985.

Electoral defeat in 1985 and a disastrous result in the 1987 election set in motion the first reinvention of the Ontario Progressive Conservative party since the early 1940s. The end result was the CSR platform that marked a sharp shift to the right where government was explicitly identified as the problem confronting Ontario. The CSR platform executed an unprecedented assault on Ontario's post-war welfare state, including: i) a 30 percent cut to provincial income taxes; ii) a 20 percent reduction to total government spending; iii) the reduction and elimination of various regulations, laws and taxes deemed to impede economic growth; iv) a shrinking of the Ontario public sector workforce as a proportion of the total economy; and v) balanced budget legislation and new marketization standards.[12] The abandonment of pragmatic centre-right politics defined the CSR.

The "Red Toryism," characterizing the Ontario Progressive Conservatives from 1943 to 1995 — one that accepted a mixed public and private sector economy, some strengthened labour rights, social entitlements and more — was gone. In the eyes of the Harris Conservatives, as with Ford, economic prosperity could only be restored by applying the legal and fiscal powers of the Ontario government toward facilitating business profits. Taxes, public expenditures and regulations had to be cut to facilitate a shift in power and resources away from workers generally to the wealthy and business community. In this regard, the CSR marked the emergence of a new party.

It is in this historical context that the Ford Nation Conservatives share continuity and change with the Harris Common Sense Revolution. First, and most obviously, the Harris and Ford governments are characterized by a certain market fundamentalism. Business interests are sacrosanct and understood as the only credible foundation to the economy. Second, with respect to public finances, both governments have been reluctant to increase public expenditures.[13] However, while the CSR sought across-the-board cuts in public expenditures and taxes, the Ford Conservatives have increased public expenditures and subsidies for private businesses, especially for large infrastructure projects, while simultaneously restraining public expenditures in health, education and other social programs. Third, while sharing parallels with Harris, the Ford government has demonstrated a particular affinity for more overtly authoritarian tendencies to override the public interest.[14]

Where the two governments differ is with respect to the strategy applied to governing. The Harris Conservatives invested heavily in policy agenda and program building which culminated in the CSR platform. The CSR was clear in framing the problems confronting Ontario — government interference, undisciplined workers and welfare cheats — and how they were to be dealt with — via tax cuts, a shrinking of the size and scope of the provincial government and labour market deregulation. The Ford Conservatives did not present the electorate with such a clear and ideologically grounded statement. Instead, it was a return to improvised policy positions with no overarching framework nor a coherent vision. Various gimmicks, like "Buck-a-Beer," free licence plate stickers, cash payouts to parents of young students and anti-carbon tax stickers on gas pumps, created the impression of a government moving from issue to issue with no overall objective.

With respect to the privatization of public assets, the Ford government has been much more ambitious than its predecessors, controversially moving to sell off or close public assets and lands, privatize and contract out health care,[15] child care[16] and education,[17] and contravene the *Canadian Charter of Rights and Freedoms* by pushing through municipal restructuring[18] and anti-labour legislation.[19] The motivation for doing so appears unapologetically to provide wide-ranging benefits — from public tax dollars to new decision-making powers — to developer and other business interests.

In contrast to the bombastic approach of the CSR, the Ford Conservatives' agenda has largely occurred via attrition, leaving vacancies unfilled and underspending—which is to say, by stealth. The Ford government quickly got to work cancelling the province's new cap-and-trade program, a process that is estimated to have cost the province more than $10 billion in lost revenues, legal fees and compensation for cancelled contracts.[20] The Financial Accountabiltiy Office (FAO) of Ontario estimates that, since forming government, the Ford Conservatives have maintained a steady state of austerity, underspending to the tune of $5.9 billion on social services annually.

Despite being the largest in the province's history, the 2022–23 budget saw Ontario's total spending per capita stagnate at $13,065, the lowest in Canada and 20 percent below the Canadian average. Ontario's program spending per capita was also the lowest — $12,138 versus an average of $15,389 — while Ontario's tax revenue as a share of GDP was the fourth lowest, declining from 15.2 percent in 2017–18 to 14 percent by 2022–23.[21] The FAO estimates that the government's planned spending would fall $3.7 billion short of what is required to fund existing programs and commitments by 2026–27. This means the Ontario government will have to choose between increasing funding, or, more likely, cutting services further in the coming years. Despite Conservatives' long-standing concerns about the *size* of government, these were always secondary to its *scope*; in this regard, public monies spent on underwriting business investment, even doubling the size and cost of premier's office staff — unlike spending on public services — is totally compatible with Ford government's use of taxpayer dollars.[22]

The FAO's Economic and Budget Outlook report for 2023–24 to 2028–29 also found that, due to continued disinvestment, government spending will fall short in virtually every sector: health care, education, postsecondary, justice and social services. The government's budget also reveals less-than-planned spending on infrastructure projects and capital funding for housing programs.[23] It is estimated the Ford government will underspend $21 billion in health care alone over the next five years as hospital capacity, long-term and home care, surgical waitlists and wait times, emergency departments, and the health-sector workforce crisis worsens. The Council of Ontario Universities has recently warned that they receive the lowest amount of operating funding of all provinces, 35 percent below the Canadian per full-time student average, which has precipitated a postsecondary crisis of unprecedented proportions.[24] In fact, a 2023 report by the Office of the Ontario Auditor General raised concerns about more than a dozen value-for-money audits, including: the higher costs of for-profit, health care staffing agencies; longer emergency room wait times and the continuing crisis in long-term care; weak environmental oversights and the lack of public inputs; absence of tourism, arts and cultural sector supports after the COVID-19 pandemic; and the decision to move the Science Centre based on "preliminary and incomplete costing information."[25]

In a similar vein, the number of Ontarians with developmental disabilities waiting for supportive housing has also grown by 10,000 since the Ford government took office, while funding for core services for children with autism covers less than 20 percent of the over 70,000 children registered in the Ontario Autism Program. More than 800,000 adults and children accessed a food bank in Ontario between April 1, 2022, and March 31, 2023 — an increase of 38 percent over the previous year and 60 percent over pre-pandemic levels.[26] In real terms, social assistance rates have never been lower. What's more, it is estimated that some 45 percent of Ontario households spend 30 percent or more of their total income on shelter, the highest on record and the highest rate across the country.

It is little wonder, then, that most Ontarians believe they are worse off today than when the Ford government came to power. A poll conducted by the Angus Reid Institute asking Ontario residents if their government was doing a "good job" on key issues like health care, inflation, housing affordability, education and more, saw that number drop from 42 percent in 2019 to 23 percent by 2024.[27] The scale and immediacy of this social crisis will inevitably leave a generational scar.

Ford Nation Populism

There has been a great deal of confusion surrounding the politics of Doug Ford, from those who argue he is neither a conservative nor a populist to others who perceive a pragmatic shift to the centre in the absence of any ingrained ideological underpinnings.[28] But, this mistakes appearance for reality. Upon Ford ascending to the helm of the Conservative party after a contentious election process that saw claims of voting irregularities and shifting alliances, a stream of articles followed arguing Ford's win signalled the arrival of Trump-style populism in Canada's most populous province. While sharing certain similarities — extreme wealth, hostility towards the press, combative rallies and anti-establishment diatribes — Ford did not share, at least on the surface, the racial intolerance, paranoia and anti-immigrant sentiment that predominated the populist movements in Turkey, Italy, the Philippines, US and elsewhere. Ford and other populists did, however, share a penchant for simple slogans, hyperbole, little regard for facts and an appeal to "folks" who felt left behind.

This is because the political imaginary of Ford Nation was from the very beginning heterogeneous and malleable. Ford's brand of "retail politics" — that is, the folksy, everyday salesmanship of government policy forged in his time as a Conservative party operator and former Toronto city councillor — offered to make life easier in small but measurable ways that expelled the special interests of elites and cleaned-up government corruption. Ford's brand of personalized, "I'll-get-this-done-for-you" politics avoided nativist and xenophobic dog-whistle politics that had characterized right-wing populism elsewhere, instead emphasizing pocketbook style "respect for taxpayers" that centred on economic insecurity. In this way, Ford's brand of conservatism falls into the long tradition of Canadian populism characterized by a fierce ideological commitment to market fundamentalism and neoliberal austerity.[29]

While populism is more of an approach to politics than it is an ideological orientation, its main function is to split society into two antagonistic groups: "the people" versus a corrupt elite, or average folks versus the "fat cats." It is in this context that the Ford government, with its rallying cry against the "gravy train," parallels the United Farmers and Maritime Rights movements, to Social Credit, the Reform Party and even the CCF.[30] Ford's own approach has contributed to a politics that views opponents as enemies, which has emboldened a greater willingness to challenge democratic norms, and even break the law, as seen with his government's repeated use of the notwithstanding clause.

Another aspect that distinguishes Ford's populism is its diversity, which includes a multiplicity of racialized groups, immigrants and religious denominations. Many of Ontario's most economically disadvantaged were central to the identity of Ford Nation. In both their 2018 and 2022 electoral victories, the Conservatives won not only in the predominantly white rural districts of southern Ontario, but especially in the multiracial suburbs of Toronto, exurban communities and industrial towns. This dominance had historical precedents for Ford. Toronto's 2014 municipal election saw his strongest support among people who identified as East Asian, South Asian and Eastern European. Ford's support was also strongest among those with religious and socially conservative views.[31] It is little surprise, then, that Ford's successes among low-income and racialized persons replicated these earlier patterns at the provincial level. The Conservatives carried every seat in the predominantly racialized communities of Brampton and Mississauga and won four seats in Scarborough where racialized persons make up three-quarters of the population.

But Ford's success also went further, transcending individualized grievances and espousing a particular form of class politics: "He doesn't deny the existence of climate change but insists that working people shouldn't be made to pay for ambitious carbon reduction schemes."[32] And herein lies Ford's success. People are motivated by a variety of issues — from faith and politics, to age, sex, economic security and more — and Ford's conservative class approach collectively mobilized people's individualized experiences. Ford's message hit home with a working class "estrange[d] from the cultural preoccupations of the left," with its "social justice rhetoric that draws heavily on academic vocabulary." As Kory Teneycke, the 2018 campaign manager put it, "'There's been a shift in the things that the progressive left used to talk about'.... 'But they've become less connected to working people.'"[33] Indeed, Conservatives were able to successfully win the votes of workers in former NDP strongholds, like Windsor, Hamilton, Timmins, London and Oshawa, areas that experienced sharp manufacturing losses.[34] Ford Nation also won support where incomes have fallen the most since the 1970s, which also tend to be among the most heterogeneous.

Revealing Ford, Resisting Ford

As the chapters that make up this book reveal, the Ford government's approach to public policy has been largely driven by the interests of business elites over regular Ontarians. This book is less the last word than it is an evolving testament to the damaging and long-term impacts of Ford Nation on Ontario. Chapters only begin to scratch the surface on issues related to gender and race relations, Indigenous communities, civil and political rights, public spaces, agriculture, manufacturing, finance and a host of other topics that no one volume could possibly cover but are equally important as the issues discussed here.

The Ford government's electoral success shows that working-class conservatism can thrive in places other than the white, Christian, rural heartlands most often imagined as the "natural" home of conservativism. Indeed, Erin O'Toole, former leader of the federal Conservative party, was explicit about chasing votes from unionized workers — a task which his successor, Pierre Poilievre, has continued with early success to run with. As Simon Lewsen explains it: "Ford's political style ... is markedly different from classical starched-collar conservatism or from the more virulent brand of right-wing populism that has recently swept the globe. It is a practical recipe, using whatever ingredients are at hand. But it may have a longer shelf life."[35] Given its success, there is growing evidence that suggests Ford's made-in-Ontario approach to populism is a recipe other conservative parties and governments in North America and elsewhere are looking to emulate.[36]

Previous governments of all partisan hues, with the exception of the 1995–2003 Conservatives, were all, in various ways, concerned with the general public interest. That is to say, they were all interested in implementing some public programs and policies that sought to integrate the social and economic interests of non-elite sections of Ontario society. While this was always limited to the acceptable boundaries of capitalism, there was nevertheless a role for the public sphere in pursuing the public interest. Of course, Ontario has always been a business-first province: patronage for party supporters, special treatment for politically and economically important interests, privileged access to the policy process for some but not others. This is just the reality in our Westminster model of colonial, parliamentary rule. But the Ford Conservatives have taken this to an unashamedly new level: deep austerity, regressive legislation and a privileging of business on all fronts.

The Ford Conservatives, no doubt unwittingly, have taken their playbook directly from the eighteenth-century Family Compact — a twenty-first-century effort to redistribute resources to a small but powerful business elite. As the Old Testament saying goes, whoever has shall be given more. It is this practice of openly allocating public assets and resources to Ontario business elites that marks a qualitative shift in the practice of governing in modern Ontario history. Processes are murky, if not simply unclear. There is little to no effort even at performative virtue signalling with the Ford Conservatives. Shrewd and calculating, the Ford Nation platform's critical part is building on the broad indifference of a large plurality of Ontario's electorate with all things political. Forty years of incremental restructuring have left a deep and pessimistic mark on the mass perception of the formal arena of government and politics. Understood historically, this cynicism is not surprising given that western, electoral systems are not, and never have been, all that democratic to begin with — assuming democracy is understood to mean something more than determining which party will govern every four to five years. Indeed, in the election of 2022, less than half of eligible Ontarians bothered to vote, the lowest participation rate since Confederation. This voter turnout is revealing and gives a good indication of how everyday Ontarians relate to and understand the role of the province in shaping everyday life.

Indeed, Ontario's working class today is more diverse and heterogeneous than ever: from unionized and non-unionized workers to public and private sector workers, blue- and white-collar workers, gig workers, the unwaged, and everything in between. Since the Ford government has come to power, Ontario is more clearly divided between those who live off the work of others, and those who must work longer and harder to keep their heads above water. But class identity, historically weak and uneven in Canada, is confoundingly weaker than ever. In the face of the wider retreat from class, especially among left and social democratic forces, Conservatives have filled this void. If hope is to be found, it will be in moving beyond forms of protest that abstractly indicate what alternatives might be capable of, to fighting back in a concrete way that unleashes the potential for that strength.[37] Organizing solely at specific workplaces or around specific issues and constituencies will not add up to the kind of strength and organization needed to surmount the new Gilded Age. Doing so requires an alternative class project with feet inside and outside of unions and firmly rooted in activist communities that can challenge the limitations of representative institutions in a way that builds class solidarity on the lived experiences of working people. Ultimately, Ontario's working class, like workers everywhere, are the owners of their history, the architects of their liberation. In that endeavour, we are beginning again. New organizations, programs and strategies will assuredly emerge and coalesce over time as an era of sharpened struggles over work, wealth redistribution and climate change push to ask serious questions about what can be done.

2

MANUFACTURING A FISCAL CRISIS

Venai Raniga

THE PAST SIX YEARS OF THE FORD CONSERVATIVE GOVERNMENT have been punctuated by a series of overlapping crises, such as the COVID-19 pandemic, health care staffing crisis, affordable housing shortage, recession and inflation. While the global crisis of declining economic growth has created pressures within Ontario, the Ford Conservative government has also authored many of its own injuries.[1] The government's narrow focus on the pursuit of profit above all else has resulted in severe consequences for struggling Ontarians who rely on the safety net of public services.

Capitalizing on these crises, the government has ushered in a wave of austerity measures and privatization. In the face of this reality, the government states it is providing record spending. However, it uses a sleight of hand by not adjusting for population growth or inflation when making such a claim. Once population growth and inflation are accounted for, it is clear that spending has not been record-breaking. Moreover, the province is wealthy and has the fiscal capacity to meet the needs of its people but deliberately chooses not to.

Economic Performance

The Conservative government's budget austerity does not reflect Ontario's actual financial capacity. As the epicentre of Canadian industry, Ontario represents 37 percent of the Canadian economy.[2] In 2022, the economy surpassed the one trillion-dollar mark. A trillion dollars is so large that it often defies comprehension. To put it into perspective, Ontario's economy is larger than those of Switzerland, Belgium or Singapore.[3] Similarly, adjusted for inflation and population growth, Ontario's economy is four times wealthier than it was 100 years ago.[4]

Economic Growth and Income Inequality

Ontario has demonstrated resilience in the face of external challenges, such as the COVID-19 pandemic and supply chain disruptions. However, the economy is not solely shaped by external forces. Self-inflicted wounds, resulting from the government's myopic policy decisions, have also contributed to the challenges. Despite Ontario's diverse economy, skilled workforce and strategic location, the benefits of its prosperity are unevenly distributed. Many families face rising living costs, stagnant wages and precarious employment in an increasingly gig-based economy.[5] There is a stark and growing contrast between those who were able to capture excess profits over the past few years and the struggles of everyday Ontarians. This disparity illustrates the outcomes of neoliberal ideology, which emphasizes free market principles and wealth accumulation for a select few. This growing inequality illustrates the consequences of prioritizing profit over investing in public services that support all citizens.

In service to this ideology, the Ford government has introduced a staggering twelve pieces of legislation over the past six years aimed at reducing corporate regulation, collectively saving businesses an estimated $1.2 billion annually.[6] These policies — from caps on developer funds used by school boards to reductions in environmental protection and limitations on occupational health and safety regulations — are designed to boost corporate profits at the expense of public services and social programs.[7] These savings are in addition to the nearly $10 billion dollars in annual tax breaks and subsidies for corporations, including mining and beer companies.[8]

Yet, prioritizing corporate interests over the well-being of working families has not boded well for economic growth. Adjusted for inflation and population growth, Ontario has seen an economic decline of 0.9 percent during Premier Ford's tenure from 2018 to 2023. This decline contrasts with the positive growth in other provinces during the same period, with British Columbia and Quebec reporting increases of 2.4 percent and 1.7 percent, respectively.[9] The strong economic performances of British Columbia and Quebec were accompanied by initiatives quite opposite to Ford's, including increasing taxes on the wealthy and businesses, enacting legislative changes to make it easier for workers to join a union and providing billions in direct cash transfers to households to help ease the cost-of-living crisis.[10]

Ontario's negative economic growth has led many commentators to raise alarm bells on issues of labour productivity. Although GDP per capita trends provide valuable information about average income, the economy cannot solely be measured by GDP growth or corporate profits. Other critical factors, such as income inequality or wage stagnation, must also be taken into consideration. Over the past four decades in much of the Global North, income for workers has declined in inflation-adjusted terms, despite economic expansion and rising GDP per capita.[11] This trend has worsened under Ford. Between 2019 and 2022, most of the income growth in Ontario accrued to the wealthiest people. If we divide households into five groups, the top group, the richest 20 percent, saw their income increase by over 13 percent from $258,400 to $291,300, while the average growth for the rest of households was 5 percent.[12] Ford's concentrated focus on the well-being of the wealthy and corporations, rather than addressing the needs of households, has resulted in the province having the highest level of income inequality among all Canadian provinces.[13] So, if one uses the indicators used by conservative economists, one finds that Ontario, during Ford's term, does not even meet their GDP standards. When using other standards, such as the economic well-being of working people, one finds that the economy has done even worse.

Labour

Under Ford's leadership, working conditions in Ontario have been systematically devalued and undermined.[14] One of Ford's first major acts as premier was the *Making Ontario Open for Business Act* in 2018. This legislation rolled back crucial employment and labour protections. Among the most egregious actions was the cancellation of the planned increase of minimum wage from $14 to $15 an hour — a vital adjustment that would have provided significant relief to low-income workers. Additionally, the bill removed Personal Emergency Leave, which previously guaranteed workers ten days of leave annually, including two paid days. This change has forced workers to choose between their health and their financial stability, which, during the pandemic, has been an ongoing choice for many. Ford also eliminated the Equal Pay for Equal Work provision, which applied to part-time, temporary and full-time workers.

In 2019, the Ford government implemented Bill 124, *Protecting a Sustainable Public Sector for Future Generations Act*, which restricted wage growth for public sector workers at 1 percent annually for three years. It has been widely criticized for exacerbating the staffing crisis within the public sector.[15] As inflation reached near-record levels, the wage cap eroded the real income of workers in critical sectors, such as health care.[16] This policy has not only diminished workers' purchasing power but has also contributed to the departure of skilled professionals from the public sector, where their presence is desperately needed. The current shortages in Ontario are forecasted to become far worse, including the need for 2,000 doctors, 33,000 nurses and 50,000 personal support workers.[17] These shortages have dire consequences; 11,000 people died in 2023 while waiting for surgeries and diagnostic scans.[18] The disconnect between unemployment and persistent job vacancies highlights a significant mismatch in the labour market, where jobs remain unfilled due to undesirable working conditions, low wages and insufficient investment in essential services. After a protracted legal battle with public sector unions, Bill 124 was ruled unconstitutional and repealed but the disregard for the rights of workers and the collective bargaining process was made clear. The Ford Conservative government undervalues the work of public sector employees and has a deep contempt for workers collectively organizing to better their working conditions.

In addition to the direct attack on labour via Ford's government policies, the labour market in Ontario has, over the past six years, faced multiple challenges that have revealed and exacerbated long-standing inequalities. During the peak of the COVID-19 pandemic in 2020, Ontario experienced an unprecedented economic downturn, resulting in the loss of over 400,000 jobs.[19] The sectors hit hardest were those already marked by precarity — namely retail, hospitality and various service industries — where workers are often underpaid, overworked and provided with insufficient benefits (most notably, paid sick days). These job losses not only underscored the fragility of employment for many Ontarians but also exposed the inadequacy of social safety nets designed to protect workers during such crises. Although most of these jobs were restored in the following year, the recovery was uneven, with many workers returning to jobs offering minimal stability or protection.

By early 2023, unemployment had fallen to near-record lows, suggesting a strong recovery. However, the subsequent rise in interest rates, a tool used by policymakers to address inflation, led to an increase in unemployment. Despite these higher unemployment rates, numerous job vacancies persist in the public sector, such as health care, education and social services.

For many employers, these job vacancies created ideal conditions to demand an increase in migrant workers to take low-paying jobs across Ontario. Rather than encourage employers to raise wages to attract employees, the federal Liberal government accommodated increasing migrant workers. This trend has raised significant concerns about the exploitation of these workers who rarely have a path to permanent residency status. A recent report by the United Nations denounced the Temporary Foreign Worker program as a "breeding ground for contemporary forms of slavery." The report highlighted egregious abuses, including wage theft, excessive work hours, limited breaks and physical abuse.[20] Accelerating these abuses in Ontario is the fact that proactive workplace inspections under the Ford government have plunged. The year before Ford took office, 3,507 inspections took place, but by 2023, this number dropped to 1,025 inspections, a decline of 71 percent.[21] This trend is symptomatic of the broader dehumanization and commodification of labour, where workers are seen and treated as disposable and their rights as negotiable. The exploitation of migrant workers not only reflects a moral failing but also weakens the labour market, driving down wages and worsening working conditions for all workers.

While some migrant workers technically have a right to unionize, many are excluded from that right or have their work permits tied to a specific employer, creating a fear of retaliation for demanding their rights. Ontario's weak labour laws are reflected in having the second-lowest union coverage rate in all of Canada, just ahead of Alberta, with only one in four workers unionized. If Ontario's unionization rate matched the national average, an additional half a million workers in Ontario would be unionized and benefiting from better working conditions. The power of unionization was recently displayed when 55,000 CUPE education workers, represented by the Ontario School Board Council of Unions, went on an illegal strike, defying Ford's use of the notwithstanding clause, which allows the government to override Charter rights.[22] The education workers' actions demonstrated the vital role unions play in protecting workers' rights. Their bold defiance of Ford's attack on Charter rights speaks to a broader and renewed sense of militancy within the labour movement, with one in two unionized workers having participated in strikes since 2019.[23]

Inflation

Opinion polls consistently indicate that the cost-of-living and inflation crises have become the most pressing issues for Ontarians.[24] Although inflation rates show a slight improvement, the soaring costs of housing, food and other necessities have left many Ontarians struggling to make ends meet. This crisis has also led to historically low levels of satisfaction with the provincial government, with three in four people expressing dissatisfaction with the way things are going in the province.[25]

At the core of Ontario's cost-of-living crisis is the persistent rise in housing and food prices. Despite a modest deceleration in inflation, these necessities of living remain significantly high, and forecasts suggest they will stay that way for some time. Real estate prices in the province have skyrocketed in recent years, rendering homeownership out of reach for many and driving rental prices to unaffordable levels.[26] Between January 2021 to July 2024, housing costs rose 23 percent.[27] The main housing solution offered by Ford's government was to open the Greenbelt nature reserve to insider real estate developers, who stand to make a profit of over $8 billion, a proposal that has resulted in significant controversy.[28]

Food prices have also remained persistently high.[29] While the overall inflation rate has dropped, the cost of groceries continues to rise, with prices going up 24 percent from the start of the pandemic to July 2024.[30] This has forced many families to make difficult budgetary choices, often compromising their nutritional needs. The impact is particularly severe for low-income households. Food bank usage has gone up by 96 percent compared to pre-pandemic levels, with 1,001,150 adults and children visiting a food bank last year, equivalent to one in every sixteen people in Ontario.[31]

The collective impact of these financial pressures is stark: Statistics Canada reports that one in three Canadians lived in a household experiencing financial difficulties.[32] The financial strain is so severe that one in three workers who hold multiple jobs do so to pay for essential needs, such as housing, food and health care. This reality underscores the inadequacy of wages in meeting the rising cost of living, even as recent data suggests that wages have begun to outpace inflation. In 2023, wages went up 5.1 percent compared to 3.8 percent for inflation.[33] It is important to note that this recent wage growth follows four decades of decline. For many workers, the benefits of these wage increases are offset by the long-term erosion of purchasing power. From 1981 to 2022, output per worker in Ontario saw a 34.9 percent increase. In contrast, during the same period, the median market earnings for working-age Ontarians only rose by 8.4 percent. Years of stagnant wages mean that, despite recent gains, workers are still struggling to catch up.

Economic growth barely raised the median income of working-age Ontarians[34]

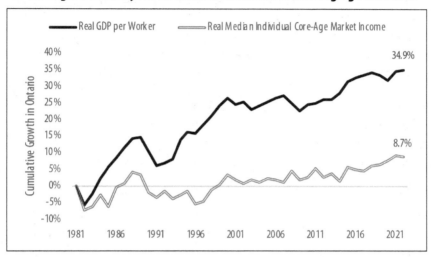

As noted above, one contributing factor exacerbating the cost-of-living crisis in Ontario was Bill 124, which limited wage increases for public sector workers to 1 percent annually over a three-year period. This legislation directly impacted approximately one in three Ontario families, many of whom depend on the income of family members who work in the public sector. By capping wage increases far below the rate of inflation, Bill 124 effectively reduced the real income of these workers via wage theft, intensifying their struggle to keep up with rising costs. The bill's effects rippled across the economy, leading to lower consumer spending and increased financial stress for countless families. While the bill was repealed after being ruled as unconstitutional, and some workers have been receiving retroactive pay, many found the back pay too little and too late. Crushing costs had already forced people into the unimaginable position of choosing between buying food or paying for rent.[35]

Ontario households have received minimal support in dealing with the cost-of-living crisis. The Ford Conservative government's signature legislation for households has been a gas tax cut of 5.7 cents per litre.[36] Based on the average tank of gas, this reduction amounts to a mere

$3.19 — basically, spare change. Drivers also received a savings of about $120 a year with the elimination of renewal fees for vehicle licence plates. Ontario's 2024 Fall Economic Statement outlined a $200 taxpayer rebate for Ontarians at a cost of $3 billion.[37] This rebate represents a classic, conservative tactic: offering voters a small but immediate payout while quietly cutting essential public services. While $200 might briefly help with groceries or bills, the Ford government's austerity measures will cost Ontarians nearly double that amount in reduced public services, with the average Ontarian facing a $385 reduction in public services once inflation and population growth are considered. This short-sighted, "buck-a-beer" style populism undermines the social infrastructure that working families depend on, from health care to education. The timing of this rebate, conveniently ahead of a potential election, makes its true purpose transparent: buying votes while continuing to underfund vital services. Ontarians deserve sustainable solutions to the cost-of-living crisis, not election-season handouts that leave them worse off in the long run.

In light of these extremely modest affordability measures, Ontarians continue to feel the financial strain, with everyday costs remaining high and many struggling to make ends meet, despite the fact that inflation is starting to moderate.

Ford's Fiscal Situation

Ontario's fiscal landscape under the Ford Conservatives paints a troubling picture of austerity and misplaced priorities, which they articulate as being driven by an ideology favouring small government. Beneath the headlines and soundbites of government press releases lies a pattern of obfuscation, underfunding and the undermining of public trust in the government's management of resources.

Provincial Budget

One of the most concerning aspects of Ontario's fiscal landscape is what appears to be deliberate manipulation of fiscal data. In the most recent audit of the pre-election budget in 2022, the Auditor General of Ontario criticized the government for both underestimating revenue and overestimating expenses. According to the Auditor General, this misrepresentation created a false narrative that the province had fewer funds available for public services than was the case.[38] This false fiscal conservatism is often used as a pretext for cutting public services, yet the audit made it clear that such measures are by choice rather than by necessity. By underestimating revenue, the government can justify austerity measures and privatization efforts, while maintaining a façade of fiscal responsibility. Manipulating fiscal data erodes public trust and shows government priorities are driven by an ideological agenda rather than by a genuine effort to address the people's needs.

One of the most striking indictments of Ontario's fiscal policy is the persistent underinvestment in public services. The Ford Conservative government has consistently brought in the lowest revenue per person and spent the least in public services per person compared to other provinces. Even at the height of the pandemic, when public spending was critical to support struggling communities, Ontario's per person spending was the lowest in the country. In 2022, Ontario spent $3,251 dollars less per person on public services than the average of other provinces.[39] Ontario spent the least in health (15 percent below the average), was average in education spending (2.6 percent above the average), and came in last in all other program spending (36 percent below the average). To match the average, Ontario would have needed to spend an additional $42 billion on public services.

Ontario is lowest in overall spending per person compared to other provinces

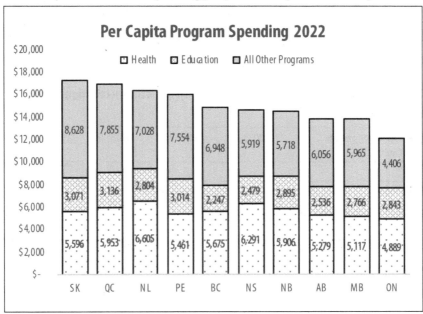

The government's claims of record spending on public services do not consider inflation or population growth. When these figures are considered, it becomes evident that spending in the public sector is on the decline. For instance, by the 2026 fiscal year, the government plans to spend $1,390 less per person on public services compared to 2020, representing a decrease of 10.3 percent.

Ford government plans to decrease spending per person by over 10 percent

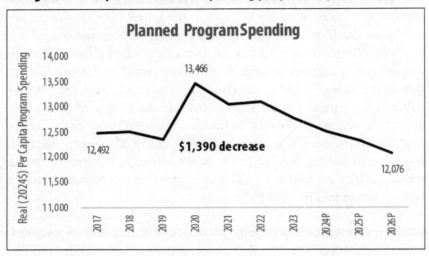

Total program spending is projected to decrease by 2.1 percent in 2024, 1.5 percent in 2025 and 2.1 percent in 2026. This downward trend is evident across all major sectors.

Taking into account inflation and population growth, sector spending is decreasing[40]

Real Spending Change per Capita (%)	2023-24	2024-25	2025-26	2026-27
Health	-	-4.5	-0.6	-1.5
Education	-	-2.4	-0.9	-2.1
Postsecondary Education	-	-8.1	-1.6	0.3
Social Services	-	-2.6	-3	-3.6
Justice	-	-8.2	-8.8	-3.6
Other	-	7.6	-1.8	-3.6
Total Programs	-	-2.1	-1.5	-2.1

This reduction comes at a time when public services are already suffering under the weight of underfunding, leading to growing waitlists and deteriorating infrastructure. Instead of addressing these critical issues, the government has chosen to cut funding or redirect public money into privatizing services, most notably in the health care sector. The expansion of private, for-profit health care has increasingly resulted in Ontarians being illegally charged thousands of dollars in extra fees for services that should be publicly funded and delivered. This shift towards privatization not only compromises the quality and accessibility of public services but also undermines the fundamental principle of universality that underpins Ontario's health care system.

Ontario has an infrastructure backlog of $16.8 billion in 2020, projected to increase to $22.7 billion by 2029–30.[41] Since the last election in 2022, the Conservative government has made infrastructure a focal point, but their approach prioritizes private profit over public good. Ford's creation of the Ontario Infrastructure Bank, later renamed the Build Ontario Fund, is a clear example of this strategy. Reflecting a throwback to private/public partnerships of earlier times,[42] this initiative encourages private investors, including large pension funds, to finance essential infrastructure projects, such as long-term care homes, affordable housing and transportation. While this may attract short-term investments, it risks eroding public control over critical services and will lead to higher costs for Ontarians through user fees, fares and tariffs.

Despite Ford's assertions of historic infrastructure spending, when adjusted for inflation, the funding in 2023 amounts to only 1.9 percent of GDP, which is identical to the levels under the last year of the previous government.[43] Furthermore, his ten-year infrastructure plan allocates $190 billion — significantly less than the $219.5 billion (adjusted for inflation) proposed by the previous government in 2017. Contrary to the rhetoric, Ford's infrastructure plans are not sufficient to meet Ontario's growing needs, particularly in the face of future challenges.

Austerity measures under Ford's administration appear to apply exclusively to public services and infrastructure, not to its own operations. Since 2018, salaries for staff in Premier Ford's office have increased by 136 percent, and wages for Conservative cabinet MPPs have risen by 72 percent.[44] These substantial increases underscore that the government's fiscal restraint is selective, targeting services that benefit the public while disproportionately benefiting the Conservative elite.

Taxes

A well-functioning public service requires adequate revenue, predominantly derived from taxation. Since coming into power, the Ford government has made several changes to Ontario's tax system, which have weakened its fairness and substantially reduced the revenue needed to pay for public services. This is a continuation of the long history of tax policy in Ontario which favours corporations and the wealthy at the expense of ordinary Ontarians.

Currently, 80 percent of Ontario's tax revenues come from just three sources: personal income tax, corporate tax and sales tax. However, there is a significant disparity between what the rich and corporations pay and the rest of Ontarians. The effective tax rates for personal income taxes disproportionately benefit higher-income individuals. For instance, a family with two young children making $50,000 has a marginal tax rate of nearly 75 percent, yet the same family with two children making over $250,000 has an effective marginal tax rate under 50 percent.[45] Economist Trevor Tombe notes, "It is fair to say that there are families in poverty who face a higher tax rate on any extra income they earn than the highest-income families in Canada do."[46]

A notable change was the decision to scrap the 2018 plan to add new tax brackets for the wealthy. This change would have increased personal income taxes by $200 for the top 17 percent of income earners while providing a $130 tax cut for those at the bottom of the income scale. Additionally, it would have generated an extra $275 million in revenue. Ford's decision to cancel this increase, which shielded the richest in the province from paying their fair share, is part of a larger shift away from progressive taxation, where higher earners pay higher rates.

The issue of tax disparity is even more pronounced when comparing personal income taxes to corporate income taxes. For every dollar individuals pay in income tax, corporations pay only 53 cents. Corporate tax rates have declined sharply over the years. In the 1970s, the total corporate income tax rate was 53.2 percent, but it has since fallen to 26.5 percent.[47]

Furthermore, this rate does not reflect the actual tax paid because corporations benefit from nearly $10 billion in tax subsidies.[48] These tax shifts and subsidies represent a massive transfer of wealth from the public to the private sector, further distorting the tax system in favour of corporations.

Since 1960, Ontario corporate taxation has dropped by half

Ontario Total Corporate Income Tax

[Line chart showing Total Corporate Tax Rate from 1960 to 2023. Values range from 59% at top to 24% at bottom. Notable points: 53.2% in the early period, declining to 26.5% by 2023.]

Another costly tax change was the increase in the exemption threshold for the Employer Health Tax (EHT), which led to a $380 million reduction in revenue. The threshold is a tax subsidy for businesses that minimizes the EHT they owe for their employees. In 2020, the Ford government raised the threshold to $1 million, which was a 104 percent increase in a single year. The EHT is a crucial revenue source for funding Ontario's health care system, and reducing it puts additional pressure on the province's finances. This move is particularly concerning given the increasing health care costs associated with the aging population. Reducing an essential source of health care funding without replacing it seems both short-sighted and reckless.

While the government has made worrisome individual changes to taxes, it is also in the second year of a comprehensive tax review, which has received little public attention or scrutiny. The review's stated goals include enhancing productivity, promoting fairness, simplifying and increasing transparency and modernizing tax administration.[49] However, these broad and seemingly innocuous objectives are vague enough to justify a wide range of potentially harmful changes to the tax system. What is particularly troubling about this tax review is the lack of transparency and public involvement. According to the government, they have consulted a select group of tax experts, economists and business leaders, but these consultations have taken place behind closed doors, with no opportunity for input from the public or civil society organizations.

If the government truly sought to promote fairness and transparency, it would have opened the process to public debate and ensured that the voices of all Ontarians, not just those of the business elite, were considered. There is a legitimate fear that the tax review will pave the way for a deeper shift away from progressive taxes, such as personal income tax, and toward more regressive taxes, such as sales taxes and user fees, which disproportionately affect low- and middle-income families. As Ontario's population ages and the demands on health care and other public services increase, the province faces a significant fiscal challenge. Several years of corporate tax cuts and subsidies have diminished the revenue base, leaving the government with limited financial resources to address these growing demands. Progressive tax reform is urgently needed to rectify the current system's deep imbalances. Such reform should include the introduction of additional tax brackets for the wealthy, an increase in corporate tax rates and the discontinuation of unnecessary tax subsidies for corporations. Additionally, a more comprehensive public consultation process is required to ensure that the opinions of ordinary Ontarians are considered, and the tax system reflects the principles of fairness and social justice.[50]

Austerity and Privatization, Not Adequate Funding

Ontario's fiscal policies over the past decade demonstrate a troubling shift towards austerity and privatization, instead of adequately funding quality public services. Issues such as a lack of transparency in the budget process, manipulation of fiscal data and the chronic underinvestment in public services all point to a government that prioritizes the "needs" of corporations and the wealthy over the well-being of its citizens. The result is a province where public services are deteriorating, inequality is growing and trust in government is eroding. To reverse this trend, Ontario will need a renewed commitment to public investment and social equity.

Characterized by sharp employment fluctuations, the labour market has also faced volatility that has disproportionately impacted workers in precarious employment situations. From the devastating job losses during the COVID-19 pandemic to the current paradox of rising unemployment alongside the widespread public sector job vacancies, combined with the unethical treatment of migrant workers — all highlight the structural deficiencies within the labour market, exacerbated by the policies of the Ford government.

What we need is a government that recognizes wage growth as a crucial tool for improving lives, rather than something to be suppressed in the name of ensuring business profitability. This government should also understand that strong public services are essential, offering support when Ontarians need it most. It is not enough to assume that if businesses and the wealthy thrive, the rest of us will automatically benefit. Now is the time for policies that truly reflect the needs and aspirations of everyday Ontarians.

3

ARTS AND CULTURE ON LIFE SUPPORT

Aylan Couchie

I BEGIN TO WRITE THIS CHAPTER ON A NOTABLE DAY — the thirtieth day of the Art Gallery of Ontario (AGO) workers' strike. As the communications and membership engagement coordinator for OCAD's (Ontario College of Art & Design) University Faculty Association (OCADFA), I've been supporting the strike by sharing updates and solidarity through OCADFA's social media platforms. Through this role, I have come to witness firsthand how cuts to arts institutions have affected precariously employed arts workers across Ontario. OCAD University (OCADU), Ontario's sole university dedicated to the arts, was where I chose to pursue my MFA in Interdisciplinary Art, Media and Design, which I completed in 2018. The following year, I began teaching at OCADU as a sessional instructor, initially teaching sculpture and installation, a commitment requiring a significant commute from Nipissing First Nation to Toronto and back each week. Until the repeal of Bill 124 and subsequent renegotiations in 2023, I, along with a vast number of colleagues, was one of the lowest-paid sessional instructors at any university in Ontario.

Over the past decade, I've supplemented my income by engaging in various side jobs and contracts. My work has included writing for publications and jurying for various arts organizations. This includes numerous stints at the Ontario Arts Council (OAC), evaluating both Indigenous and non-Indigenous grant applications. I've curated exhibitions, and I've spearheaded and organized large-scale arts events. In 2018, I was appointed by Wanda Nanibush, Indigenous curator at the AGO, to be the Indigenous curatorial intern within AGO's newly renamed Department of Canadian and Indigenous Art.

I've juggled side jobs and community work for the past twelve years while balancing my roles as a single mother to three young men and a grandmother to four. Alongside family commitments, I've maintained an interdisciplinary creative practice while pursuing an academic education. The breadth of my experience within the arts and culture industry frames my insights into the challenges facing arts workers — employment precarity, insecure housing and institutional instability, exacerbated by provincial budget cuts and policy changes.

Under the previous government, the Ontario arts community was on an upward trajectory through the creation of new funding streams, such as the Indigenous Culture Fund (ICF) and funding increases to support artists and arts workers through the OAC, the main funding body for most arts organizations and workers in Ontario. As an example, in September 2017, the previous government had announced a new funding strategy for the OAC that would see an incremental increase over four years, bringing the OAC's operating budget from $60 million to $80 million by 2020–21.[1] Sadly, under Doug Ford, none of these newly announced OAC supports came to fruition. In fact, the opposite occurred.

(Un)Welcome to Ford Nation

In June 2018, Doug Ford was sworn in as Ontario's twenty-sixth premier. His administration quickly enacted austerity measures that sharply cut funding and cancelled programs across various sectors, including the arts. Ford's reductions have deeply affected the arts and culture community while disproportionately and repeatedly impacting marginalized groups, especially those who benefit from arts and culture initiatives. As an example, in August 2018, just two months after Ford was sworn in, the Ministry of Tourism, Culture and Sport cut $500,000 in promised funding to a free, after-school music program for at-risk youth in Toronto. Described as "devastating" by the program's operators, this cut severely limited their capacity to serve communities and children burdened by poverty.[2]

Vulnerable communities were targeted again in December 2018, when Conservatives set their sights on the province's largest arts funding body: the OAC. They slashed $5 million from the OAC, bringing its funding back to the 2017–2018 level of $64.9 million.[3] Alongside announcing the $5-million OAC cut, Conservatives also targeted the OAC's newly formed ICF, slashing its relatively modest $5-million annual budget by almost 50 percent to $2.25 million.[4] The government also placed the ICF under review and froze new grant applications.[5]

Ford's cuts to the OAC tightened an already small and fiercely competitive funding pool for creative and arts organizations. I've juried many OAC grant assessments. In an assessment process, jurors may review say, forty applications, but of those, only eight to ten may advance for full or partial funding. From these, just a few may receive full funding, with the rest possibly receiving partial amounts. Consequently, many excellent applications are rejected, simply due to a lack of funds, including feasible community projects that engage youth and marginalized groups through the arts.

Supporting the OAC is not merely about cultural enrichment; it is also vital for economic growth and community development across Ontario. The Ontario branch of Canadian Artists Representation/Le Front des Artistes Canadiens (CARFAC) reports that arts and culture contribute $27 billion to Ontario's GDP, with $5.5 billion generated by sectors such as arts education and performing arts, which rely heavily on OAC support.[6] Additionally, the OAC highlights that arts and culture activities attract 9.5 million overnight tourists annually, contributing $3.7 billion to the provincial GDP.[7] Moreover, a study by NANOS (a North American research and strategy organization), commissioned by the OAC, revealed that the arts significantly enhance the quality of life, mental health and community identity, with 78 percent of respondents recognizing the arts as a vital area for government investment.[8] The substantial economic and societal benefits provided by the arts highlight the essential role of OAC funding.

Initial Cuts and Community Responses

A few months prior to the OAC funding cuts, I'd moved back to the reserve to learn Nshnaabemwin (the Anishinaabe language) in evening classes held weekly at our community's high school. Language revitalization and preservation have been a key concern and priority for many First Nation communities, especially as we attempt to recover from the ongoing impacts of Indian Residential Schools and the systematic destruction of our cultures and languages, enacted and enforced through the schools and other governmental policies and legislation. Nipissing First Nation speaks a dialect of Nshnaabemwin unique to our community, and every time we lose an Elder, it's like losing an entire catalogue of linguistic knowledge that connects us to land, cosmologies and ways of being. Our Elders' remaining time with us is precious and limited. Ford's actions have already cost our communities essential and valuable opportunities to revitalize and preserve. Cultural continuity is important, and yet, our languages are endangered and governments fail to make this issue the priority it should be. Our languages are being lost over time through political apathy.

The ICF was created in 2017 as a response to the Truth and Reconciliation Commission's Calls to Action. Its stated purpose was to "support cultural priorities and activities as defined by Indigenous peoples and communities, including on and off-reserve, urban, rural and remote."[9] The ICF was unique because, although administered by the OAC, it was a granting stream not focused solely on art or arts projects: it provided opportunities for non-arts-related initiatives intended to support language and cultural revitalization and preservation to be identified and developed by Indigenous community members. During its short lifespan, the ICF went through two rounds of project funding in November 2017 and May 2018. These produced projects designed to revitalize Indigenous communities, connecting youth and Elders in an attempt to reclaim endangered Indigenous knowledge systems and cultures. The scope of potential projects that could have stemmed from the fund was limitless.

Back home, in 2018, I'd recently learned of the newly created ICF and had already started brainstorming ideas for projects that could contribute to preserving Nipissing Elder knowledge. I was shocked when I heard the ICF, *a new program* that was just starting to get its legs, was already on Ford's chopping block. To add insult to injury, the loss of the ICF looked to put four Indigenous women, some of them single mothers themselves, out of work. I quickly began to organize, reaching out to others in the Indigenous arts community for support. No stranger to politics, I knew the initiative would likely be a losing battle, but I couldn't let the ICF be ghosted into a distant memory without fighting for it, and, at the very least, putting Ford on blast for his anti-reconciliatory and harmful decisions.

Support came swiftly from Danis Goulet, Kerry Swanson, Gisèle Gordon, Melody McKiver and Jesse Wente. Together, we drafted an open letter and scripts for emails, letters and talking points constituents could use to urge their MPPs to fight for the ICF. I hosted these materials on my website, and our group, alongside many from the arts and Indigenous community, used social media to direct supporters to these advocacy resources. We received media attention which helped garner statements of support from Nipissing First Nation (NFN) Chief Scott McLeod and other notable figures, like Cree artist Kent Monkman, who took time during an interview to advocate for the fund. Additionally, NDP MPPs Sol Mamakwa, the reconciliation critic, and Dr. Jill Andrew, the arts and culture critic, initiated legislative petitions and helped organize a rally and news conference at Queen's Park.

Despite garnering over 1,870 signatures in support of our open letter, our efforts to spotlight this issue were often overshadowed by unions from other sectors who were also contending with Ford's cuts. On the day of our press conference and rally at Queen's Park — a significant event to which I personally drove a youth leader from NFN to speak — other union rallies dominated the downtown core. As a result, our news conference attracted just a single reporter from Queen's Park, limiting our ability to reach a wider audience.

In response to our open letter and petitions, Michael Tibollo, then Minister of Tourism, Culture and Sport, provided a list of alternative "Indigenous" funding initiatives. Despite the ICF's broader cultural scope, Tibollo's suggestions focused primarily on Indigenous arts grants and museum funding. Tibollo also referenced the Trillium Grant, a competitive funding stream not earmarked for Indigenous people, and besides, they'd also recently slashed that fund by $15 million. Finally, and perhaps most offensive, Tibollo listed the Ontario Cultural Attractions Fund and Indigenous Tourism Ontario. I don't have the words to express how insulting it is, post-TRC, to have our languages and cultures — here since time immemorial — relegated to a tourism commodity. Tourism funding was soon to be on the chopping block too, and if we thought 2018 was bad, we quickly learned that Ford was just getting started.

WTF?!: A Year of Significant Reductions

In the spring and early summer of 2019, the arts, culture and tourism sectors were rocked by another slew of Ford cuts still being felt today. In May, to no one's surprise, Ford finally terminated the ICF, sending a message to Indigenous people that the Ford government wasn't (and still isn't) interested in reconciliation on any level.[10] Also cut was $17.5 million from Ontario tourism funding, affecting major cities like Toronto and Ottawa.[11] This wasn't just a time for cuts, though; this was a time for the

Ford government to begin overhauls: gutting, shuffling and renaming grant and funding programs.

To "modernize" the Ontario Music Fund (OMF), established in 2013, a whopping $8 million was slashed from its $15-million budget in April 2019 — over *half* its budget.[12] The OMF was initially created to "support new digital and record production and distribution of Canadian music, to increase partnership opportunities and to promote Ontario's music industry in Canada and around the world."[13] In its first year, the fund generated $24 million "in additional revenue for music-related businesses," alongside the creation or retention of 2,000 jobs.[14] Renamed the Ontario Music *Investment* Fund, the program has also been restructured under Ontario Creates, a government agency that funds and supports the book, magazine, film, television, music and interactive industries.

Many large-scale arts festivals rely on more than one funding stream to make annual events happen. In the OMF cuts, a noted concern was that "slashed funding will have an impact on some of Hamilton's local music festivals, including Supercrawl."[15] This is important because, over the past five years, large-scale festivals like Supercrawl have been negatively impacted through provincial cuts to more than one funding stream.

Another important festival funding stream, Celebrate Ontario, offered "funding to festivals, events, and cultural organizations that will host tourism-focused events in the province."[16] Applicants to the now-closed Celebrate Ontario program once had the ability to apply for up to $250,000 in funding. Celebrate Ontario has now been replaced by Experience Ontario. This new funding stream only funds up to $125,000 per applicant.[17] In June 2019, Celebrate Ontario's funding was cut by $3 million. This reduction could have been more manageable for festival organizers, who had relied on this funding for years, had they been informed earlier. According to *CBC News*, the notification of these cuts came too late, leaving many organizations to scramble for alternative funding. Some events were only weeks away and others had already taken place when the news broke.[18]

Moreover, some festivals didn't lose part of their funding, they lost all of it. For example, Supercrawl in Hamilton, which previously received $275,000, found itself with nothing, mirroring the situation faced by Toronto's Inside Out 2SLGBTQ+ Film Festival, which also saw its funding drop from over $152,000 to zero. One arts advocate noted how "the change means the province is being less transparent about how the funding is allocated, making the full impact of the cuts harder to assess."[19] As the pandemic unfolded, the arts and culture sectors faced unprecedented challenges. With funding foundations intertwined and severely eroded by cuts and restructuring, the industry entered a period of uncertainty. The sector would soon be tested as they navigated new realities of lockdowns and closed galleries, theatres, music halls and other arts venues.

Remix 2019: The Pandemic and Beyond

The arts community is still struggling to recover from the pandemic. With public spaces and galleries closed during lockdowns, many organizations shifted their programming to incorporate online talks, panels and workshops. Some galleries, like the Art Gallery of Sudbury, evolved, building entire new sections onto their websites dedicated to digital exhibitions. Other galleries, like North Bay's decades-old White Water Gallery, lost their physical locations during the pandemic. Only recently has the White Water Gallery obtained a new, smaller space in the city's downtown core, but not all galleries have fared as well.

CARFAC Ontario reported:

> Growth of Ontario's culture sector since 2010 was reversed by the pandemic. Between 2010 and 2019, Ontario's cultural economy saw a real per capita increase of 4%; this was followed by a 7% decrease in 2020. Job trends in the sector follow a similar trajectory, increasing by 8% between 2010 and 2019, only to decrease in 2020 by 11%.[20]

In spite of the sector's attempts at recovery, March 2023 saw yet another Ford cut to the Ontario Arts Council's one-time arts grants in the amount of $5 million.[21]

A few months later, the festival community experienced a pre-pandemic flashback when their arts funding, now through Ontario's newly renamed Experience Ontario program, was again cut with little notice to organizers. If you'll recall, the province had already cut Celebrate Ontario by $3 million in 2019, and cancelled/revised Celebrate Ontario, rebranding it as the Experience Ontario program, with only half the original funding offered through Celebrate Ontario.

In summer 2023, festival organizers were once again left scrambling with little time to manoeuvre when Experience Ontario cut funding to several key summer arts festivals that have become annual staples in their respective regions. Orillia's Mariposa Folk Festival, for example, learned only after their festival had taken place that they would be receiving $112,500 less in funding than the previous year's amount of $210,000.[22] Sudbury's Up Here Festival was also hit hard. Less than a month before launching, event organizers learned their expected $100,000 in funding was denied.[23] They told *CTV News*:

> We had anticipated and budgeted for some funding reductions, due to the government of Ontario reducing the total envelope [of grant funding] from $50M in 2022 back down to $19.5M this year, but with Up Here's proven track record, growing out-of-town attendance, and an overall economic impact of over $5M to date, we never imagined our funding would be eliminated entirely.[24]

General manager Jayme Lathem also noted funding application timelines are whittled down to a small window in April each year, and by the time they learn if they've been approved and for how much, they wind up making hard decisions to adjust programming to compensate for shortfalls.[25] This means organizers have had to cancel several weekend shows, a much-anticipated mural, an act from overseas and were forced to scale back artistic installations. Up Here Festival co-organizer Christian Pelletier told *CBC News* that they would normally hear back about funding by the end of April, which gave them plenty of time to reorganize the event. However, Pelletier notes, since the COVID-19 pandemic, Ontario has "completely shifted their deadlines," leaving organizers in "an impossible situation."[26]

Hamilton's Supercrawl also voiced frustration about the application dates for Experience Ontario. Organizer Tim Potocic told *Global News* that applying for funding in April means organizers aren't notified of funding approvals until mid-summer.[27] Supercrawl once again felt the impacts of funding shortfalls from Experience Ontario, receiving just $65,000 in 2023 from a grant that had provided them with "closer to $300,000 in recent years."[28] In an April 2024 *Toronto Star* article, Kelsey Jacobson, an assistant professor of drama at Queen's University, said funding models relied upon by festivals are "particularly at risk" because they offer once-per-year programming that makes it hard to maintain loyalty from attendees.[29] Further, during the pandemic, many found other new hobbies and diversions. Jacobson commented further that "many arts organizations, which planned for a two or three-year recovery, didn't see financial returns that they were anticipating." The *Star* also noted, "Because of the number of arts organizations in the industry and their disparate disciplines, it's difficult to quantify how many have ceased operations due to the pandemic."

At the beginning of 2024, Toronto's theatre sector raised the alarm, calling attention to the post-pandemic crisis happening within their industry. The Toronto Alliance for the Performing Arts says it lost about 46 percent of its members with only 89 companies surviving in January 2023, compared to the original 164 members. Meanwhile, the Toronto Fringe Festival cited "low attendance and a loss of financial support from a provincial grants fund" as the reason for their significantly reduced summer 2024 programming. The *Star* has reported low attendance, reduced funding and even the increased cost of softwood lumber used to build sets as having also contributed to the crisis many theatre companies find themselves in.[30]

OCAD University: A Microcosm of Wider Policy Impacts

OCADU hasn't escaped Ford's cuts and policy impacts. In April 2019, Ontario cancelled $20 million of funding for a $60-million Creative Campus revitalization expansion that would add much-needed 50,000 square feet of new, modernized space for students and faculty. Former OCADU president Sara Diamond said the $20 million cut was a "negative decision on the part of the government."[31] Diamond highlighted the new space as essential for providing "high-quality education in design and digital media and creative industries critical for Ontario's economy." It's clear OCADU's forward-thinking strategy aligns with the evolving needs of a rapidly increasing digital society. Conversely, the deputy minister of training, colleges and universities justified the budget cuts as part of a "thorough review" to ensure investments are "sustainable and modernized."[32] However, this reasoning is contradictory since the drive towards sustainability and modernization is precisely what academic institutions need, as technologies like artificial intelligence and augmented and mixed reality become increasingly integral to our lives. This highlights the Conservatives' lack of understanding, creativity and foresight needed to navigate these current and future challenges.

In January 2020, OCADU students organized a protest over cuts to the Ontario Student Assistance Program (OSAP). A prominent feature of this protest was a large mural in the main campus lobby, named the "Ford Tracker." This mural displayed a detailed timeline on digitally created posters printed and arranged side by side on the lobby wall, outlining the impact of the Ford government on arts students. Some posters included creative caricatures of Ford, while others used straightforward text on plain backgrounds to convey their message. One of my personal favourites simply read, "IS PAINT A FOOD GROUP?"

Mural installed in the lobby of OCAD University in 2020[33]

The ripple effects stemming from Ford's cuts and policies impact art students in a myriad of ways. Many struggle to keep food in their cupboards and often must make hard choices between purchasing art supplies for their coursework and paying rent. Some struggle with inadequate and/or unaffordable housing, bed bugs and renovictions while living off meagre funding models that no longer meet the needs of today's students in an increasingly unaffordable economy and rental market. Megan Feheley, an ililiw (Cree) artist, curator, arts worker and one of my former students, summarized the student experience best in a Facebook comment to me:

> I always think about how [Ford] gutted education, his impact on funding for education in arts, fallout impact on universities in

Ontario (OCADU losing a huge part of its funding for what was supposed to be an extensive campus revitalization). I remember my OSAP funding being cut so drastically after the Ford govt was elected that I had to scramble for additional supports on short notice, I had about half my typical funding to cover rent and food for Jan-April and had to work two jobs while a full-time student while also not making too many hours to lose my funding altogether.

Arts educators haven't escaped Ford's policy changes either. I'll be brief regarding Bill 124, as it is discussed elsewhere throughout this volume (given that the bill impacted *all* public sector workers).[34] What I'll provide is a brief snapshot of Bill 124 as it relates to how things rolled out for workers at OCADU.

In 2019, the *Protecting a Sustainable Public Sector for Future Generations Act* was introduced by the Ford government. It capped public sector salary increases to 1 percent annually despite rising inflation and housing challenges. OCADFA joined a large coalition of unions, alongside the Ontario Federation of Labour, to contest the legality of the act in court. In November 2022, it was deemed unconstitutional. In his ruling, Justice Markus Koehnen said, "On my view of the evidence, Ontario was not facing a situation in 2019 that justified an infringement of Charter rights."[35] On the same day this ruling was made public, the government announced it would be repealing the bill.[36] In a joint statement issued on March 30, 2023, the presidents of OCADFA and Ontario Public Service Employees Union (OPSEU) Local 576 relayed to their members, "Bill 124 has been profitable for [OCADU] as they realized significant savings from a union-busting piece of legislation that froze your wages and has now been deemed unlawful."[37]

The challenges faced by OCADU, its students and faculty exemplify broader systemic issues that extend into the realms of unaffordable housing and unsustainable futures for emerging art students who will be encountering industries enhanced by technologies, like AI, for which few are prepared. Further, arts workers typically rely on more than one stream of income to maintain artistic practices. The continual defunding results in lost opportunities, such as those offered by festivals, exhibitions and other arts events. This loss of opportunities impacts already precariously employed arts workers, making it harder to continue to create and support themselves and their families.

A Society Without Art?

The continuous gutting of funding programs that artists, festivals and organizations have historically relied upon has disrupted the industry's ability to sustain itself under these financial pressures, most especially as housing costs soar and the cost of living continues to rise. If the industry were having to adjust based solely upon the austerity measures of a careless Conservative government, it would likely be able to make do. However, the unprecedented global pandemic changed not only the landscape economically but also the way in which the public engages with arts and culture in Ontario. Arts festivals will not be sustainable if the current funding models are not properly restructured so as to ensure annual festivals, relied upon by businesses and municipalities for tourism income, exist. The Ford government is playing a risky game of chicken in its defunding strategies because, believe it or not, people *will* notice if the industry collapses and their community's annual festivals, cultural events and spaces are gone.

Every single person is impacted by, and benefits from, the arts, every single day. When you turn on your radio, pick up your phone, buy new clothing, navigate street signs, read books, marvel at architecture or make purchases based on product design — you are interacting with what has been created by artists. During the pandemic, the arts saved many people, as video games and Netflix binge-watching provided mental health escapes from long days of isolation. Even COVID-19 infographics, seen online or posted in public spaces, delivering crucial, life-saving information through visual communication, were created by artists who were also once art students or people who relied on arts grants or took on side jobs to support their practice, many of them doing so while juggling a family. Some may have begun in community-based art or writing workshops held at their local library or artist-run centre — or perhaps they simply discovered their love of music at a free after-school program for at-risk youth. The arts matter and so do those who keep these valuable — and I assure you, *very necessary* — industries alive.

Consider the arts community as the canary in the coal mine, the one on the front lines. Since 2022, advancements in AI models and hardware have increased exponentially. By the time this book is published, in fact, the AI landscape will have likely evolved several times over from the time of this writing. AI has the potential to be more economically disruptive to our society than even the pandemic. This is a current discussion happening among industry experts who are discussing the implementation of universal basic income. Some say AI will lead to job loss, others say it will create jobs; I'm skeptical of the latter given the current trend toward the corporatization of AI technologies. Every political leader, in every level of government, should be planning for how *all* job sectors will deal with the impending, inevitable, disruption AI will have upon employment and the economy. Here in Ontario, we have seen a government with a flagrant disregard for arts and culture working to defund and destabilize the sector over and over again. Even post-pandemic, we've seen Ford's negligence when it comes to supporting Ontario's struggling arts and culture industries.

As Ford continues to weaken a sector that will likely continue to see the impacts of this growing AI threat, Ontarians will need to consider whether they are willing to forsake the arts and culture sector, allowing it to be destroyed by Ford's lack of funding and support. The drastic cuts and restructuring initiatives have been mind-boggling and inexplicable. It is clear these decisions come from a place of ignorance to just how important arts and culture are to the general public and to marginalized communities. Under Ford, we can anticipate further crises within organizations struggling to stay afloat. This not only impacts vulnerable workers, but many of the events brought to cities and towns throughout the year. Imagine, if you will, an Ontario with little to no public arts offerings; the outcome would impact the quality of life for most, including families with young children, not to mention future generations of artists, musicians, writers, dancers, actors and performers … the list goes on. Is this the drab and colourless future you want for this province?

4

SCHOOLS FOR SALE

Chris Chandler

DOUG FORD'S HISTORY OF ANTAGONISM towards progressive ideas and institutions, and his populist appeals to the lowest common denominator, predate his time as premier of Ontario. His record in Toronto municipal politics yields evidence enough of both. In education, one can start the story of Ford's attacks on public schools after the wreckage of his and his family's immediate influence at city council had cooled, and before he took the controls at Queen's Park. Ford's ascendance to the leadership of the Progressive Conservative Party of Ontario, at its convention in March of 2018, is where we can trace the beginnings of his education policy and his attitudes toward public elementary and secondary schooling. The genesis of Ford's agenda in public education is revealed in the machinations which saw him defeat Christine Elliott for the reigns of their party. The seeds of that agenda took root in the soil of reactionary social conservatism and the denial of a shared, common good.

The kingmaker in the 2018 Tory leadership race was Tanya Granic Allen. She was the leader of "Parents as First Educators," a self-styled, grassroots organization devoted to home schooling, "parents' rights" and defeating curriculum that addressed gender identity and sexual consent.[1] Ford won on the third ballot after Granic Allen encouraged her supporters to "vote based on their issues." The point of this story is not the internal intrigues of a party leadership convention. Rather, it serves as a symbolic reminder of the crucible in which Doug Ford's education policy was formed, namely by pandering to populist social conservatism where his conservative fiscal policy could already be taken for granted by his base.

It is worth remembering that Patrick Brown used a similar campaign for the Conservative leadership in 2015, but backtracked by

September 2016, pivoting his messaging to a critique of the Liberal government's lack of public consultation, and leaving the content of the changes in the curriculum alone.[2] In the end, Ford also had to soften his regressive zeal for the repeal of gender identity and consent curriculum in the face of a massive public backlash, allowing much of the content of Kathleen Wynne's 2015 revisions to remain in his government's curriculum updates in 2019.[3] But opportunity arose in 2023. He weighed in on the conservative premiers in Saskatchewan and New Brunswick who were legislating "parental consent" for a student's use of their own choice of pronouns at school. Ontario's minister of education Stephen Lecce returned to the original Ford playbook, stating in a press conference that the "overarching value system" of our schools should not guarantee any privacy or safety for students who were not open about their identity at home.[4]

Setting Up Public Education for Privatization

Similarly, quick upon the heels of taking office in July of 2018, Ford decided to cancel curriculum revisions to implement the education-related Calls to Action issued by the Truth and Reconciliation Commission.[5] Those revisions had committed to the long overdue process of infusing into Ontario students' learning the history and perspectives of Indigenous Peoples, including the largely erased history of residential schools, a national shame needing direct redress in Ontario classrooms. The Ford government's framing of this cancellation was to "run government more efficiently" and to ensure that all ministries "carry out initiatives in the most cost-effective way possible."[6] Yet, it is impossible to miss the context which tied this decision to Ford's earlier manoeuvres in gender and consent education on the campaign trail. In both cases, divisive and reactionary politics were the order of the day, at the expense of the most vulnerable and deserving students in Ontario's schools and communities. Insofar as this pattern marked the very beginnings of his party leadership and premiership, it can be seen as foundational to his education policy.

It would be a mistake, however, to conclude that the Ford agenda in public education has only been devoted to cancelling Liberal initiatives, or that it has not positioned itself as the progenitor of new curriculum development. Ministers of Education Lisa Thompson and Stephen Lecce did take marching orders from the premier to attack any curriculum that advances and protects the interests of historically oppressed or marginalized communities. It is also true that the neoliberal, pro-business bent of the Ford government has shaped curriculum reform projects devoted to economic individualism and corporate boosterism, often masked in the rhetoric of "back to basics," especially in what is now termed STEM (science, technology, engineering and mathematics).

The hallmarks of this program have been the scapegoating of teachers for a supposed lack of numeracy skills — the insidious implication that students' future financial prospects and well-being can only come from improved "financial literacy" skills and better business studies courses, and that students must choose more marketable career paths. The not-so-subtle message has been to dump the entire responsibility for their own future welfare onto the shoulders of individuals (as discrete, lonely agents in the economic order). The systemic economic and political forces of neoliberalism, which have produced soaring corporate profits, higher postsecondary costs and an explosion of income inequality, are to be shuffled behind the curtain as embarrassing realities not fit for analysis or discussion in schools.[7]

Take, for example, the *Safe and Supportive Classrooms Act,* which in 2018 sought to introduce a mandatory Math Proficiency Test (MPT) for all those seeking certification to teach in Ontario, regardless of their area of subject specialization. While pretending to support a broader effort at math curricular reform, this move amounted to little more than a demonizing of education workers as being incapable of teaching anything. This initiative went beyond the normal and stereotypical union bashing one might expect from a conservative party. It was an attack on those not even yet certified to teach at all. The Ontario Education Quality and Accountability Office (EQAO) — the government agency charged since 1996 with ensuring "accountability" in Ontario public schools via standardized testing — had determined that student math achievement declined in Ontario from 2015 to 2019.[8] According to EQAO's research, there was little to no evidence that compulsory teacher competency testing had any impact on the quality of mathematics instruction or on student learning outcomes.[9]

However, even if it was reasonable for the Ford administration to develop and implement a new mathematics curriculum to address a decline in student achievement, what were the grounds for asserting that educators were personally to blame? There were none. The MPT was hatched to confer political advantage to Doug Ford and to Stephen Lecce by implying a generalized lack of teacher competence in the context of a broader battle with organized labour, and to diminish the electorate's faith in public institutions more broadly. Thankfully, the MPT was challenged in the courts by the Ontario Teacher Candidates' Council, a group representing students in teacher education programs, on the argument that it would disproportionately impact racialized teacher candidates, thereby violating equality rights under section 15 of the Charter. Indeed, an Ontario Divisional Court ruled in 2021 that the MPT did just that, based on the data collected during the EQAO's piloting of the test in 2020.[10]

The Court also considered the MPT to be unjustified because other, more sound alternatives existed, which might achieve the government's own stated goals, such as "requiring a minimum number of hours of math instruction or a math course in B.Ed. programs, requiring an undergraduate math course as an admissions requirement for B.Ed. programs or waiting to see the effects of the other parts of the [Crown's] four-year math strategy."[11] While the Ford government has since successfully appealed this Divisional Court ruling, and though the MPT will proceed, the Court of Appeal's ruling in Ford's favour addressed only the question of whether the test discriminated against racialized teacher candidates, which the Court ruled it did not so long as candidates could take the test repeatedly to pass it.[12] This later appeal decision does not affirm that the MPT will improve mathematics instruction or student achievement; but the legal battle *does* show that Ford will happily spend large amounts of public money in the courts to achieve partisan goals unrelated to the quality of education — namely, the goals of vilifying education workers and defending a public relations posture designed to paint himself as the strong, uncompromising boss who demands the best candidates for the job, an approach more befitting of a reality TV-show host than that of a premier.

In the realm of more substantive curriculum reform, and in the subject area of mathematics, Ford has pushed a platform of neoliberal creep. In 2020, Minister Lecce released a supposedly extensive revision to math instruction in order to undo the damage allegedly done by previous Liberal governments. This rollout was but one installment in a careful messaging campaign dating back to Ford's promise on the 2018 hustings to undo the destruction wrought by the so-called experimental pedagogy of "discovery math,"[13] a campaign which was maintained by press releases from the Ministry of Education bemoaning worsening standardized test scores,[14] and a March 2019 ban on student cellphone use in schools (without any substantial implementation plan, and which was revived again by Lecce in the spring of 2024).[15]

This "new" curriculum for Grades 1 to 8 was to be the cornerstone of a "back to basics" promise and a key part of Ford's "Four Year Math Strategy." According to the Ministry of Education's press release, this curriculum would teach "the value and use of money through mandatory financial literacy concepts;" coding skills starting in Grade 1 to "prepare students for jobs of the future;" and "fundamental math concepts and skills," such as the memorization of number facts.[16] Notwithstanding that some academics had already questioned the validity of Ford's caricature of math pedagogy in Ontario's schools, stating that it did not accurately depict teaching practices in classrooms nor the existing curriculum,[17] the 2020 math curriculum rollout was billed as a wholesale change by the minister of education. Critics of the new curriculum, like Mary Reid at the Ontario Institute of Studies in Education, were quick to point out that there were other variables detracting from student achievement in math, such as anxiety around math, and that aspects of the new curriculum might actually impair student comprehension.[18] Regardless, such critiques missed the point. As a politician steeped in the art of spin (as the former director of media relations for Stephen Harper), Minister Stephen Lecce's work on the math education file was as much about diversion as any real change.

As it has been with Ford's changes to technological and skilled trades education in Ontario's public schools, the goal is less about improving the quality of math education in the public interest and more about posturing to a socially conservative and politically nostalgic base as a cover for defunding the public education system and for the introduction of back-door privatization schemes. This agenda starts with the characterizing of public schooling as driven by misguided liberal eggheads who cannot be trusted to focus the students on the "real world" demands of the job market, and who eschew the teaching of basic skills which every employer now supposedly demands. Such a communications plan not only undermines public confidence in Ontario's schools, but also slyly strengthens standardized testing regimes, which pit schools against one another irrespective of the highly diverse communities they serve, to introduce market ideologies into the delivery of a public good. Ford's vaunted "math strategy" has played these familiar tunes perfectly, and stands as a model of his government's approach to curriculum in Ontario public schools.

Financial (il)Literacy

Nowhere has this corporate policy bent been stronger than in Ford's fixation on "financial literacy" curriculum. Fulfilling the promise laid out in the 2020 "Four Year Math Strategy," to increase student understanding of finances and money, Minister Lecce announced further curriculum reforms on May 30, 2024, in what he billed as the first "modernizing" overhaul in a quarter century of the requirements for a high school diploma, "ensuring students graduate with practical learning that leads them to better jobs and bigger paycheques."[19] Some of this announcement was a recycling of previous policy planks, including the MPT, but the cornerstone of this initiative was to be a new requirement that students complete a financial literacy component as part of their mandatory Grade 10 math course, with a minimum 70 percent score. The irony of such a posture couldn't be more profound, considering the Ford government's aggressive legislative programs to roll back employment standards, like his October 2018 repeal of Bill 148, intended to improve minimum sick leave provisions, the minimum wage and other provisions of the *Employment Standards Act*, or his unconstitutional Bill 124, which imposed a cap of 1 percent on public sector wage increases for three years in 2019.[20]

Any claim by the Ford government that it aimed for bigger paycheques for the average Ontarian, or for improving their working conditions, is laughable. The subtext in Lecce's announcement was that a student and their teachers are to be held responsible for the ravages of conservative policies on the worsening financial prospects of Ontarians, and that the growing income gap could be best explained by disparities in individuals' knowledge about personal financial planning rather than an economic system which produces obscene degrees of inequality. The deeper irony is that the research shows that Ontario's "financial literacy" achievement is well above the global average, according to the recent international tests available. Ontario ranked above the OECD average on both the 2015 and 2022 financial literacy assessments conducted by the Programme for International Student Assessment, which measured

15-year-olds' ability to "apply their accumulated knowledge and skills to real-life situations involving financial issues and decisions." Indeed, Ontario students fared better than many other western industrialized nations on those same tests.[21] An older 2014 study of global levels of adult financial literacy conducted by Standard and Poor's indicated that Canadians ranked among the top ten scores in the world.[22] Since Ontarians are not financially illiterate, and in a rapidly changing economy where inflationary pressures, rising corporate profits and increasingly unaffordable housing form the backdrop for education policy, it is fair to conclude that Ford's direction amounts to blaming the victim. The insult here is that a child's future prospects, for say home ownership, depend on them better understanding personal credit and mortgage amortization more than it would on economic or labour market policies from Queen's Park to improve the incomes of working people, or to put a lid on skyrocketing housing costs without shovelling billions of dollars to Greenbelt land developers.[23]

Nowhere in Doug Ford's vision of "financial literacy" did we hear a demand for learning how yearly postsecondary tuition costs in Canada on average required only 293 hours of minimum wage work in 1990, but needed 505 hours of such work in 2018,[24] or why the average undergraduate tuition in Canada in 2023 was more than twelve times higher than it was in 1972, and that this increase is almost double what inflationary increases would account for.[25] Would studying the collapse of robust public subsidy for postsecondary education qualify as "back to basics" learning in Ford's vision? Would investigating mounting student debt and its adverse effect on young people's ability to finance a first home exercise numeracy skills?[26] Apparently not.

Minister Lecce's May 2024 rollout of the new graduation requirements in Ontario also included a supposed "wholesale revitalization of guidance and career education," claiming that students would "benefit from modernized career education programming in their schools with more exposure to the skilled trades and priority economic sectors."[27] The same ideological drift is at the core of the Ministry of Education's July 2024 revamping of the secondary school business studies curriculum, the centrepiece of which is the replacement of a Grade 9 and 10 course to help students learn business-related software applications ("Introduction to Information and Communication Technology in Business"), with one leaning heavily towards a focus on private business ventures ("Building the Entrepreneurial Mindset"). It should come as no surprise that a Ford government would prefer that a student developing skills in spreadsheet software, for example, see that new ability as part of a push to "take initiative, adapt to change, find creative solutions, and understand the financial considerations of entrepreneurship,"[28] instead of seeing it as something useful more generally, or needed by a well-paid employee of a larger business, where they earned a decent wage, with predictable hours of work, a pension and benefits coverage.

Here, Ford sings the same neoliberal ditty situating public schooling as a training ground not just for the job market, but for a market where "business" means students must survive on their own, whether as an employer or employee. Ford's concentration on financial literacy and business studies helps expunge from public schools the goal of developing a student's broadest understanding of and engagement with the world, to nurture skills for active and critical citizenship. Of no consequence, it appears, is research by the Conference Board of Canada and the University of Ottawa's Education Policy Research Initiative, among others, which indicates that the soft skills of communication, collaboration and critical thinking best developed in liberal arts and science degrees are in renewed demand by employers.[29] But again, to query Ford's educational reforms on the assumption that he and his ministers of education base their work on a careful consideration of academic research in pedagogy, or in sincere attempts to better the economic prospects of Ontario graduates, is to miss the point. The conservative goal is to treat the system as a generator of diversionary headlines for reactionary purposes, to cast the purpose of the system in purely corporate terms and to distract (unsuccessfully) from defunding and privatization.

Funding Shortfalls

On the question of funding for public education, the Ford saga has been a finely wrought public relations campaign which claims increased investments in public education, while real dollars spent have dropped since he came to power. In a summary of the misrepresentations and obfuscations by the Ford government since 2018, Ricardo Tranjan, economist at the Canadian Centre for Policy Alternatives, notes: "For the 2018–19 school year, [Ontario] school boards counted on an average of $14,700 per student in inflation-adjusted terms; for the [2024–25] school year, they will have to make do with $13,200."[30] The bottom line is that since Doug Ford's government came to power, constant dollar-per-pupil funding in Ontario has dropped $1500, or roughly 9 percent.[31]

As for how the Ministry of Education under Ford's watch has funded school staffing needs, Tranjan calculates that for the 2024–25 school year, Ontario's public schools will be funded for at least 4,990 fewer frontline classroom educators than was the case for 2018–19.[32] Any efforts that school boards in Ontario make to maintain staffing levels beyond what the ministry pays for, to keep their class sizes manageable or to abide by caps negotiated in education worker collective agreements must be paid for either with money allocated by the Ministry of Education for something else, by school boards generating revenue by other means or by the spending of reserves. It is worth remembering that the reductions in funding for school staffing complements are better than what they might otherwise have been, thanks to a largely successful fight by education unions in 2019–20, waged with broad public support, against Ford's plans to cut funded pupil-teacher averages even more.[33]

Ford's financing of public education from the start has been marked by a strategy of political opportunism. Funding streams for public schools were yanked immediately after his election victory in 2018, before he delivered his government's first budget. In July 2018, as part of the fulfilment of Ford's campaign promise to dismantle the cap and trade carbon pricing system implemented by the Liberals, he cancelled the Greenhouse Gas Reduction Fund (GGRF), a revenue stream created via the sale of carbon credits worth $100 million a year to school boards, and used to fund upgrades and repairs to school buildings to lower their energy consumption (such as new windows, LED lighting, EV charging stations, or more efficient heating and cooling systems). To take just two examples: for the Toronto District School Board, the GGRF provided $25 million a year (about 8 percent of its overall budget for repairs),[34] while for the Ottawa-Carleton District School Board, the GGRF afforded $5 million a year (again, about 8 percent of its budget for all repair and upgrade work).[35]

While the loss of the GGRF was part and parcel of the Conservatives' repeal of Regulation 144 under the *Climate Change Mitigation and Low-Carbon Economy Act,* and the scrapping of the cap and trade auctions which funded it, some hoped that a sum as small as $100 million (that is, one-sixteenth of 1 percent of Ontario's public expenditures in 2018–19[36]) would be worth keeping, for the greening of the province's public schools if not for the savings in lower utility costs following such retrofits. But for Ford, this was not just an opportunity to extinguish efforts to lower the carbon emissions of buildings held in the public trust where our children learn. It was more. It was a chance to send an immediate message to school boards, by whatever means, that the tap was being turned off and that what was already a $15-billion backlog in school building repairs by the time Ford took office[37] would only get worse, which it did, as that figure grew to $16.3 billion by November of 2019,[38] and to $16.8 billion by 2022.[39] The Ford government did not create the school repair backlog crisis, but its cynicism about an existing revenue source devoted to fixing some small part of it (and devoted to fighting climate change, too) was amply demonstrated when Ford's spokesperson, Simon Jefferies, referred to the GGRF as a "slush fund" on the day it was axed.[40] The absurdity of such a statement is beyond reckoning, from an Ontario government under criminal investigation by the RCMP for arranging over $8 billion in profits for Greenbelt land developers.

The crisis of the underfunding of public education at the hands of Doug Ford's Conservatives, as bad as it has been, must properly be understood as part of a deeper neoliberal experiment that twins such cuts with new forms of privatization. Much analysis has already been devoted to the funding cuts to public education implemented by Conservative premier Mike Harris,[41] but for all of the devastation wrought by the Harris education reforms, he was comparatively timid on the privatization of public schooling, despite his appetite for the sale of long-term care, the 407 highway or Hydro One. Perhaps the brain trust advising Doug Ford was smart enough to learn a lesson from John Tory's loss in the 2007 Ontario general election, partly blamed by some on his 2006 promise of tax credits for Ontarians sending their children to religious private schools, or his further pledge on the hustings to allow faith-based private schools to receive public funding directly.[42] Either way, by the time Ford came to power, the Progressive Conservatives had become too savvy to invite public backlash against promises of, say, charter schools of the kind found in Alberta or of the voucher systems so prevalent in the United States.

The *modus operandi* for privatization of public schooling for Doug Ford was to be crasser than either of these older methods and would instead take the form of direct cash payments to families. Over the span of a mere two years, the Ford government contrived to pay out via four distinct programs more than $1 billion to almost 6 million parents, with no rigour in the application process beyond the requirement to provide a name, a school and a postal code in the online form.[43] While the ostensible rationale for these programs was to support parents with personal education-related expenses, which may have arisen as a result of the academic disruptions of the COVID-19 pandemic (like supports for student mental health, home schooling or tutoring), no receipts were ever required to verify that the money was spent by families in any particular way at all. Indeed, the dollars spent on hot dogs at any of the premier's infamous "Ford Fests" are likely better accounted for, and perhaps we err here in dignifying such Tammany Hall hucksterism with the term "privatization" at all. Regardless, these casually administered but grossly expensive voucher payments enraged hundreds of Ontario families, many of whom discovered that unscrupulous fraudsters (or other family members) claimed the cash before they could point and click their way onto the ministry website themselves. Not surprisingly, in December 2023, Ontario Ombudsman Paul Dubé commenced an investigation into these programs, noting: "People have complained to us about this issue through successive iterations of these programs, and the latest version is likely not the last."[44] It would appear that even Ombudsman Dubé knows a plan for further vouchers when he sees one.

Betraying Children's Futures

To look back on the record of Doug Ford's concerted, six-year attack on public education is to see the trends of systemic underfunding, partisan tinkering with curriculum and the denigration of education workers all converge with the dangerous development of siphoning public money from depleted Ministry of Education coffers to be tossed about in a barely concealed attempt at buying votes. Meanwhile, a school system that was once an exemplar to other jurisdictions the world over has been pushed to the point of dangerous dysfunction. While leaking roofs of aging schools,[45] critical staffing shortages of frontline education workers[46] and epidemic levels of workplace violence[47] all crowd the headlines, the concerns of Ontario families for their children's futures — economically, socially and environmentally — grow more acute.

All the while, Ford has played divisive politics in our schools, attacked education workers when they needed support, decimated the funding of our system and pandered to corporate and privatizing interests bent on destabilizing a civic good. As we contemplate a possible third term with Doug Ford at the wheel, we owe it to ourselves to remember that he has not simply failed to guard the sacred trust we as citizens place in our government to educate our children and to prepare them for a prosperous, sustainable and inclusive future; he has, in fact, willfully betrayed that trust. The people of Ontario deserve a public education system where the real assessment of students' needs — and of the common good itself — determine how schools are funded, how curriculum is developed, how learners and education workers are supported and how communities are strengthened by a rich and sincere investment in meeting their needs. Fully funded public schools should not be a frill, a thing denied by reactionary governments to siphon resources to pay for handouts to corporate interests under the cover of so-called "reform" agendas. Fully funded schools are our collective right.

5

PRIVATIZING ONTARIO'S UNIVERSITIES

David Leadbeater

FURTHER THAN IN ANY CANADIAN PROVINCE, Ontario governments since the late 1970s have driven the public university system down the neoliberal road of privatization and corporatization. The central economic device in this transformation has been provincial reductions in per-student grants to universities, coupled with increases in tuition fees for students.

By the time the Ford Conservatives came to power in 2018, Ontario spent less per university student than any province in Canada and had among Canada's highest tuition fees. Ontario governments had reduced public grants for university operating revenues from about 80 percent in 1980 to around 50 percent in 2004, and to only 38 percent in 2017.[1] Over this period, domestic and international tuition fees and miscellaneous fees paid by students jumped from 15 percent of operating funds in 1980 to 56 percent in 2017, to become the largest source for operating funds. By the 2010s, some government policy analysts and senior university administrators were using the terminology of "publicly assisted" or "publicly supported" universities, rather than public universities.

The Ontario public system was also highly unequal in terms of university size and regional disparity, and it became more so as total enrolment grew. Between 2,000 and 2018, the average size of Ontario public universities grew from 13,462 students (for eighteen universities) to 23,515 students (for twenty universities). In these, the University of Toronto nearly doubled in size to 83,554 students. By contrast, the average size of universities in Northern Ontario changed from 3,681 to 4,747 students, of which two were under 1,000 students. Well before 2018, the total number of full-time students in all the northern universities had peaked and started to decline absolutely.

The Ford Conservative government has furthered public university decline, undermined their claimed priority of "financial stabilization" of the postsecondary system in the wake of the Laurentian–CCAA debacle, spread indebtedness among universities and students, and heightened the exploitation of international students. This does not deny the roles of preceding Conservative, Liberal and NDP governments since the late 1970s — all supported neoliberal policies and bear major responsibilities for the decline of public university education in Ontario. So do federal Liberal and Conservative governments.

The Ford Conservative government has deepened and created new crisis conditions in the public system. Their populist rhetoric is a phony cover for more openly anti-democratic efforts to subordinate and fuse university education to corporate direction, "values" and objectives. A democratic response requires breaking from the neoliberal policy direction as a whole, particularly privatization and corporatization, by asserting principles of universal, free and democratic public education in the postsecondary system in all regions of Ontario.

Phase One: Destabilizing Cuts and Privatization

While the processes of privatization and corporatization were not complete when the Ford Conservatives came to power, the public universities already formed a tuition-dependent, corporative-competitive system.

In that system, incremental reductions in provincial, per-student funding were typical, along with an expectation from universities of some respite through increases in tuition fees, incidental fees, international recruiting, external research funding and ancillary revenues. Institutional indebtedness, along with inter-university and external competition, had not reached such destructive levels as to threaten the system's scope and stability. Concerns about student accessibility were ignored or downplayed by claiming students could get student assistance.

For the Ford Conservatives, however, this gradualist decline did not go far enough. In 2019, the government reduced domestic tuition fees by 10 percent, proclaiming with populist bravado: "Government for the People to Lower Student Tuition Burden by 10 percent."[2] Yet this same government also cut student assistance, including the elimination of a program of free tuition for low-income students. The then-minister of training, colleges and universities Merrilee Fullerton, a physician, commented, "The Ontario Student Assistance Program grants had become unsustainable, and it was time to refocus the program to provide help to students in the most financial need." Such neoliberal talking points hark back to the "less eligibility" call of the capitalist accumulators of the Industrial Revolution. Of course, the province would determine who were the lower number of "deserving poor" among students — as Ontario lurched further backwards from universality and education as a right.

Crucially, the Ford government did not compensate universities for revenues lost due to the tuition reduction. Then for the following years, the Conservatives doubled down on defunding by maintaining both domestic tuition freezes and reduced real per-student funding to public universities — while university costs continued to rise at rates higher than average inflation. Such financial pressures against the public system were destined to reduce program quality, cut faculty and staff jobs, worsen working conditions, and increase university indebtedness and vulnerability to external "shocks," such as in international student enrolment numbers on which the system was increasingly dependent.

Further, the Ford government encouraged more intensified competitive pressures against public universities, particularly through increasing degree-granting powers to the colleges, and through facilitating the spread of private, postsecondary programs. Public universities had already established joint programs with colleges in which students were charged higher university-level tuition fees while receiving lower-cost, college-level services. This field for university profit-making at the expense of students was now being partially turned over directly to the colleges. As well, politically, college control would mean fewer concerns about collegial governance, academic freedom and faculty research — key characteristics of the public university system largely not present in the college system.

As for private competition, signs soon appeared of how private for-profit universities might profit from the high tuition fee levels and exploitation of international students in Ontario's public system. The University of Niagara Falls (UNF), owned by Global University Systems (GUS) Canada, a Netherlands-based corporation, has planned its first class for 2024: "UNF will have a strong but not exclusive focus on the international student market, offering five undergraduate and master's programs in business management, data analytics, digital media and biomedical sciences."[3] The corporation said it plans to set tuition "broadly in line with similar programs in Ontario."

By privatization in this context, I mean a process by which the costs of education services are shifted to students (and their families) — that is, students pay individually for their university programs, primarily through tuition fees. A key indicator of the privatization of public universities is the portion of the cost of provision of the education services that is from private sources. The set of education services becomes defined increasingly as a commodity with a partial or full price (tuition) and subject to competitive pressures among universities based on maximizing net revenue (or profit). Generally, for each production unit, privatization requires either break-even or high net revenues, which reduces and eliminates the role for government funding. Full privatization implies not only higher tuition and/or reduced costs or quality, but also the closure of programs and institutions unable to raise tuition revenue and/or reduce costs or quality.

While the emphasis here is on education services as primary, these are not the only services in universities subject to privatization. Long before Ford, Ontario universities have pursued other avenues of privatization, particularly in ancillary services (internet technology, catering services, food courts, residences, conference venues, parking, merchandise, etc.). These already have turned many campuses into glorified platforms for landlordism, for contracting out and for monopolistic forms of profit extraction. The current direction in privatization is to cut even more deeply into core education functions.[4]

The privatization of university programs and other operations does not necessitate that the capital costs and means of provision (the university's land and facilities) are predominantly privately owned or held by private, for-profit corporations. Control and effective ownership of the land and facilities still remain ultimately with the Ontario state through legislative charters of incorporation, powers to amend, appointments, financial coercion and information access.

Privatization hits unequal institutions differently. During the three decades following the late 1970s, as university fees were raised across the board, they were also "differentiated" — raised even higher — for international students and for professional and graduate programs. More prestigious universities and programs with greater student demand and market power saw even higher increases in some differentiated fees.

As a result, elite universities, particularly the University of Toronto, came to have a much higher tuition (private) share and lower government share in their operating revenues than, say, small Northern universities. For example, according to the 2016–17 operating revenues, the University of Toronto received 64.7 percent from tuition and miscellaneous fees and 29.6 percent from provincial grants and contracts; by contrast, Lakehead University received 49.7 percent and 46.1 percent, respectively, and Nipissing University received 41.3 percent and 55.2 percent.[5] In this way, the leading elite university in Ontario, the University of Toronto, was much further along the road to full privatization compared to two much smaller Northern Ontario universities; in this way, too, the latter are relatively more vulnerable to public funding cuts.

Hence, destabilizing financial attacks like those of the Ford Conservatives are more likely to further privatization in better endowed institutions and increase impoverishment among the rest, including program closures. In the Ontario context, with its uneven regional educational and employment conditions, some fees in certain universities were already so high that they were beginning to choke off enrolment in some programs, such as in arts and basic sciences, or to lead students to study at other institutions or jurisdictions.

This is already an aspect of the decline in relative demand for arts programs.[6] The effects appear earlier in universities and programs lowest in the hierarchy of demand, such as universities in Northern Ontario. The general effect of this is that arts programs (especially fine arts and humanities), and some basic sciences, become increasingly streamed as studies for privileged elites or academic luxuries.

One might ask here if Ford's one-time tuition reduction and freeze of tuition fees is some sort of populist halt to the privatization process? Given Ontario students now pay on average well over half of operational costs,[7] the Ford reduction and freeze of fees is insufficient quantitatively to change the system's tuition-dependent, corporative-competitive conditions. Short of mass closures, the Ford government's sharpened financial degradation of public universities is more likely to accelerate the privatization process for better endowed universities,[8] while elsewhere precipitating class streaming, quality cuts, program closings and increased regional disparity.

Despite their declining — yet highly privatized and corporatized condition — Ontario's public universities remain fundamentally public in terms of assets and control in an overall public system. Indeed, the terms "publicly assisted" and "publicly supported" are misleading in that they suggest the universities are private but receiving assistance, while actually they are still public but being denied adequate public funding support.

Phase Two: Laurentian–CCAA Debacle and Anti-Democratic Education Politics

The second phase of the Ford government university policy was dominated by the Laurentian University–Companies' Creditors Arrangement Act (CCAA) debacle, which revealed not only the government's gross negligence in financial oversight but also a range of their anti-democratic education politics.

The Laurentian–CCAA process obtained for its supporters an unprecedented, radical downsizing and extraordinary corporate centralization of a public university — now sometimes called "the Laurentian model." While the Ford government did not initiate the corporate hijack, they supported it, covered for it and used it to give the impression of a concern for "stabilization," while driving forward with their continued degradation of the public system.

I characterize the Laurentian–CCAA event as a debacle in that the strategy of the Laurentian University senior administration and Board of Governors was widely exposed and discredited, and most of its characters driven from the scene. Then, after the program closures and mass terminations were executed, the Ford Conservatives moved in to reduce and replace Laurentian's Board of Governors in their own narrowly corporatist image so as to ensure their ideology of down-sized provision, top-down management and "market-aligned" education would be carried through and maintained long-term.

The events of the Laurentian–CCAA debacle and its leading characters are too many to name here. Articles written by my colleagues Reuben Roth (2021) and Ron Srigley (2021) give valuable context.[9] A key statement and petition emerging from the struggle is the N'Swakamok Reconciliation Declaration.[10] From a different angle, Ontario consultant Alex Usher has taken apart elements of the mismanagement of Laurentian University, not least that of President Robert Haché ("a guy like that should never have been in charge of a university"), in several blog posts.[11]

Compared to other public universities in Ontario, Laurentian (chartered in 1960) is a relatively small, significantly first-generation and working-class university, located in Sudbury, a hard-rock mining community. Its mandate prominently claims bilingualism (English- and French-language programs, services and administration) and triculturalism (English, French and Indigenous). Laurentian is often viewed as a "regional" university in Ontario.

The crisis broke out into public view on February 1, 2021 — in the midst of the COVID-19 pandemic — when the Laurentian Board of Governors sought and obtained bankruptcy protection under the CCAA.[12] For the first time in Canadian history, this corporate bankruptcy legislation was applied to a public, postsecondary institution. New profitable territory was opened up for corporate lawyers, consultants and corporations desiring to profit from the privatization of public institutions.

By supporting the CCAA process, the Ford government enabled the Laurentian Board to:

- break collective agreements and slash over 200 faculty and staff positions;
- eliminate 76 academic programs directly affecting over 932 students, mainly but not only in arts and basic sciences;
- destroy Huntington University, Thorneloe University and the Université de Sudbury, three small, federated universities who provided mostly arts programs and had been founding partners with Laurentian University;
- cut the second oldest Indigenous studies program in Canada without any consultation with Indigenous communities;
- cut a disproportionate number of programs vital to the Franco-Ontarian community, including the well-enrolled Sage Femme/Midwifery program;
- wipe out individual and institutional donations to Laurentian for teaching and research;
- end or disrupt research activities, including research with community and third-party obligations;
- close important cultural and sports activities with destructive community effects;
- inflict massive reputational damage on the institution, including internationally.

An Unnecessary and Costly Process

At the outset, it needs to be emphasized that the entire CCAA process was unnecessary, enormously costly and could have been ended by the Ford government who instead supported it through to the present day.

The Laurentian administration started planning secretly nearly a year in advance, and took advantage of the weak bargaining approach of Laurentian's faculty association to delay negotiations and manoeuvre the university into an even more desperate situation. Months in advance of the CCAA onslaught, the provincial government was aware that Laurentian was considering a CCAA strategy, and weeks before, the ministry had formal communications with Laurentian about financial assistance.[13]

Even after February 1, 2021, the CCAA process could have been brought to an end by provincial financial intervention or by facilitating a takeover or trusteeship by another university. Although it was often said that the province could not intervene, the province could and did intervene, at least three times publicly, such as with taking over Laurentian's $35 million debtor-in-possession (bridging) loan. The province also intervened to protect the Northern Ontario School of Medicine and the Université de Hearst from being dragged down by their connections with Laurentian — while it did nothing for Laurentian's three federated universities.

Any responsible government should have been alarmed by expenditures for CCAA legal and financial consultants, as well as by their possible self-serving role, on which the Auditor General commented gently: "In our view, Laurentian's actions in this regard were significantly influenced by these external parties."[14] The Auditor General observed that by September 12, 2022, Laurentian had incurred over $30 million for "legal and other financial consultant fees associated with its insolvency." It is remarkable that then Minister Ross Romano, himself a lawyer, or his advisors, would not have questioned sharply such a waste of student tuitions and public funds.

The CCAA's final scenes would be played without Romano. On June 18, 2021, after presiding over the most visible destruction and before the pending provincial election, Romano was dumped and replaced by Jill Dunlop, a former faculty member of Georgian College. Dunlop would continue government support of the CCAA and its anti-community consequences, all while extolling her "love and appreciation of rural Ontario and community engagement."[15]

Foremost a Ford Government Failure

The Laurentian–CCAA debacle was treated by the Ford government as a local failure, but it was foremost a provincial failure, in financial oversight, in funding and governance policies, and in regional representation for Northern Ontario. Such failure was used to increase more centralized, corporate, financial oversight — not greater community oversight or democratic engagement.

The CCAA process itself lent support to the dominant framing of the crisis as primarily one of local conditions by restricting most issues to those that were immediate and interior to Laurentian. The Auditor General's report had a larger scope, but it still placed the primary responsibility on Laurentian, particularly putting a major responsibility on the previous president, Dominic Giroux, and his overspending on capital projects and top-heavy administration.

However, the Auditor General also showed that the ministry had been aware, for over a decade, of Laurentian's situation — that it could be facing long-term enrolment issues. Most striking, the ministry was "not effectively overseeing the financial sustainability of the university sector."[16] Her report contained eleven recommendations to the ministry and two about lobbying requirements to the Office of the Integrity Commissioner. Unfortunately, other factors affecting Laurentian (and other northern universities) were not addressed, such as the impacts of rising tuition on enrolment and the province's inaction on satellite campus expansion outside the region.

A New Anti-Labour Extreme

The Ford government's support for the CCAA enabled a new anti-labour extreme in public universities. The Laurentian Board strategized using the CCAA to break the collective agreement with the faculty association, especially on financial exigency and severance, "to terminate more senior, fully tenured professors and avoid paying them full severance entitlements in cases where they were terminated before their retirement," as well as to clear many union grievances and to be "less transparent."[17]

This was evident in the termination protocol which was accepted by Laurentian's faculty association by a majority vote of members. The first Board target was faculty on limited-term contracts, usually the most vulnerable to predatory administrations. Then came faculty of pensionable age. This was a direct attack on tenure and seniority using age. It was not about any *bona fide* occupational requirement or inadequate performance. Nor was it even about years of service, which might at least recognize the reality that some scholars start permanent university work later in life, or have career interruptions for children or other family obligations, most especially women. The protocol expressed flagrant ageism and was fed by a long-held Ford attack on older professors claiming "the growing average retirement age among university faculty is 'limiting turnover that would bring in earlier career professionals with new teaching methods and increase diversity,'" while ignoring provincial responsibilities for cuts to new hiring and non-replacement of faculty who do retire, leave or die.[18] This attack, which included stigmatizing senior professors as "double-dippers," is part of a larger reactionary effort to reverse the ending of mandatory retirement and to absolve neoliberal government for the decline of public universities.

After older faculty, the terminations turned to faculty in alleged low-enrolment programs. "Low enrolment" was determined by a Senate committee meeting in secret, led by the administration's data and threats, without possibility of appeal. No questions were allowed as to why enrolments were low. In rapid turn, there followed a brief debate and vote by Senate, a spectacle in which Senate faculty members and students under administrative eye and pressure voted in the majority to dispatch their colleagues. The faculty association took the position of abstaining.

Ignoring Rights

The Ford government's responsibility in the devastation of Laurentian included negligence in protecting national rights and consultation, and in representing regional concerns in education.

The Laurentian–CCAA debacle led to the closing of the second oldest Indigenous studies program in Canada. At no point did the Ford government raise publicly their own or Laurentian's responsibility to consult Indigenous communities, especially neighbouring First Nations, about such a closure.

Nor did the Ford government offer any defence of Franco-Ontarian national minority rights and education against Laurentian's disproportionate slashing of French-language programs. For instance, Laurentian closed the French department/ Études françaises (but not the English department), and other programs crucial to Franco-Ontarian cultural reproduction, such as history/Histoire and theatre/Arts dramatiques.

The closure of English-language programs showed the utter hypocrisy of Ford's populist job rhetoric. While praising the importance of STEM (science, technology, engineering and math) education for jobs, the Ford government raised no concerns regarding Laurentian's closure of both its math and physics departments, the latter associated with the Sudbury Neutrino Observatory and the 2015 Nobel Prize for physics.

In my view, it is unlikely that the Ford government would have supported a Laurentian-style scorched campus policy in a GTA university. Provincial policy with its metropolitanist outlook treats Northern Ontario primarily as a place for resource extraction and transportation corridors.[19] For Ford Conservatives, the priority for Northern Ontario is resource mega projects, like the Ring of Fire, not major educational, scientific and cultural needs, including public university education and research.

Federal Government Irresponsibilities

Although the Ford government had foremost responsibility for the Laurentian–CCAA debacle, the federal Liberal government too had major areas of direct responsibility. In public, there were federal expressions of concern. In a historical first, on April 15, 2021, on the initiative of NDP MP Charlie Angus, the Liberal government held an emergency debate in the House of Commons around the Laurentian University crisis. But while much was said, nothing was done to end the Laurentian–CCAA process; quite the opposite.

While the most general federal responsibility lies in the long-term reductions in federal transfers for health and social programs, including education, there were areas where urgent federal action was needed, but absent. In particular, there was no firm federal challenge demanding consultation with Indigenous peoples in closures of Indigenous programs, nor against closures affecting the national minority education of Franco-Ontarians.

Another major issue was the federal government's failure in the oversight of millions of dollars of public research funds at Laurentian, particularly through the federal Tri-Council agencies, such as the Social Sciences and Humanities Research Council (SSHRC). One of the travesties at Laurentian was the "intermingling" and loss of research funds into general revenues. The federal Tri-Council agencies could have stood openly behind the researchers to whom they had awarded funding, as well as the community partners and third-party funders of the research, by directly guaranteeing all federal research funds and even transferring their administration to another university. Despite its high-sounding concerns about ethics, community commitments and support for researchers, SSHRC and the other Tri-Council agencies continued to allow Laurentian to control research funds, despite all the risks, research disruptions and public discredit of Laurentian. Indeed, the federal agencies even took the shameful step of joining the CCAA credit table with a claim of over $7 million — in competition against faculty severances and community claims against Laurentian.

Phase Three: Hardened Neoliberalism and Blue-Ribbon Delusions

On March 2, 2023, over two years after the Laurentian–CCAA crisis broke out, the third Ford minister of colleges and universities, Jill Dunlop, appointed a blue-ribbon panel "to help keep the postsecondary education sector financially strong and focused on providing the best student experience possible." The exercise was headed by Alan Harrison, the same special advisor on the Laurentian–CCAA debacle whose advice still remains hidden from the public and who was a known proponent of anti-collegial views of university governance.[20]

On the central issue of system funding, the blue-ribbon panel proposed a one-time increase of 10 percent in per-student funding for colleges and universities, to be followed by increases in line with the consumer price index, with a minimum of 2 percent per year for three to five years. Though the report was titled "Ensuring Financial Sustainability for Ontario's Postsecondary Sector," the amount was not even close to being able to make up funding losses under Ford, so its recommendations would ensure not sustainability but decline and sharpened conflict.[21]

But even this low-ball proposal was too much for the Ford government. In February 2024, Minister Dunlop announced only a $1.3 billion one-time increase for *both* universities and colleges. The CBC reported, "The freeze on tuition fees will be extended for Ontario students until at least 2026–2027, the year of the next provincial election, although institutions will be allowed to increase tuition by up to 5 percent for domestic, out-of-province students."[22]

The Council of Ontario Universities, representing senior university administration, responded with unusual sharpness:

> Our universities are at a breaking point. In fact, Ontario universities receive the lowest per-student funding in Canada and are only funded at 57 percent of the national average. The 10 percent tuition cut in 2019 and ongoing freeze, declining real per-student operating funding and the more than $345-million impact this year in repealing Bill 124, are further placing the education, programs and services students rely on at risk.[23]

The Ontario Confederation of University Faculty Associations was "glad" for the continued tuition freeze, but threw up its hands over the $1.3 billion, calling it "an inadequate investment in Ontario's postsecondary institutions" and "a drop in the bucket." They did not take issue with the 5 percent increase against domestic, out-of-province students.

Beyond such clashes at the highest levels of Ontario university politics, there are significant forces moving in a fundamentally opposed direction to the Ford Conservatives. The Canadian Federation of Students (CFS) Ontario has long advocated for free postsecondary education, including federal funding, with their most recent campaign being "Fight the Fees." The CFS was also a signatory, along with over 300 individuals and organizations, including the Ontario Public Service Employees Union (OPSEU/SEFPO), to the N'Swakamok Reconciliation Declaration. In the wake of the Laurentian disaster, the Ontario Federation of Labour too has been giving a wider working-class voice and organization to the struggle for "a post-secondary education system that is publicly funded, universally accessible and publicly administered — just like health care."[24]

Despite opposition from multiple quarters and despite major destabilizing risks to the system, the Ford Conservatives hardened on funding cuts with their limited fallback being tightened central financial oversight, along with delusional talk about major cost efficiencies without quality reduction.

On the issue of public university governance, the blue-ribbon panel followed a crude, corporatist, political direction without serious evidence or discussion of alternatives. The Australian corporate consulting firm Nous Group, well-known for re-treading neoliberalism to order, was given a privileged role in panel deliberations. This was the same consulting corporation inserted into the Laurentian–CCAA debacle. Alex Usher, an Ontario consultant, had this to say about the managerialist line pushed in the Nous Group governance report produced for Laurentian:

> Both the Senate and the Board are to be reduced in size by about 40 percent but, more importantly, the powers of Senate are to be circumscribed, leaving it as little more than an academic quality assurance body, able to make recommendations on individual programs, but not to make recommendations about the academic direction of the institution as a whole. Instead, unbelievably, this power is to be reserved to the Board, a body whose proposed skills matrix includes sixteen different areas, only one of which is to have the first freaking clue about higher education actually works.
>
> In fact — get this — Nous thinks that Laurentian's administration thinks that an external body (I'm guessing Nous has themselves in mind here) should conduct "performance reviews" of Senate. I'm honestly unsure if I've ever heard of a weirder perversion of the idea of academic self-governance....
>
> This is a plan which would make Laurentian's Board — a Board which, recall, made all the key decisions that ran the institution into the ground in the first place — more powerful than it currently is, and probably the most powerful Board in the province. And its Senate, concurrently, will be turned into the weakest in the province. And this is all based on a highly torqued email survey.[25]

Much of this would be comical in its crude, self-serving character. But the forced, managerialist rationalization of privatization and corporate power has anti-democratic consequences for public university education and research.

On more circumscribed issues, the panel showed no depth of analysis or evidence, such as on "regional universities" or on the panel's faith in the cost-reducing effects of institutional "differentiation." Also treated uncritically was the related ministry process of "Strategic Management Agreements," an undemocratic process encouraging patron-client relations between government officials and university administrations, diminished collegial governance and opaqueness to public scrutiny.[26]

On the issue of Indigenous postsecondary education, the panel report noted defensively that they were aware of the existence in the postsecondary sector of nine Indigenous Institutes but were precluded from making recommendations. However, there also exist Indigenous students and faculty and Indigenous programs in the public university system, but apparently these did not warrant the panel's attention. The panel discerned not a single noteworthy lesson from the Laurentian–CCAA debacle and its treatment of Indigenous programs, students and faculty.

The panel appeared less worried about venturing recommendations on Francophone postsecondary education. The report is marked by an exaggeration of Francophone university opportunity without any accurate data, a singling out of the low enrolments of two Francophone institutions, a blithe sense of the success of bilingual universities, particularly the University of Ottawa, and a dissent from key recommendations — by the panel's one Francophone and Northern Ontario member.

There is a long history of debate within the Franco-Ontarian national minority over education rights. Within the community, the leading position today is for independent Franco-Ontarian postsecondary institutions ("par, pour et avec"), not excluding Anglophones but not "bilingual" institutions. Not all Franco-Ontarians support this, such as the key Laurentian misleaders pushing the CCAA debacle who were Francophones. But for many Franco-Ontarians, the Laurentian–CCAA debacle was yet another failure of the bilingual university model. The main Francophone student organization in Ontario (*le Regroupement étudiant franco-ontarien*) has called for one independent Franco-Ontarian university with campuses at Ottawa, Sudbury, Hearst and Toronto and the transfer of existing Francophone programs to the newly consolidated university. This would resemble the Université du Québec. It is an important proposal, one not addressed by the panel.

The panel did manage to touch briefly on something that is serious in its consequences for the public postsecondary institutions — the remarkable disconnection and inadequacy of public system statistics. But the panel's concern was limited to comments about the situation *within* the ministry and managerial collaboration, not about public access, including for students, researchers, policy makers and education advocates.[27] This touches on one of the most debilitating elements of the corporatization of public universities: the proprietorial restriction of information about university conditions, educational and financial, in ways that block or limit public scrutiny and community participation in policy debates about their public universities.

The situation is especially backward even for enrolment statistics, which are crucial not only for educational policy but also related directly to revenue issues. Currently, the only public source of enrolment data for individual Ontario universities is through the Council of Ontario Universities (COU), and their data organization Common University Data Ontario (CUDO). But the COU is without any publicly defined mandate or accountability in how they organize, verify and make public the program enrolment and other data of member university administrations. For example, Ontario does not yet publish annual data on Indigenous student enrolments or programs, let alone have a public commitment to working with Indigenous communities to decolonize the CUDO data system. On the question of language, CUDO has a complete absence of data for program language and student language, such as would be useful for the Franco-Ontarian community.

In the end, the Ford government's hardened position on real funding cuts to Ontario's public university system rendered the blue-ribbon panel into window dressing for pushing the crisis forward. The closest to a public rationale for squeezing down public universities was left to Minister Dunlop to deliver: "The province needs to ensure schools are operating efficiently before it will boost their budgets or allow tuition fees to increase."[28]

A Truly Public Education

Advocates for public university education face in the Ford Conservative government both deepened crisis conditions and a hardened neoliberal drive that seeks to reduce public funding while furthering privatization and corporatization. This is consistent with capitalist accumulation — not "stabilization" — including class streaming and forcing the costs of education on to working people.

The effects of Ford's hardened neoliberal policies against the public university system are being felt in spreading indebtedness, vulnerability to instability and closure threats — especially to smaller and regional universities and to the arts and basic sciences. It is also leading to more authoritarian, anti-collegial and anti-labour administrative measures within the universities. As 2024 began, the COU already had announced "urgently" that: "Almost half of Ontario's universities are now running deficits, with schools warning that student services will face cuts if the government does not provide a bump in funding and also allow tuition to rise by at least 5 percent this fall."[29] Then came a change to federal immigration policy to reduce the number of international student study permits that triggered further cries about the conditions of Ontario's postsecondary institutions.[30] Neither of the COU measures would alter the overall direction of public decline, nor by itself will the federal prohibition of the CCAA against public postsecondary institutions. A real danger exists that the actual crisis conditions in the Ontario public system will be used to advance the Laurentian model by other means.

The degradation of Ontario's public university system makes even more crucial the struggle for democratic public education, including universal free access, respect of Indigenous and Franco-Ontarian national rights in education, collegial governance, reduced regional disparity, and, not least, community accountability and accessible, accurate statistics. Policy responses need to include:

- the reduction and eventual elimination of tuition fees (without means-testing) for all domestic students and the elimination of differential fees against international students, with universities compensated, per student, by the Ontario government;
- increased federal responsibility for funding free, universal postsecondary education across Canada, including fulfilling treaty responsibilities for full educational funding of Indigenous students, strengthened support for minority-language programs, regional research capacity, increased arts and cultural program support and assuring a non-exploitive approach to international education and student exchange;
- to counter uneven development among public universities, the province should regionally balance the allocation of system enrolment to stabilize northern and regional enrolments and capacity utilization; clarify regional mandates and end extra-regional satellite campuses; and consolidate the northern English-language universities as a strengthened, regional, multi-site university with a full range of programs;
- increased democratic community accountability and engagement; elections in regional university board representation; and reform for independent, accurate and accessible public statistics of postsecondary institutions.

6

EVERYDAY JUSTICE IN FORD'S ONTARIO

Kathy Laird

WHEN THE FORD GOVERNMENT FIRST TOOK POWER in June 2018, Ontario had a relatively well-functioning tribunal justice system that was widely recognized as a model for other jurisdictions. It offered reliable access to dispute resolution services, including mediation and adjudication, for a range of legal disputes experienced by many Ontarians, particularly low- and middle-income households. Since 2018, the quality and accessibility of justice at several of Ontario's dispute resolution tribunals (commonly referred to as adjudicative tribunals) have taken a precipitous drop.

Ontarians who need to interact with the justice system have always been much more likely to find themselves at one of its adjudicative tribunals rather than at a civil or criminal court. Across Canada, provincial tribunals deal with everyday situations where stressful legal conflicts can arise, including landlord and tenant relations, eligibility for disability benefits and social welfare, employment and labour relations disputes, discrimination and harassment claims, environmental issues, compensation for workplace injuries, land use planning, automobile injury insurance claims and child welfare conflicts. Adjudicative tribunals are an essential part of civil society, designed to offer low-cost, low-barrier access to dispute resolution services.

One of Ontario's most important tribunals is the Human Rights Tribunal of Ontario (HRTO); it hears and decides cases involving discrimination and harassment, including in employment, in housing, in education, and in government services. Ontario's busiest tribunal is the Landlord and Tenant Board (LTB); it holds hearings to resolve tens of thousands of rental-housing disputes every year, including eviction applications. The Conservative government, early in its first term, moved both tribunals into its newly created umbrella adjudicative body,

Tribunals Ontario. Tribunals Ontario functions under the oversight of the ministry of the Attorney General. The Ford government has established and maintained a leadership team at Tribunals Ontario that is dominated by individuals with close ties to the Conservative Party.[1] At the same time as new leadership was installed, the government moved to replace experienced adjudicators who had first been appointed by the previous Liberal government.

By replacing experienced leaders and adjudicators early in its mandate, the Ontario government began a process that, as will be discussed below, has diminished the quality and accessibility of justice at these two tribunals. Cumulatively, the changes introduced under the Conservative government at the HRTO and the LTB have had a devastating impact on hundreds of thousands of Ontarians who must go to either tribunal to resolve a legal dispute. Other Ontario tribunals, including those dealing with land use and environmental issues, have suffered similar fates, affecting access to justice for a broad cross-section of Ontarians.

Jeopardized Human Rights Enforcement

Delays have become endemic at every stage of the human rights enforcement process in Ontario. The backlog of unresolved cases at HRTO has doubled under the Ford government, even as the number of incoming cases has fallen. The backlog is now a three-year queue. Equally alarming is the way the HRTO is dealing with its backlog. At an unprecedented level, 93 percent of all final HRTO decisions have seen the applications completely dismissed, without the applicants having an opportunity to make oral submissions or attempt mediation. Most of these dismissed applications, referred to as "jurisdictional or procedural" dismissals, have been stuck in the HRTO backlog for years. In the past, the applicant would, at minimum, have had the opportunity to attempt settlement at a mediation meeting or to explain at a summary oral hearing why they believed they had suffered discrimination or harassment.

Justice Delayed and Denied to Tenants and Landlords

Members of the public who need the assistance of the LTB have received increasingly diminished service every year since the Ford government was first elected. Despite higher funding, more staff and a larger complement of adjudicators than ever before, the delays are crushing and the number of cases resolved each year has continued to drop, notwithstanding that every year since 2018/19, the LTB has received fewer new applications as compared to pre-2019 levels. A typical arrears application now takes ten times longer to be resolved — often up to one year. Tenant applications take much longer — often two years. An investigation by Ontario's Ombudsman found one tenant application that had been stalled in the LTB backlog for six years. That report from the Ombudsman described the delays as "excruciatingly long" and cited many examples of tenants "forced to live in unsafe and substandard conditions" and landlords "facing financial ruin."[2]

Understanding Tribunals

Before examining in detail what has gone wrong at the HRTO and the LTB under the Ford government, I will provide some helpful background on Ontario's tribunal system. Adjudicative tribunals are supposed to be "arm's length" or semi-independent agencies of the provincial government. They are governed by provincial legislation and operate under the broad oversight of a cabinet minister. An agency head, appointed by provincial cabinet, usually named the chair or executive chair, has a quasi-reporting relationship with a deputy minister and has an overall responsibility for budget planning, financial and annual reporting, risk management and functional efficiency. The responsible minister makes recommendations to provincial cabinet on persons to be appointed and reappointed to sit as chairs and as adjudicators at the tribunals within their authority. The chair or executive chair is generally involved in recruitment and recommendation of candidates for appointment. The appointments process is overseen by the Public Appointments Secretariat, which operates out of the Premier's Office. Adjudicators are the tribunal's decision-makers, appointed to conduct hearings and to make determinations in individual cases. At some tribunals, including the HRTO, adjudicators also chair mediations.

Within this framework, it is a fundamental principle of law that the integrity of an adjudicative tribunal rests on the expertise and independence of its leadership and its decision-makers. Particularly because the government is often a party to proceedings before its tribunals, including in housing, human rights and land use disputes, for example, it is vital that the public is confident that tribunal adjudicators will make decisions based on the evidence and not based on the interests of the government that appointed them and the tribunal leadership to their positions. Simply put, to ensure fair and independent decision-making, an adjudicator must be appointed based on demonstrated qualifications and not on the basis of ties to the government of the day.

This principle of adjudicative independence and expertise rests uneasily within the framework of the justice system when a government politicizes the appointments process, as has happened in Ontario today. Although there is legislation requiring that appointments to tribunals be merit-based,[3] there is no oversight to ensure this. In contrast to court judges, tribunal adjudicators in Ontario have typically been appointed for two, three and five-year terms, and, in the past, renewal has been routine if performance reviews are positive. It is when the government changes that the integrity of the system is most at risk. A review of the qualifications of appointees under the Ford government, available on the website of the Public Appointments Secretariat, suggests a pattern of replacing experienced adjudicators with appointees who lack comparable or demonstrated subject-matter expertise and adjudicative experience, and of rewarding Conservative party loyalists with leadership positions at tribunals.

Early Days under the New Ford Government

When the Ford government first took office, there was an unusually high number of vacancies and potential vacancies as adjudicators waited for their appointments to be renewed following the election period. The new Conservative government needed to act quickly to renew the expired or soon-to-be-expired terms of experienced adjudicators at most of its tribunals. It also needed to fill vacancies with new appointees with demonstrated subject-matter expertise (that is, knowledge of the relevant area of law) and prior case resolution experience. Instead, the government dragged its feet in making new appointments for months and declined to renew a significant majority of adjudicators at many Ontario tribunals. In the end, many Ontario tribunals lost almost all experienced decision-makers who had previously been appointed by the prior Liberal government.

The loss of experienced adjudicators meant a massive loss of substantive law expertise and case resolution skills that had been developed over years. For example, the Ontario Environmental Review Tribunal was amalgamated into a new Land Tribunal, and soon lost all its adjudicators with expertise in environmental issues. At several tribunals, it was easy to identify newly appointed adjudicators with little to no demonstrated experience relevant to their new responsibilities, but with, sometimes, connections to the Conservative Party.

By 2020, this policy of the Ford government left many tribunals in chaos, with only a skeletal group of adjudicators.[4] Adjudicators who were not renewed, and so went on to find new employment, still had hearings to complete and decisions to write. Sometimes, hearings days had to be repeated, with parties required to give their evidence again in front of a new and inexperienced appointee. At the HRTO, where hearings can last for multiple days, decisions were often delayed for four or more years after completion of hearings, as the few remaining adjudicators laboured under an overwhelming caseload and former adjudicators struggled to write lengthy decisions while engaged in other full-time employment.

Governments do not, of course, replace judges in the criminal or civil justice system when a new political party is elected. Discarding well-qualified and experienced adjudicators in the tribunal justice system predictably created dysfunction. Tribunals Ontario, including the HRTO and the LTB, were particularly hard-hit. The number of adjudicators fell drastically — the HRTO lost over 50 percent of its full-time adjudicators and the LTB lost an estimated 30 percent, between 2018 and 2020. In the 2023 report on the LTB, *Administrative Justice Delayed, Justice Denied*, Ontario's Ombudsman identified the drop in the number of LTB adjudicators after the 2018 election as a significant factor contributing to what he described as "an extraordinary backlog of applications" at the LTB.[5] In early 2024, Ted Hsu, MPP for Kingston and the Islands, introduced a private member's bill, the *Fewer Backlogs and Less Partisan Tribunals Act*, that, if passed, would have significantly reformed the appointment process for Ontario tribunals.[6]

Leadership Tainted by Patronage

The Ford government's policy of replacing experienced tribunal leadership was particularly marked at Tribunals Ontario. According to analysis by the Investigative Journalism Foundation, six of the nine senior chairs at Tribunals Ontario have either donated money to, served as a high-ranking staffer for, or ran for political office under the banner of a Canadian conservative party.[7]

The executive chair of Tribunals Ontario is a case in point. Sean Weir was first appointed in June 2020, without a posting or competition, and then renewed as executive chair until December 2025, again without the position being posted. Instead, there was a posting for executive chair of the Licence Appeal Tribunal, a position which does not exist and to which, accordingly, he may have been the only candidate. Sean Weir is a former Conservative candidate at the federal level. Although he was an accomplished pensions and corporate lawyer at one of Canada's largest law firms, he had no tribunal experience and had never led a public-serving justice sector body, let alone one with a mandate to deliver accessible dispute resolution services to a disproportionately lower-income population. He also had no apparent subject matter expertise in key areas now falling under his responsibility, including anti-discrimination legislation, rental housing law and child welfare and social assistance eligibility.

Removal of the Right to In-Person Hearing in Your Own Community

Before examining the current state of the HRTO and the LTB in detail, there is an important policy shift introduced across the board at Tribunals Ontario that deserves special mention —the loss of the right to an in-person hearing in your own community.

During the pandemic, most, if not all, of Ontario tribunals and courts moved temporarily to electronic hearings — by video or telephone — as a public safety measure. Tribunals Ontario never looked back. In November 2020, it announced that "digital" hearings would be the default hearing format for its thirteen tribunals, with almost no exceptions. For example, in its last published annual report, Tribunals Ontario reported that the LTB held only seven in-person hearings in 2022/23, compared to over 43,000 electronic hearings.[8] The decision to make electronic hearings the almost-mandatory hearing format was tied to another Tribunals Ontario decision to close 46 regional offices and hearing centres across the province. In the past, with very limited exceptions made for Ontario's far north, parties were afforded an in-person hearing at a regional centre in, or close to, their own community.

Ontario courts and other tribunals, like the Ontario Labour Relations Board, pivoted back to offering in-person hearings, with electronic hearings remaining as an option. This is particularly true at tribunals comparable to those at Tribunals Ontario, like the federal Social Security Tribunal, which also serves a high percentage of lower income parties who are unrepresented by counsel and who may lack adequate internet access. The Canadian Bar Association has cautioned that imposing an electronic hearing format will often have a negative impact on people living in poverty or facing other challenges to electronic participation.[9]

Tribunal Watch Ontario, an advocacy group promoting fairness and accessibility in Ontario's tribunal system, has published extensively on the barriers created for a broad cross-section of Ontarians who have no choice but to try to seek remedies at tribunals like the LTB and the HRTO, concluding that the electronic format has a disproportionately negative impact on marginalized communities.[10] Notably, over 60 percent of LTB applications are arrears evictions. Households that are living in precarious financial circumstances, that are unable to pay their rent, will often also lack adequate internet access. The LTB's solutions to this — setting up computers in a handful of regional centres, offering loaner phones or suggesting the use of the public library — fail to address the issue adequately.[11]

The Human Rights Tribunal

The unresolved caseload at the HRTO has doubled to 9,527 cases since 2017, according to the most recent data reported in Tribunals Ontario's latest Annual Report, released August, 2023. The backlog has ballooned despite the HRTO receiving, cumulatively, almost 2,000 fewer cases since 2020, as compared to pre-Ford government years. The HRTO's unresolved caseload currently amounts to a three-year queue, based on its historical record of closing approximately 3,000 applications a year.

Twice as Many Dismissals

The HRTO is now dismissing twice as many cases without mediation or hearing, most often on its own initiative, not on the basis of a dismissal motion brought by the opposing party. By 2023/24, the HRTO had increased the number of applications dismissed without mediation or a hearing by more than 100 percent, as compared to pre-Ford government years. In 2017/18, 610 applications were dismissed without a mediation or hearing (on "jurisdictional or procedural" grounds: see discussion below); by 2023/24, that number had grown to 1,344.[12]

In most cases, these dismissals are precipitated by the HRTO delivering a Notice of Intent to Dismiss or a Request for Additional Submissions to an applicant whose case has been stalled for years in its backlog. Research has documented a threefold increase in the number of HRTO-initiated dismissal motions since the HRTO was moved under the current leadership at Tribunals Ontario.[13] In many cases, after years of delay, the HRTO has moved to dismiss an application without even taking the mandatory first step of delivering the application to the responding party named in the application.

The Human Rights Code requires that the HRTO not dispose of cases that are within its authority under the legislation (referred to as its "jurisdiction") without an opportunity to make oral submissions.[14] However, under the Tory-appointed leadership at Tribunals Ontario, the HRTO now applies a new test for dismissing these cases: whereas before the HRTO only dismissed applications without a hearing if it was "plain and obvious" that the claim was outside its authority or jurisdiction, it now dismisses applications on a lower threshold: if it is "more probable than not" that the claim is non-jurisdictional. The applicants in many of these cases would have been afforded, in the past, the opportunity to attend mediation to try to achieve a settlement, including financial compensation, or been granted an oral summary hearing.

In addition to applying this lower threshold for dismissal, the HRTO has in recent years conflated the question of whether it has jurisdiction to hear a case with the question of whether the written application form demonstrates that the applicant will be able to prove discrimination. The HRTO is now basing hundreds of dismissals on a determination that it has lost authority or jurisdiction over an application because the applicant has not clearly articulated how they will prove that there is a link between the described negative treatment and a claimed Code-protected ground.

An estimated 80 percent of applicants are not represented by counsel when they file their applications. The statutory scheme, implemented in 2008, was designed to be accessible to self-represented applicants, with a comprehensive form that allowed the applicant to "tell their story," in their own words. The Human Rights Legal Support Centre (HRLSC) was established under the same legislation to provide advice to human rights claimants in filing an application, and then representation once mediation and/or a hearing was scheduled. The HRLSC has not been funded at a level that would allow it to accept retainers to draft the over 3,000 new applications that are typically filed annually. In fact, provincial government funding for the HRLSC has been virtually frozen since it first opened its doors in 2008.

Under previous leadership, the HRTO recognized that its process was designed to be accessible to self-represented parties and that it was its job under the legislation to determine if the negative treatment was Code-related. In fact, in discrimination cases, it is not unusual for the deciding evidence of discrimination to come from a witness's oral testimony at a hearing or from documents in the sole possession of the respondent that are only disclosed before a hearing. By imposing a new requirement to file additional written submissions, on the legal and factual basis for the claim, the HRTO is guaranteeing that some applications with merit, filed by self-represented applicants, will be unfairly dismissed.

The overall picture that emerges is stark. Under Tribunals Ontario's leadership, the HRTO is attempting to reduce its growing backlog, not by prioritizing prompt access to mediation and hearings, but by implementing a coordinated strategy that hits unrepresented and unsophisticated applicants particularly hard. It has ramped up dismissal motions on its own initiative and doubled the number of dismissals without a hearing. By requiring largely unrepresented applicants to file written legal submissions, often years after filing their application, the HRTO has erected new barriers to a previously accessible process, allowing it to dismiss hundreds of applications stalled in its backlog.

Human Rights Claimants Are Giving Up

Perhaps even more alarming than the twofold increase in "jurisdictional and procedural" dismissals — but not surprising — is the almost threefold increase in the number of abandoned applications that has occurred under the leadership put in place by the Ford government. In 2023/24, 1,083 applicants abandoned their applications, up from 374 abandonments in 2017/18. According to a review of the first fifty dismissal decisions based on abandonment in 2024, as reported by the Canadian Legal Information Institute,[15] all but a handful of the dismissed applications were filed in 2020 or earlier, including applications that were six and seven years old. When a tribunal leaves applications languishing in its backlog for years at a time, it is not surprising that an unrepresented applicant would fail to respond effectively to a newly imposed deadline to file additional materials. Many applications are dismissed at this point because the adjudicator is not satisfied with the new submissions filed.

Few Discrimination Hearings

Very few applications now make it to a hearing to decide if discrimination has occurred. The HRTO released 40 final substantive decisions in 2023/24, up from 33 decisions the year before, and 16 in 2021/22. But in the five years before this government was elected, the Tribunal was issuing an average of 103 final substantive decisions annually.[16] A final substantive decision (also called a "merits decision") is one that is issued after the applicant has been granted a full hearing where both parties have the opportunity to lead evidence and make oral arguments.

Of the forty merits decisions issued in 2023/24, only a handful were issued after an in-person hearing. Although full data for 2023/24 was not available at the time of writing, the Tribunals Ontario website reported only four in-person "hearing events" in the first three-quarters of 2023/24, as compared to 1,342 electronic hearing events and ninety-one written hearings over the same period.[17] The HRTO has almost entirely abandoned an in-person format, even for full evidentiary hearings.

The 40 merits decisions represent only 2.7 percent of final human rights decisions issued in 2023/24. To place this in context, the data for 2023/24 shows that the HRTO issued 1,450 final decisions in all, of which 1,344, or 93 percent, were "jurisdictional or procedural" dismissals without a hearing. Of these dismissals, 1,083, or 81 percent, were based on abandonment. A positive finding of discrimination was made in thirteen of the forty final merits decisions.[18]

There is something deeply wrong at a human rights tribunal when 93 percent of final decisions are no-hearing dismissals, mostly of aging cases in a multiyear backlog; when 81 percent of those no-hearing dismissals are because the applicant has given up, and only 2.7 percent of all final decisions are substantive decisions after full consideration of the evidence of the parties. This record proves that, if a tribunal fails over multiple years to effectively move applications toward resolution, it can count on the majority of applicants moving on or giving up, especially when the applicant is self-represented. It can now be said that the Human Rights Tribunal is the place where discrimination cases in Ontario go to die.

It also seems entirely likely that this track record is the key reason for the drop in incoming cases. Why bother filing an application when the record shows that you are unlikely to have your application heard and decided for years? Certainly, the cumulative drop of approximately

2,000 cases over the past two reported years cannot be explained by any drop in the incidents of discrimination or harassment in Ontario. It is, for example, contrary to a well-reported notable increase in reported incidents of anti-Semitism and Islamophobia. The fact that fewer Ontarians are turning to the HRTO for remedies can only mean that it has lost credibility as an effective body that can address and resolve human rights and discrimination claims.

The Landlord and Tenant Board

Despite increased funding, more staff, [19] and more than twice as many adjudicators as compared to the pre-Ford years,[20] delays at the LTB are now crushing and the number of cases resolved each year has continued to drop. As of the last Tribunals Ontario annual report, the backlog stood at over 53,000 cases. According to recent media statements by Tribunals Ontario, the backlog has increased by another 1,000 cases in 2023.[21] This has occurred despite the fact that every year since 2018/19, the LTB has received fewer new applications than pre-2019 levels. Cumulatively, the LTB has received over 57,000 *fewer* new cases over the last three reported fiscal years than under the previous leadership, which was able to manage the larger caseload with half as many adjudicators and without creating a significant backlog.[22]

LTB Wait Times Increased by as Much as Tenfold

The average wait for an order on a landlord's arrears eviction is now 342 days, according to Tribunals Ontario's most recent website data, as compared to 32 days during the same period in 2018.[23] This means that, whereas previously a landlord could expect to get an eviction order for arrears while still covered by a tenant's last month's rent, the same landlord will now be without rent for almost a year before obtaining a repossession order. While landlords with larger portfolios may be able to weather these delays, a small landlord with rising financing costs may be forced out of the market. This result is inconsistent with the government's stated goal of increasing the housing stock. Small landlords have historically contributed a disproportionate number of affordable units to the rental market.

For tenant applications, Tribunals Ontario reports that the average wait time from filing to order is even longer — 427 days — with some tenant applications, including applications seeking a maintenance order, taking over two years to be resolved. This can be compared to an average of 70 days for a tenant application to be resolved in a comparable period in 2018. Ontario's Ombudsman stated in a 2023 report, "Administrative Justice Delayed, Justice Denied," that his investigation had found tenant applications stalled at the LTB for as long as six years.[24]

It is also worth noting that the most recent Tribunals Ontario Annual Report records that when a member of the public tries to telephone the LTB seeking assistance, they now wait more than three times as long on hold as compared to the three-year average wait time reported in the 2018/19 Annual Report, even as the LTB now answers half the number of calls.

Fewer LBT applications resolved year after year[25]

Fiscal Year	Applications Received	Applications Resolved	Outstanding Applications
2018/19	82.095	79,476	14,276
2019/20	80,874	72,064	22,803
2020/21	48,422	35,983	34,731
2021/22	61,586	61,868	32,800
2022/23	73,208	52,986	53,507

Notwithstanding this clear record of growing dysfunction at the LTB since 2018, the Attorney General has repeatedly claimed that his government has been working diligently to fix a tribunal that was dysfunctional under the previous Liberal government. For example, on May 15, 2023, in answer to a question from NDP Justice Critic Kristyn Wong-Tam, Attorney General Doug Downey rose in the Legislature to falsely claim that Ontario's Ombudsman reported that the Liberals had left the LTB in "shambles."

In fact, the Ombudsman's report on the LTB traces the origins of the growing backlog to the change in government. The Ombudsman stated:

> Over the past few years, the Board has proven itself unequipped for the task of reducing its extraordinary backlog of applications. More importantly, those applications represent tens of thousands of Ontarians suffering hardship caused by the Board's inability to provide timely service…. Excruciatingly long delays have had immense negative impacts on thousands of landlords and tenants who depend on the Board to resolve their tenancy

issues. We heard from many of those trapped in the queue on both sides of the landlord/tenant relationship — some forced to live in unsafe and substandard conditions, and others facing financial ruin.[26]

In-Person Hearings Virtually Eliminated at LTB

One contributing factor to delays at the LTB, recognized by Ontario's Ombudsman, is the decision by Tribunals Ontario to move the LTB, and all its thirteen tribunals, from in-person hearings in 46 local regional centres across the province to video and telephone hearings. LTB hearings are now scheduled in multiple, daily, simultaneous, province-wide hearing blocks. This move, together with the unnecessary introduction of an expensive but flawed new case management system, was found to have resulted in "chaotic hearings," inefficiencies in the management of the caseload, and compromised fairness for tenant households who had more difficulty accessing legal assistance and who often lacked the ability or resources to connect to video hearings.[27]

Although Tribunals Ontario states in its annual report that the LTB and all its tribunals "will continue to provide alternatives for users who do not have access to technology or who need other supports to participate fully in tribunal processes," the numbers on its website, in fact, indicate otherwise. In the first nine months of 2023/24, there were only 15 in-person LTB hearings across Ontario, as compared to 53,891 electronic hearings.[28] Experienced counsel report that the electronic hearing model is simply not effective in managing a high-volume tribunal with a large number of unrepresented and often computer-illiterate parties. Over 90 percent of tenants are not represented by counsel and approximately 60 percent of all LTB applications are landlord applications to evict a tenant household for unpaid rent. Households living in precarious financial circumstances are less likely to have the IT resources and internet access to be able to participate effectively and on an even footing with a better-resourced landlord party on the other side. The move to electronic hearings has eroded fairness for Ontario tenants facing eviction.[29]

In addition to undermining fair process, the switch to electronic hearings has been identified as a key factor contributing to the backlog. Mediators are no longer present at all LTB hearings and mediation is much less effective in the rushed and impersonal electronic hearing format, particularly when one party (almost always the tenant) is on the phone and the other (the landlord) is participating by Zoom. Legal clinics report that, when hearings were conducted locally and in-person, up to 30 percent of matters could settle on the hearing day without the need for adjudication.[30]

Reduced Access to Legal Assistance for Tenants at LTB

The move to electronic hearings scheduled in province-wide hearing blocks has also made it more difficult for tenants to obtain legal assistance from the tenant duty counsel program funded by Legal Aid Ontario. From 2002 until 2020, regionally based, legal-clinic, duty counsel consistently attended all regularly scheduled LTB hearing days in locations throughout Ontario. Duty counsel lawyers were able to work effectively with LTB mediators, local landlords, municipal rent banks and housing inspectors to negotiate settlements on hearing days, diverting cases from adjudication and reducing the adjudicator's workload.

With province-wide hearing blocks and electronic hearings, legal clinic lawyers now waste an enormous amount of time sitting in on virtual block hearings, attempting to identify and connect online and by telephone with tenants who need immediate legal assistance at their LTB hearing. Because the hearing blocks are not organized regionally, clinic duty counsel struggle to identify local resources, such as rent banks, that can support settlements and save tenancies. This has resulted in a less effective legal assistance program for tenants facing eviction. In addition, by wasting the time of clinic duty counsel, the new system reduces the overall capacity of legal clinics to provide low-income households with legal assistance and representation.

Making Justice Inaccessible

The Conservative government, under Premier Doug Ford, has presided over the demise of accessible justice at two of Ontario's most important tribunals: the Human Rights Tribunal and the Landlord and Tenant Board. Since moving the HRTO and the LTB into its newly created Tribunals Ontario, and appointing new leadership that is notable for its Conservative party connections but not for its related expertise or experience, access to justice at both tribunals has suffered greatly. Ballooning backlogs and excruciating delays have caused significant hardship for hundreds of thousands of Ontarians who need the services of these two tribunals. All this has been allowed to happen when the solutions are in plain sight: these are tribunals that were, after all, functioning quite well, without significant delays, just a few years ago. The expertise to course-correct is readily available.

Why has the Ford government allowed this disaster to unfold on its watch? Whose interests does it serve when ordinary people cannot access justice? Will the dysfunction at the LTB be used as an excuse to move away from having any kind of hearing model for eviction applications? Will the human rights enforcement system keep shrinking, as Ontarians lose faith in its effectiveness? The questions go beyond these two tribunals; there are, for example, increasing indications that land use disputes are becoming the exclusive domain of developers and municipalities, with few avenues for public participation.[31] Ultimately, when a government reduces the opportunities for people to seek justice in everyday disputes, it also reduces confidence in our democracy. The ramifications over time may be most unfortunate for civil society.

Premier Ford has repeatedly said that he cares about "the little guy." Apparently, that does not include the predominately low- and middle-income Ontarians who can no longer access timely, expert dispute resolution services — a fair and efficient hearing — when facing critical legal disputes and challenges.

7

HEALTH CARE SOS

Michael Hurley and Doug Allan

IN THE EARLY 1990s, the Bob Rae New Democratic Party government removed almost ten thousand hospital beds in Ontario. Despite this, the Mike Harris Progressive Conservative (PC) government cut another 8,100 beds between 1995 and 2003. Dozens of hospitals were ordered closed or merged. The PCs cut nominal hospital funding in 1997 by 3.6 percent — or $348 million. But, after public outrage at the problems that ensued, the PCs quietly reversed their policy and began to improve hospital funding, increasing it by 33.4 percent between 1998 and 2002 (and by 12.6 percent in 2000 alone).[1] Public pressure forced even a right-wing government to moderate its cuts. Ontario hospitals and long-term care (LTC) capacity did not keep up during the Liberal reign. Liberal austerity meant that there were 31,736 hospital beds in 2005 and 30,301 hospital beds in 2017 — a decline of 4.5 percent.[2] Likewise, there were 74,000 LTC beds in 2005 and 78,664 in 2019, with 6.3 percent nominal growth, while the population aged 75 years and older grew by 43 percent.[3]

For decades, there has been a consensus in ruling circles that Ontario hospital capacity should be constrained despite a rapidly growing population, societal aging and pressures arising from health care utilization. When the Liberals were elected in 2003, this ideology spread to LTC. But with repeated capacity crises, the COVID outbreak and many years of campaigning by labour, local communities and the Ontario Health Coalition (OHC), this consensus has broken down. By the 2018 election, even the right-wing PCs campaigned on promises to end hospital hallway health care and to add 30,000 LTC beds. Despite those promises, the PC government has actively undermined hospital capacity and has miserably failed to build LTC capacity. The capacity crisis has gotten worse.

Funding

Provincial government funding of hospitals is lower in Ontario than in any other province, according to the latest data.[4]

Ontario had the lowest per capita spending on hospitals in Canada in 2023

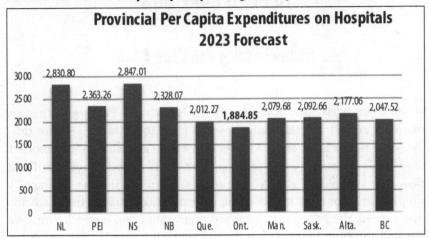

For many decades, Ontario followed the Canada-wide funding pattern, but starting in the 2000s, Ontario began to fall behind.[5] According to the latest Canadian Institute for Health Information (CIHI) figures, Ontario is 6.7 percent behind the Canada-wide average for provincial health expenditures per capita.[6]

Much of this is due to hospital underfunding, where Ontario is 7.9 percent behind the Canada-wide average.[7]

Hospital Staffing

Ontario hospitals are drastically understaffed. If at the same levels of staffing per capita as other provinces, Ontario would have an additional 34,292 extra full-time staff.[8] The province has low levels of staff in the following key areas: 12,133 are missing in support services (cleaning, food, maintenance, etc.); 842 in intensive care; 2,367 in operating rooms; 1,909 in emergency departments; and 15,396 in nursing inpatient services.[9]

The overall 34,292 full-time equivalent (FTE) staffing shortfall in Ontario occurs despite higher hospital staffing levels in Ontario in non-traditional hospital employment, such as research, education and community health.

Ontario hospitals need tens of thousands more full-time staff

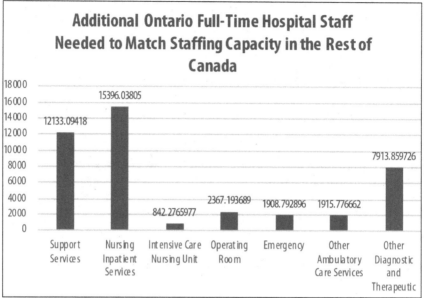

In addition, Ontario hospitals currently have a large number of vacant positions, with job vacancies now at 534 percent of the number of vacancies in 2015. The increase in hospital vacancies has occurred regardless of a sharp fall in job vacancies across all industries since 2022. The increase in hospital job vacancies has also corresponded with an ongoing decline in the percentage of hospital spending on employee compensation, going from 64.3 percent to 58.9 percent between 2005 and 2022.

Hospital Bed Capacity

Consistent with low hospital staffing in Ontario, there is also a very low number of staffed hospital beds. In 2023, there were 34,931 Ontario hospital beds staffed and in operation, which is 2.23 beds per 1,000 people.[10] This is virtually identical to the level it was at when the PC government — with their promises to end hallway health care — came to power in 2018, when there were 31,720 beds and a ratio of 2.21 beds per 1,000 population. Between 2005 and 2023, hospital beds in Ontario increased by 10 percent. However, the population increased 24.6 percent. As a result, hospital beds per 1,000 people decreased from 2.53 to 2.23, a 12 percent decrease.

To return Ontario to the same capacity relative to the population as in 2005, an additional 4,699 hospital beds would have been required in 2023. These 4,699 extra beds would not account for the additional need created by societal aging. Between 2005 to 2023, the 65-years and older population increased by 1.25 million (an increase of 77.5 percent).[11] This population growth also requires a significant increase in hospital capacity.

The Ontario number of beds per 1,000 population compares poorly with the rest of Canada: 2.23 versus 2.59 (16.9 percent fewer beds).[12]

Ontario hospital-bed capacity lags behind the rest of Canada and far behind other western nations

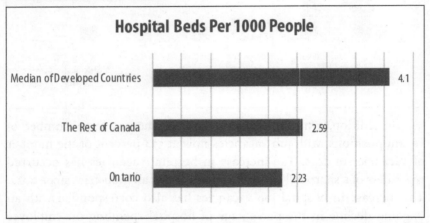

Internationally, Ontario is an outlier. The median among rich nations is 4.1 hospital beds per 1,000 population, which is 84 percent higher than Ontario's capacity.[13]

The Current Situation and Future Plans of the PCs

The PCs promised to end hallway health care. This promise is now almost forgotten, given the many hospital capacity failures during this government's reign. However, the government is making some promises to increase capacity. These promises do mark a change in policy. After decades of shrinking capacity, the promise now is to increase it. The problem is that what has been done and what has been promised for the future are inadequate to meet care needs. The promise to increase LTC capacity remains officially in place — but the government's execution has been inept and inadequate.

Hospitals

The government has claimed that it increased hospital capacity during COVID-19 by 3,000 beds. It further claims that it will increase hospital capacity by another 3,000 beds by 2032. If true, this would be a capacity increase of 18.3 percent over thirteen years, or 1.3 percent per year. There are several problems with this claim, however.

First, the hospitals themselves report an increase of only 2,161 beds since the COVID-19 pandemic (since 2019). If 3,000 additional beds are added to that, it means an increase of 15.7 percent, not 18.3 percent. Second, the demand pressure for hospital and other health care capacity is growing much more quickly than 1.1 percent (or 1.3 percent) per year.

Part of the failure of the government to solve hospital capacity problems lies with its unwillingness to keep up with population growth. According to Statistics Canada, Ontario's population in the second quarter of 2018 (when the Ford government was elected) was 14,251,136. This number rose to 15,996,989 by the second quarter of 2024, a 12.3 percent increase.[14] Just to keep up with population growth, the government would have needed to add 6.3 percent more capacity over the last two years and 12.3 percent since the Ford government was elected in 2018. This increase in health care demand is exclusive of other health care pressures, such as aging and increased utilization of health care.

Health care needs are very sensitive to aging. About 60 percent of hospital beds are occupied by people aged 65 or older. This group is growing at a very rapid pace: between 2018 and 2023, its population grew 18.4 percent, or, on average, 3.4 percent per year. To maintain a comparable capacity for this age group, the total number of beds would need to increase by 2.04 percent each year.[15]

Health care utilization, demand for health services outside of population growth and aging have all been rising. For example, a new medical discovery increases utilization as Ontarians are then able to take advantage of a previously unavailable service. Diseases and conditions that could not be treated now can be. Health care utilization is estimated to increase at a constant annual rate of 1.5 percent.

One new factor also affecting utilization is COVID-19. COVID-19 bed occupancy over the last year ranged from a high of 1,753 beds in November 2023, to a low of 249 in March 2024. Average COVID-19 bed occupancy remains far above occupancy for influenza, even during the flu season when the flu has regularly caused hospital capacity problems.

Notably, CIHI data indicates patients with COVID-19 stay three times longer and cost three times as much as the average inpatient.[16]

The health system is also impacted after people no longer have the COVID-19 infection. Trisha Greenhalgh and her colleagues write in *The Lancet* that post-COVID-condition "can affect multiple organ systems and lead to severe and protracted impairment of function as a result of organ damage. The burden of this disease, both on the individual and on health systems and national economies, is high."[17]

Combined, current population growth, aging and increasing utilization create significant pressure for growth — over 4 percent per year. That is over four times the annual planned hospital bed growth over the next ten years. Increasing utilization will add another 1.5 percent. Along with the population growth of those aged 65 and above, the total estimated demand pressure is just over 4 percent.

It is important to note that this increase does not deal with the staffing crisis, the workload crisis, the bed shortages or the emergency room back-ups, and it does not offset inflationary cost pressures. This is simply to maintain the current inadequate service levels. The 6.6 percent increase (or an average annual increase of 1.6 percent) in hospital beds over the four years since the beginning of COVID-19 (2019 through 2023) falls well below this — it is less than half of the needed extra capacity. This likely helps explain the deepening problems faced by our hospital system.

However, the existing PC government plans are even worse. Their plan to increase hospital capacity by another 3,000 beds over ten years (approximately 8.6 percent) falls much further behind demand pressures, as illustrated in Figure 7-4. Ontario is already thousands of beds behind the capacity it had in 2005, and the current PC plan will create even more problems.

Worse still, a 2023 Financial Accountability Office (FAO) report indicates that, based on government plans, few new beds will be added between 2022/23 and 2027/28 — 1.8 percent over five years. The immediate future is especially bleak.[18]

Further, the government trumpets new money for home care — but the FAO projects a decline in the number of nursing and personal support hours per Ontarian aged 65 and over, from 20.6 hours in 2019/20 to 19.4 hours in 2025/26. This is a decline of 5.8 percent. Unless this improves, there will be no relief through home care — in

Ford's planned hospital capacity falls far short of need

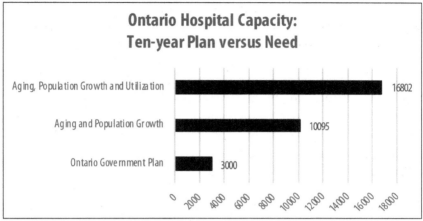

fact, just the opposite. The FAO sees a slight improvement in the ratio of LTC beds to elders aged 75 and over — from 71.3 beds per 1,000 in 2019/20 to 72.1 in 2027/28. This amounts to a 1.1 percent increase over eight years, or 0.1 percent per year. This very slight increase is the plan despite nearly 43,000 elders currently on the LTC waitlist and the government having passed legislation requiring hospital patients to move into long-term care. With this modest increase, Ontario will still be short of the 90 beds per 1,000 elders aged 75 and older that existed in 2010/11 — 20 percent fewer beds.

There is no relief coming for the capacity crisis from the current plan for LTC. Worse, as we shall see, LTC development is going very slowly.

Another concern, reported in January 2024 by the Ontario Medical Association, is that the number of Ontario residents who don't have a family doctor — currently around 2.3 million people — will nearly double in the next two years.[19] This is up from 1.8 million people in March 2020. The government responded in the 2024/25 budget by promising $546 million over three years, claiming this increase will connect 600,000 people to primary care. Notably, however, over the last three years, Ontario's population increased from 14.8 million to 15.99 million, an increase of almost 1.2 million people.

Once again, the government announces impressive-sounding numbers that do not stand up under scrutiny.

Even the government's frequent boasts about its plans to build new hospitals and new LTC beds fall far short under examination. In real dollar terms, the FAO reported in 2023 that the ten-year planned increase in health infrastructure funding amounts to a 10.8 percent increase in spending over the previous decade. While this sounds impressive, the population grew 18 percent between 2014 and 2024. That is two-thirds more than the increase in health infrastructure funding. Moreover, aging and utilization pressures further increase the demand for health care infrastructure. The hospital capacity crisis is also compounded by a lack of new LTC beds. Despite a promise to increase beds by 15,000 by 2023/24 and by 30,000 by 2028, the government records show in the 2024/25 budget to have only opened 2,246 new beds. This is only 7.5 percent of their promise to add 30,000 beds over ten years (that is, by 2028), and just 15 percent of their promise for 2023/24.

If the addition of 2,246 beds is a *net* increase in beds, it amounts to a 2.9 percent increase in the total number of LTC beds. However, the population of the relevant age group (aged 75 and older) increased by 21 percent between 2018 and 2023. As with hospital infrastructure, LTC infrastructure development has fallen *far* short of need — and government plans. It is unlikely, however, that there has even been a *net* increase of 2,246 beds, as some LTC operators are closing facilities and beds. In Toronto, six LTC facilities have closed entirely or have announced their closure since 2022. This means the loss of 650 beds. Guelph, Niagara Falls and Burlington LTC homes have also announced closures of their facilities.[20] The government is having serious difficulties with LTC development. In the 2022/23 budget, the government claimed 3,689 new LTC beds would be created by 2023. Now, in the 2024/25 budget, they note that 2,246 new beds have been created. Given the lack of new beds, the waitlist for LTC has grown to 43,000 people, about 20 percent more than when the PCs were elected in 2018 on a promise of adding LTC beds. The current government's failure to meet its promises to increase LTC capacity in a timely way contrasts with the previous PC government. It promised in 1998 to add beds, and by 2005, 17,000 new beds had been added.[21]

Health Care Privatization

Since the election of the Mike Harris PC government, health care privatization has been a major threat. But the inherent problems of privatization and significant popular resistance from the OHC, labour and the broader community have tempered the privatization push, leaving mixed success for corporations. Under the

PC government, public-private partnership (P3) hospital projects were started in the early 2000s. The OHC responded with public referendums in cities across the province, with people voting overwhelmingly for fully public hospitals. Eventually, the government dramatically cut back the extent of privatization that came with P3 hospital development. However, private clinics began to intrude on public health care.

On September 20, 2007, Krista Stryland died after undergoing liposuction at a private clinic. Stryland bled excessively following the surgery. The College of Physicians found that one of the doctors involved delayed calling 911, and when paramedics finally did arrive, they found Stryland lying in a pool of blood with no vital signs. The family doctor who performed the liposuction was ultimately publicly reprimanded and told that her "dangerous" behaviour was an "obvious betrayal of the public trust." "Emboldened with time and experience, you proceeded to perform more and more invasive procedures and ultimately major surgeries without the benefit of formal surgical training," she was told. The government had let much of the emerging industry slip entirely free of public reporting and oversight. After this, the government was forced in 2010 to require the industry to face some modest oversight. Unfortunately, this was not by a public authority, but through self-regulation by the doctors. Problems with transparency and public accountability of this method of oversight became headline news.[22]

The PC government also tried to set up private MRI and CT clinics. Community/labour campaigns however were able to stop this expansion of privatization. A key factor was that the private clinics were allowed to bill private patients for a certain number of hours each week. As the public insurance system must pay for all "medically necessary" hospital services, the government was left to try to explain why private clinics subject patients to tests for medically unnecessary reasons.

Over the summer of 2013, the previous Liberal government of premier Dalton McGuinty got into a messy dispute with private physiotherapy clinics. The government stopped 94 physiotherapy clinics from directly billing OHIP. Ontario Health Minister Deb Matthews said that, over the years, licences to provide these services have been bought up by large corporations. Moreover, she charged, the "existing 94 clinics have had an unlimited ability to bill the government and have become very creative in the way they bill."[23]

The government claimed that an audit of 15,000 records from the clinics found that 58 percent of them failed to support OHIP billings.

Five-minute exercise classes were sometimes billed as physiotherapy, care plans did not measure up, record keeping was incomplete and physician referrals were sometimes lacking. "There is extraordinary growth in expenditures and the audit was one of those factors that just demonstrated to me that there were companies who were just taking advantage of the way the program was set out and taking advantage of their unlimited ability to bill," Matthews told the *Toronto Star*. The government was back at war with another group of private clinics in early 2014, this time the newly established private plasma clinics. The government, opposed to their plan to pay people for their plasma, wanted to shut them down.

But the clinics refused. In the face of this open defiance, Matthews was reduced to calling in inspectors and threatening to get a court order. New legislation was also threatened. Matthews told the *Toronto Star*, "I expect any company operating in Ontario, and especially in the health care sector, to operate within our laws."[24] As a result of these struggles, private expenditures on health care, after increasing in the 1990s, have hovered at roughly the same level, only taking a temporary dip when COVID-19 forced the provincial government to inject more money into health care.

Over 30 percent of health spending in Ontario is private payments[25]

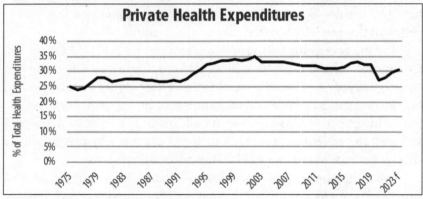

Whether this will continue is an open question. The OHC has repeatedly revealed extra billing of patients by existing private clinics for a decade. Private clinics have pushed hard to allow extra billing for medically necessary services, appealing all the way to the Supreme Court. Notably, increased privatization does not mean a reduction in public spending. Governments in the US spend about twice as much per capita for their largely privatized care as Canadian governments do.

New Hospital Privatization in Ontario

The PC government passed legislation in 2023 to turn hospital surgeries and diagnostic tests over to for-profit clinics. Prior to the 2022 election, they vehemently denied claims made by the OHC that the PC government would privatize hospital services.[26]

The government says this action is to increase capacity. But in the one area where surgical privatization has been used in Ontario to a significant extent — cataract surgery — Ontario fails to meet the national delivery time standard more often than other provinces (59 percent versus 66 percent Canada-wide). For hips and knee replacements, Ontario meets the national standard more than any other province. The PC government plans to privatize these surgeries next.

Research shows that increased funding for private, for-profit cataract surgical centres was associated with a large increase in the number of surgeries performed for those in the highest income quintile, even as the number of surgeries in total declined. The highest income category was "the only group that saw an increase in cataract operations."[27]

CBC News reports the rates being paid to the privately owned Don Mills Surgical Unit Ltd. are noticeably higher than what the province provides public hospitals for the same procedures. "The overpayment for these minor things is egregious," said the chief of surgery at a large Ontario hospital. "If I were running that centre, I would be a millionaire," said the director of surgery at another hospital. "There's a tonne of money to be made.[28] Meanwhile, the government plans to *cut* hospital funding for 2024/25.

Surgery at for-profit clinics can be 2 to 3 times higher than public surgery

Private/Public	Cataracts	Knee Arthroscopy
Don Mills Surgical Unit	$1,264	$4,037
Public Hospitals	$508	$1,273–$1,692

The government plans to provide public dollars to for-profit clinics to build new operating rooms, while hospital operating rooms sit completely unused or closed for much of the year. The government plans to give $20 million to these clinics for buildings in 2024/25, up from $2.7 million in 2021/22 — a 95 percent annual growth rate. For-profit clinics are attracted to larger urban centres where more business and profit are found. This is where they duplicate operating rooms —

while small and rural hospitals face unprecedented closures and capacity shortages.

A 2022 study by University of Oxford researchers concluded that private sector outsourcing in England corresponded with significantly increased rates of what is termed "treatable mortality" (deaths that can be avoided through timely and effective health care interventions). The study found that an annual increase of one percentage point in outsourcing to the private for-profit sector corresponded with an annual increase in treatable mortality of 0.38 percent in deaths in the following year.[29] A 2024 *Lancet* study by the same researchers found that "aggregate increases in privatization frequently corresponded with worse health outcomes for patients" and that "outsourced cleaning services corresponded with higher rates of inpatient infection than internal cleaning services."[30]

There has been creeping privatization in hospitals for years and the results have not been good. Contracting out costs have consistently gone up as a percentage of total hospital spending.[31]

Spending by hospitals on contracting out has tripled over twenty years

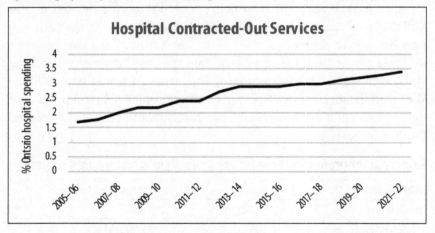

The Auditor General showed how P3 hospitals introduced twenty years ago ran up costs by billions of dollars. And now we see that building costs are eating up twice the share of hospital spending as they were when the P3 privatization experiment started twenty years ago. The result? Spending on employees has gone down dramatically.

A powerful BC for-profit clinic took the BC government to court — right up to the Supreme Court — to win the right to charge patients extra for medically necessary services. The logic is plain: the more for-profit clinics can charge, the bigger their profits. Worse, the bigger the for-profit providers get, the harder they can push to undermine public health care.

The Consequences of PC Policy

In 2018, the PCs ran on a promise of ending hospital-hallway health care. In fact, the problem has gotten worse. The number of inpatients being cared for in hallways has hit 1,326. This is an all-time high: 25 percent higher than when the government was elected in June 2018.[32]

In an unprecedented development, Ontario now has hundreds of unplanned hospital emergency department closures every year, often due to staffing problems. Prior to the Ford government, this happened rarely. Small-town and rural hospitals are especially under threat. After the cancellation of tens of thousands of surgeries because of COVID-19, hospital bed occupancy fell from 96 percent in 2018/19 to 84 percent in 2020/21 — an almost safe bed occupancy level. However, hospital bed occupancy returned to 93 percent by the first quarter of 2023, a dangerously high level (because high-bed occupancy can result in treatment delays, long waits in emergency rooms, problems with infection control and cancelled surgeries).[33] With so few hospital beds and staff, patients who turn up at emergency departments must wait. Currently, the average wait time is nineteen hours before a patient can be admitted to the hospital.[34]

This average wait time is well over twice the target of eight hours. Only about a quarter of patients admitted to hospital via emergency rooms are admitted within the target time set by the government which is about a 75 percent failure rate. This is not because of unusual increases in emergency department admissions. In fact, admissions via emergency departments have been stable and highly predictable over the past year.

Consequences for Health Care Workers

The health care system is sustained by exploiting the compassion of its largely female workforce. Staff work through breaks and lunches, arrive early and stay late, without any claim for overtime pay. They work extra shifts constantly. Scheduling is blind to its responsibilities for child care, with twelve-hour workdays, rotating shifts and few weekends off. Vacations and unscheduled days off (for a wedding or a graduation, for example) are hard to obtain given the level of understaffing across all health sub-sectors.

Health care workers are denied civil liberties, like the right to strike or to refuse unsafe work. Removing these rights ensures that the workforce is less powerful. During COVID-19, no work refusals were upheld by the Ministry of Labour of hundreds initiated, including that of a pregnant woman who was asked to clean a COVID-19 patient's room without real protective equipment — despite the known risks to mothers and fetuses. This worker and many others were forced to do work that was unsafe. Officially, seventeen Ontario health care staff are known to have died during this time, and many will never work again.

Health care work is increasingly part-time — 50 percent of hospital work and 60 percent of long-term care jobs are part-time or casual. These workers depend on the goodwill of their supervisors for hours of work and for the quality of their assignments. Full-time employees depend on that goodwill, too, for the quality of their work assignments and for unscheduled time off. It is less expensive to employ full-time workers, but employers favour part-time work because it leaves the workers more vulnerable and less resistant to ever-increasing workloads. Increasing part-time staffing has been key in shifting away from work assignments, which were stable and covered absences, to schedules that plan for the absence of several staff on each unit, every shift.

This power over the workforce has impacted health care through austerity and downsizing. Health care management compensates for the shortfall in staffing and capacity by guilting and coercing caregivers to treat greater and greater volumes of very sick patients and residents without complaint — despite staff shortages that are ongoing and worsening. Those who speak out about the conditions of work are often harassed, disciplined and sometimes fired (like a nurse from North Bay who spoke out against violence against staff in our hospitals).

Compensation for health care workers has been restrained by successive governments using wage rollbacks, limitations on bargaining and provincial wage mandates limiting funding for wage costs to employers. As a result, the income of Ontario health care workers has been cut consistently in real terms. Bill 124 in Ontario, which limited public sector workers' compensation increases of all kinds to a total of no more than 1 percent a year for a three-year period, was introduced shortly before inflation began to soar in Ontario. It coincided with the pandemic, so health care workers who were asked to put their lives and well-being on the line and to work without adequate protection took significant real wage cuts.

Not surprisingly, Ontario is experiencing a retention crisis across health care as the workforce leaves in record numbers, driven by aging, workloads and the lure of jobs with an equivalent after-tax income, reasonable hours of work and less emotional stress or risk of injury or violence.

Based on the government's existing capacity plans, the Financial Accountability Office predicts a shortage by 2027/8 of 33,000 nurses and personal support workers (PSW) in Ontario. The FAO also estimates that the total complement of nurses and PSWs must be expanded by 53,700 by 2027/28.[35] Brutal working conditions and low pay mean there will be an especially large shortage of PSWs. Approximately 40 percent of PSWs leave the health care sector after graduating or within a year of training.[36] Having the fewest number of hospital staff to patients and the second-fewest number of long-term care staff to residents of any province in Canada means workloads are backbreaking and unsustainable. As vacancies grow, workloads increase. Anxiety, depression, stress and dread of going to work are feelings reported by most workers in a Nanos poll of Ontario hospital staff. Fuelling these emotions is a moral injury caused by the guilt of failing to provide patients with the quality of care that staff know they should be providing.

Health care staff also face a pandemic of workplace violence. Tens of thousands have been assaulted physically, sexually, racially or verbally in the last few years. Polling of hospital workers and long-term care workers in Ontario reveals shocking levels of assaults of all kinds and a toxic environment for women in these workplaces. The *Globe and Mail* ran a powerful series on the violence that women in Canada experience. It found that violence is rampant, and that racialized and Indigenous women are particularly vulnerable. The victim is usually blamed. The police rarely press charges. The courts fail most victims. In a female-dominated, largely racialized work environment like health care, societal attitudes towards violence against women inevitably permeate the institutions. This work is inherently unsafe.

Living with the most under-resourced health care system in Canada (measured by beds to population, staff to population and overall spending) has a profound impact on the quality of care available to the people of Ontario. When aging, population growth and utilization are figured in, the capacity of the Ontario health care system is completely strained. The waiting time for surgeries for many Ontarians is much longer than is medically recommended; thousands die on waitlists for procedures;

people are pushed out of hospital while acutely ill; more than 1,300 people a day are on hallway stretchers; people wait months for a long-term care bed; home care is strictly rationed; and many people have no access to primary care.

Make Health Public

This current situation leads to increasing frustration and a thirst for solutions. Unfortunately, the only solutions offered by the Ford government have been: to increase private delivery, including lucrative subsidies and high mark-ups to do so; to provide modest incentives for nurses to work in Ontario; to expand nursing programs; and to continue to underfund the public system. We believe the following could be solutions to our current health care crisis: Firstly, end private sector delivery of acute, long-term care and community health services — it is much more expensive than public delivery and less efficient in terms of quality and mortality. Right now, the lion's share of new long-term care beds is being given to the private sector to operate. Surgeries for cataracts and for hip- and knee-replacements are being privatized, with the province paying three times more for the service privately provided as it does when performed in public hospitals.

Secondly, capacity must be increased significantly in acute care, complex continuing care, rehabilitation care, mental health care, palliative care, long-term care and home care to meet the needs of an aging and growing population. The standards of care in long-term care must be lifted to the four hours of care per resident, legislated but not implemented. The chaos of home care in Ontario must be addressed by returning to public delivery of the service, as envisioned in legislation introduced by the 1990s NDP government, but never passed. Compensation must be standardized across the health sector, as it is in BC, to ensure that nurses and other staff in home care and the community sector do not gravitate to work for higher pay in hospitals and long-term care. Medical school placements and residencies, as well as nursing programs, must be significantly expanded. Student physicians, nurses and other scarce professions should receive support for living expenses while studying, in return for agreeing to practice in Ontario.

The use of nurse practitioners to lead primary care clinics should be significantly expanded. Outreach should be made to the thousands of staff who are no longer working, with incentives to recruit them back to work. All staff should work to their full scope of practice. This would alleviate some of the current pressures. Moreover, the government needs to ban the use of staff from nursing agencies. These agencies charge two to three times what institutions pay their own staff, bleed away resources from round-the-clock and weekend staffing, worsen morale and weaken the continuity of care. Real wages must increase. In any other labour market with skill shortages, wages would increase to retain and recruit. But real wages are being cut for Ontario's female health care workers and this policy is leading to demoralization and an exodus of staff.

Another solution to improve nurse morale and retention, and to significantly improve patient satisfaction and outcomes, is by moving to nurse-to-patient ratios, as BC has done. The government needs to increase the percentage of full-time work in the health sector to 70 percent as recommended by the Severe Acute Respiratory Syndrome (SARS) Commission. Turning part-time work into full-time will increase health care capacity and create a more stable and attractive work environment. The government must also address violence in health care. Adding staff, creating a culture of zero tolerance for abuse, restricting staff working alone, providing whistle-blower protection and prosecuting those who attack health care workers are all part of the solution to the problem of violence.

Despite problems brought on by the Ford government's consistent underfunding and moves toward privatization, our health care system in Ontario remains a vital social program but it must be defended and supported. With help, it can do so much better for the people of this province. We are very fortunate that the Ontario Health Coalition is such a fierce defender of quality care. All of us have a responsibility to actively support its great work.

8

UNEQUAL ONTARIO

Carlo Fanelli and Katherine Nastovski

THE DOUG FORD-LED CONSERVATIVE GOVERNMENT'S dismantling of existing labour regulations has been as swift as it has been brutal. Since 2018, Ontario has become a more unequal and divided province, characterized by growing precarity of job tenure, low wages and insecure work. At the same time, profits and wealth have skyrocketed for Canada's business class and corporations. While many of these tendencies precede the Ford government, the policies and practices put in place since their coming to power have accelerated and deepened these trends.

Whether through the use of the law to suspend the right to strike and bargain collectively, or the weakening of employment standards legislation, the Conservatives have played an active role in upending wage growth across the province. The legislative assault against workplace protections has exacerbated income and wealth inequality, financial hardship and the affordability crisis across the province. In the face of these challenges, there have been a number of labour-community efforts to challenge the draconian policies of the Ford government. Strengthening and rebuilding worker bargaining power and solidarity will be crucial if the trend toward more precarious, low-paid and insecure work and living conditions is to be confronted.

Legislating Worker Precarity

Within weeks of coming to power, the Conservatives moved quickly on several labour issues. The government's first action was the omnibus Bill 2, which included the *Back to Class Act* that legislated 3,000 striking CUPE 3903 contract faculty, teaching assistants, part-time librarians and graduate students at York University back to work. In suspending the right to strike, the government gave itself the power to fine any individuals and the union $2,000 and $25,000 per day for not complying with the Act. In a punitive action following the strike, the university administration sought to circumvent worker protections and punish striking student workers for allegedly violating the university's code of conduct. The Act was challenged in court by CUPE 3903, with the Superior Court of Ontario ruling unanimously that the university does not have jurisdiction to arbitrarily punish workers as students, thereby circumventing the collective agreement. While sombre solace, the decision does take some steps to protect student-workers' rights to strike and bargain collectively.[1]

The Ford government's next move was to undo the previous Liberal government's late-term labour reforms. With the passage of Bill 47, *Making Ontario Open for Business Act*, the Conservative's legislation repealed major provisions of Bill 148, *Fair Workplaces, Better Jobs Act*, including:

- cancelling a planned $15 per hour minimum wage increase and freezing it instead at $14 per hour for two years before tying it to inflation;
- repealing increased penalties for employers contravening employment standards legislation;
- removing the extension of card-based certification into home care, building services and temporary help agencies;
- removing the entitlement of ten days annual personal emergency leave, the first two of which are paid, and its replacement, with a limited patchwork of unpaid leave;
- eliminating the right to equal pay for part-time, contract, temporary and temporary help agency workers;
- scrapping provisions that put the burden of proof on an employer to demonstrate that a worker is an independent contractor and not an employee.

In addition, the Act also removed provisions that granted trade unions access to an employee list upon demonstrating 20 percent support in the proposed bargaining unit; eliminated the ability of the Ontario Labour Relations Board (OLRB) to amend or consolidate bargaining units; took away first collective agreement mediation and first agreement arbitration as a right; restricted the circumstances under which the OLRB can remedially certify a trade union without a vote; removed enhanced successor rights protections for unions in "contract flipping" scenarios where employers award contracts and then change providers in an effort to de-unionize their workplaces outside the building services industry; and eliminated the requirement for an employer to reinstate a striking employee following six months of a strike. Improved scheduling protections for workers, such as minimum pay requirements for being on-call, the right to request scheduling changes and the right to refuse demands to work on days off were also eliminated. Whereas Bill 148 was introduced against the backdrop of two years' worth of consultation with labour, community and employer groups, Bill 47 was preceded by little consultation outside of the business community and represented an unabashedly pro-business perspective.[2]

In keeping with Bill 47, the government also implicitly implemented a public sector hiring freeze by leaving job vacancies and retirements unfilled. The result was to increase workloads, reduce frontline staff and effectively shrink the quantity of the labour force and quality of public services without direct layoffs. The increased use of for-profit consulting and accounting agencies soon followed (at a significant increase in cost to taxpayers), as would privatizing and contracting out public services like Ontario Works (OW) and the Ontario Disability Support Program (ODSP).[3]

Soon after came Bill 66, *Restoring Ontario's Competitiveness Act*, which removed a requirement in the *Employment Standards Act* that required employers to ensure an informational poster be present in the workplace regarding that Act's regulations. It also removed the requirement that employers obtain approval from the OLRB to make agreements that allow their employees to exceed 48 hours of work per week and overtime pay averaging. In submissions to the government, labour and community groups argued workers in precarious and low-wage jobs, which are disproportionately occupied by youth, racialized and non-status workers, would be most negatively impacted.[4] This argument and others like it went unheard.

The Ford government's second intervention into a legal strike came in December 2018 with Bill 67, the *Labour Relations Amendment Act*. Bill 67 was pre-emptive back-to-work legislation aimed at Power Workers' Union members at Ontario Power Generation (OPG) who had voted for a strike mandate. The central issue in the dispute was the refusal of the employer to grant contract workers at the Darlington and Pickering nuclear power plants equivalent rights to full-time workers. The legislation prohibited both strikes and lockouts, and the dispute was sent to binding arbitration for resolution. In a Canadian tradition as old as maple syrup, the Conservatives ran roughshod over constitutionally protected rights to free collective bargaining.[5]

The Ford government's farthest-reaching intervention into collective bargaining arrived in November 2019 with the tabling and passage of Bill 124, *Protecting a Sustainable Public Sector for Future Generations Act*. This legislation applied to over 1 million predominantly unionized as well as non-union public-sector workers and limited pay increases to 1 percent on any collective agreements or arbitration awards occurring. The Act also prohibited any retro- or pro-active compensatory wage increases before or after the legislation came into effect, and ensured the wage freeze implementation by removing the jurisdiction of both the OLRB and labour arbitrators to enquire into the constitutionality of the Act or its congruence with the Ontario Human Rights Code. To make doubly certain that full compliance would be achieved, the minister of labour was given the discretion to void any agreement or award that did not conform to Bill 124. It should be noted that several exemptions were written into the legislation, including police, firefighters and management, leading education and health worker unions to criticize, among other things, the differential treatment of feminized work and male-dominated sectors.[6]

The Ontario Federation of Labour (OFL), as part of a coalition of over 70 public and private sector unions, spearheaded a Charter challenge against Bill 124 in December 2019. The unions argued that the bill undermined the right to free collective bargaining under the freedom of association guarantee in the Canadian *Charter of Rights and Freedoms*. While the case was making its way through the courts, the Ford government introduced, on October 31, 2022, *The Keeping Students in Class Act*, which used the controversial notwithstanding clause of the Charter to impose a contract and remove the right to strike from 55,000 education workers across 2,000 schools and 67 separate union locals with CUPE's Ontario School Board Council of Unions (OSBCU).[7]

The Act imposed a 2.5 percent salary increase for workers earning under $43,000 annually, and 1.5 percent for those earning above that, as inflation neared 7 percent (meaning a 4.5–5.5 percent real pay cut in the first year alone). The legislation backed this up with individual fines of

$4,000 for workers and $500,000 for the union per day in the event of a strike — a sum equal to the annual salaries of about half the workforce after just two weeks. As part of the legislation, the government also insulated itself from any challenges under the Human Rights Code or the *Ontario Labour Relations Act*. It is worth noting that this was only the second time in Ontario's history that the notwithstanding clause was used.[8]

While the pre-emptive move by the government to criminalize the rights of workers to bargain and strike if necessary was nothing new, the collective response by education workers to challenge this subjugation was significant. Education assistants, early childhood educators, librarians, office staff, custodians, maintenance workers and safety monitors from across the province disobeyed the legislation and walked off the job on Friday, November 4, 2022. Public support lay largely with OSBCU workers who were joined on the picket lines by teachers, parents and the wider labour movement against Ford's mounting authoritarianism.[9] By the weekend, whispers of a general strike across the province proliferated. However, before this could happen, on Monday, November 7, 2022, Doug Ford announced the Conservatives would repeal the Act in exchange for CUPE returning to the bargaining table. The OSBCU agreed, and the next day, on November 8, bargaining talks with a mediator resumed.

On November 16, the two sides announced they had reached a new agreement. The proposed four-year settlement included a flat $1-an-hour per year pay increase, or an annual increase of roughly 4 percent for the lowest-paid union members, and around 1.8 percent increase for those earning more than $70,000. The vote on a tentative agreement quickly became a source of high drama, with OSBCU president Laura Walton stating: "As a mom, I don't like this deal. As a worker, I don't like this deal. [. . .] I think it falls short.... It [$1 wage increase over four years] falls very short of what workers need in this climate."[10] Indeed, the agreement was a far cry from the $3.25 per hour increase that the union had initially demanded just to catch up to a decade's worth of wage erosion and rising inflation. While 70 percent of the membership eventually voted in favour of the new agreement, the process was marred by claims of national union interference and contrasting labour philosophies. In the end, there are strong arguments to support the claim that the outcome of this round of bargaining was both a victory and a defeat.[11] Regardless, there is no denying that the years spent organizing internally, including OSBCU workers' ready solidarity to strike — legally or not — was nothing short of remarkable.

Little more than a week after reaching a settlement with OSBCU, the Ford government received a scathing rebuke from Ontario Superior Court Judge Markus Koehnen, who found Bill 124 to be unconstitutional. In his ruling, Judge Koehnen said that:

> The Act ... interferes with collective bargaining not only in the sense that it limits the scope of bargaining over wage increases, but also...prevents unions from trading off salary demands against non-monetary benefits, prevents the collective bargaining process from addressing staff shortages, interferes with the usefulness of the right to strike, interferes with the independence of interest arbitration, and interferes with the power balance between employer and employees.[12]

The Ford government immediately announced it would appeal. This was in spite of the fact that the government's own internal reports found that Bill 124 was deepening the staffing crisis across the Ontario health care sector.[13]

On February 12, 2024, the Ontario Court of Appeal released its decision. In a split 2–1 decision, the court reaffirmed Bill 124 to be unconstitutional. Writing on behalf of the majority, Justice Favreau added:

> Because of the Act, organized public sector workers, many of whom are women, racialized and/or low-income earners, have lost the ability to negotiate for better compensation or even better work conditions that do not have a monetary value. Considering these impacts against the Act's purported benefits leads me to conclude that, on balance, the Act's infringement cannot be justified. By imposing a cap on all compensation increases with no workable mechanism for seeking exemptions, the deleterious effects of the Act outweigh its salutary effects.[14]

After reviewing the decision on February 23, 2024, a frustrated Doug Ford announced his government would rescind the legislation.

While the court's decision reaffirmed the (always uncertain) Charter-protected right to free collective bargaining, the long history of Canadian labour shows that a reliance on the law is a weak foundation from which to build worker power. Increasing worker bargaining power requires more than just knowledge of the law; it also requires a political vision and active solidarity that can effectively mount a challenge to government decrees and the power of employers. In fact, were it not for a swing vote, the case could have easily gone in the other direction.[15] By the midway point of 2024, broader public sector workers in Ontario had recouped more than $6 billion in retroactive pay increases.[16] However, this has coincided with wider cuts to virtually all program spending.[17] For roughly five years, Bill 124 — in the depths of the COVID-19 pandemic — devasted public sector workers and the quality of public services, leading to an exodus of health care professionals, education, disability support workers and others, exacerbating work-life conflicts, stress and worker burnout. In this way, the social costs of Bill 124 — and its crushing impacts on the lives of all Ontarians — cannot be easily measured.[18]

Rich Get Richer, Rest Get Poorer

While workers across the province struggled to make ends meet, the election of the provincial Conservatives has coincided with explosive income and wealth accumulation for the very rich, while most Ontarians' wages stagnate and fall. In 2022, Canada's top 100 CEOs set a new, all-time high earning, on average, of $14.9 million — more than double what they were earning in 2008.[19] Corporate pre-tax profits also hit a new record of $685 billion in 2022, 54 percent higher than 2019, and over double the average profit levels of the pre-pandemic decade.[20] At the same time, as a share of Canada's gross GDP, after-tax corporate profits reached a sixty-year high, accounting for 20 percent and more than double the average between 1960 to 2000. A study done by the *Globe and Mail* found that revenue at more than 200 publicly traded Canadian companies was up 37 percent, and net income up 40 percent, between 2019 to 2022. Total dividends paid over that period also rose 24 percent, close to $70 billion.[21] Profits at Canada's Big Five banks reached a new record of $61 billion in 2022, triple what they were earning little more than a decade ago.[22] Business prices rose close to 20 percent as the "shrinkflation" of goods across Ontario reduced product volume by around 20 percent between 2019 to 2024, while costs stayed the same or rose.[23] Unsurprisingly, these findings reinforce widespread public sentiment, which rose from 19 to 38 percent between 2018 to 2023, that Canada had become the land of extreme inequality.[24]

In Ontario, the average wage of executives and other senior managers, including high-level government officials, proved recession-proof as their inflation-adjusted hourly wages rose from $53 in 2006 to $87 by 2022. In other words, senior managers have seen a 64 percent wage increase over those sixteen years, with the bulk of it happening between 2018 and 2022.[25] The top 1 percent of Canadians is estimated to control an astounding 26 percent of the country's wealth, while the top 20 percent accounted for nearly 68 percent of the total net worth across the country. On the other end, the bottom 40 percent held just under 3 percent. The poorest 20 percent had a 0.2 percent negative share of net wealth, meaning total assets were outweighed by debt and liabilities. A Statistics Canada report also found that the debt-to-income ratios of core-working age groups (aged 35–64 years) hit their highest rates on record as debt accumulation outpaced disposable income.[26]

In Ontario, teachers, nurses, warehouse workers, retail workers and tradespeople, among others, all saw below-average wage growth between 2006 and 2022. Machine operators, assembly line workers and inspectors had the slowest wage growth among Ontario workers. For these workers, wages grew 32 percent on average — exactly half of the wage rate growth of Ontario managers and executives.[27] By 2022, workers' purchasing power dropped 3.4 percent, or close to $2,000, the largest drop in over a decade, as consumer prices outpaced wage growth. It was only at the midway point of 2023 that average real wages in Ontario for all workers finally nudged higher than they were in January 2020.

Troublingly, wage growth occurred predominantly among non-union workers. While the level of unionized wages has historically been higher than those of their non-unionized counterparts, non-union wage growth has risen faster than union wages since 2017. From 2019 to 2023, average annual pay increase for unionized workers was 3.8 percent compared with 4.7 percent for non-unionized workers. Though most of those modest gains were eaten up by inflation, the union-to-non-union wage gap has since narrowed from $4 to $5 per hour to $3 per hour in 2023.[28] Whether unions will be able to restore their wage premium moving forward in the absence of new strategies and tactics remains an open question. Weak wage appreciation across the province has also been buttressed by the continued exploitation of migrant workers whose numbers have swelled from 109,000 in 2018 to 240,000 in 2023. The stated aim of bringing in these workers was to help businesses with alleged "labour shortages." However, the result has been to undermine employer competition for workers and to disincentivize businesses from investing in productivity-enhancing technologies, which drove wages down for all workers. What is more, wage theft, excessive work hours, limited breaks and physical abuse predominate among migrant workers who are deemed "disposable" and given limited pathways to citizenship.[29]

Low-waged workers are increasingly being priced out of cities as minimum wages fall short of what is actually needed in order to meet basic food, shelter and transportation costs.[30] Between 2020 and 2022, Ontario workers filed more than 8,400 claims for employer wage theft, including claims of not receiving overtime pay, minimum wages, severance, termination pay and other entitlements. By the end of 2022, less than 40 percent of the $36 million owed to workers had been paid out. The number of proactive workplace inspections by the Ministry of Labour has also dropped dramatically from 2,800 in 2017, the year preceding the Ford government, to a low of 790 in 2022. The number of serious prosecutions for violations of employment standards legislation also fell, from 79 to just 7 over that same period. Smaller fines are down fourfold.[31]

Despite a new Gilded Age for some, it has been the so-called excessive worker demands that have been largely blamed for rising inflationary pressures. There is, however, little evidence to support such a view. Former Bank of Canada governor Stephen Poloz has recently argued that growing income inequality is distorting traditional economic relationships so standard economic models of supply and demand struggle to explain what is going on. He notes that the share of total worker income in the economy has "never been lower than it is today," adding that wage increases can be mitigated by rising productivity or reduced corporate margins which continue to exceed historical norms.[32] Reports from both Scotiabank and BMO confirm Poloz's arguments, finding that labour costs have had a negligible impact on price inflation, which is being driven largely by historically unprecedented profit margins and, to a lesser degree, geopolitical challenges like supply bottlenecks, Russia's invasion of Ukraine and other matters.[33]

Today, one in three Canadians say they are living in a household that is experiencing financial hardship, while four in ten Ontarians — the most of any province — say they are considering leaving the province due to low wages, rising debt and unaffordable food and housing costs. A recent survey found growing dissatisfaction at work, with some 70 percent of Ontarians dreaming about quitting their jobs.[34] More than four in ten workers reported feeling burnt out and unable to balance their work and personal lives, with unreasonable workloads due to understaffing, lack of communication and managerial supports most commonly cited. One in five Ontarians are now spending over half their income on housing, the highest of any province.[35] In short, Ontario is more divided between the rich and the rest than at any point in recent memory.

Workers' Struggles Ahead

In the context of the legislative and material assault against workers, rising inflation and a growing unaffordability crisis, it has been labour and community groups that have responded in the most sustained and collective ways.[36] Across the country, a number of high-profile strikes by 155,000 Public Service Alliance of Canada federal public sector workers, more than 7,000 port workers in Vancouver, 600,000 workers in Quebec and 4,000 workers at Metro supermarket stores across the Greater Toronto Area inspired hope that a reinvigorated labour movement could reverse more than a quarter-century's worth of labour's declining fortunes.

In 2020, Ontario hit a decade high with close to 850,000 person-days not worked due to work stoppages, which rose to just over 1 million in 2022. While the high point of the decade, it was notably lower than the 1.5 million person-days lost in 2009, let alone the elevated period from 1968 to 1988, which reached an annual peak of more than 5 million.[37] Nevertheless, growing labour militancy has been quite a contrast to what has been a relatively dormant decade for the labour movement over the last decade or two, where major wage settlements, the number of work stoppages and person-days not worked all fell. Part of this is explained by the decline in total unionization rates in Ontario, which fell by more than one-third from 37 percent in 1984 to 24 percent by 2023. The decline in union coverage in the private sector has been particularly pronounced, falling nearly 14 percent (a decline of roughly 27 percent since 1997), whereas union coverage in the public sector has remained significantly higher and more stable at around 70 percent.

This decrease in unionization is, in part, the result of declining manufacturing work and the shift to an increasingly services-oriented economy. But, as the foregoing discussion has shown, it is also the result of changes to labour law and the wider industrial relations system that has made it more difficult to organize and sustain union drives at individual workplaces, as well weakened employment standards legislation. These changes emboldened employers who not only resisted unionization, but came to rely on government's growing willingness to intervene on their behalf. Unions themselves are also accountable as they increasingly came to rely on the law and the courts to sustain rights gained in the political arena. Perhaps the biggest limitation, however, has been a lowering of expectations amidst a general acceptance of "representative" unionism, where labour leaders speak and act on behalf of members rather than building worker capacities (organizing, educating and mobilizing) from the ground up in ways that workers can themselves enact change.

In this regard, the OSBCU, despite its economic limitations, provides an important political lesson. It also raises critical questions about how union organizing needs to change to confront the escalating assaults on workers and working conditions. How then did this turn into a struggle that threatened the government with the possibility of a general strike? How did these workers come to defy a labour relations framework designed to criminalize resistance? In the years preceding negotiations, the OSCBU devoted considerable resources to build up the capacities of all union members to engage in collective action. From educational and political campaigns to organization and mobilization strategies, the aim was to build worker solidarity and a collective consciousness to resist further demands for concessions. This was a crucial departure from conventional organizational approaches that only mobilize members during contract negotiations. The OSBCU went beyond the day-to-day business of maintaining the union. While organizing rallies, engaging in issue-based coalitions, developing campaigns to oppose specific bills and supporting candidates in by-elections mattered, they reconceptualized the work of unions as a mechanism for building class identity which connected struggles at work to struggles outside of it.

In other words, the OSBCU struggle was the result of a strategic decision made by the union to go beyond the duties assigned by the law to trade unions and to allocate resources to build active resistance. This translated into a plan to organize workers across the province, show how the game is rigged and build worker confidence to resist. The organizing plan was based on a recognition that the only way to confront the compounded impacts of years of austerity was to refuse to take part in the usual motions and its practices, which would have had them strike a bargaining mobilization committee sometime around the start of bargaining. Long before the repressive tactics of the Ford government's use of the notwithstanding clause, organizers had honest conversations with members about what they were up against, and what it would take to achieve their ends.

For public sector workers, when your employer also makes the law, this means preparing to reject the law if they have no other choice. There is a long history of the criminalization of workers' resistance, where unions have been subject to everything from criminal conspiracy and injunctions to fines and jail time. Unlike in many union campaigns, where strike votes are framed as a last resort, organizers laid out the terrain clearly and workers approached their struggle prepared that they would likely have to defy legislation. If they had not been organizing and building solidarity in the years prior to negotiations and prioritized the need to prepare to defy repressive tactics, they would never have been able to build the trust and mobilize such massive participation in defiance of the Ford government outlawing the right to strike.

The organizing process was itself a site of learning and skill-building that radically shifted the understanding of power, politics and what "the union" is. This organizing put the industrial relations regime, its processes and laws in the background and centred aims and goals. The strategy relied on the ability of workers to mobilize their fellow workers and communities, map their workplaces and see themselves and their actions as the basis upon which they could win. This is in stark contrast to the ritualized movement through the industrial relations processes, where workers may (or may not) fill out a survey, get updates on bargaining and then vote for a strike or a tentative agreement. As a transformative site and process, internal organizing can become the basis for a different vision of workers' struggle where workers themselves are at the centre, rather than being reliant on external actors, like lawyers, union staffers, the bargaining team, leadership or even a particular political party to come and save the day.

What's Left?

If a union ultimately doesn't support the goal of mobilizing workers to fight for justice, then what are we left with? The dilemma is that when we centre the power of workers to organize solidarity, the union as an institution comes under threat by the power of employers and government. Thinking through this tension demands critical consideration of the nature and function of unions as institutions and to what extent they build workers' capacities to understand and interpret events and act themselves. There are significant political limitations to hiring better lawyers and technicians to wade through collective agreements and/or launch Charter challenges (as important as this is). These processes are set up to reinforce the economic and political advantages of employers vis-à-vis employees. Accepting this regime places a duty on the union to approach issues of worker exploitation and oppression through grievance procedures that individualize collective issues and remove the worker from the process of resolution.

It is little wonder that in this context, many workers see their union as a kind of insurance policy that has financial means and technical knowledge to process their issues. Nor is it a surprise that some union leaders, having not been schooled in a culture of organizing and resistance, understand leadership as being good managers that see their success in their ability to avoid strikes. This frame accepts and reinforces the confines of the industrial relations system and the ways it weakens possibilities for solidarity and building collective worker power. Left to themselves, it is questionable whether or not unions will be able to develop a culture of organizing within the confines of their duties to process individuated grievances. And so, it is also important to think about workers organizing outside of unions.

Unions and organized labour cannot be conflated. Many unions are not organized and many workers are organized who are not in unions. We see this in cases of community unions but also worker collectives like Justicia for Migrant Workers and the Naujawan Support Network. These forms of independent worker organizations, which spend the majority of their time, energy and resources on organizing the power of workers themselves, have a lot to teach in terms of how to put organizing first. This includes placing workers and their power to resist at the centre of their strategies and their understanding of the struggle with employers, and this is done by going to where workers are actually located, engaging in one-on-one conversations, using direct action and creating spaces for building solidarity.[38] In short, a knowledge of rights and procedures is not going to shift the power imbalances between workers and employers because most workers in Ontario are not in unions or organized collectively. Accordingly, this will mean thinking about changes beyond individual workplaces — changes such as improved statutory minimum wages and employment protections; the removal of barriers to unionization; and equal pay rules that are spread more evenly across the labour market. Wider measures include more supportive unemployment insurance; income protection during parental leave; extended child and elder care benefits; access to affordable housing; and enhanced public services. These improvements will not be possible, of course, without reversing Canada's shift to a more regressive tax system that has workers picking up the tab in place of corporations and economic elites.[39]

Despite the continued attacks against working people and a growing cost-of-living crisis that has defined so much of the Ford government's time in power, there are some reasons to be optimistic. The last number of years has shown an increasing willingness of rank-and-file workers to challenge their leadership's lack of ambitiousness, and to put new goals, aims and initiatives on the table. This shift was seen on display when striking Metro grocery store workers in the Greater Toronto Area, Ford plant workers in Windsor and members of the Ontario Secondary School Teachers Federation rejected tentative deals that their local bargaining teams had recommended. And on July 3, 2024, for the first time in its nearly 100-year history, more than 9,000 unionized workers at the Liquor Control Board of Ontario (LCBO) shut down hundreds of stores across Ontario after Doug Ford announced plans to accelerate province-wide alcohol privatization.

After two weeks on strike, LCBO workers were able to secure a new deal that includes wage increases of 8 percent over three years, plus an additional 7.8 percent for the lowest-paid workers and a special wage adjustment for warehouse workers. The new deal also includes converting 1,000 casual workers to permanent part-time and hiring 60 permanent full-time workers. It also limits contracting out and improves access to benefits for casual part-time employees. Despite the gains at the bargaining table, however, the Ford government's privatization, contracting out and sale of public assets have continued apace, with the government spending $250 million in order to get alcohol in grocery and convenience stores a year early. Such actions are not the result of economic laws but political decisions that vividly reveal the contradiction between crying "fiscal crisis" for workers, while doling out hundreds of millions to private corporations.

All things considered, these experiences show that workers fighting back against their employers, and even governments, matters. They are also timely reminders of how we need to rethink and reframe what workers are up against, where power lies, what constitutes workers' justice and how we work to achieve it. The worsening reality for Ontario workers calls attention to the urgent task of rebuilding and renewing worker power inside and outside of our unions, and of fostering a collective sense among workers that things do not have to be this way.

9

WHY ARE PEOPLE IN ONTARIO HUNGRY?

Maria Rio

FOOD INSECURITY IS THE POLITICAL HOT POTATO no one wants to be left holding. Hundreds of thousands of Ontarians are accessing food banks as they run out of other options, such as credit card debt or predatory payday loans. They turn to emergency services like drop-in meals, food bank hampers and mutual aid. With ongoing issues like precarious work, economic insecurity and shrinking social supports, the demand for emergency food services is rising at an unprecedented pace —demands that non-profits are ill-equipped to meet, let alone address systemically.

In Ontario, power, politics and philanthropy create a complex landscape that exacerbates hunger. Power dynamics among the government, corporations and non-profits directly impact and sustain food insecurity. For example, large grocery chains determine food prices and availability. Within the non-profit sector, power dynamics also affect how food and funds are distributed and who ultimately benefits. Instead of working collaboratively to solve the issue of hunger, non-profits often compete for donors and dollars. Politics play a crucial role, particularly in resource allocation and policymaking. Decisions about minimum wages, social assistance rates and employment laws directly affect household economic stability. Governments viewing poverty as inevitable — rather than an emergency or an ongoing injustice — combined with their growing dependence on the non-profit sector to manage systemic issues without adequate supports (or worse still, deference to "the market") exemplifies the challenges in addressing food insecurity.

Philanthropy, while critical in providing immediate relief, is not the answer to systemic issues. Relying on philanthropy to "solve" food insecurity diverts attention from the need for comprehensive government policies and reforms. These three forces—power, politics and philanthropy—are interconnected, creating a system where immediate needs are met while underlying causes persist. Unfettered capitalism allows problems to grow despite significant efforts and resources.

Before Ford

On December 16, 1966, the International Covenant on Economic, Social and Cultural Rights was signed by the United Nations and later ratified by Canada in 1976, solidifying the right to adequate food as a fundamental human right. In response to the 1996 World Food Summit, Canada released its Action Plan for Food Security in 1998, aiming to alleviate hunger across the country. The Ontario government's 2009 *Poverty Reduction Act* mandated the development of a new strategy every five years, emphasizing the need for continuous efforts to reduce poverty and improve food security. In 2018, the Market Basket Measure (MBM) was adopted as Canada's "Official Poverty Line," providing a standardized approach to measure and address poverty nationwide.

So, with all of these policies in place, *why are people still hungry?* Simply put, governments put the onus of solving systemic issues on non-profits and corporations, who at best offer piecemeal solutions and at worst contribute to the problem. In a market-driven economy, essential items, including food, are treated as commodities, subject to the law of supply and demand and the differential power relationships that they express. This approach inherently conflicts with the notion of food as a fundamental human right.

Social assistance rates and minimum wages, which are set at the provincial level, have been shockingly low for decades.[1] Instead of increasing them, politicians have patronized those in poverty with budgeting advice and "welfare diet" shopping lists, perpetuating the false narrative that poverty is a personal failing. The gap between social assistance rates and a livable wage has been studied repeatedly, with little action from the provincial government. Incremental increases to minimum wages and social assistance, along with discretionary funding to charities, do little to address legislated poverty. Charities — which are run by unelected leaders, have no formal responsibilities to the public and no sector-wide governing body — are the frontline of food insecurity. It is an enormous responsibility that, if done by government employees, would be compensated fairly through wages, pension funds, matching RRSP contributions, and suitable vacation times — benefits that most non-profit employees view as rare luxuries.

On top of these concerns, non-profit board members often lack a basic understanding of poverty's causes and symptoms, often because they lack lived experience themselves. Boards of non-profits hold the most power, yet have the least sector knowledge or diversity. In 2021, Statistics Canada reported board members were 59 percent women (mostly white), 14 percent immigrant, 11 percent racialized, 8 percent LGBTQ+, 6 percent disabled and 3 percent Indigenous. These numbers matter. Leadership teams shape an organization's communications, public policy, fundraising and programming. "Systemic racism produces deep inequities with respect to food insecurity in Canada. For example, Black households are 3.56 times more likely, and Indigenous communities 3 to 5 times more likely, to be food insecure than white households."[2] Without leaders who share lived experiences with the communities they serve, an understanding of the nuances, barriers and needs of those experiencing hunger is missed.

For over forty years, food banks and drop-ins in Ontario have provided immediate relief to those facing food insecurity. However, the data collected by these services often lack the depth and breadth needed to fully comprehend who is impacted by hunger, preventing accurate resource allocation at non-profit and governmental levels. For instance, many food banks only track the metrics required for grant applications, neglecting critical demographic information such as languages spoken, income levels, racial background and accessibility needs. Drop-in centres typically record only the quantity of meals distributed, not distinguishing whether, for example, 10,000 meals were served to 5,000 or 8,000 unique individuals. While some charities might use sophisticated software, others operate without such resources. Numerous groups are also not registered as non-profits — they are non-qualified donées — meaning their service users remain uncounted. In addition, households often access multiple services to meet their needs, with different family members utilizing various forms of aid. We must also remember that not all individuals facing food insecurity seek or can access aid; they may instead resort to frequent meal skipping or purchasing less nutritious food. Some are turned away from help due to a non-profit's lack of resources or arbitrary policies, such as frequency of service use or their status as international students. This dispersal of data collection dilutes the ability to form a cohesive picture of food insecurity and thus hinders effective and equitable service provision.

While non-profits struggle, regulatory failings in the corporate and government sectors are also evident. A prime example is the bread-price-fixing scheme (2001–2015), exposed in 2018, involving major grocery retailers like Loblaw, Sobeys, Metro and Walmart. This scandal revealed a coordinated effort to inflate bread prices and highlighted the challenges of holding corporations accountable without a mandated Code of Conduct, regulatory oversight, or even price controls. Grocery price inflation acts as trickle-up economics, shifting wealth from the poorest consumers to the wealthiest supermarket owners, exacerbating economic inequality and food insecurity. The scandal underscored the potential for abuse when a few corporations control a significant market share. After the scandal, demands for a government-mandated Canadian Grocery Code of Conduct grew louder. However, without a binding framework, the risk of market manipulation and its impact on food affordability remains.

The relationship between major grocers (like Loblaw, Sobeys, Metro and Walmart) and charitable organizations is complex, involving both benefits and ethical dilemmas. While these corporations help mitigate food waste by donating unsellable but consumable items to food banks, thereby addressing immediate needs in food-insecure communities, they also gain significant advantages, such as the benefit of tax incentives, a boost to their corporate images, and the avoidance of waste management fees. As John Lowrey, an assistant professor at Northeastern University's D'Amore-McKim School of Business, puts it: "when you are faced with leftover food, you can either pay a per-pound pickup fee to waste management companies … or remove it for free and donate it to the food bank."[3]

Indeed, partnerships between corporations and non-profits, while practical, raise concerns both about the corporations' intentions and the quality of donated food. For instance, items rejected by the market, like ranch-flavoured ice cream, are often donated in bulk. Moreover, donating food that is near or past its best-before date, though still safe, perpetuates a cycle of reliance on lower-quality donations that fail to address the root causes of food insecurity. Non-profits may feel pressured to accept whatever quality is offered, fearing they will be passed over for future donations if they do not accept what is offered. Grocers have the option to donate, discard, or even sell these items as animal feed, and some organizations prioritize reducing food waste in landfills over providing dignified food access, ensuring there is always a charity willing to accept such donations.

As an added benefit, brands often use charity partnerships to enhance their image, as mentioned above. For example, Walmart Canada's "Fight Hunger, Spark Change" initiative with Food Banks Canada helps Walmart appear socially responsible. However, the irony is clear. Walmart's low wages and anti-union practices contribute to food insecurity among its own employees. Since 2017, this strategy has allowed Walmart to position itself as a leader in the fight against food insecurity, raising questions about the role of corporations in addressing social issues they are viewed as complicit in creating. Similarly, companies like Loblaws, Metro and Amazon are touted as food security champions by major food security organizations, like Daily Bread and Food Banks Canada, despite the infamous poor working conditions and price-fixing scandals of these corporations.

When Food Banks Canada, Daily Bread, or other large organizations align themselves with problematic donors, they pass down this relationship to their partner agencies, who may then be pressured to promote companies that contribute to poverty. If they refuse, they risk losing funding or access to donated food. These constraints create barriers for those with the most lived experience of poverty — racialized individuals, the working poor and those on social assistance — who struggle to access the wealth or power needed to effect systemic change independently. They are forced to rely on those with little to no lived experience to grant them funds and dictate how they operate, stifling innovation, reinforcing white supremacy in the non-profit sector and chilling advocacy.

The Ford Era

Doug Ford was sworn in as Premier of Ontario on June 29, 2018 — six months after the Loblaws bread-price-fixing scandal broke. Since then, the provincial government has not taken significant action to address food insecurity, despite having immense power and resources at its disposal. This inaction has allowed the crisis to escalate, leaving many without adequate support. The main policy meant to reduce poverty in Ontario, the 2020–2025 Poverty Reduction Strategy, centres around the dubious notion that increased employment is the solution to poverty. While this may look good on paper, it is flawed in many ways. It is completely out of touch with the reality of those living in poverty and those who serve them.

Expecting people who access the Ontario Disability Support Program (ODSP), who have been deemed too disabled to work, to gain employment is unrealistic, especially when doing so can result in claw backs or loss of benefits. Similarly, those already working multiple jobs cannot simply "work harder" to escape poverty. The only actions that have the ability to lift people out of destitution are vast increases to minimum wages, strengthening unions, improving labour protections and significantly raising social assistance rates. No amount of side hustles and gig work will be enough to resolve systemic issues. Stagnant wages and rising living costs are making urban living increasingly difficult, forcing more and more people to rely on community programs and mutual aid.

Because of the flawed foundation of the Poverty Reduction Strategy, the Ford government has made no progress in alleviating hunger. The resistance to mandating a livable minimum wage or indexing social assistance rates has only caused the crisis to grow, pushing small, non-profits past their limits. In fact, the Ford government has overwhelmingly benefited from several initiatives recently put in place by the Liberal federal government, though the provincial Conservatives are happy to take credit.

Federal and provincial governments have a pattern of commitment followed by insufficient action. In 2019, Federal Minister of Agriculture and Agri-Food, Marie-Claude Bibeau, launched "A Food Policy for Canada," the nation's first comprehensive food policy. This policy's vision is that "all people in Canada are able to access a sufficient amount of safe, nutritious, and culturally diverse food. Canada's food system is resilient and innovative, sustains our environment and supports our economy."[4] Despite the policy's goals, the Canadian Food Policy Advisory Council created alongside it has only met nine times since 2021, seven of those meetings happening before 2023 — a significant accountability gap.

This shortfall in action could raise questions about the effectiveness of the council. Speculation and conjecture about its priorities may also arise. As an example, Lori Nikkel, CEO of Second Harvest, an organization focused on keeping food out of landfills, serves on the council. While her inclusion brings non-profit experience to the table, it also introduces the appearance of a potential conflict of interest. Under her leadership,

Second Harvest saw a 255 percent increase in revenue from 2019 to 2022, primarily through fundraising efforts focused on food rescue. The council's advocacy for measuring food loss, eliminating best-before dates and recognizing food waste leaders may align with Nikkel's organization's model, potentially benefiting large grocery donors rather than addressing the root causes of food insecurity. Outside of meeting summaries, the council's lack of transparency — no public meeting minutes or detailed records — further complicates accountability, leaving the public in the dark about decision-making processes and priorities.

Another issue is the continued reliance by governments on the Market Basket Measure (MBM) for determining Canada's Official Poverty Line. The MBM has been criticized for not adequately reflecting the true cost of living, particularly in high-cost areas like Toronto. However, this shortcoming has been adopted and weaved through provincial policy around poverty. The way in which the MBM is calculated is difficult for a layperson to understand. The calculated MBM for each region is available only through direct contact with the government, and the variety of terms describing incrementally different notions are plenty.

The MBM bases the estimated cost of a basic standard of living using a specific basket of goods and services, which includes food, clothing, shelter, transportation and other essentials for a family of four. This cost is compared to a family's disposable income in order to determine whether or not they fall below the poverty line. For 2022, the MBM calculates that a single person in Toronto needs over $27,631 in disposable income annually to maintain a modest standard of living, while a family of four needs $55,262.[5] Disposable income is defined as total income (including government transfers), after deducting not only income tax, but also several non-discretionary expenses, including contributions to Canada Pension Plan and Employment Insurance. Disposable income is a malleable term, but in broad strokes, a Torontonian earning $37,500 pre-tax is at the poverty threshold, and a family of four requires $78,000 pre-tax to meet that same threshold.

As of October 2024, the minimum wage in Ontario is $17.20 per hour, or just over $33,500 annually before any tax deductions for full-time workers. In Toronto, this is $5,000 less than the pre-tax income needed to meet Canada's Official Poverty Line. In contrast, the Ontario Living Wage Network has calculated the living wage in the Greater Toronto Area (GTA) to be $25.05 per hour, or just under $49,000 annually before any tax deductions. This means that there is a $13,500 gap between the minimum wage and a living wage. Moreover, 70 percent of minimum wage workers are adults, not youth with other financial support. Notably, two-thirds of food-insecure households in Canada rely primarily on employment wages, highlighting the strong link between low-wage work and hunger. The Official Poverty Line, used by both federal and provincial governments, fails to accurately reflect how many individuals and families are living paycheque to paycheque, leading to misleading data on poverty and the effectiveness of anti-poverty measures.

Social assistance provided by ODSP and Ontario Works (OW) falls far below both Ontario's deep poverty threshold, which is set at 75 percent of Canada's Official Poverty Line, and the actual cost of living, perpetuating poverty and food insecurity among the most vulnerable. As of March 2024, the maximum monthly amount for a single person receiving ODSP is approximately $1,308 for basic needs and shelter — $15,696 a year. For a single adult on OW, the maximum monthly amount is around $733 for basic needs and shelter — $8,796 a year — with a mere $390 monthly shelter allowance. Ontario's deep poverty line is significantly higher than ODSP and OW rates, creating annual gaps of $12,429 and $19,329, respectively, for single-person households in Toronto. Even by its own metrics, the provincial government's failure to significantly increase social assistance rates leaves many unable to escape deep poverty.

A one-person household in Toronto being paid minimum wage or one on disability/social assistance falls far short of the living wage.

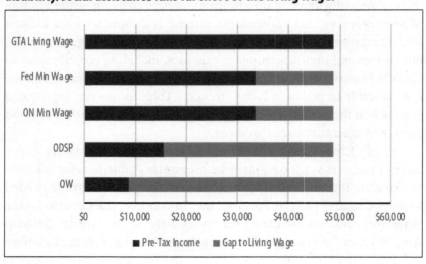

For many on ODSP, living in poverty funnels them towards drastic decisions, like Medical Assistance in Dying (MAID). This issue is worsened by the 2021 legislative amendments in Canada, which expanded the access to MAID to individuals with chronic illnesses or disabilities — even if they are not terminally ill. As one woman living with debilitating pain noted: "If I wasn't on ODSP, would I be seeking MAID? I don't know that answer, but I'm leaning towards no, because my quality of life would be so much better." Rabia Khedr, national director of Disability Without Poverty, commented further: "What are we giving [people with disabilities]? The option to line up at a food bank? The option to choose medical assistance in dying?"[6]

Challenges for the Non-Profit Sector

In the pursuit of addressing food insecurity and poverty, many well-positioned organizations have paradoxically focused on bolstering their respective brands rather than fulfilling their collective mission. This has created a stark disparity in the level and quality of support provided in Ontario, where food bank access is contingent on one's catchment area. This can mean the difference between receiving ten days' worth of food a month or just three. Such inequities could be reduced if organizations prioritized collaboration over isolated efforts. While ideally charities should aim to render themselves obsolete, the reality is that many food security organizations are instead expanding their operations, working in silos and accumulating resources. This expansion often becomes a fundraising metric, attracting donations and media to a select few rather than distributing resources equitably. Large, white-led organizations have notably used COVID-19 emergency funding to dramatically increase their scale.

Such dynamics force smaller non-profits to make a dire choice: focus on systemic advocacy to address the root causes of food insecurity or merge with larger entities to ensure their immediate survival and essentially double the food they can provide to their communities. This latter option not only diminishes the diversity of perspectives and approaches in tackling food insecurity but also centralizes power in ways that may not align with the needs or wills of the communities served. The resulting landscape is one where power is entrenched not in the hands of those most impacted by food insecurity, but in their self-appointed rescuers.

From 2019 to 2022, Community Food Centres Canada (CFCC) scaled their revenue, expenses and reserve fund by over 300 percent, going from a $7-million organization to $28 million. In the same period, Second Harvest ballooned from a $64-million organization to a $230-million one — with a 255 percent increase in revenue, a 300 percent increase in expenses and a 134 percent increase in their reserve fund. Mississauga Food Bank went roughly from $8 million to $20 million in revenue and expenses, and increased its reserve fund from $1.2 million to $7.5 million. Collectively, Food Banks Canada, Second Harvest, CFCC, Daily Bread and Ottawa Food Bank had over $159 million in their reserves by the end of their 2022 fiscal years.

It is important to note that some organizations may also open endowment funds at banks or community foundations, depositing significant amounts that are then excluded from their audited financial statements. This, along with other accounting and tax receipting practices, makes it difficult to assess an organization's true financial resources. While the leadership of organizations like these may highlight increased expenses, it is important to note that they have been well-resourced to scale — and have chosen to do so — while many lesser-known but much-needed non-profits have been forced to close.

The unequal distribution of resources results in the uprooting of local organizations that have served their communities for decades. This corporatization of non-profit efforts promotes a model of operation that is fundamentally capitalistic, contradicting the altruistic mission organizations claim to uphold. It also reflects the monopolistic behaviours seen in large grocery chains, where the concentration of power within a few large entities undermines the diversity and richness of smaller, community-based approaches and groups. Take for example CFCC's $23-million capital campaign to purchase a location in downtown Toronto, where many other organizations are already serving the community and know it well. Instead of ensuring the sustainability of existing organizations in the Moss Park area, or even providing more food or funds to the community or their non-profit partners, CFCC opted for self-serving real estate worth millions.

Organizations must not only contend with inequitable resource distribution but also with a hesitancy to advocate for systemic change. Due to a reliance on external funding, non-profits often refuse to "bite the hand that feeds them," choosing instead to focus on "safe, non-political" issues that will not challenge existing societal power structures or upset funder expectations. This approach is often dictated by the desire to maintain funding and appease donors, rather than to drive real change. There is an evident conflict within the non-profit sector: it exists to challenge unjust systems yet is funded by those very systems. When a non-profit relies heavily on government support, it is less likely to criticize government policy. "Fighting hunger" is palatable to both left- and right-leaning folk and avoids making those in power uncomfortable. The irony is clear when Justin Trudeau, Doug Ford and Olivia Chow tour food bank warehouses, charity-washing their images, and asking the public to donate, despite having significant power to enact meaningful change themselves. Similarly, leaders in Ontario's food security non-profits continue to wear the mask of social activism while silently enabling systemic oppression. By focusing on non-controversial issues like food, rather than addressing the politically charged roots of income inequality — capitalism and racism — these leaders avoid challenging the status quo. Politically charged topics like taxation of the rich, systemic oppression, white supremacy, monopolies in the food industry and non-profit governance never have to be discussed. Instead, the sector encourages the wealthy to reduce their tax obligations by funding programs serving people in legislated poverty — all without holding government leaders accountable.

Organizations that do get political face many challenges, as recently seen with the muzzling of charities by the Ontario Trillium Fund (OTF), an agency of the Government of Ontario. In his 2023 investigation for "Future of Good," Gabe Oatley noted that Michael Diamond, the campaign manager for Ford's successful PC leadership bid, joined the OTF board in January 2019, six months after Doug Ford was sworn in. In April 2020, the foundation's advocacy policy was changed and three more volunteers who had previously run for or represented the PCs in the provincial legislature joined Diamond on the OTF board. Non-profit grantees were required to "agree not to engage in any activity meant to bring about change in law or government policy, including public policy dialogue and development." If non-profits refused, they were not eligible for funding. This illustrates a critical problem within non-profit work: the need to balance immediate organizational survival against the imperative to advocate for deeper, systemic solutions.

Non-profits face an uphill battle in solving hunger due to operational, staffing and persistent challenges associated with low-wage and precarious work. Record-breaking inflation rates have made buying food at scale more expensive. However, non-profits are not able to similarly increase staff salaries, forcing non-profit workers to take on additional responsibilities and jobs, leave the sector, or access charitable services themselves, causing a sector-wide human resources crisis. Similarly, donors are facing their own fiscal limits and therefore contributing less, leaving most non-profits unsure of their future sustainability.

While a handful of food security organizations thrive, reports of food bank locations in states of disrepair, with issues ranging from pest infestations to unsafe buildings, highlight the severe underfunding and neglect that pervades the sector. The expectation for non-profit employees to work under such conditions, fuelled by a culture of self-sacrifice, overlooks the basic needs and rights of workers and often leads to burnout and reduced organizational capacity. Most organizations are suffering from the aforementioned unequal distribution of food and funds. In its 2024 "Hungry for Change Report," Second Harvest reported that 36 percent of non-profit organizations providing free food currently have a waiting list and are turning people away due to lack of resources. Undoubtedly, these are 1,400 smaller organizations that do not have the same connections as the big non-profits, but that does not mean they are any less essential in their respective communities. This trend is concerning, not just for its immediate impact on communities but for its broader implications.

On a brighter note, it does seem like Canada will have a voluntary Grocery Code of Conduct soon. To provide some context, Loblaw Companies Ltd. own a range of grocery stores, including Loblaws, Real Canadian Superstore, No Frills, Freshmart, SuperValu, T&T Supermarket, Zehrs, Valu-Mart, Provigo, No Name, Your Independent Grocer, City Market, Fortinos, Wholesale Club, Maxi, Extra Foods, Dominion Stores, Shoppers Drug Mart and more. The 2024 boycott against Loblaw was initiated due to the company's decision to end its price freeze on certain No Name brand products. This move was criticized amid rising food prices and cost-of-living concerns, leading to public frustration and calls for a boycott. The boycott started on May 1, 2024, days after CEO Per Bank sent out a statement to all employees saying there were "misconceptions about our role in the ongoing food affordability crisis." Bank continued: "Not only are we being unfairly blamed, we're also not getting credit for the value we are providing."[7] On May 17, 2024, *CityNews* reported that after years of negotiation, Loblaw was now ready to sign the proposed Grocery Code of Conduct, contingent on other grocers doing the same. By August, holdouts Walmart and Costco had also agreed.

It is too early to gauge the impact of this "agreement to agree." The Grocery Code Adjudication Office is set to run as a non-profit, with its primary funding coming from annual fees collected from its members. This setup could lead to typical non-profit issues, such as a reluctance to challenge funders and outsized control by corporations and government.

From Palliative Care to Hunger Cure

The stark reality faced by hundreds of thousands of Ontarians relying on food banks each month highlights the inadequacy of current measures to address poverty. Governments often delegate poverty reduction to non-profits, whose efforts, though significant, are insufficient to address systemic issues and growing income disparity. Hunger in Ontario exemplifies how power, politics and philanthropy can perpetuate systemic inequalities, with temporary solutions overshadowing the pressing need for substantial systemic change. As the Ontario Nonprofit Network has noted, "There is an urgent need for a coordinated sector response and long-term public policy solutions to not only mitigate challenges non-profits are facing now, but also to prepare us for future emergencies. Without action, the erosion of Ontario's critical social infrastructure will only speed up."[8]

The power of major grocery chains, combined with constraints within the non-profit sector, often reduces philanthropy to a palliative care role rather than a cure. Political decisions that prioritize the status quo over addressing the root causes of poverty exacerbate the situation. Inadequate minimum wages, insufficient social assistance and weak labour protections directly contribute to the cycle of food insecurity in Ontario. It is evident that income-based, institutional interventions are transformative: improving quality of life through greater agency, better health and dignity. Legislation has the unique power to enable such changes, and without significant policy shifts, the demand for essential services will continue to rise, along with social isolation and poor health outcomes.

Addressing food insecurity in Ontario requires both immediate action and long-term structural changes. In the short term, governments can take crucial steps by increasing incomes for those most in need, especially those on social assistance and workers earning less than a living wage. Economic inequality drives food insecurity, and policies must focus on wealth redistribution, such as taxing the wealthy to fund income-based supports. At the same time, enforcing rent control or tying rent to income will provide immediate relief to those struggling with high housing costs, a key driver of food insecurity. Corporations, especially those paying poverty wages, must also be held accountable for ensuring all full-time employees earn a living wage. This will immediately ease the pressure on working families, particularly in high-cost areas like Toronto, where many spend a significant portion of their income on rent, leaving little for food.

Long-term solutions, however, are essential to truly eradicate food insecurity. First, we need to move away from the outdated and insufficient food bank model, which was never intended as a permanent solution. Food insecurity is an income issue, not a charity issue, and only systemic solutions will address its root causes. Governments must focus on policies that treat food access as a human right, ensuring that the food supply is not monopolized by private corporations focused on profit. Instead, the food chain must be regulated to ensure fair access for all Ontarians. Additionally, addressing food insecurity requires tackling housing insecurity, which is intertwined with hunger. Governments must treat affordable housing as a basic right, implementing policies that cap rent at a reasonable percentage of income to ensure people are not forced to choose between food and shelter.

Non-profits also have a critical role in pushing for these systemic changes. They must move beyond small, symbolic charity efforts and instead advocate for deeper reforms. Non-profit boards must be reformed to reflect the diversity and expertise of the communities they serve, ensuring they are equipped to tackle complex issues like poverty. Non-profits must also demand that Donor-Advised Funds, which allow the wealthy to store money indefinitely without taking action, are better regulated to ensure immediate deployment of resources. Charity cannot replace justice. In the long run, the solution to food insecurity will only come through systemic reforms: taxing the rich, enforcing rent control, raising wages and holding corporations and non-profits accountable for their roles in perpetuating poverty. Only through comprehensive, systemic reforms can we hope to eradicate hunger and poverty in Ontario.

10

BULLDOZING INDIGENOUS LANDS

Dayna Nadine Scott and Dania Ahmed

The Breathing Lands

The "Ring of Fire" is a significant deposit of minerals discovered in the far north of Ontario in 2007.[1] Successive provincial governments have hitched their hopes to the idea that the region can become the next big driver of Ontario's economy. Developing mines in the Ring of Fire "is a generational opportunity to transform our economy," according to the former mining executive and current Minister of Mines, George Pirie.[2] The deposit was once hyped for the presence of chromite. Now, it is nickel — a crucial component of electric vehicle (EV) batteries, and said to be necessary for the transition to a green economy — that is attracting the most attention.

The so-called Ring of Fire is located in Treaty No. 9 territory, on the homelands of several small, remote Anishinaabe and Anishini nations, who are the region's sole occupants. The lowlands here are said to contain the largest and last intact boreal forest remaining in the world, as well as a globally significant wetland and a massive carbon storehouse.[3] The landscape has sustained the lifeways of its Indigenous stewards since time immemorial. Some Elders call the peatlands "the Breathing Lands," because they act as "the world's lungs."[4]

As a result of seemingly intractable tensions and a distinct lack of infrastructure that could connect the mineral deposits to the provincial highway and rail network, the deposits have remained undeveloped for years. On the campaign trail in 2018, Doug Ford promised to build a road to the Ring of Fire, even if he had to "hop on a bulldozer" himself. Ontario Regional Chief Isadore Day responded by saying, "[First Nations have the] ultimate authority when it comes to resource development," and adding, "The principle of free, prior and informed consent must be implemented.... If our Nations and communities agree to any development, they must be full partners in prosperity."⁵

Positioning the mining of this new "frontier" as being "critical" for transitioning to green energy, addressing the climate crisis and building a "clean economy," the government announcements now increasingly emphasize "inclusion" and "partnership." Ford Nation is trying on a new green cape, casting itself as part of a progressive corporate movement for bringing First Nations into prosperity by enlisting them in the struggle to save the climate through the production of EV batteries.

Legal and Historical Context of Indigenous-Provincial Relationships

Major tensions with Indigenous communities of Treaty No. 9 emerged very early in Ford's term, as the Regional Framework Agreement (RFA) was torn up and a divide-and-conquer strategy took shape. The RFA was struck after a period of constructive negotiations between Ontario and the Matawa First Nations, a collection of nine communities close to the Ring of Fire mineral deposits and likely to be impacted by the infrastructure necessary for its development. The negotiations, led by former Ontario premier Bob Rae for the Matawa and the former Supreme Court of Canada Justice Frank Iacobucci for Ontario, focused on resource-revenue sharing and environmental assessment. They were eventually hung up on the disagreement over "jurisdiction" and control over permitting. On the Matawa side, the approach was built on the solid foundation of a solemn "Unity Declaration," insisting that the nine communities were "one Nation" and would "stand together" based on the principle of Mamow-Wecheekapawetahteewin — a reflection of the Nations' pre-existing and continuing jurisdiction over their homelands.

While Ford's government made a point of publicizing the termination of the RFA in 2019, proclaiming it was moving too slowly, in reality, it was the previous Liberal government that initially signalled a shift away from the negotiations with a united Matawa group in favour of bilateral deals with individual nations.⁶ Indigenous Affairs Minister Greg Rickford explained that the Ford government preferred a pragmatic approach, pursuing individual agreements with First Nations seen as ready to move at the "speed of business."⁷ The government stated that the RFA had "come off line," lamenting that over $20 million had been spent without "shovels in the ground."⁸

In the background to all of this was long-standing contestation over the treaty relationship and the now-defunct *Far North Act*, which was a land-use planning exercise undertaken ostensibly to enable community-based, land-use plans and conservation in the far north but seen by many Indigenous nations as a land-grabbing exercise. The question of whether or not the free, prior and informed consent of all affected Indigenous communities is required before major resource extraction can proceed on their homelands was and remains the central sticking point. Here, the evolving constitutional jurisprudence on the Crown's "duty to consult and accommodate" Indigenous peoples and its relationship to the United Nations Declaration on the Rights of Indigenous Peoples is crucial.

This part of Ontario is inhabited almost exclusively by remote Indigenous communities, who continue to maintain and renew their connection to their homelands by exercising their rights to hunt, fish, harvest food and medicines, practice ceremony and continue to care for the lands and waters as they have since time immemorial.[9] First Nations in the region state that they "depend on the [James Bay Lowlands'] biodiversity and the richness of its fish, wildlife, and plants for food, medicine, cultural and spiritual values, and economic livelihoods."[10] Community members from Neskantaga First Nation, one of the small remote communities near the proposed mining district, state repeatedly that the Attawapiskat River system is the "lifeline," the "lifeblood," of their people. The Attawapiskat River will need to be crossed by a new, all-season road if the minerals in the Ring of Fire are to be extracted and brought to markets in the south.

At the time Treaty No. 9 was signed, Indigenous communities understood that it was an agreement to share the land in exchange for specific treaty benefits and the protection of the Crown.[11] In contrast, from the Crown's perspective, Treaty No. 9 was a land surrender intended to open Northern Ontario for resource development.[12] Indigenous communities throughout Treaty No. 9, however, firmly dispute that they ever ceded, sold or surrendered their homelands or their inherent jurisdiction over their territories and people.[13]

In regard to lands and resources, mineral exploration permits are often the vector through which settler state law is inserted into Indigenous territory, in Treaty No. 9 and elsewhere. According to settler state law in Canada, the provinces are assumed to have jurisdiction over natural resources within their boundaries and ownership of all ungranted minerals. The "free-entry" principle is "understood as the right to stake a mineral claim without consulting with private landholders or Indigenous peoples."[14] The mining lease, then, has been treated as a tenure instrument that authorizes mineral extraction — with or without the consent of affected First Nations.

Structural Changes in the Ford Government

In the settler colonial state, structural changes within the government's cabinet reflect that government's priorities. The Ministry of Indigenous Affairs and the Ministry of Northern Development were consolidated in 2018 under one minister, Greg Rickford.[15] This change despite the fact that the Ipperwash Inquiry of 1995 recommended that Ontario should have a stand-alone Ministry of Indigenous Affairs with a dedicated minister.[16] As the "minister of everything," Rickford's extensive portfolio dilutes attention and resources essential for meaningful engagement with Indigenous issues and raises concerns about his ability to effectively balance competing interests.[17] Kiiwetinoong MPP Sol Mamakwa points out that Rickford's multiple positions place him in a clear conflict of interest, signifying a concerted effort from Ford's government to "undermine any momentum towards meaningful Indigenous consultation and regulatory environmental processes."[18] Indigenous leaders interpreted the move as signalling a clear "disregard" for Indigenous voices.[19]

In 2022, Ford established mining, previously under Rickford's direction in Northern Development, as a standalone ministry, led by former mining executive George Pirie, with a specific mandate to develop the Ring of Fire region.[20] Pirie aims to align mining objectives with the broader economic initiatives supporting EV battery creation, emphasizing domestic supply for minerals being currently sourced from abroad.[21] Multi-billion dollar investments have been allocated to battery "giga-factories" in southern Ontario, with Pirie promising to supply these facilities with the essential raw materials required for the creation of clean technologies.[22]

Ontario's approach to engagement with Indigenous communities affected by mining projects in the Ring of Fire has continuously emphasized the economic benefits that could be realized by these communities. The government is focused on the creation of jobs for Indigenous youth in the area, casting the development of the mineral resources as "economic reconciliation."[23] Pirie says that revenue-sharing agreements can incentivize Indigenous communities to participate fully, claiming that it is "the easiest and quickest way that the Indigenous communities can participate in the real economy."[24]

Fast Tracking Critical Mineral Extraction

In the energy transition, access to critical minerals is positioned as the bottom line: according to Minister Pirie, "You can't be green without mining. You can't develop as Ontario wants, and transform the economy into a green economy, without accessing critical minerals out of the Ring of Fire."[25] In other words, the future of Treaty No. 9 is taken for granted: it is an extractive landscape, with the so-called "transition minerals" at the forefront.

The common rhetoric surrounding the Ring of Fire confirms its status as nothing more than an extractive frontier. It is seen as full of resource potential and as "lawless," empty of order.[26] Finding ways to "open up and "unlock" the potential of Ontario's far north, to "access the wealth" and to build a "corridor to prosperity" are common refrains. Nonchalant statements, such as how "the promising" Ring of Fire will some day supply much of the world's primary minerals," appear regularly in trade publications.[27] An illustrative example of the government's thinking, with echoes of *terra nullius*, is seen in a 2024 interview with Minister Pirie in which Pirie states, "Nine-tenths of the province is Northern Ontario, one-tenth is southern Ontario; [southern Ontario has] nine-tenths of the population, [the north has] one-tenth. So, it's largely empty and begging for exploration drill holes."[28]

The deep entanglement of state and industry actors in relation to the critical minerals portfolio has opened space for a rare alignment between federal Liberal and Ford government priorities. Premier Ford is keen to promise a return of manufacturing glory to small southern Ontario cities in decline. Prime Minister Trudeau is onside with this message: in March 2023, when Volkswagen announced its first North American giga-factory for St. Thomas, Ontario, the Prime Minister applauded the news, stating, "We're not just bringing back manufacturing ... we're delivering a national anchor for Canada's electric vehicle supply chain."[29] Trudeau described it as "a win for workers, for the community, and for the economy," noting that the project promises to be "the largest manufacturing plant in the country," part of a larger "made-in-Canada plan" to deliver "a strong economy" and "clean air for our kids and grandkids." Pirie continued the pitch, stating that the deposit represents a $1-trillion project — a vastly exaggerated claim about the Ring of Fire which drew attention. When challenged, the minister's office doubled down, saying it has an "economic potential that is limitless."[30]

The Integrated EV-Supply-Chain Dream

The vision Ontario is putting forward today is of an integrated, fully domestic supply chain for EVs. It features the mining of critical minerals here in Ontario in order to support battery manufacturing for vehicles that will also be assembled here. Premier Ford states that he aims to create opportunities for Indigenous communities to prosper from these supply chain "opportunities." As such, the impacted Indigenous communities are navigating not just the enthusiasm for the energy transition in the sense of the policy mandate to reduce greenhouse gas emissions, but also the deliberate decisions taken to "fast track" this extraction in pursuit of the public good.

To succeed in seducing Ontarians to buy into this vision, state and industry actors must differentiate critical minerals mining from other conventional forms of extraction. This marketing campaign is active in Treaty No. 9. For example, Wyloo Metals, the Australian subsidiary of Fortescue Metals Group that owns the most advanced claims in the Ring of Fire, has made various ambitious promises to "meet the highest environmental and social standards."[31] It proposes a mine that is "net-zero," disturbs less than one square kilometre of sensitive peatland, uses recycled water and has no above-ground tailings pond.[32]

Conveniently, in March 2023, Pirie introduced two main changes to mining law in Ontario with the *Building More Mines Act*. One amendment lowered the standards for land reclamation, stating that environmental conditions must be "comparable to or better than it was before the recovery, as determined by the minister."[33] Not only does this change eliminate the obligation to *enhance* the affected land's condition, but it also places the responsibility for determining how mine tailings are dealt with squarely at the discretion of the minister.[34] Critics say it may result in less stringent remediation efforts, given the already inadequate requirements for mining companies to clean up their operations.[35] This change has understandably sparked concerns among Indigenous communities, particularly those with historical grievances related to mining activities on their lands.[36]

Another amendment to the legislation consolidates decision-making powers previously held by non-political staff solely into the minister's hands. The change grants the minister authority over mineral exploration, permitting and mine closures — a departure from precedent.[37] Pirie has stated that the changes will "streamline the process, make the ministry more efficient and effective so we can get on to building the mines that are required."[38] Under previous legislation, government staff with technical expertise reviewed closure plans of mining projects to ensure compliance with mining regulations.[39] In April 2023, the Matawa Chiefs Council released a formal statement, expressing how the provincial government has failed to consult them regarding the Act's amendments, signalling a blatant disregard for "meaningful partnerships and reconciliation."[40]

From some Indigenous communities' perspectives, it is easy to see how the "critical minerals" angle is just the latest colonial rationale in a long chain of rationales strung out to justify extraction in their homelands. In their recent memory, it was chromite, not nickel, that was billed as "critical," rare and in strategic demand.[41] This legacy gives rise to the awareness that any tactic will be used to gain access to Indigenous lands for settler purposes and that it will be justified in whatever language current politics demand. The push for critical minerals, cloaked as a climate-mitigation measure, is yet another ruse in the long history of extractive colonial relations.[42]

Indigenous Resistance and Assertions of Jurisdiction

Indigenous communities across Treaty No. 9 have asserted their own inherent jurisdiction on the land for generations. They have denied would-be miners access to their "assets" through direct action,[43] and have declared and enforced moratoriums on development activity on their territories.[44] In the early days, proposals for development in the Ring of Fire met with resistance from an allied group of Indigenous communities in the region. The Matawa Tribal Council affirmed their commitment to work together on land, resource and water issues in the 2011 Unity Declaration. Since those discussions fell apart, various First Nations have continued to oppose development in the Ring of Fire. For example, in January 2021, the Mushkegowuk Council Chiefs called for a moratorium on development in the Ring of Fire until a proper protection plan could be implemented.[45] In April 2021, Neskantaga First Nation, Attawapiskat First Nation and Fort Albany First Nation took the next step and jointly declared a moratorium on any development in, or on facilitating access to, the Ring of Fire.[46]

In May 2021, in the midst of the global pandemic, when most of Ontario was still very much "disrupted" by COVID-19 restrictions, the leadership of Neskantaga First Nation called publicly for a halt to the environmental assessment processes for the Ring of Fire roads. The leadership noted that the community was already overwhelmed by compounding emergencies, including a major drinking water crisis that had prompted a full community evacuation. Their view was that it was callous and unreasonable to expect environmental assessments to proceed in that context.

Then Chief Wayne Moonias, in a letter to government officials and the road proponents, stated that Neskantaga's decision-making protocols were being undermined during a pandemic. Moonias wrote: "It is obvious that Ontario has 'weaponized' the environmental assessment process to further repress our Aboriginal and Treaty Rights. We are under duress."[47] He cited the ways the pandemic had made the situation in Neskantaga even more precarious — the health emergency exacerbated the ongoing water crisis — and he expressed resentment that the community should be expected to "engage" on a road project during this time. As debate raged in Ontario about which services were "essential" and should remain open during the lockdowns, Moonias stated:

> We reject the claim that an environmental assessment of a mining road should be treated like an essential service during a pandemic.... By downplaying the real threats of the pandemic in our community, continuing to run the process by any means available and ignoring the fact that it is more challenging for Neskantaga to get information to participate, Ontario is weakening the already limited measures, which do not exist to address meaningful participation by Indigenous communities in environmental assessment.[48]

Post-pandemic, resistance to Ford's vision continued. Discussions about the Ring of Fire at the 2022 Fall Assembly of the Chiefs of Ontario was recorded as follows:

> Sentiments expressed ... were overwhelmingly against the project, as Chief declared his community will do everything in its power to prevent the project unless it gets a "big say" in how

the Ring of Fire will be operated." Moonias continued, "If the industry and the government want to proceed without our free, prior, and informed consent, we will defend our right. We will defend our lands . . . We're going to fight." "I will tell you this," he continued, "Neskantaga First Nation will be there to stop Premier [Doug] Ford if he gets on that dozer."[49]

The Land Defence Alliance, formed in January 2023 by five First Nations communities, including Neskantaga First Nation, is an organized effort to stop Ford's bulldozer.[50] The alliance aims to fight against the "unwanted encroachments on their territories" by rejecting the Ontario government's continued implementation of the "free-entry" system with its blatant disregard for free, prior and informed consent. Chief Rudy Turtle of Grassy Narrows emphasizes that the alliance's concerns stem from the desire to maintain their traditional way of life and to protect Mother Earth from the "scars" of mining. He also referenced the traumatic legacy of mercury poisoning in Grassy Narrows, citing further industrial developments as too risky.[51] Alliance leaders call Ford's willingness to bypass Indigenous consent and ignore repeated calls by the Land Defence Alliance to meet them at the negotiation table, "an aggressive colonial feeling of entitlement."[52]

Meanwhile, there has also been ongoing contestation about a possible "Regional Assessment" for the Ring of Fire region to be conducted under the federal *Impact Assessment Act*.[53] A Regional Assessment is a broad, regionally focused environmental assessment intended to look at all possible cumulative effects from multiple and anticipated developments on social, economic, cultural and ecological systems.[54] Ontario was firmly opposed to the idea, saying it would only slow things down further. Probably due to Ontario's influence, the Impact Assessment Agency of Canada's (IAAC) first attempt at drafting a Terms of Reference for the Regional Assessment was roundly and rightly rejected by Indigenous nations and non-governmental groups for failing to recognize the inherent governing authority of Indigenous peoples of the region.[55] They called upon Canada's new "activist" environment minister, Steven Guilbeault, to dissolve the Draft Agreement and to establish an Indigenous-led Regional Assessment process.

As a result of the significant opposition, the minister released a statement in April 2022, that he would be "carefully considering" feedback received during the public comment period. Many Indigenous communities in the region were willing to work with the IAAC and the minister to develop a better model. In June 2022, the Chiefs of the Matawa First Nations announced that they were collaborating to develop a mutually agreeable process to establish an Indigenous governing body to co-lead the Regional Assessment of the Ring of Fire in joint partnership with the IAAC.[56] Mushkegowuk Council came out in support of this proposal shortly thereafter.[57] Minister Guilbeault finally met in person with the Chiefs of both tribal councils early in 2023 in Thunder Bay. Following the meeting, he stated, "It's clear to me that there is no access to critical minerals in Canada without Indigenous Peoples being at the table in a decision-making position."[58] As of September 2024, work is ongoing to "co-develop" a Terms of Reference for the Regional Assessment, but this is amid talk from both federal and Ontario cabinet ministers that mine approval processes need to be "fast-tracked" in order to get mines built more quickly. To add even further layers of complexity, the *Impact Assessment Act* was found to be largely unconstitutional by the Supreme Court of Canada in November 2023, and Ontario is actively opposing its application to major development projects in the province.[59]

Indigenous Sovereignty and the Future of Lands and Resources in Ontario's Far North

Ten First Nations groups launched a "game-changing" lawsuit against Canada and Ontario in April of 2023. Litigation challenging the interpretation and implementation of Treaty No. 9 has long been anticipated, with the resources required to bring such a challenge as the main impediment. The plaintiff First Nations argue that Canada and Ontario have continuously acted as if the Treaty No. 9 Nations ceded all their jurisdiction to the Crown, contrary to the actual agreement made at treaty time. They argue that this unjustified infringement of their treaty rights has had profound and devastating effects on their capacity for self-determination. The lawsuit is seeking declarations and injunctions, urging the court to compel Canada and Ontario to negotiate a co-jurisdiction regime.[60] They also request declarations that Canada and Ontario have breached Treaty No. 9 by "regulating the land" without their consent, as well as the striking down of several statutes, including the *Mining Act,* as unconstitutional. The plaintiffs seek equitable compensation and damages for breaches of Treaty and Duties, amounting to $95 billion,[61] determined in part by a portion of the total revenue generated by resource extraction activities on Treaty No. 9 territory over the past century.[62]

If successful, the lawsuit will have wide-ranging and serious implications for not only Ford's plan to kickstart mining in the Ring of Fire, but for lands and resources governance across the province more generally. Neither the provincial nor federal government has commented on the lawsuit. Minister Rickford provided an evasive response, highlighting how his government intends to "continue to focus on the economic development projects ... and Indigenous business leaders who want to transform the region."[63] But the case undoubtedly serves as a warning to mining companies operating in Ontario, signalling the need to obtain consent from Indigenous communities. Kate Kempton, lead counsel for the plaintiffs, emphasizes that the Crown will need to negotiate a co-jurisdictional regime that ensures Indigenous oversight and participation in resource extraction projects. The lawsuit has significant implications for how regulatory regimes now taken for granted — such as free-entry mining — may become inapplicable to Treaty No. 9 territory.[64] It has the potential to challenge the long-standing status quo of unilateral Crown jurisdiction. The legal and historical context of the relationship between Indigenous nations and the provincial government is instructive, with both direct action by the Land Defence Alliance and litigation on treaty implementation contributing to the potential for dramatic changes to those relations over the next several years.

By approaching the far north of the province as a resource frontier, "an empty, unoccupied wilderness with rich resources freely available for the taking, [as if] the rightful wealth [is] owed to those representing the interest of civilization and progress," as Sarah Hunt (Tłalilila'ogwa) puts it,[65] the Ford government's right-wing populism belatedly embraces EVs as a means to selling a narrative of a return to (auto)manufacturing glory in Ontario. It is a cynical and instrumental use of the climate crisis to justify further extractivism in the old-economy model. It is also an expression of a divide-and-rule approach to Indigenous peoples that is short-sighted and fails to grasp the true challenge that Indigenous self-determination presents.

11

CHILD CARE WHEN CONVENIENT

Rachel Vickerson, Carolyn Ferns and Brooke Richardson

THE DOUG FORD-LED CONSERVATIVE ERA in child care has been devastating to the early childhood educators, child care workers and the families and children that rely on child care. Since its election, through the COVID-19 pandemic and the implementation of the Canada-Wide Early Learning and Child Care (CWELCC) agreement, the Ford government has been characterized by a profit-driven agenda and cancellations fuelled by a privatization ideology. New federal leadership on child care has decreased costs for families since 2022, but the Ford government has been an unwilling and stagnant partner at best, and, at worst, has actively subverted the federal program's goals to create affordable non-profit and public child care for Ontario families. This has also been an era of an increasingly organized coalition of educators, families and community members demanding accessible child care and good working conditions. New advocacy alliances, including those incorporating municipalities and the federal government, continue to fight against a marketized child care system where this essential service is sold for profit.

Child Care in Ontario

Child care is not, and has never been, universally accessible in Ontario. Despite the current federal government's recent investment in a national child care system, there are enough licensed child care spaces in Ontario for only 21.3 percent of children under five years of age. Families typically face long waiting lists to access a child care space. Up until the CWELCC program, enacted in 2021, licensed child care in many places in the province easily cost families more than $2000 per month. There have been significant changes in parent fee affordability since CWELCC, and parent fees are currently frozen at 50 percent of what they were in March 2022, in centres enrolled in the CWELCC program (which is 92 percent of licensed child care spaces).[1] In line with CWELCC's promises, it is the current goal of the Ontario government to have parent fees reduced to an average of $10 per day by the end of 2025–2026 fiscal year.

In Ontario and across Canada, the province acts as the regulator of licensed centre-based and home child care programs, almost all of which are privately operated as either for-profits or non-profits. Regulatory responsibilities include determining the training levels of staff, health and safety protocols, group sizes and ratios of educators to children, and overseeing licensing and regulatory compliance. Ontario is unique to other Canadian provinces and territories in that municipalities act as service system managers. This means municipal, rather than provincial, authorities are responsible for managing and administering the provincial funds to centres. Similarly, Ontario municipalities are responsible for determining and managing fee subsidies for families and special funding related to supporting children with disabilities.

On the whole, funding to child care in Ontario (and other provinces/territories) under a neoliberal system has had to compete with other social and educational services for a slice of limited provincial dollars, and generally, it comes out short. Except for a brief period from 2015 to 2017, Ontario has never prioritized allocating funds to child care.

Ontario Child Care Pre-Ford

Under the government previous to Ford, there were significant changes in child care. In 2017, a new report based on comprehensive community consultations, Ontario's Renewed Early Years and Child Care Policy Framework, hinted towards a massive re-organization of child care. In March 2018, the government announced a $2.2-billion investment in a free, universal preschool program (targeted at three- and four-year-old children). At the June 2018 election, child care was still a private market-based system in which parents paid extraordinarily high fees and early childhood educators (ECEs) were underpaid and felt undervalued. However, there was a sense that there was momentum for change and positive steps towards an increasingly publicly funded and managed system of early learning and child care.

These changes, first discussed in the 2017 report, included:

- The introduction of new governing legislation, the *Child Care and Early Years Act*, and *How Does Learning Happen*, a new play-based curriculum for licensed child care and full-day kindergarten;
- A much-needed child care workforce strategy to address the recruitment and retention crisis in the sector, with a commitment to create a province-wide wage grid by April 2020 to provide fair compensation to the woefully underpaid ECEs and child care workers;
- A commitment to create 100,000 new child care spaces for children ages zero to four by 2021, doubling the number of available spots;
- A commitment to make child care for preschool-aged children free by 2020.

CARE Tax Credit: 2018–2020

As had happened with the shift from the Liberals to the Conservatives at the federal level in 2006 (reflected in the shift from the Early Learning and Child Care Foundations program to the Universal Child Care Benefit), a comprehensive, supply-side-funded child care system — where child care programs themselves were operationally funded — was "replaced" with a tax credit by Ford's newly elected Conservative government. In a major step backward from a public system to one of enhanced privatization and marketization, the child care policy narrative shifted from one of universality back to one of "parental choice." Conservative MPPs claimed that their government was "putting parents back in charge of child care" and "respecting the choices of parents."[2] Following an election campaign focused on parental choice in child care, Ford cancelled monumental work underway to build a sustainable, universal, preschool program in Ontario. This included the cancellation of the hard-fought-for ECE wage grid, child care growth plans and parent-fee reduction plans. In its place, the Conservatives enacted a new child care tax credit. The Ontario Child Care Access and Relief from Expenses Tax Credit (cleverly referred to as "CARE") was announced in the 2019 budget and promised to provide up to 75 percent of child care expenses.[3]

Instead of funding an increase of licensed child care staffed by qualified early childhood educators, the CARE tax credit could be claimed for babysitting and other forms of unlicensed care. This was touted as a more "flexible" option for parents and aligned with MPP Stephen Lecce's assertion: "We don't believe that one style fits all child care, for example. We don't believe in just a state-run system."[4] This plan may have had immediate appeal to parents who relied at the time on unlicensed child care — a relatively common phenomenon when licensed care is scarce.

To no child care policy expert's surprise, a September 2019 report by the Financial Accountability Office (FAO) on the CARE tax credit found it did not deliver on its promise of supporting access to child care for middle- and low-income families. The average benefit of a family receiving the CARE tax credit was $1,300, less than one month's child care expenses for most families with children below school-age.[5] The FAO report also found that the CARE Tax credit disproportionately benefited middle- to high-income families, as they were already spending more on child care and could use these monies for occasional babysitting or recreational programs that they would have enrolled their children in anyway. Perhaps most surprising was that only 3 percent of the total CARE tax credit benefit was distributed to families with incomes below the twenty-fifth income percentile ($21,400 or less).[6] In other words, CARE was anything but caring for Ontario families who required care most — it was a political decoy successfully diverting attention (and funds) away from the urgent need for systemic planning and funding for child care.

Municipal Cost Sharing

Ontario's upper-tier regional and municipal governments serve as local early years and child care service system managers. In contrast to other jurisdictions in Canada, Ontario municipalities play a critical role in child care planning, administration, quality "assurance" (itself an increasingly marketized concept) and operation. In 2019, the Ford government announced two major child care cuts to municipalities. The first was to reduce cost-share arrangements for child care administrative funding from 100 percent provincial to 50/50 provincial-municipal cost-share. The second was to reduce the allowable administrative funding threshold from 10 percent to 5 percent. For the City of Toronto, this could cut into their child care budget of $84.8 million in 2019, including a $28.6-million reduction in direct provincial funding and a $56.2-million reduction due to cost-sharing changes.[7]

The government's key political tactic to justify these cuts was a focus on (in)efficiencies. Minister of Education Lisa Thompson declared in the legislature: "[City staff] go around to make sure the seasonal decorations are in place in daycares. Honestly, Speaker, is that the best use of taxpayer dollars?"[8] Again, this line of thinking was a distraction from the reality that 6,166 subsidized licensed child care spaces in Toronto would be lost to funding cuts. When child care advocates (tired and deflated after the near-universal preschool program enacted by the previous government) and municipal politicians pointed these losses out, Ford announced that he was backing down, but he, in fact, only delayed the changes. Following "transitional funding" over several years, Ford's government proceeded with the cuts in 2024, resulting in an $85.5-million cut to municipal budgets.

Blaming municipalities has become a running theme for the Ford government. In 2024, the Ford government announced that they were requiring value-for-money audits of municipally operated child care programs, but not for for-profit or private non-profit programs. Furthermore, they would now require municipalities that wanted to expand a public, child care program to prove it to be a "last resort" and that no private operator was available. This initiative followed closures of municipal child care programs in Peel and Waterloo, where Conservative councillors had convinced local governments to hold their own audits or service reviews carried out by private consultants like KPMG. Given the important role of municipal child care as a model ("lighthouse") child care program in Canada, this government has led a direct attack on the quality of licensed child care programs in Ontario. Indeed, municipally run, public, child care programs disproportionately represent the few programs that provide decent wages and working conditions for educators, which supports a high-quality environment for children and families.

2020–2022: COVID-19

The Ford government's gutting of both child care and municipalities was partially put on hold during the COVID-19 pandemic. Following initial closures of child care programs, it became clear that emergency child care would be necessary for health care and other vital community workers to operate "essential services." And it was municipal child care administration and operations that stepped up to offer emergency child care programs quickly. For example, within two weeks of the declaration of the pandemic, the City of Toronto had organized to open free, 24/7 emergency child care services. Having publicly administered and organized child care in the City of Toronto (even if it did provide less than 5 percent of licensed child care in the city) was invaluable to mobilizing and coordinating public resources to act in an emergency.

The pandemic years, especially 2020 and 2021, were financially uncertain and stressful for Ontario child care operators, as months of closures and low enrolments put many programs into deficit and the Ford government provided little support. For the first time in Ontario, in 2020–21, more child care programs in Ontario closed than opened, and if it wasn't for federal Safe Restart funding, many more programs would surely have shuttered.

Across Canada, the pandemic was a turning point for the acknowledgement of child care as an essential community service. The Ford government's previous parental choice narrative no longer made sense in a context where there were zero child care options. This narrative was replaced with another political discourse favoured by Conservative governments: the immediate economic importance of child care. With a tanking economy due to the pandemic, Ford's Conservatives suddenly claimed to "know the integral role child care plays in the restart of Ontario's economy, especially when it comes to enabling parents to return to work."[9]

One issue that the Ford government has consistently ignored, even when the importance of child care gained prominence, is the importance of ECEs and child care workers. During the pandemic, this became apparent by failing to recognize ECEs as "essential workers." Working ECEs and child care workers therefore did not receive the financial benefits ("pandemic pay") of being an essential worker, nor did they have priority to the early release of vaccines. Furthermore, ECEs and child care workers were not initially eligible to enrol their own children in emergency child care services. In the end, ECEs and child care workers became eligible for vaccines only a few days before vaccines were rolled out to the general public.

Canada-Wide Early Learning and Child Care Agreement: 2022–2024

On April 19, 2021, the federal government introduced an unprecedented new funding commitment for child care. It allocated $30 billion to create a Canada-Wide Early Learning and Child Care (CWELCC) program.

The goal of CWELCC was to lower parent fees to an average, $10-per-day, and to create 250,000 child care spaces by 2026. The 2021 budget also stated that the federal government would work with provinces and territories to support "primarily not-for-profit sector child care providers to grow quality spaces across the country."[10]

As child care is a provincial responsibility, the federal government set out to sign bilateral funding agreements with each province and territory and to negotiate separate agreements under the Indigenous Early Learning and Child Care Framework with First Nations, Métis and Inuit governments. This news of a Canada-wide system was met with widespread enthusiasm and excitement by child care advocates, who had been pushing for the federal government to become involved in child care since the 1984 Federal Task Force on Child Care.

Most provincial and territorial governments were quick to demonstrate they too were on board with "$10-a-day" child care and willing to work alongside the federal government. In July 2021, British Columbia — which already had its own provincial $10-a-day pilot program — became the first province to sign a CWELCC agreement. The Ford government was not so enthusiastic, and would be, unsurprisingly, the last province to sign on. In June 2021, Education Minister Stephen Lecce complained, "To date, the federal Liberals contribute a whopping 3 percent of the child care budget. They must do much more, and we're going to negotiate in the best interests of families to provide the flexibility and affordability that parents deserve."[11] The 3 percent, however, was the previous funding commitment, *prior to* the significant new federal involvement and it was nowhere near the billions the federal government was currently proposing to transfer to Ontario. The themes of flexibility (the so-called "parental choice") and that the federal deal "may not be a good one" became central to the ongoing negotiations between the two levels of government.

Each province and territory had their own process in negotiating with the federal government. In almost all cases, negotiations appeared to happen with integrity behind closed doors. In Ford's Ontario and Jason Kenney's government in Alberta, however, negotiations became a pathway to political grandstanding. Throughout the negotiations, Education Minister Lecce was relentless in his messaging around "fairness." Lecce repeatedly called for a "fair deal" — one that took into account "our full-day kindergarten program" (with the implication being that these funds could be used for an already existing program) and one that didn't "discriminate against for-profit child care owners." Essentially, Lecce wanted a deal that gave Ontario more money and with fewer strings attached than the rest of the provinces and territories. This was despite the fact that the funds were to be distributed on a per-child basis. So, the amount was never, in fact, up for debate; the terms of the agreement, such as child care space creation targets, were all that could be negotiated.

As other provinces and territories inked deals with the federal government and began to reduce fees immediately for families, the Ford government continued to grandstand and refused to provide any information regarding the status of negotiations. Time was running out: the first year of federal funding would be voided if a deal couldn't be reached by March 31, 2022, and every other province and territory had signed an agreement. At the very last hour, on March 28, the Ford government finally announced they had come to an agreement. When the agreement was released, it was obvious that there had been significant concessions to the for-profit child care lobby, and, as to be expected, complete neglect of early childhood educators and their wages and working conditions.

Unlike the majority of other jurisdictions, Ontario did not commit to a wage grid for ECEs, whose wages were now significantly publicly funded. They instead opted for a complicated system of a new wage floor of $18 per hour for registered ECEs and an additional separate wage enhancement of $1 per hour for registered ECEs making under $25 per hour — not be to be confused with the existing provincial wage enhancement, which provided $2 per hour for those making under $27 per hour. While a wage grid would have provided an increase in transparency for ECEs making low wages, this new system caused further confusion and distrust in the government on the part of the sector.

The federal government initially announced that the new, Canada-wide child care system would be primarily public and non-profit, and that capital funding for new child care spaces would be specifically for public and non-profit child care — something the child care advocacy movement had been calling for, for years. This, of course, clashed immediately with Ford's "Open for Business" messaging and privatization/marketization campaign. Child care, instead of being seen as a public good and social service, was positioned as another opportunity for profit-making, usually at the expense of ECE wages. International experience, such as in

Australia's embrace of for-profit child care, has shown that the expansion of "big box" corporate child care chains increases costs for government (in their case, ultimately leading to a multi-million-dollar government bailout), while failing to provide improved access, affordability or quality. There has been an increase in private equity investment in for-profit child care companies to access lending institutions' financial capital and increase expansion and/or the "competitive edge" of child care companies in many countries.[12] Concerns about private equity investment, "an opaque form of for-profit enterprise that boasts remarkable returns to investors in short time periods," are being raised in Ontario, though they have yet to reach public policy discussions.[13]

The federal government's preference for non-profit expansion was one of the issues that Minister Lecce consistently raised during the negotiations, and resulted in concession by the federal government in the final agreement. As opposed to a complete restriction on federal funding for for-profit expansion, Ontario was the only province allowed to maintain its existing ratio of 30 percent for-profit spaces for children under six years. That meant that as long as non-profits continued to expand and provide 70 percent of the child care spaces, funding could also flow to the for-profits. As the province is aiming to create 86,000 new spaces, this could mean as many as 25,800 new for-profit spaces. Time and again, the Ford government has demonstrated their enthusiasm and support for an increasingly market-based child care sector in Ontario despite evidence that families prefer licensed child care and are better off financially with funding going directly to support these programs.[14] Three years before CWELCC, the Ford government removed the requirement that in-school child care centres must be non-profit or publicly run, and they removed too the "For-Profit Percentage Threshold," a provincial policy under the previous government that had put a cap on overall for-profit expansion.

Soon after the agreement was signed with the federal government, owners of existing for-profit child care centres began to push for changes to the funding guidelines of the new Canada-wide funding in order for them to also become a CWELCC centre. The initial funding guidelines required all child care operators to provide audited financial statements and limited them in "undue profit-making." Through their quick and successful lobbying of the Ford government, for-profit centres had these requirements removed so that they were able to use public funding with little accountability to serve their profit-making business. Minister Lecce justified this by saying the province needed to support "small-business women entrepreneurs who are the majority of for-profit owners."[15]

In the two years since the CWELCC agreement was signed, Ontario has resisted making transformative changes to the way child care is funded. Unlike several other provinces, Ontario still has not introduced a wage grid, pension or benefit plans for ECEs, and it has been slow in developing a new funding formula for child care programs. Also, in contrast to other provinces, Ontario has put little of its own money into developing the child care system. The Ford government's provincial allocations to child care are lower in 2024 than when they were first elected in 2018. Funding increases have been made possible by the new federal funding, and as of 2024, more than 50 percent of child care funding in Ontario has come directly from the federal government's Canada-wide child care agreement. But as Ontario approaches renegotiation with the federal government in 2025, Minister Lecce is conveniently attributing funding increases to his government and funding shortfalls to the federal government: "While Ontario will continue to increase funding annually to operators, starting this month, we will commence a review of the federal deal and vigorously advocate for a long-term increase in funding to better support operators and families."[16] It is worth noting that federal funding has increased from 3 percent (when Minister Lecce first made this argument in June 2021), to 55 percent of the child care spending in Ontario as of March 2024.

In July 2024, newly-in-place Minister of Education Todd Smith sent a formal request to the federal government to remove the for-profit percentage cap completely from Ontario's child care agreement so as to allow for an unlimited number of new, for-profit spaces.

Advocacy in the Ford Era

Ontario has, and always has had, a vibrant child care advocacy community, largely coordinated by the Ontario Coalition for Better Child Care (OCBCC) and the Association of Early Childhood Educators of Ontario (AECEO). The OCBCC is a member-based organization (parents, labour unions, educators and child care centres/programs), established in 1981 to "advocate for universal affordable, high quality, not-for-profit child care in Ontario."[17] The AECEO, whose members are early childhood educators and child care staff, has a more focused mission: "To build and support a strong collective voice for early childhood educators

(ECEs) so they can participate in and influence positive change that benefits ECEs, children, families and communities."[18] The role of the AECEO has shifted drastically with the establishment of the College of Early Childhood Educators in 2007. While it historically acted as the professional organization overseeing the qualifications and professional development of educators (the College of ECE now does that), today, it is primarily concerned with ensuring the voices and lived experiences of educators have a space in public policy discussions and practice. Currently, the AECEO is funded through both membership fees and project funds related to decent work and anti-racist, anti-oppressive and inclusive pedagogical practice.

The child care movement in Ontario dates back to the 1970s, with close ties that continue to this day to the larger feminist movement. Child care was first advocated for by women, mostly white middle-class mothers, as an essential tool for gender equity and female economic independence. Child care as a feminist issue for working mothers has been a predominant narrative of advocacy, yet early childhood educators and other child care workers were often left out of the conversation and not included in advocacy campaigns. In recent years, this has changed significantly, with the workforce growing in prominence as a key advocacy issue and as advocates themselves. Addressing the workforce crisis in child care is, and has been, a central plank of both the OCBCC's and the AECEO's advocacy efforts for the past decade.

Indeed, in 2014, the OCBCC and the AECEO came together to focus their advocacy efforts on advancing decent work for the child care workforce. Under Kathleen Wynne's government, both organizations were actively sought after by the Wynne government for their perspectives and they also sat on the minister's Early Years Advisory Committee and Early Learning and Child Care Advisory Group. The organizations were still publicly critical of many decisions by the previous Liberal government — for example, its attempts to increase child care group sizes. Child care advocacy organizations repeatedly called for the government to do more to expand child care and support the child care workforce. This helped yield the late mandate commitments to 100,000 child care spaces, free preschool-aged child care, a workforce strategy and a wage grid.

Of course, with Ford's election, the child care advocacy landscape has shifted dramatically and efforts have gone from envisioning and building a universal preschool program to disaster management — literally and figuratively. Figuratively, advocates were unsuccessful in preventing the removal of the "For-Profit Percentage Threshold" and the requirement that child care in schools be non-profit, both key policy mechanisms of preventing the further marketization of child care. Disaster management became quite literal during the pandemic when child care advocates had their work cut out for them in terms of ensuring the physical safety of children and staff in programs (let alone decent work and/or respect for educators during this time).

In contrast to the previous collaborative relationship between the AECEO, OCBCC and the Wynne government, child care advocacy organizations have been effectively shut out of the policy process by Ford's Conservatives. The child care advocacy community was extremely disappointed when a new Minister's Advisors Table in 2022 was convened with a confidential membership. Neither the AECEO nor the OCBCC was invited to participate. The membership of this secretive table was only revealed through a Freedom of Information request. The request confirmed what advocates had suspected; there were three separate, for-profit lobbying organizations at the table, two of which had only formed that year: the Association of Day Care Operators Ontario, and the newly formed Private Operators Group and Ontario Association of Independent Childcare Centres. For a government that claims to support parents and families, this situation was, and continues to be, very troubling.

Blame and Credit-Taking

Child care is a policy area of somewhat murky jurisdiction, which has been explicitly exploited for political gain by the Ford government. Under the Canadian constitution, child care is a provincial responsibility, and thus, funding and regulation are all managed at the provincial level. Nevertheless, child care advocates have long called for a federal role in funding and in leading the country in a universal system. In Ontario, municipalities also have a mandated role as service system managers, coordinating all subsidy administration and funding. Child care is operated in a variety of locations, with 65 percent of spaces located in schools, so school boards are also involved in managing child care, acting as the landlord for independent child care programs leasing the space.

This multi-level governance structure has provided ample opportunity for the Ford government to both transfer blame and take credit for others' investments. Ford's government blamed the federal government when thousands of families in Ontario failed to receive child care fee reductions months after the rest of the country. This delay, however, was due to Ford's government leaving their negotiations of the agreement to the eleventh hour. More recently, Ford has blamed the federal government for delays and funding challenges faced by operators in the rolling out of CWELCC. Ford also likes to take aim at municipal governments regarding child care issues, blaming wasteful and inefficient spending on public child care quality assurance programs or the slow rollout of CWELCC's expansion. In 2023, the Toronto District School Board called out the province's failure to fund and begin construction in their buildings for the 28 new child care centres that had already been approved. Deflecting yet again, Ford's government claimed this was the school board's fault for changes to the project's timeline. In July 2024, the province formally cancelled 56 previously approved school-based child care projects across Ontario, causing a loss of approximately 3,500 potential child care spaces and $11 million in sunk costs. Child care centres and ECEs themselves were blamed in 2020 for the slower speed of re-opening child care centres during COVID-19, as they scrambled to rework their entire operations to facilitate the safety and well-being of children and staff. Truly, any issues that emerged in relation to child care policy implementation and funding became proverbial balls in a game of dodgeball. Once again, the onus fell on child care advocates to point out the true origin of the mounting child care policy failures in Ontario.

At the same time as Ford's government is dodging balls, they have had no trouble throwing others. Ford was eager to take credit for any gains in child care affordability and accessibility that resulted from CWELCC. In the 2022 budget and subsequent provincial election, the federal Canada-wide child care plan was touted as a major accomplishment of the provincial government. In December 2022, Minister Lecce proudly announced, "The Ontario government is increasing access to child care spaces and delivering needed financial relief for families."[19] The degree of hypocrisy in this statement is palpable, given this government's refusal to seriously negotiate CWELCC with the federal government until the threat that a year of federal funding would disappear. Furthermore, the reality is that the provincial government has not kept their child care funding at pace with inflation, resulting in an actual provincial funding decrease. Any policy "successes" in terms of lower parent fees or new child care spaces are entirely a result of increased federal funds to child care.

Uncovering Ford's Real Agenda and Protecting Hard-Won Gains

The first few years of the Ford administration were dominated by a focus on a public message of parental "choice" while making cuts to supply-side funding and abandoning the previous government's child care plans. But when the COVID-19 pandemic and the federal government's new child care policy and funding made it impossible for Ford's government to toe the marketized "parental-choice" line, Minister Lecce signed the CWELCC agreement at the last minute and proclaimed himself as a leader of licensed child care expansion and affordability in service of the economy.

Throughout these shifts, what has been consistent is the Ford government's support of for-profit child care (both owner-operator and corporate). Thus, the next years will likely see another major shift, as Ford's government will attempt to undo CWELCC's progress on child care affordability and a publicly funded child care system in favour of more *laissez-faire* funding that provides more flexibility (and bigger profits) to for-profit child care. Profit-making and privatization will continue to be sold as providing "choice," while true choice and stability for Ontario families, found only in a universal, publicly funded and managed child care system, is undermined.

From beneath the public messages, it is essential to uncover and shine a light on Ford's true, for-profit, child care agenda in order to protect advocates' hard-won gains on child care affordability and public funding. And in order to gain a system that addresses both the chronically poor material conditions of child care workers and the well-being of children and families, it will be necessary to keep organizing parents and educators, building their solidarity with each other, so that they can jointly advocate for a system that finally puts their interests ahead of profit-making.

12

RIDING THE "GRAVY TRAIN"

William Paul

THE GRAVY TRAIN WAS READY TO GO upon the victory of the Ontario Progressive Conservative Party (PC) in June 2018. Doug Ford wasted no time. Far from his claim that "the party with the taxpayer's money is over," it was just beginning.[1] He got rid of Liberals in comfy patronage posts only to replace them with loyal Tories at higher pay. Ian Todd, Ford's head of tour during the election, landed a job as Ontario's trade envoy to Washington along with a $75,000 annual bump in salary.[2] Todd was a Tory insider from his days with the Harper government and later went on to be chief of staff for Pierre Poilievre. It wasn't important that Ford search for someone with merit and qualifications. Connections were enough for a government imbued with the ethics of the feeding trough.

Early Start

Ron Taverner, a superintendent with Toronto police, was appointed in December 2018, as head of the Ontario Provincial Police, a job paying $270,000 per year, for which he was not qualified — until the Ford government changed the relevant criteria.[3] In the ensuing uproar, Taverner withdrew his name from consideration for the post. Dean French worked for Rob Ford, Doug Ford's brother, when he was mayor of Toronto. French was Doug Ford's friend and campaign manager and was appointed chief of staff. This lasted little more than a year until he was caught making his own patronage appointments, one to his son's friend, another to his wife's cousin, each with salaries of over $165,000 annually.[4]

It was a homecoming party with gifts. Guests included unsuccessful PC candidates, such as Sandie Bellows, who was appointed chair of the Niagara Parks Commission, and Cameron Montgomery, who landed at the Education Quality and Accountability Office (EQAO). Charles

Harnick, attorney general under Mike Harris, climbed aboard to lead the cuts to Legal Aid Ontario. PC Ontario president Michael Diamond joined the Ontario Trillium Foundation that doles out over $100 million annually to non-profits. Head of the lobbying group Upstream, Diamond managed Ford's leadership campaign. Gavin Tighe, who did legal work for the Fords, was appointed to the $166,000-per-year post as head of the Public Accountants Council.[5]

Carmine Nigro, head of Craft Development Corporation, assumed the chair of the Liquor Control Board of Ontario (LCBO) shortly after the 2018 election, concurrent with his role as vice-chair of the PC Ontario Fund. He hosted a fundraiser for loyalists to attend a pay-for-access "Evening with MPP Vic Fedeli," who, as Minister of Finance at the time, was in charge of the LCBO. Nigro went on, in 2022, to lead Ontario Place through the murky waters of the Therme Spa private development. He's close to the premier, sitting at the family table, for instance, during the 2022 wedding reception of Ford's daughter.

The party rolled on during the most vicious cutbacks and assaults on democracy since the Mike Harris years, with the Ford government capping public sector wages at 1 percent annually; cancelling a surtax on the highest-earning Ontarians; holding the minimum wage at $14 per hour; ending the cap-and-trade agreement; and cutting Toronto Public Health funding.[6] The government also cancelled the writing team working on an Indigenous curriculum,[7] severed Toronto City Council[8] and threatened to use the Canadian Constitution's "notwithstanding clause" when it lost a challenge to the local council cut in the Ontario Superior Court. It nixed the basic income pilot project, cut the advanced age allowance and slashed education funding while increasing class sizes across the province.[9]

Still, the train kept taking on passengers. By July 2023, it was passing out titles to Tory friends, thanks to its revival of the "King's Council" honorific for lawyers. Considered to be "corrupted" patronage, it had been dropped in 1985.[10] No surprise that this list included many PC friends, donors, loyal supporters, government ministers and potentates. Ottawa lawyer Michael Spratt aptly described this move as a "reckless dive into the sewer of patronage appointments"[11] that brings the Ontario justice system into disrepute. Plumbing these depths was the appointment of Tory minister Caroline Mulroney, who was hurriedly called to the Ontario bar so she could be recognized as a lawyer and get her "K.C."

Most illuminating of all Doug Ford's patronage appointments were those of ex-political staff Matthew Bondy and Brock Vandrick to the Judicial Appointments Advisory Committee, the panel charged with recommending lawyers to become provincial judges. That neither of them had any qualifications for the job was immaterial. Ford said proudly: "I'm appointing like-minded people that believe in what we believe in — keeping the bad guys in jail."[12] The appointments were unabashedly political.[13] In a few words, he spelled out what Toryism is in Ontario: a club of like-minded people who support the party with well-founded expectations of returns. If neoliberalism is the structure of market-governed thinking behind so many of the Ford government's decisions, cronyism provides the nails that hold it together.

Highway 413 and the Bradford Bypass

This waste of asphalt started as a proposal to connect the Niagara Region with Vaughan, shelved by the Liberals because it would cost between $6 billion and $10 billion and save drivers less than a minute per day. That didn't stop the PCs. In 2018, they revived a plan that would cross 85 waterways, pave 2,000 acres of farmland, encourage sprawl and pump out more carbon emissions, claiming it would save drivers thirty minutes per day. Each of those minutes is worth a fortune to eight of Ontario's largest developers, who own thousands of acres of land along the route.[14]

Developer John Di Poce owned 663 acres of land at the eastern end of the highway. He bought much of it in the early 2000s, and maybe had keen foresight. He also has good connections. One of them, Tony Miele, goes back to the scandal-ridden Ontario Realty Corporation (ORC) under the Mike Harris government. Before that, Miele worked for Canada Lands Corporation managing a deal with Di Poce in 1997–98 to sell federal land in Brampton[15] at less than a quarter of the going rate. Di Poce nearly tripled his investment within a month, ascribing it to "luck." Miele left the ORC and went to work as a consultant for Di Poce while heading up the party's fundraising organ, the PC Ontario Fund.

Other prominent developers included the Cortellucci, De Gasperis, Guglietti and De Meneghi families. Also involved were Benny Marotta, as well as Argo Development and Fieldgate Homes. Altogether, they owned 39 properties embracing 3,300 acres of land. Potential profits were huge. The University of Guelph pegged the cost per acre in the York

Region, through which Highway 413 will run, at $17,500 per acre in 2020. The following year, the price leapt to $40,000 per acre.[16]

The web of connections between these landowners and Tory friends is impressive. Former Conservative house leader Peter Van Loan was chair of PC minister Caroline Mulroney's bid for the party leadership in 2018. He's a registered lobbyist, who has clients like Fieldgate Homes with land along the route. The De Gasperis family owns The Amazing Construction Company (TACC), and Argo Developments is headed up by Gord Buck. Lobbyist Amir Remtulla, once Rob Ford's chief of staff, worked for TACC, as well as the De Meneghi family, between 2019 to 2020. His name appears as a lobbyist for them in connection to the Greenbelt and Minister's Zoning Orders (MZOs). TACC's Stephen De Gasperis kindly hosted Doug Ford and Tory minister Stephen Lecce in his private box at a Florida Panthers Game in late 2018.[17] All together, these developers donated $813,000 to the PCs between 2014 and 2021. Not bad, considering the size of the return.[18]

Like Highway 413, the Bradford Bypass will cut through environmentally precarious areas like the Greenbelt and the Holland Marsh on its way between Highways 400 and 404. The major problem, however, was that it would slice into three holes at the Silver Lakes Golf and Country Club, co-owned by Tory MPP Stan Cho's father. So, the bypass was rerouted. The NDP referred the matter to Ontario's Integrity Commissioner, citing insider information and influence breaches, but the Commissioner dismissed the complaint.

Greenbelt Follies

In September 2023, Doug Ford admitted he broke his promise not to touch the Greenbelt: "for that, I'm very, very sorry." It was a mistake, he said. His government moved too fast, causing people "to question our motives." The government cancelled the removal of lands from the Greenbelt, along with its unilateral decision to alter municipal plans and expand their boundaries into rural areas to open them up to development friends. There was a lot more to these stories than Ford's folksy apology could obscure.

The Greenbelt is 7,200 square kilometres of protected land, wrapping around municipalities from the rich "Golden Horseshoe" running from the western end of Lake Ontario east to Cobourg. It includes the Niagara Escarpment and the Oak Ridges Moraine, and was created by the Liberals in 2005 with the passing of the *Greenbelt Act*. During the 2018 election, Ford listened to disgruntled developers who owned land there, said he would allow development, then facing public outcry, he reversed his statement, saying, "The people have spoken — we won't touch the Greenbelt. Very simple."

Well, not so simple, as we've come to realize. By November 2022, after a rushed process of choosing properties, Ford announced that he would be reversing his reversal, opening 7,400 acres of Greenbelt lands to developers. This was done through regulation, with little public consultation. Tim Gray, head of Environmental Defence, said that it was clear from the beginning that such a radical change, of course, was ordered from a very high level, politically. No one in the civil service saw it coming.[19]

Altogether, fifteen parcels of land throughout the Greater Toronto and Hamilton areas, near the Highway 413 route, were opened for development. While the Tories hyped the move as a plan to build 1.5 million homes by 2031, an Environmental Defence report claimed there were already 350 square kilometres of land in the Golden Horseshoe area ready to be developed. Significantly, eight of the fifteen properties to be removed from the Greenbelt had been purchased in the years since Doug Ford was elected premier in 2018.[20]

These properties included 100 acres near Canada's Wonderland, purchased by the TACC group of companies in May 2021 for $50 million. The De Gasperis family group already owned 4,300 acres in the Duffins Rouge Agricultural Preserve, the largest plot on the list for removal, along with thirty-two other properties affected by opening the Greenbelt. Michael Rice, head of Greenlane Bathurst Inc., paid $80 million for 700 acres in September 2022, months before land removals were announced. These companies and others, like Torca II Inc., 502 Winston Rd Inc., and three numbered companies with land purchased since 2018, somehow fathomed it was worthwhile to purchase land in these Greenbelt areas that the Tories were about to open up for development.[21]

There was money to be made on land flips alone. Ford's friend Shakir Rehmatullah, owner of Flato Developments, paid $15 million for land in Markham in 2017. He received a Minister's Zoning Order (MZO) for the property in 2021 to allow him to build houses. An MZO is a powerful tool with which the government can overwrite local regulations as though they never existed. In 2023, Rehmatullah sold two sections of this property for $62 million.[22] So much for housing. These developers paid a lot of money for land they figured would be removed from the Greenbelt, but the potential rewards were enormous. In her August 2023 report, Auditor General Bonnie Lysyk estimated that they would rake in about $8.3 billion in profits from land sales.[23] She added: "At least 92% of the acreage removed from the Greenbelt was from five land sites passed on from two developers (which included a land site associated with a third developer) who had direct access to the Housing Minister's Chief of Staff."[24] She was referring to the TACC group, Greenlane Bathurst and Fieldgate Homes, with land in Hamilton.

Ryan Amato, the newly appointed chief of staff at the Ministry of Municipal Affairs and Housing (MMAH), bent over backwards to make land removal work. At his direction, Lysyk reported, assessment criteria for land removal were altered so that requirements including access to roads, schools and utility hook-ups were set aside. Site selections were changed to meet the criteria for removal. Even basic considerations were ignored, like whether a property up for removal was needed for a specialty crop or was part of the Natural Heritage System. Amato simply dropped that requirement for thirteen of the fifteen sites chosen by him.[25]

The developers involved were close to PCs in power. Pending an RCMP investigation into the Greenbelt affair, there is no proof that illegal acts occurred. But party donations certainly helped a few people get the ear of the government. A *Toronto Star/Narwhal* investigation revealed that nine of the developers donated about $572,000 to the party between 2014 and 2022.[26]

The Elections Ontario website details the size of contributions developers were willing to donate to the PC party and candidates since 2014. Familiar names on the list include Silvio, Carlo and Michael De Gasperis who, with TACC Developments, donated $116,875. Fieldgate Homes, with its owners Jack Eisenberger and Dennis and Tom Kohn, donated $75,174, along with Michael Rice, who gave $21,531.[27]

Ontario Integrity Commissioner (OIC) David Wake revealed the importance of having an inside track in his August 2023 report. It was clear from his 2022 mandate letter that MMAH Minister Steve Clark needed to remove land from the Greenbelt. There was no call for public discussion, Wake noted in his report, but developers who caught wind of the change and had access to Amato gained an advantage for their lands to be removed. The question left hanging was how that wind happened to be blowing the right way for some.

Ryan Amato was a loyal Tory who had worked in various capacities for his party. He had no experience as a chief of staff, though Wake claimed he was the "driving force behind a flawed process which provided an advantage to those who approached him."[28] Amato certainly did some driving, according to the report. He went to the "Building Industry and Land Development" dinner in September 2022, picking up a package there from Silvio De Gasperis containing information about removing a huge plot of land in Pickering, referred to as Cherrywood, from the Greenbelt. He also stopped by Michael Rice's office to pick up information about his Greenbelt property. He didn't wait for developers to give him information, but actively pursued it between September and November 4, 2022, when the removal plan was announced.

According to Wake's report, developers like Shakir Rehmatullah knew something profitable was in the works. His lawyer requested the removal of ten acres of his property from the Greenbelt, a little more than a month before the plan was announced. Rehmatullah first told the OIC he didn't know why his lawyer would make such a request, then backtracked and said it was "normal" to keep submitting removal requests. Yet none had been made since 2017. Why now?[29]

Rehmatullah was close friends with Kaleed Rasheed, a PC Minister until he resigned from the party in 2023. The two met briefly in Las Vegas in 2020 with Amin Massoudi, Ford's principal secretary, though Rasheed initially got the date wrong. Rehmatullah told the commission that neither he nor Massoudi socialized or visited each other's homes, a claim contradicted by text messages obtained by *The Trillium* from three government insiders.[30]

There was the mysterious Mr. X, who turned out to be former Clarington mayor John Mutton. He said he wasn't a lobbyist, but he helped developer Peter Tanenbaum rezone his Greenbelt lands near Nash Road in Clarington. For his help, beginning in August 2022, Mutton was to receive $6,000 per month and another $1 million once the land was approved for housing.[31] According to Tanenbaum, Mutton met with Ryan Amato and senior MMAH staffer, Kirsten Jensen, in September 2022, to discuss the file (as well as taking them to play golf and attend a Toronto Raptors game). This was all before the Greenbelt removal became public.

Tanenbaum's lobbyist Nico Fidani-Diker was to be paid $10,000 monthly. He is a Ford family friend and fourth vice-president of PC Ontario.[32] He was former Toronto Mayor Rob Ford's assistant in 2012–13 and Doug Ford's executive assistant in 2018–20. From there, he went on to launch the lobbying firm, ONpoint Strategy. Other clients included Fieldgate Homes and Penta Properties, both seeking to remove Greenbelt lands near Hamilton.[33]

Wake criticized the lack of oversight on the part of Minister Clark who allowed Amato to "leave it with me" as he rushed ahead in chaos. But it was much more than chaos. As Tim Gray of Environmental Defence explained: "You're creating a situation where you are entrenching risk of long-term corruption because it's very clear to anyone that if you want to get ahead, you better have influence with the right people because the process isn't a process anymore. It's just influence peddling."[34]

Boundary Issues

Meanwhile, MMAH staff worked feverishly to prepare as the Ford government extended municipal boundaries into rural areas to allow for the development of surrounding areas like Hamilton, Halton Hills, Waterloo, York Region, Niagara and Peel. Late in 2023, Environmental Defence obtained thousands of heavily redacted documents from the MMAH, showing ministry staff working through September and October 2022 with developers and lobbyists to review flurries of requests to change land use rules in order to open areas up for housing and commercial development. In one email, Ryan Amato, with no municipal planning experience, ordered certain building height limits to be deleted from Hamilton's official plan.[35] All this work was ongoing before November 2022, when the ministry announced that it was going to change boundaries.

Much of the work done on behalf of developers, seeking a way to avoid the hassles of planning regulations, comes in the form of MZOs. The Tories are keen on them, issuing 114 between 2018 and the end of 2023. By contrast, only eighteen were issued during the previous fifteen years. The bulk of MZOs conferred include the names connected to the developers listed above, like TACC, Argo, Flato, Cortel Group, Orca Equity and the Rice Group. Flato, for instance, scored eight of them.[36] Orca Equity got an MZO in 2021, so it could build 1,500 houses near land belonging to Flato Developments that were removed from the Greenbelt in November 2022. There's a fortuitous connection between

MZOs and friends of Ford who attended his daughter's wedding, people like Carmine Nigro, who received a MZO for Craft Developments' 200-home project in Lindsay; and Mario Cortellucci, whose Cortel Group received six of them over the years.[37]

Whose Health?

The train runs not only through "undeveloped" land; it also makes its way through health care. In May 2023, the Ford government passed *Your Health Act,* which gave greater access to private health care facilities to charge for services, such as hip and knee replacements, MRI and CT scans, as well as long-term care (LTC). Touted as a way to reduce wait times and surgery backlogs, *Your Health Act* might be viewed by skeptics as being more about privatization, given government changes that include shrinking control of local health care, cutting funding for mental health and cancelling free prescriptions for young people.[38]

Critics argued that more private health clinics would improve profit margins rather than health. Only three private hospitals in Ontario were allowed to operate after 1971 legislation ended the practice. One of them, Clearpoint, not only continues to thrive, but built three new operating rooms in the past few years. It helped that between 2017/18 and 2021/22, Clearpoint received a 278-percent increase in payments and much higher rates from the government for its services.[39] Cataract surgery costs $508 in a public hospital versus $1,264 at Clearpoint, which also charges $4,037 for arthroscopic knee surgery compared to the $1,200 to $1,600 cost in public hospitals.[40]

It happens that Christine Elliott was the deputy premier and minister of health at the time, leaving politics in 2022 to lobby on behalf of Clearpoint and other companies for Fasken Law. The *Member's Integrity Act* forbids former members of the cabinet from lobbying the government in which they were a member. Questioned about this, Elliott responded that, as a minister, she didn't take part in funding decisions about institutions.[41]

The conflict between being a senior member of cabinet and lobbying for a private clinic speaks volumes about the cozy relationship between Tories and those who can afford to hire them. Natalie Mehra, executive director of the Ontario Health Care Coalition, commented: "[It] stretches the bounds of credibility that a health minister would not be part of a decision to expand a private hospital."[42] Clearpoint gets help from other party insiders, like former PC policy director Francesca Grosso and senior policy advisor Michael McCarthy, who lobbied to increase Clearpoint's government funding.

The prize goes to LTC homes when it comes to rewarding unconscionable negligence. Terrible overall care and few precautions regarding COVID-19 plagued private LTC facilities. The Canadian military was deployed to deal with conditions, including bleeding fungal infections, patients left in soiled diapers and a "general culture of fear to use supplies because they cost money."[43] Remarkably, in 2020, two large private companies, Extendicare and Sienna Senior Living, were able to pay out $74 million in profits to shareholders.[44]

In 2021, in the midst of this disaster, companies with the highest death rates received more money and licences to expand their operations. Rykka Care Centres, second on the death-rate list (8.6 per hundred beds), received the go-ahead for 160 new beds, along with provincial funding to develop them;[45] Southbridge Homes, with the highest death rate (9 per hundred beds), and the disgrace of having the military intervene in one of its homes, received tens of millions of dollars in government funding to add 733 new beds, along with thirty-year licences to run them.[46]

It's a mystery how these operations continued to thrive but there might be some clues in the company they keep. For example, Alanna Newman, former Ontario PC party's ninth vice-president, who worked for Caroline Mulroney during her time as attorney general, lobbied various government ministries on behalf of Southbridge over the damning military report about the treatment of residents. She got help from former Tory MPP Rob Leone, now head of Earnscliffe Strategies.[47] Stephanie DiNucci, who worked in the minister's office at MMAH between 2018 and 2023, lobbied for construction subsidies on behalf of Sienna Senior Living,[48] along with Cody Mallette, who worked in the premier's office between 2020 and 2022. Both work with Atlas Strategic Advisors, whose principal, Amin Massoudi, received $237,000 in 2022–23 for "caucus support" for the Tories after he left the premier's office.[49]

This influence of corporate operators is overwhelming as far as Natalie Mehra is concerned: "What we're seeing is unprecedented." Sure, there was corporate influence under the Liberals but "that was nothing compared to what we're seeing now."[50] Privatization of health services is proceeding at an astonishing rate.

Buying Influence

Lobbying provides tracks for the gravy train. PC party executives mentioned above lobbied their party's government on behalf of high-paying clients. Chris Loreto is first vice-president of PC Ontario and head of StrategyCorp, which lobbied on behalf of Arch Capital to explore the LTC market. StrategyCorp lobbyist Kyle Sholes, PC Ontario's third vice-president, left his job as chief of staff to the Associate Minister of Transportation in order to lobby on behalf of the Mayors and Regional Chairs of Ontario; it apparently needs to use citizens' tax dollars to hire someone to lobby the provincial government.[51] Others have made good use of the connections developed while working with the Tories. Mark Lawson was a policy advisor and chief of staff in several government ministries before he joined Therme, the company redeveloping Ontario Place. He's both vice-president and a lobbyist for the company. Kory Teneycke, co-founder of Rubicon Strategies, was PC campaign manager for both 2018 and 2022 elections. Rubicon lobbied for KWG Resources in 2019, exploring chromite resources in the Ring of Fire, part of Doug Ford's future mining plans.[52]

These are just some of the PC government workers who are finding green pastures in the world of lobbying. Their work doesn't break Integrity Commission lobbying rules. Former ministry employees aren't allowed to lobby their former ministries for twelve months, but it's acceptable to lobby other ministries.[53] In-house lobbyists who work for a company seeking to influence the government need not register until they've lobbied for fifty hours per year. So, lobbyists can do their jobs quietly, according to Ian Steadman of York University. He explained this rule suits companies — mindful of how lobbying has blossomed — that want to keep their lobbying efforts away from the public eye.[54]

Among the thousands of lobbying registrations on the Integrity Commission's website, you won't find many not-for-profits or community groups unless they have money. The homeless, the poor, the underfed don't get lobbyists. Even those who advocate for them would be hard-pressed to find the money to hire one. This is in sharp contrast to those who can afford to pay for access to their government, something itself, that represents corruption of the democratic process. Rules are stricter elsewhere: the federal government restricts such lobbying for five years for designated officials, including all parliamentarians, ministerial staff and most senior government officials.[55]

Lobbying must be curtailed. Ministry staff and others officially involved in party activities should not be able to lobby for one election cycle. In-house lobbyists don't need a fifty-hour free pass to lobby without registering. Meeting notes between lobbyists and government officials should be publicly available. Lobbying goals should clearly state what clients plan to gain from the exercise. Lobbyists must be prohibited from donating to politicians or their parties. Should something go awry and complaints are made to the Integrity Commission, details, as well as adjudication, need to be made public.

Lobbying and donations are the Tweedledum and Tweedledee of cronyism in politics. The boundary between politicians and cronies who want special treatment from them is muddy. Democracy Watch is highly critical of the Ontario Integrity Commission's blessing on giving gifts, like sports tickets, for fundraising and help for politicians and their election campaigns. It's just too cozy. Between 2014 and 2024, familiar names of donors on the Elections Ontario website keep cropping up: friend and beneficiary Carmine Nigro ($15,556), lobbyist Amir Remtulla ($16,962), along with lobbyist and fourth PC vice-president Nico Fidani-Diker ($21,755). Tory insider and lobbyist Christopher Froggatt chipped in $25,486, joined by StrategyCorp's Chris Loreto, whose name is beside $17,349 in donations.[56]

Money makes the wheels of Ontario politics go round. Money from individuals or corporations may go to the central political party, to individual candidates in ridings across the province, as well as to riding associations. Fundraising is central to the process. Doug Ford topped everyone before him with the largest fundraiser in Canadian history in February 2023. His Tories raised $6 million when supporters paid $1,500 each to listen to him speak at the Toronto Congress Centre. We'll never know what he said; the event was closed to the media. Perversely, in February 2021, Ford made it harder for third-party organizations to spend money on political advertising, but improved Tories' prospects for fundraising with the *Protecting Ontario Elections Act*. The PCs rely heavily on individual donations, receiving 63 percent of them from 25 percent of their donors giving $1,000 or more.[57] Individual donation limits doubled from $1,650 to $3,300 annually, an amount that can be donated to candidates, the party *and* riding associations — thereby lifting the actual limit to $9,900.[58] Government in Ontario is permeated by the influence of expensive lobbyists and political contributions: leadership by buddies driven by the needs of cronies, large donors and people who think like them.

There's much room for improvement. In Quebec, individual annual donations are capped at $100, with the government compensating political parties for that limitation. Ontario should have the same limit. Donors should be allowed to contribute only to candidates for the riding in which they reside. Elsewhere in Canada, professionals like lawyers or lobbyists must declare related work on behalf of a party as a political contribution. That ought to happen here. Elections Ontario needs to audit donations to ensure they aren't subsidized by businesses to which donors are somehow connected. If someone likes a party, they can donate their own money, not someone else's.

For the People

The passengers on Doug Ford's gravy train characterize not just the people his government is for, but its belief in the inherent value of a province "open for business." Ford is *for* some people —those who can pay either directly to his party or for the public goods he is so eager to privatize.

To that end, his government cuts education spending, leaving school boards to slash staff, programs and basic maintenance; maybe parents will consider private options. Health care undergoes relentless assault as this government chooses to support private clinics, while forcing people in long term care to move to homes not of their choosing. It chooses to build a highway that, while profiting some, will cost billions, greatly increase car travel and lay waste to the rivers and forests it crosses.

For others, there is austerity. Ford shutters supervised drug consumption sites, rails against safe bike lanes and tells homeless people to get off their "A-S-S and start working." He squeezes local democracy by pushing strong mayor powers on cities so they can better pursue his government's agenda.

For six years, Ford's Tories have faced loud opposition from different groups across the province in efforts to stave off the worst of their actions. These people need to come together in a common front that can relentlessly counter the fantasies about privatization and austerity the PC party wants to sell. Parents should not have to turn their kids over to child services because they can't afford to provide the help they need. Cities need not scramble to find housing for citizens while developers concentrate on building expensive condos. There is no sane argument that places the car ahead of preservation of land, water and air. Neoliberal austerity and primacy of markets are not prerequisites for government. It should not run on the fuel of friendship, party loyalty and payment for access.

13

LOCKING IN UNSUSTAINABLE DEVELOPMENT

Mark Winfield

THE SUMMER OF 2023 was defined by unprecedented episodes of smoke and smog in major southern Ontario cities, the by-products of record wildfires burning in northern areas of the province and across Canada. The impacts of a changing climate were becoming very real for Ontarians. The significance of these developments was further reinforced by a provincial climate change impact assessment published at the end of that summer, outlining the grim future consequences of a changing climate.[1]

But Doug Ford's Ontario continued to lack any meaningful climate strategy of its own. Instead, the province escalated its attacks against the federal government for its efforts to implement substantive climate policies, particularly carbon pricing.[2] The Ford government's behaviour in this regard comes as no surprise. The Ford era has been defined by an unparalleled period of retrenchment on the environment and climate change, turning the institutional and legislative clocks back, in some cases, to the immediate post-WWII era and beyond.

Following its June 2022 re-election under its banner of "Getting It Done," the Ford government doubled down on its first-term themes of urban development and expansion, energy and transportation infrastructure megaprojects, and resource extraction, particularly the "Ring of Fire" mineral deposit in Northern Ontario. In many cases, these initiatives are deepening the environmental challenges facing the province, including the loss of prime farmland and ecologically significant areas, and leading to major increases in the release of greenhouse gases (GHGs) and other pollutants, particularly from the electricity and transportation sectors. The infrastructure megaprojects being pursued by the government in those sectors may lock in environmentally and economically unsustainable development pathways for decades, if not centuries, to come. At the same time, increasingly aggressive use has been made of provincial authority to exclude or suppress dissenting voices from decision-making, avoid any meaningful reviews of provincial initiatives and to support favoured, private, economic interests.

The First Ford Government: 2018-2022

The Ford government arrived in June 2018 on a relatively thin platform focused on cutting taxes, particularly the carbon "tax" from the previous Liberal government's GHG cap and trade system and hydro rates.[3] What followed was the most significant period of reversal in environmental and climate policy in the province of the post-WWII period. The new Conservative government moved swiftly to dismantle the former government's climate change strategy. The GHG emission cap and trade system was terminated, along with initiatives related to building retrofits, electric vehicles, and other adaptations related to industry and climate change that would have been funded through the estimated $3 billion in revenues the system was to have generated over the first three years of its existence.[4] The province then joined Alberta and Saskatchewan in challenging the constitutional basis of the federal government's "backstop" carbon pricing system. Without the provincial cap and trade carbon pricing regime, that system now applied to Ontario. The provincial challenges ultimately ended in a decisive loss before the Supreme Court of Canada. Their attempt to require that gas stations apply stickers to their pumps to indicate the impact of the federal carbon price on gasoline prices ended in an embarrassing fiasco. The initiative was ruled to be unconstitutional, and the stickers failed to stay affixed to the pumps.

With respect to electricity, the government moved to cancel all the renewable energy projects that were then under development. This amounted to more than 700 projects being halted, most of them small-scale and community-based. The total cost of the cancellations ultimately exceeded $230 million.[5] The province's largely successful existing strategy on energy efficiency was terminated in 2019, and the requirement that the province develop any long-term energy plans at all ended, leaving the system to operate solely on "directives" from the minister of energy. This meant that there was no need to explain or justify, before any sort of meaningful public review process or regulatory body, the costs and risks flowing from the government's increasingly nuclear and gas-fired orientation around electricity.[6]

Urban development quickly emerged as a central focus for the new government. Although having to retreat repeatedly in the face of municipal and public opposition to efforts to open the Greenbelt to development, provincial planning rules were extensively re-written in favour of developers. The use of Ministerial Zoning Orders (MZOs) and similar instruments to override local planning decisions and rules became commonplace, again almost exclusively in response to development industry demands. The authority of Conservation Authorities within the planning process was significantly constrained, even in relation to areas subject to flooding or other hazards.

The province's land-use planning interventions were accompanied by an aggressive push for the expansion of the provincial highway network, particularly within the Greater Toronto Area. Many of these projects, like the Vaughan to Milton 413 Highway and Highway 404 to 400 Bradford Bypass, revived concepts originally proposed under the previous Harris government and subsequently rejected as unnecessary and likely to induce additional automobile-dependent urban sprawl. New transit projects were also pushed forward aggressively, although many, like the Ontario subway line in Toronto, seemed poorly conceived and politically motivated.[7] Protections for endangered species were significantly weakened, particularly with respect to urban development and natural resources, especially forestry.[8]

On pollution-related issues, Ontario's toxics use reduction legislation was repealed. The Municipal Industrial Strategy for Abatement regulatory framework for controlling industrial water pollution, initiated and completed in the 1980s and 1990s, was dismantled. The regulatory system was effectively returned to the largely ineffective 1960's and 1970's approach of negotiating discharge limits on a facility-by-facility basis. Rules around agricultural pollution of drinking water sources, particularly nutrients (e.g., fertilizer and manure), which had been a key factor in the Walkerton, Ontario, water treatment disaster, were weakened.[9] A restructuring of the province's municipal waste recycling regime, in theory to increase the costs carried by packaging and waste producers, seemed instead likely to strengthen increasingly monopolistic positions held by certain well-connected waste management companies. The province's previously independent Environmental Commissioner's office, created through the 1994 *Environmental Bill of Rights*, was folded into that of the Auditor General.[10]

The government's agenda continued, and, in many ways, accelerated under the cover of the COVID-19 pandemic and subsequent recovery efforts. One of the PC's first moves in response to the pandemic was to suspend the application of the *Environmental Bill of Rights* notice and comment requirements regarding changes to environmental laws, regulations, policies and approvals.[11] The application of the province's environmental assessment process, mandatory for public sector projects since its establishment in 1975, was made discretionary, and the content of the assessment process significantly weakened. Broad powers were given to provincial agencies, most notably the provincial transit agency Metrolinx, allowing them to override any potential objections to their projects and effectively giving them the authority to approve their own undertakings.

A "Made in Ontario" environment plan was released at the end of 2018. The plan was motivated in large part by the government's (unsuccessful) attempts to stave off the application of the "backstop" federal carbon price introduced under the auspices of the 2016 federal-provincial Pan-Canadian Framework on Green Growth and Climate Change. The federal carbon pricing system was only to apply in provinces without systems of their own. Although relying on an ill-defined incentive system in place of a carbon pricing system, the plan did include some potentially interesting elements. These related to climate change adaptation, linkages among land-use planning, transportation and climate change, distributed energy resources (e.g., renewables and energy storage), and community energy and climate change planning. However, virtually nothing was done to implement the plan.[12]

As the 2022 provincial election approached, the Ford government added a new form of post-pandemic activism to its "market populist" governance style.[13] This focused on cutting red tape further and increasing spending to "get it done," in terms of infrastructure development, particularly highway construction. At the same time, a populist focus on short-term affordability — through moves such as the removal of road tolls and vehicle licencing fees, and a promised gas tax cut — responded to public concerns over rising living costs.

All three major opposition parties presented election platforms which included detailed provisions around the environment and climate change.[14] There was substantial and sustained coverage in the mainstream media of environmental issues throughout the campaign, particularly the implications of the 413 Highway project and climate change, more generally. The environment was consistently identified in media commentary as an area of vulnerability for the PC government.[15] The government, in response, presented nothing new on environmental issues, and retained its steadfast commitments to infrastructure expansion, especially the GTA highway network.

In the end, environmental and climate change issues seemed to fail to connect with the provincial electorate, with the election ending with a strengthened PC majority. The vote was, however, marked by a historically low voter turnout, with the result that the PC victory rested on the votes of fewer than 18 percent of those eligible to cast a ballot.[16] The outcome suggested underwhelming enthusiasm for a renewed Ford government on the part of the electorate, but also pointed in the direction of the weakness of the primary opposition alternatives.[17]

The Second Ford Government: 2022+

Urban Development and Housing

A defining feature of the Ford government in the aftermath of the 2022 election was a deepening of the emphasis on re-writing the province's planning rules in favour of the development industry. In fall 2022, the government brought forward a housing plan consisting of several major components. Bill 23, the *More Homes Built Faster Act*, further limited the authority of the province's Conservation Authorities in the planning process; proposed to remove upper-tier (i.e. regional or county) governments whose roles included the provision of major infrastructure from certain types of planning approvals; curtailed the ability of municipalities to impose changes on new developments to finance the required infrastructures; provided authority to remove requirements that rental units lost or demolished to facilitate new development need to be replaced; and weakened the rules around built heritage conservation. The natural heritage conservation provisions within the planning process were dramatically downgraded. Provisions baring third party (that is, public) appeals to the Ontario Land Tribunal (OLT), the successor to the Ontario Municipal Board, were eventually dropped, but other legislative changes and alternations to the OLT's rules have made appeals and participation by community or public interest-based parties almost impossible.[18] The 2006 Growth Plan for the region, with its emphasis on "smart" growth and "complete" communities, was repealed. Additional legislation gave mayors extraordinary powers when implementing provincial policies, including the ability to pass measures with the support of only one-third of council members.[19]

The second major component of the Housing Supply Action Plan — the removal of 7400 acres of land from the Greater Golden Horseshoe Greenbelt and the imposition of urban boundary expansions, covering over thousands of additional hectares of farmland, despite the objections of the affected municipalities — would lead to one of the most serious political challenges faced by the Ford government so far. The government's own development industry-dominated Housing Affordability Task Force had acknowledged that an adequate supply of land was already designated for urban development to meet the 1.5-million-homes target, noting: "A shortage of land isn't the cause of the problem. Land is available both inside the existing built-up areas and on undeveloped land outside greenbelts."[20]

Subsequent analyses confirmed that adequate land was designated for development to support over 2 million housing units in the region, rendering the Greenbelt removals, urban boundary expansions and many elements of Bill 23 — particularly as they related to natural heritage conservation and the roles of Conservation Authorities — unnecessary from a housing supply perspective.[21] Investigations by the province's Auditor General and Integrity Commissioner around the Greenbelt removals concluded that the process by which the lands had been identified for removal had been "improper," "madcap,"[22] and "biased" in favour of certain well-connected development interests, with potential to provide more than $8 billion in windfall profits to the developers involved.[23]

The fallout from the Greenbelt removals would lead to the resignations of the minister of municipal affairs and housing and his chief of staff, the minister of public and business service delivery (over a "mani-pedi" "meeting" in Las Vegas with one of the developers involved), and the premier's housing policy advisor. The government was eventually compelled to reverse the Greenbelt removals and involuntary urban boundary expansions, and to provide a partial replacement of the infrastructure funding lost through the Bill 23 restrictions on development charges through general provincial revenues.[24] Despite all of this, and suggestions that the government's target of 1.5 million homes was itself excessive relative to the region's actual housing needs,[25] further legislation (Bill 162 — the *Get It Done Act*), adopted in May 2024, seemed to reverse the government's previous reversals on urban boundary expansions.[26] Bill 185, the *Cutting Red Tape to Build More Homes Act*, adopted in June 2024, established a ban on third-party appeals to the OLT, originally contained in Bill 23. Third-party appeals (i.e., public appeals) are the primary mechanism through which the natural heritage protection provisions of planning policies, which protect forests, wetlands, streams, rivers, species at risk and source water areas, are enforced, especially in rural areas. Similar questions would arise around the protection of existing affordable rental housing.

In effect, the Ford government transformed the province's land-use planning system — including the Greenbelt and growth plans for the GTA (once the subject of international acclaim for its management of intense growth pressures while protecting farmland, housing affordability and natural heritage areas) — into an instrument wielded by the province to serve the interests of well-connected developers. The result, for all its negative consequences for ecologically important areas and endangered species, watershed management and flood prevention, prime agricultural lands, climate change adaptation, built heritage conservation and long-established democratic norms in local governance, has been the utter failure to meet the need for affordable housing.[27] The "tall and sprawl" development patterns of hyper-intensive, investor-owned, high-rise condominium development in certain urban centres and the sprawling, low-density development onto prime agricultural and natural heritage lands at the urban periphery, both brought about by the Ford government's approach, have done little to improve housing affordability, particularly for lower-income people.[28]

In some areas, the government's development-industry-driven model is leading to significant losses of existing affordable rental housing, particularly where there is good transit access. It is being displaced by investor-owned condominium developments —textbook examples of gentrification.[29] At a fundamental level, the government failed to grasp the reality that private capital was unlikely to ever build dedicated affordable rental or otherwise deeply affordable housing, particularly with more lucrative investment options, like high-rise condominium construction, available. Scrapping the planning rules and letting developers do as they pleased, in the hope that some affordable options would "trickle down," was a futile and counterproductive strategy.

"Getting It Done" — Infrastructure Megaprojects

With respect to infrastructure projects, the "get-it-done" mantra was a central element of the Ford government's 2022 election platform. Announcements made in February 2024 further expanded the types of major projects that would be subject to a minimal, "streamlined" review, including all new highways (provincial freeways and municipal expressways), rail projects and electricity transmission lines and stations.[30] Transit and electricity projects were already covered by *de facto* exemptions or self-assessment processes. Many of the projects at the centre of the government's 'get it done' efforts, including Highway 413, the Highway 404–to–400 Bradford Bypass and the refurbishment of Pickering B nuclear station, had been subject to previous reviews (either under the environmental assessment or other planning processes) and determined to be unnecessary and uneconomic. In the case of the highway projects, they were seen as likely to induce further urban sprawl.[31]

For transit projects, serious questions remained, including how the Ontario Line Toronto subway project expanded from a modest and long-planned-out Pape-to-Queen Station line to provide downtown relief into a nearly $20-billion megaproject stretching from Ontario Place to the Ontario Science Centre. The sudden decision to transfer the Science Centre to Ontario Place, with little economic or operational rationale in the midst of a controversy over the province's signing over a 95-year lease on the Ontario Place site to a private spa developer, further reinforced questions about how the province was making decisions about major infrastructure.

On the energy and electricity front, the province's July 2023 energy plan committed to a major expansion of the role of nuclear energy, including 4800 megawatts of new generating capacity at the Bruce Nuclear facility, and four 300 megawatts of new reactors at the Darlington site. This would be on top of the ongoing refurbishments of six reactors at the Bruce Facility and four reactors at Darlington. To this was added the refurbishment of four reactors at the Pickering B facility, a project assessed more than a decade earlier as uneconomic. The resulting nuclear construction program will involve costs in the range of at least $100 billion, making it the largest such program in North America or Europe.[32] It will also commit the province's energy system to a technological pathway that carries enormous economic, technological, safety and security risks, that is associated with the generation of up and downstream waste streams that will require management on timescales of hundreds of millennia, and that will leave little flexibility for the adoption of more environmentally and economically sustainable options in the future.[33]

At the same time, the province is also seeking to add 1500 megawatts of new natural gas-fired generation to the system. The role of existing natural gas-fired plants is growing rapidly at the same time to replace nuclear facilities that are being refurbished or retired. Emissions from gas-fired generation have more than tripled since 2017, and are projected to continue to increase dramatically, thereby significantly eroding the gains from the 2013 coal-phaseout in terms of emissions in GHGs and smog precursors. The government's approach advanced the interests of deeply entrenched incumbents. The overwhelming beneficiary has been the provincially owned utility Ontario Power Generation, the successor corporation to Ontario Hydro, which has expanded its already dominant portfolio of legacy nuclear and hydro facilities to include new large gas-fired generation facilities. The other big winner has been Bruce Power, the private consortium which operates the Bruce nuclear facility on behalf of Ontario Power Generation.

The changes to the environmental assessment process further reinforced a situation where the province undertook major infrastructure projects with enormous long-term economic and environmental implications, but with little to no meaningful external review or oversight. The government's initiatives seem instead designed to avoid and prevent any serious scrutiny. In the past, when such projects have been subject to meaningful review, it has not been unknown for their rationales to collapse.[34] Ontario Hydro's original "supply planning" nuclear expansion plans of the 1960s and 1970s, its nuclear- and gas-heavy electricity demand-supply plan of the 1990s, the Ontario Power Authority's equally nuclear- and gas-focused 2007 Integrated Power System Plan and the 413 Highway project are leading examples of such outcomes in the province. In these cases, meaningful and substantial reviews derailed projects with the potential of becoming immensely costly programs of "white elephants."

Megaprojects Trump the Environment

The Ford government's record on environmental issues is best understood as an extension of its wider approach to governance. It has been observed that the government's agendas seem driven by "instinct more than ideology."[35] The government came to power with little vision for what a provincial government should do, other than cut taxes, red tape and hydro rates. It struggled when confronted with more complex problems, like the COVID-19 pandemic, that required the province to play a more active role. The resulting governance model remained fundamentally reactive and grounded in relatively short-term perspectives.[36] Issues like the environment and climate change, as with health and child care policy,[37] were destined to do poorly under such a model.

To the extent that the government has developed a longer-term vision, it is focussed on urban expansion and the "get-it-done" megaprojects. Unfortunately, its approaches in these areas, like almost everything else it has done, have been defined by a tendency to accept uncritically whatever business lobbyists (with the necessary access) have asked the government to do. This pattern has been evident around the handling of COVID-19, housing and infrastructure, mining, gravel pits and quarries, energy and long-term care. The overall decision-making model that has emerged seems based on connections and political whim, rather than evidence, analysis and transparency. The voices of the public, civil society organizations, local governments and the provincial public service have been aggressively marginalized as red tape.[38] The Greenbelt land removal scandal of 2023 was, in many ways, a culmination of this ethos.

The decisions flowing from this governance model have also shown, unsurprisingly, a distinct tendency to make the problems they are supposed to address, worse. This is perhaps most evident in the electricity sector, where emissions of GHGs and smog precursors are rising dramatically, and higher, long-term costs are being embedded through an unexamined and unassessed nuclear construction program reminiscent of that which led to the downfall of Ontario Hydro. With respect to housing, the "free-for-all" that occurred because of developers with the "right access" has reinforced the problems of financialization, speculation, gentrification, urban sprawl onto prime agricultural and ecologically important lands, and it has undermined basic norms of local democracy, while doing little to nothing to improve housing affordability.[39]

Despite all of this, the government has demonstrated a remarkable capacity for political survival and recovery. Even the Greenbelt episode only produced a temporary dip in public support for the Ford government. This could be seen as validating the government's apparent assumption that a significant portion of Ontario voters, especially those who are likely to vote for the Ford government (and have come to be known as the "Ford nation"), care more about immediate affordability issues than with abstract values such as evidence-based policy-making, good planning, legal correctness and political accountability — values that were emphasized by the legislative opposition and mainstream media throughout the Greenbelt saga. Whether the situation reflects a failure of the electoral alternatives to provide a compelling, alternative vision for the province, or a deeper shift in the province's political culture, remains an open question.[40]

That said, one of the defining features of the environment as public policy is its fundamental grounding in biophysical reality. Environmental issues do not go away just because a government chooses to ignore them. As highlighted by the extraordinary presence of forest fire smoke in the GTA over the summer of 2023, the impacts of a changing climate are likely to become more and more apparent in the form of extreme weather events, flooding, extended ranges of disease vectors and cyanobacteria blooms.[41] Long-standing issues related to air and water pollution, and losses of biological diversity, natural heritage and prime agricultural lands to resource extraction and urban development, continue to worsen, and in many cases, seem likely to accelerate as a result of the decisions made in the Ford Era.[42]

These fundamental biophysical realities may ultimately reinforce the status of the environment and climate change as key points of vulnerability for the Ford government. The broad civil society and institutional response resulting in the reversal of the fall 2022 removal of lands from the GTA Greenbelt, particularly in the 905 region around the City of Toronto, highlighted these risks. The government's approach to environmental issues emphasized a second point of vulnerability as well: the question of who actually wins under the Ford regime — "the people" or certain well-connected interests, like the developers, resource industries and incumbents in the energy sector? The latter question could ultimately prove fatal but will also require the articulation of a vision for the future that responds to the dynamics flowing from the province's economic and social transitions over the past two decades, which laid the groundwork for the appeal of Ford's "market populism" in the first place.

14

DE-DEMOCRATIZING ONTARIO

Tom McDowell

THE FORD GOVERNMENT'S EXTENSIVE INSTITUTIONAL AND POLICY REFORMS have significantly transformed Ontario's political and social landscape. To implement its agenda, the government has employed various approaches and strategies aimed at evading legislative scrutiny and insulating its policies from democratic influence. These restrictive procedures have become crucial instruments in its efforts to overcome institutional opposition and pursue a radical policy agenda.

The Ford government's approach to the legislature amounts to the most aggressive parliamentary implementation plan in Ontario's history, smashing several constitutional and legislative norms. These actions have established new precedents that, taken together, weaken the capacity of the legislature to hold the government accountable, heightening the power of the executive branch in Ontario politics.

The curtailment of constitutional and legislative processes, therefore, is a fundamental aspect of the Ford government's approach to governance, without which many of its most contentious neoliberal reforms likely would not have been realized. The government utilized five primary procedural instruments to "streamline" democratic institutions and secure its neoliberal reforms: delegated legislation, time allocation, closure, omnibus legislation and the use of constitutional authority.

Parliamentary Democracy

Parliamentary democracies are characterized by dual, and at times, contradictory roles. In Ontario, the executive is composed of the monarch (represented by the Governor General), Premier and cabinet ministers. While the executive seeks to advance its agenda through the legislative process, parliament concurrently upholds a responsibility to scrutinize the executive's actions to represent the public interest.¹ Consequently, a delicate balance between the executive's prerogative to enact its agenda, and the legislature's authority to scrutinize and potentially impede government proceedings, must be struck.

Procedural rules within a parliamentary system are established through two mechanisms. Firstly, formal rules, known as "Standing Orders," govern the legislature's procedures. Secondly, a set of unwritten norms, similar to common law principles, guide the assembly based on historical precedents from both its own activities and those of other Commonwealth nations.

Given the finite time available to governments dictated by election cycles, the relationship between the executive and legislature often revolves around the allocation of parliamentary time for debating and scrutinizing contentious legislation.² The governing party controls the programming of the legislature, meaning that the only instrument available to the opposition to protest the government is to use procedural mechanisms to temporarily obstruct house proceedings to impede government initiatives. The executive retains an escape hatch against permanent stasis in the form of closure, which allows it to conclude debates and proceed to a vote on any matter.

The equilibrium between the executive and legislative branches, then, constitutes the essence of parliamentary governance. An optimal balance entails a functional government subjected to perpetual and effective parliamentary scrutiny, where the majority acknowledges the executive's right to govern, while the government respects the opposition's duty to oppose and hold it accountable. However, recent trends indicate a problematic shift toward executive abuse of authority, undermining the legislature's role in ensuring accountability and oversight.

Ford Government and Parliamentary Procedure

Legislative procedure in Ontario has evolved in a manner consistent with "neoliberal parliamentarism," which is a deliberate strategy to reform democratic procedures as a means of securing the implementation of neoliberal policies that do not have sufficient support to be put into place through usual democratic procedures. ³ This process can be dated back to the early 1980s in Ontario, when the PC Davis government established the precedent of strict time allocation to secure the passage of its *Inflation Restraint Act*. In following decades, the curtailment of legislative procedure became a critical instrument in the closing of space for democratic dialogue and sheltering controversial reforms from democratic interference. These circumstances required a streamlined institutional form adequate to the implementation of radical, unpopular policy reforms.

The Ford government has used five main primary procedural tactics to carry out its policy objectives. First, it has expansively interpreted its regulatory authority under the Royal Perogative to assign legislative powers to the cabinet through *delegated legislation*. Delegated legislation is a type of law made by the executive, without direct consultation with the legislature, under the authority granted by an enabling or parent statute. Recent trends have seen delegated legislation misused to confer substantial authority to the executive for implementing significant reforms, shielding them from democratic oversight. Second, the government has also made use of the *authority granted to the provinces under Canada's constitution* as a deliberate strategy to shield its policy objectives from institutional interference. It specifically made use of section 92(8) of the constitution, which grants provinces authority over the affairs of municipalities, as well as section 33, the notwithstanding clause. section 33 enables provinces to declare sections 2, and sections 7 to 15, of the *Charter of Rights and Freedoms*, "notwithstanding" for a period of up to five years, making it possible to disregard unfavourable court rulings.[4] Prior to 2018, Ontario had never applied the notwithstanding clause for any matter.[5]

Third, the strategy of *omnibus legislation* involves bundling unrelated reforms under a single legislative umbrella, allowing the executive to pass multiple bills within the timeframe allocated for one. While historically used for streamlining public administration, omnibus bills have increasingly become a tool for pushing through numerous reforms simultaneously, contributing to concerns about democratic accountability.[6] Fourth, *time allocation*, which establishes fixed time limits for debate on issues before the legislature, has been routinely employed by the government to impose formal time limits on both committee and house proceedings.

Finally, the government has frequently resorted to *closure*, a procedural mechanism allowing it to promptly conclude legislative debates with a simple majority vote in the legislature. The Ford administration notably escalated the use of closure during its second term, employing it extensively to expedite the passage of government bills. These approaches were essential to the government's privatization of health care and its restructuring of municipal government in Ontario.

Dismantling Public Health Care

Shortly after assuming office, the Ford government began developing the institutional architecture for privatizing health care services in Ontario.[7] It accomplished this objective by granting significant regulatory powers to the cabinet through delegated legislation, giving the government the capacity to restructure health care without consulting the legislature. The first significant step towards privatized health care was established by Bill 74, *The People's Health Care Act* (2019), an omnibus bill amending dozens of different laws that restructured Ontario's health care system, undermining the control of the Local Health Integrated Networks (LHINs) with a centralized Super Agency, later called Ontario Health. The bill empowered the Super Agency, which was appointed by and accountable to the minister of health, with substantial power to oversee the administration of the planning, implementation and assessment of the provincial health system, including the management of labour relations.

Included among the significant regulatory powers granted to the minister was the right to facilitate the "integration" of health services in the province.[8] This included the broadly worded authority to "designate a person or entity, or a group of persons or entities, as an integrated care delivery system," thus preparing the ground for the introduction of private sector actors into the province's health service model.[9] The government has also made explicit efforts to privatize aspects of home care services in Ontario. Following Bill 74, the Ford government brought forward Bill 175, the *Connecting People to Home and Community Care Act*, reconfiguring the structure of home-based health care by removing critical oversight of patient care and granting the cabinet authority to facilitate the inclusion of for-profit organizations as home care service providers.

Bill 175 established what it called "Ontario Health Teams," which can include representatives from private sector organizations to plan and administer home care in the province.[10] Legislation brought forward in 2023 further facilities privatization by transferring authority from the LHINs, which were public entities, to a new organization called Ontario Health at Home. Bill 135, the *Convenient Care at Home Act* (2023), delegates authority to this organization to contract out home care services to privately run client service providers. This inserts the fox into the henhouse, enabling private sector stakeholders, with an interest in undermining the public system, to influence health care policy decisions.

The most substantial steps towards the dismantling of public health care in Ontario, however, occurred with Bill 60, *Your Health Act* (2023), an omnibus bill that granted substantial power to the minister of health to delegate authority to a director to authorize the establishment of private health clinics throughout the province. The director, who is not required to be an employee of the Ontario Public Service, is accountable only to the cabinet and has wide latitude to facilitate privatization. Furthermore, since the director need not belong to the public service, they are exempt from typical freedom of information or financial disclosure requirements.[11]

Perhaps the most significant use of omnibus legislation under the Ford government has been its application to undertake the privatization of universal health care. The four major pieces of legislation enabling the privatization of health services in the province are: Bill 74, *The People's Health Care Act* (2019); Bill 175, *Connecting People to Home and Community Care Act* (2020); Bill 135, *Convenient Care at Home Act* (2023); and Bill 60, *Your Health Act* (2023). All were omnibus bills, each amending or repealing several existing laws. The most significant of these was Bill 74, which made changes to thirty-three laws, establishing the institutional scaffolding for the establishment of private health care in Ontario.

Efforts to privatize health care have been aided by a variety of procedural mechanisms, which provide a political shell for its reforms, placing them beyond the reach of accountability measures that could interfere with their implementation.

Constitutional Authority and the Restructuring of Local Government

As in health care, the Ford government has wielded its constitutional powers in municipal affairs to shield its undemocratic practices from political opposition.[12] In utilizing section 92(8) of the constitution, which grants the provinces complete authority over municipalities, the Ford government rewrote municipal governance arrangements across the province.

Shortly after assuming office in July 2018, the Conservatives took the unprecedented step of redistributing the ward boundaries of Toronto City Council. With almost no public consultation, Bill 5, the *Better Local Government Act*, moved to reduce the seats on council by nearly half, from 47 to 25. The legislation also enabled the cabinet to make regulations for the transitional period during which the boundaries were being changed, granting the province considerable authority to manage and supervise the establishment of the new council structure.[13]

Bill 5 was ultimately struck down at the Ontario Superior Court for having "clearly crossed the line," by undermining the freedom of expression of council candidates who were in the middle of an election campaign at the time the bill was brought forward.[14] The Ford government responded immediately, bringing forward Bill 31, the *Efficient Local Government Act*, which was substantively the same as Bill 5, with the exception that it included a provision to invoke the notwithstanding clause in Canada's constitution. The government ultimately withdrew their threat to use the clause when the Court of Appeal for Ontario overturned the lower court's decision.[15] However, the precedent of using constitutional brinksmanship to avoid checks from other branches of government demonstrated that it was possible to violate long-standing norms to secure the passage of its signature legislation.

In 2021, the Ford government formally invoked the notwithstanding clause for the first time in Ontario's history to override an Ontario Court of Appeal decision that ruled against limits on advertising in the months prior to an election. Ostensibly seeking to stop the Working Families Coalition, which opposed the Progressive Conservative Party in previous elections from purchasing advertisements, the government amended the *Elections Finances Act* to restrict third-party advertisements to expenditures of up to $600,000 in the year before an election.[16] After winning its second majority in 2022, the Ford government continued its use of the notwithstanding clause to shelter its reforms from unfavourable court decisions. In part to gain bargaining leverage in its negotiations with more than 50,000 public sector education workers, the government brought forward Bill 28, the *Keeping Students in Class Act* (2022), which contained a provision enabling the government to declare sections 2, 7, and 15 of the Charter as notwithstanding.[17] The legislation undermined collective bargaining rights, taking away the capacity of CUPE employees to collectively bargain for their wages and benefits by forcing a new four-year contract on them with only modest pay increases.[18]

After considerable public backlash, the Ford government changed course and reversed its decision to invoke the notwithstanding clause on education workers, bringing forward Bill 35, *An Act to Repeal the Keeping Students in Class Act* (2022), just a few weeks after Bill 28 received Royal Assent.[19] Despite abandoning this initiative due to political pressure, the Ford government continues to use the notwithstanding clause as a key element of its legislative strategy. It has allowed them to charge ahead with the confidence that they can bypass court decisions.

The government also used its constitutional authority over municipalities to make substantial reforms to the structure of local democracy in Ontario. In August 2022, the government brought forward Bill 3, the *Strong Mayors, Building Homes Act*, which extended an initial series of strong-mayor powers to Ottawa and Toronto. The new strong mayor powers granted mayors substantial authority at the expense of council, including a veto, as well as control over the design process for the city budget. The veto would enable the mayor to override any council resolution or bylaw that interferes with "provincial priorities," which are determined by the provincial executive.[20] This would enable the mayor to pass bylaws with as little as a third of the total support of council.

Bill 3 also contains a provision enabling the provincial cabinet to designate to which municipalities the legislation applies, meaning that it can designate new cities for strong mayor powers through regulation. In 2023, the government used its regulatory authority to expand this authority to nearly fifty cities across the province. These reforms make Ontario mayors among the most powerful government officials anywhere in North America, empowering them to govern with just a fraction of the support of council members, while marginalizing city council by undermining their capacity to impact policy and to scrutinize the executive.[21] The Ford government has thus made use of its constitutional powers to further close off space for democratic deliberation and accountability, providing a political armour that previous governments had been hesitant to employ.

Marginalizing the Legislature

Upon assuming office in June 2018, the Ford government inherited a legislative environment already primed for the swift execution of its policies. The procedural architecture established during the PC Harris era was largely left in place by the Liberals from 2003 to 2018.[22] This meant that the Ford government did not have to make major reforms to the structure of legislative procedure to achieve their agenda. Instead, they found a procedural apparatus already organized to accommodate their populist radicalism. Despite these circumstances, the government still adopted a tone of hostility in the legislature unprecedented in its disregard for the role of the opposition. Before the house even began sitting after the election in 2018, the government revised the Standing Orders to increase the threshold for recognized party status from eight to twelve. This was clearly a deliberate ploy to keep the Liberal Party, which had been reduced to just seven seats and third-party status in the assembly, from being officially recognized.

The Ford government also continued the use of omnibus legislation to bundle major reforms together. Although the Ford government did not bring forward omnibus legislation to the scale that the Harris government did in the 1990s, it followed the same approach of using it to establish the legal and administrative architecture necessary to de-democratize the legislature.[23] Brought forward early in the Ford government's first term, Bill 57, the *Restoring Trust, Transparency and Accountability Act* (2018), made changes to fifty-six existing laws, affecting almost every government department. Bill 57 also dissolved three offices of the legislature — the Ontario Child Advocate, the Environmental Commissioner of Ontario and the Office of the French Language Services Commissioner of Ontario — which limited independent oversight of the executive.[24] It also preserved the approach used under the Conservative Harris/Eves and Liberal McGuinty/Wynne governments of bringing forward omnibus legislation to carry out deregulation under the auspices of "red tape reduction." Legislation such as Bill 139, the *Less Red Tape, More Common Sense Act* (2023), Bill 91, the *Less Red Tape, Stronger Economy Act* (2023), and Bill 69, *Reducing Inefficiencies Act* (2023) were all substantial omnibus bills that made changes to dozens of laws and regulations.

The Ford government also continued the use of time allocation as a conventional aspect of house business. During its first two years in office, the Ford government used time allocation on nearly every bill passed by the legislature, applying it to 95 percent of government bills passed between July 2018 and March 2020. Only the most benign legislation, such as supply motions to fund the government, were passed without the use of time allocation during these initial years.

Ford's time allocation approach ended in March 2020, as the COVID-19 pandemic led to a scaling down of the operations of the legislature and a temporary truce between the governing PCs and the opposition NDP. During the final months of the First Session of the 42nd Parliament, there was a significant decrease in the utilization of time allocation by the government, with only about one-third of government legislation being subjected to it. This pattern continued in the Second Session, with only one out of the fourteen government bills passed being subjected to it, marking a notable departure from traditional practices at Queen's Park in recent decades.

Prior to COVID-19, the Ford government extensively used time restriction to ram through their agenda

Parliament	Date	Number of government bills passed	Number of time allocation motions	Percentage of time allocation motions to government bills passed %
42nd Parliament, First Session, *before* March 2020	July 2018– March 2020	38	36	95%
42nd Parliament, First Session, *after* March 2020	March 2020 –September 2021	37	13	35%
42nd Parliament, Second Session	October 2021–May 2022	14	1	7%
43rd Parliament, First Session	July 2022– March 2024	37	8	22%

Although the Ford government's deployment of Orders-in-Council remained generally consistent with their application in the pre-COVID period, there was a heightened reliance on long-term emergency orders, some lasting for more than two years.[25] This strategic approach afforded the government the ability to manage a significant portion of the crisis through enabling legislation, reducing the necessity of seeking regular approval from parliament. While this arrangement largely held through the balance of the Ford government's first term in office, the question was whether it would continue after the PCs won an even larger majority in 2022.

Incidences of time allocation after 2022 have remained low compared to the Ford government's first two years in power, and its application by other governments over the last three decades.[26] This, however, does not indicate a renewed commitment to legislative accountability. Instead, it conceals the degree to which the Ford government has largely replaced the use of time allocation with "closure," making increasingly common use of the legislature's bluntest procedural instrument.

By contrast with time allocation motions, closure offers two clear benefits to the government. First, closure spares the government from needing to dedicate legislative time to discuss the merits of its implementation, unlike time allocation motions. Additionally, it grants the government the authority to conclude debates at its discretion, without the need to fulfil prior commitments to debate, thereby providing maximum "flexibility" in scheduling house proceedings.

From July 2022 to March 2024, the government applied closure to 16 of 37 — or nearly half — of the total government bills passed by the legislature. This included its most controversial legislation, such as Bill 3, *The Strong Mayors, Building Homes Act*, Bill 39, *The Better Municipal Government Act* and Bill 60, *Your Health Act*. If the Ford government's actions do indeed indicate the adoption of closure as a regular procedural tactic, it will represent a substantial step towards the erosion of the legislative process in Ontario.

Reaching for Authoritarianism

Although reforming parliamentary procedure to carry out restructuring is not a new phenomenon in Ontario, the Ford-led Conservative era has been characterized by the intensification of the approaches to parliamentary and institutional reform pursued by previous governments at Queen's Park.[27] The Ford government has accelerated the use of restrictive procedural mechanisms, making closure a standard method for passing controversial legislation. It has also increased the employment of extra-parliamentary constitutional provisions, such as the notwithstanding clause, and expanded its jurisdictional authority over municipalities. This willingness to use mechanisms, considered too controversial and undemocratic by previous governments, heralds a new chapter for Ontario. It concentrates power in the executive and marginalizes the legislature to a degree never before witnessed in the province's modern history.

The Ford government's approach to lawmaking in Ontario has prioritized speed over accountability, leading to increased executive dominance and a weakening of the legislative function. The government has made extensive use of delegated legislation to achieve many of its objectives through regulation. This is to the benefit of the government, shielding reforms from the democratic and administrative processes that could dilute their content. From the restructuring of municipal government to the privatization of health care, the abuse of regulation has been an essential instrument in the Conservatives' legislative toolkit, applied widely to secure the implementation of a variety of important measures.

The Ford government has also established a new standard by utilizing the notwithstanding clause to shield its policies from the courts, enabling it to violate aspects of the Charter at its discretion. Although the notwithstanding clause had never been used in Ontario's history prior to 2018, the Ford government has used, or threatened to use it, on at least three occasions.[28] The government's use of its constitutional authority over municipalities is also likely to have substantial long-term impacts on local democracy. By granting some mayors the capacity to govern with only a fraction of the support of its council, the Progressive Conservatives have enshrined executive dominance at the local level. This enables a squeeze on democracy at the municipal as well as the provincial level.

The Ford government also created new precedents that expand executive dominance, undermining the capacity of the provincial legislature to scrutinize the executive. First, it applied time allocation at a rate never seen before at Queen's Park, then, after its re-election in 2022, it turned to the use of closure, the most extreme instrument a government can use to end debate.

Taken together, these approaches amount to the most aggressive policy implementation effort by any government in Ontario's history, breaking several constitutional and legislative norms in the process. The

Ford government has gone even further than their radical predecessors, using virtually every procedural and constitutional instrument at its disposal to secure passage of its right-wing, market-fundamentalist reform program.[29] These tactics have been a critical instrument in the Ford government's legislative blueprint, empowering them to overcome institutional and political opposition and to secure the implementation of reforms that were broadly opposed by the public.[30]

As has been the case with other conservative reformers around the world, Doug Ford and his government have sought to reshape the form of legislative institutions rather than compromise on their policies to achieve a political consensus.[31] Viewed this way, the Ford government's approach is a domestic manifestation of a global trend towards de-democratization, as right-wing governments around the world prioritize a strong executive capable of acting without public scrutiny and accountability.[32]

15

STRONG MAYORS, WEAK CITIES

Carlo Fanelli and Ryan Kelpin

IN ONTARIO, THERE IS A LONG AND CONTROVERSIAL HISTORY of municipal restructuring and experimentation stretching as far back as Confederation.[1] Yet, the Doug Ford–led Progressive Conservative government has taken constraining the scale and scope of municipal administration to new levels. Collectively, the measures implemented by the PCs have usurped local decision-making, concentrated power in the hands of local executives and provincial ministers, and heightened municipal fiscal pressures owing to weak municipal revenue-raising capacities and governance arrangements.

In this regard, there is an element of both continuity and change. Starting in the mid-1990s, the Mike Harris-led Conservative government — in which Doug Ford, Sr. was a sitting member — controversially reduced the number of municipalities in Ontario from 815 to 447, including the amalgamation of six cities and seven governments to form the new City of Toronto in 1998. In doing so, the number of municipal councillors was reduced from 4,586 to 2,804, along with school board trustees, their numbers falling from 1,900 to 700. This restructuring also involved a massive downloading of program spending and responsibilities onto municipalities without an equivalent transfer of funding or new fiscal powers to pay for them. Ever since, municipalities have been on the hook for such things as social services, public school services, non-profit housing, roads, public infrastructure, long-term care, child care, shelters, children's aid societies, ambulance, fire and police services, waste collection, public health and transportation — to name but a few.

From 2010 to 2014, Doug Ford was a Toronto city councillor when, in 2014, he unsuccessfully ran for mayor after his brother, Mayor Rob Ford, pulled out of the race after a cancer diagnosis. It is little wonder then that Premier Doug Ford has long expressed a particular fascination with municipal governance. He wrote in his 2016 book, *Ford Nation: Two Brothers, One Vision*: "If I ever get to the provincial level of politics, municipal affairs is the first thing I would want to change. I think mayors across this province deserve stronger powers. One person in charge, with veto power."[2] As premier of Ontario, Ford immediately set upon establishing this vision. His government's authoritarian approach to local democracy and governance arrangements has been especially damaging.

Upending Local Democracy

For four years, from 2013 to 2017, the City of Toronto and the province engaged in a series of public consultations, committee and council meetings to determine how best to represent the City's diverse wards leading up to the May 1, 2018, municipal election. Both City Council and the Ontario Municipal Board formally approved a plan that would see ward seats increase from 44 to 47 seats to improve voter equity. On June 7, 2018, the PCs were elected with a majority. On July 27, 2018, just one month after being sworn in as premier, and halfway between the start of the municipal campaign and election day, Premier Ford announced his government would undo years of consultations and reduce Toronto City Council from 47 to 25 seats.[3] The Ford PCs gave no indication of their intent to do so during the provincial campaign, nor did they provide notice or consult with the City prior to announcing the changes. In so doing, not only did they contravene the duty to consult with the City, as laid out in the *City of Toronto Act*, but they also gave their first indication as to what was to come: a top-down, undemocratic and authoritarian approach to municipal governance.

One day before the deadline for candidate nominations registering to run in cities and towns across Ontario, the *Better Local Government Act* (BLGA) cancelled the elections of regional board chairs in Peel, York, Niagara and Muskoka. The BLGA changed the rules in the middle of the game and undermined the democratic process by removing from local residents the ability to elect their regional chairs. Instead, the provincial government gave itself the power via the minister of municipal affairs and housing to rule by fiat.

In response to the BLGA, Toronto City Council voted in August 2018 to legally challenge the bill, in addition to a parallel legal challenge launched by Council candidates. In September 2018, Superior Court Justice Edward Belobaba struck down the provincial bill on constitutional grounds, citing interference with municipal candidates' and voters' freedom of expression. "It is only when a democratically elected government has clearly crossed the line that the 'judicial umpire' should intervene. The province has clearly crossed the line," Belobaba wrote in his decision.[4] Premier Ford immediately announced his government would appeal.

In the meantime, unwilling to wait for the judicial process to play out, the Ford government also announced its intentions to draft a new bill that would invoke, for the first time in the province's history, the controversial notwithstanding clause of the Canadian Charter of Rights and Freedoms in order to override the lower court's ruling. In a rare, overnight sitting that was met with significant public backlash and demonstrations at Queen's Park, the Ford government introduced and quickly passed Bill 31, the *Efficient Local Government Act*.[5] On September 19, 2018, the Ontario Court of Appeal granted a stay of the original ruling, paving the way for a 25-seat Toronto municipal election. In response, the Ford government shelved Bill 31. While accepting the ruling, the City also announced it would appeal to the Supreme Court of Canada. In a narrow 5–4 decision in 2021, the Supreme Court found Bill 5 did not violate the Charter. The majority highlighted the "creatures of the province" provision and the unquestioned power of provinces over municipalities. Bill 5 was not only legally justified, but to rebut Ford's authority over municipalities would require amending the Constitution. In a dissenting opinion, Justice Abella wrote: "No pressing and substantial objective exists for this limitation, and it cannot, therefore, be justified in a free and democratic society. The legislation is [. . .] an unjustified breach of s. 2(b) [freedom of expression]."[6] While the high drama of the BLGA vividly detailed the Ford government's contempt for local democracy, it also revealed the limitations of the courts and the law as a vehicle for defending, let alone extending, democratic rights in the electoral field.

Six months later, in April 2019, the Ford government continued its aggressive assault against the autonomy and independence of local government in the City of Toronto. Most notably, they announced $1 billion in cuts to cost-sharing arrangements for Toronto Public Health and Paramedical Services. The cuts were met with harsh criticism by councillors, residents and the City's chief medical officer of health who noted that infectious disease initiatives, communicable disease surveillance, immunization programs, food safety and water quality initiatives would all suffer. Amidst the public backlash, the Ford government announced it would pause the cutbacks.[7] But this did not stop them, as the provincial government would continue seeking to expand its control over local government and agencies province-wide.

At the peak of the COVID-19 pandemic, in April 2021, the PCs passed the *Accelerating Access to Justice Act*. The perversely titled legislation actually reduced individual residents' and municipalities' access to justice, amalgamating five former land-use review bodies into a new singular entity named the Ontario Land Tribunal (OLT). The aim was to create a more "efficient and effective" system for building new homes, though expediency came with great public costs. In consolidating the Environmental Review Tribunal, Conservation Review Board, Local Planning Appeal Tribunal and Mining and Lands Tribunal, the Ford government's OLT replaced specialized legal bodies and experts with adjudicators who often had no training or experience in the industry they were supposed to be regulating. The Act also removed the requirement for municipalities to hold public meetings for all development draft plans and limited third-party appeals by individuals and community groups at the OLT to only those "directly involved." Not only did this consolidation weaken public safeguards and environmental protections,[8] it also shifted the balance of power away from local municipal democracies to the development industry.

The impact was immediate. Developers and other private companies soon had a 97 percent success rate in challenging municipal decisions over planning, zoning, conservation and forced growth targets on towns, regions and cities.[9] A regulation change — a common occurrence of this government[10] — filed by the Attorney General, allowed Ford's government to hand-pick Marie Hubbard to be the head of the OLT, skipping the usual competitive, merit-based appointment process, including a public job posting.[11] Under her leadership, the Tribunal's "mission warped from objective decision-making to rubber-stamping projects," precipitating an exodus of adjudicators and a review by the Attorney General as a result of a "toxic" workplace.

In August 2022, the Ford government introduced the *Strong Mayors, Building Homes Act* (SMBHA). The bill reversed the long-standing and widely supported view of majoritarian decision-making at council.

In practice, SMBHA said little about actual housing, but it did grant the mayors of Toronto and Ottawa the power to unilaterally appoint the chief administrative officer (CAO), to hire and dismiss senior municipal managers, chairs and vice-chairs of agencies, boards and commissions; to reorganize the city's administrative structure; and to direct municipal employees to "undertake research and provide advice, including actions to implement them, directly to the head of council." Before the ink was dry on SMBHA, the PCs passed the *Better Municipal Government Act* (BMGA), which boosted strong mayoral powers in Toronto and Ottawa. While certain restrictions were placed on these new powers — for instance, the mayor cannot hire and fire employees with special legal authority like the clerk, treasurer, chief building official, accountability officers and the heads of health, police and fire services — it did extend the power of these mayors to veto decisions by council if it is to do with the budget or, in the mayor's words, with what has been vaguely defined as "provincial priorities."

The BMGA granted new veto powers to the mayor by lowering the approval threshold for passing bylaws to just one-third of council. Council may override the mayor's veto by a two-thirds vote, but, in the case of Toronto, for example, this means the mayor can now pass bylaws with the support of only eight councillors, the same number which makes up the mayor's hand-picked executive committee. The mayor will now also present the budget, formerly proposed by the CAO, and can unilaterally put matters related to provincial priorities directly on the council agenda. The effect of this legislation is to ensure that provincial priorities determine and control municipal politics and decision-making more explicitly. It also fits within Ford's idea of what governance should look like under neoliberalism,[12] embracing the imagery of a boardroom of corporate executives as the ideal model of efficient decision-making when he stated: "Good governance in any corporation is seven to nine because you can't get anything done if you have 20 people around the table."[13]

Together, SMBHA and BMGA reject the basic democratic principles of legislative debate and public scrutiny.[14] Instead, they accelerate authoritarian tendencies by concentrating powers in the hands of the mayor and a hand-picked executive, essentially enshrining minority rule. Considerable democratic processes were erased under the guise of "timeliness" and "efficiency," with little to actually show for it, trumping principles of accountability, representation and deliberative decision-making. This led five former mayors to argue that the strong mayoral veto power eliminates any meaningful role of councillors and the voices of those who elected them.[15] With new strong mayor powers, local politics moved firmly into anti-democratic territory. This is a part of recent anti-democratic reforms worldwide, designed to centralize power as much as possible in the executive.[16] In this way, the mayor has the executive power of a prime minister and the veto power of a US president, alongside none of the formal oppositional checks and accountability measures built into either of those systems of government.[17]

Mayor of Ontario, Premier of Toronto

In November 2022, the Ford government extended these powers further by passing the *More Homes Built Faster Act* (MHBFA). The omnibus bill consolidated dozens of laws to meet, according to Ford, the government's stated aim of building 1.5 million homes by 2031. MHBFA rewrote extensive regulations related to the *Development Charges Act, Planning Act, Municipal Act, Ontario Heritage Act,* and others. The MHBFA exempts site plan control for developments with ten or fewer units, exempts affordable and inclusionary zoning from development charges and discounts to community benefits, and limits the parkland developers need to offer in new housing developments. It also removes the costs of studies from development charges, reduces costs associated with rental residential construction, weakens environmental protections and grants developers the right to take any dispute to the OLT for resolution. In short, the MHBFA turns on its head the widely accepted view that "growth should pay for growth."[18]

It is important to note that while development charges assist in supporting new infrastructure — things like roads, sewers, stormwater, waste management, public transit, parks, libraries, recreation spaces, community centres and so on — they do not support long-term operations, maintenance and replacement costs. The effect of the MHBFA is to transfer the costs of infrastructure away from for-profit private developers and onto municipalities and local taxpayers who pay twice (for building, then for maintenance). In response to the legislation, the Association of Municipalities of Ontario, and Ontario Big City Mayors group noted that municipal services and employment would either need to be cut or local taxes raised significantly to offset the new costs.[19]

While developers have shifted the costs of development onto "taxpayers," municipalities are estimated to come up more than $5 billion short over the next decade. This shortage led even the usually cautious AMO to criticize the "faulty assumption" that savings will be passed on to homeowners and renters: "It is more likely that the bill will enhance the profitability of the development industry at the expense of taxpayers and the natural environment."[20] Right they were. These changes are estimated to have put more than $400 million back into the pockets of the development industry in Ontario, with no discernable savings passed on to consumers. In exchange for a pledge by municipalities to adopt the provincial building target of 1.5 million homes by 2031, the Ford government extended "strong mayoral" powers to twenty-six large municipalities in June 2023, and to twenty-one small and medium-sized ones in August 2023. Four municipalities, citing concerns related to undemocratic powers and the impossibility of meeting these housing targets (Haldimand, Norfolk, New Tecumseth and Newmarket), rejected the offer. To sweeten the pot, the Ford government announced a Building Faster Fund, worth $1.2 billion over three years, that will provide annual funding for municipalities that meet at least 80 percent of the annual housing targets assigned by the province. Those that do not will get nothing.

As of March 2024, the 46 municipalities in Ontario that have accepted strong mayoral powers have issued 637 decisions using their new powers.[21] In just one controversial example among many, Caledon's mayor, Annette Groves, cited provincial priorities when she pushed through the development of 35,000 homes across the township. The decision was met with widespread criticism from across the community. One resident noted the "complete subversion of how to build complete communities," and the need for the public to be an integral part of planning with staff and council based on "democratic principles."[22] It was only when the provincial government discovered that six of the twelve proposed development sites would interfere with the planned Highway 413 that provincial pressures led the mayor to withdraw her bylaw amendments.[23] The provincial government has also overridden local municipal decisions in Hamilton and the Halton Region when they rejected urban sprawl, forcing these communities to develop vital farmland, greenspace and pockets of the Greenbelt. Only after the Greenbelt scandal did the provincial government reverse course.[24]

There has been a recurring tendency by the provincial government of Doug Ford to make decisions concerning municipal governance without consultation only to have to reverse them later. In May 2023, the Ford government announced plans to break up Peel Region into three independent cities by January 2025. A report by KPMG pegged the cost at over $1 billion, in addition to an expected property tax increase of nearly 40 percent.[25] By December 2023, the Ford government announced it was abandoning plans to dissolve Peel and that it would revise the mandate of the Peel Region Transition Board to focus instead on speeding up home-building. By May 2024, the provincially appointed five-member Transition Board had cost Peel Region taxpayers more than $4.4 million, leading to an exodus of staff as employees braced for potential layoffs. To date, the province has refused to pick up the tab despite being the source of its costs.[26]

The PC government also announced financial audits for Brampton, Caledon, Mississauga, Newmarket, Toronto and Peel Region, with no explanation as to why those six jurisdictions were chosen. A financial analysis of the impacts of MHBFA began in the summer of 2023 and was completed in the fall. The government then cancelled the audits and has since refused to share the findings with the public or municipalities.[27] In March 2024, the provincial government announced a new $1.8 billion Municipal Housing Infrastructure Program to support core infrastructure projects, like roads and water infrastructure, to enable housing development.[28] The new funding ostensibly aims to make municipalities "whole" again, given the combined effects of Bills 23 and 39, and to at least partially make up for fees that would have otherwise been funded by development costs. In short order, taxpayer subsidies have upended the long-standing principle that development should pay for growth.

This has exacerbated the City of Toronto's recurring fiscal challenges — a crisis imposed from above by federal and provincial devolution without matching fiscal supports in the context of weak governance powers. The Ford government announced in November 2023 the *New Deal for Toronto Act* (NDTA). It is important to note that $1.1 billion of Toronto's annual property tax revenue, the primary revenue-raising mechanism for Ontario municipalities, is spent on extensions of federal and provincial responsibilities, like social assistance and health services, social housing, fire and policing, to name but a few.[29] The 2023 new bill enacts two pieces of legislation, *Recovery for Growth Act (City of Toronto)* and *Rebuilding Ontario Place Act*. Contingent on matching fiscal supports from the federal government, the NDTA sees the province take control of two Toronto highways (the Don Valley Parkway and Gardiner Expressway), equal to $6.5 billion in spending relief to the city over the next decade. In exchange, the City approved the province's sell-off and re-development of the publicly owned Ontario Place to a private spa operator of which Ontario taxpayers are estimated to pay between $1 billion to $2 billion in direct and indirect subsidies.[30] The City also agreed to drop its request for a municipal sales tax. The NDTA also provides the City with one-time fiscal injections worth $758 million for new subway cars and $600 million over three years for housing/shelter support. In December 2023, the federal government announced close to half a billion dollars for the City of Toronto for 12,000 housing units over the next three years and 53,000 over the next decade. Municipalities outside Toronto did not see any additional fiscal injections.

The NDTA also expands the powers of the minister of infrastructure under the *Planning Act*, exempting the province from the *Environment Assessment Act* and stating that the *Ontario Heritage Act* will not apply to portions of Ontario Place. The Acts grant the province, via the minister of municipal affairs and housing, the ability to issue ministerial zoning orders, thereby circumventing the need to hold public meetings and consult. Since 2018, the Ford government has issued more MZOs than all the preceding governments combined since 1995.

Municipal Futures

If the last seven years of Conservative rule has shown anything, it is a seething contempt for local democratic processes and the governance autonomy of municipalities small and large. Power has increasingly been concentrated in the hands of mayors and councils or, worse, unelected technocrats that adopt provincial policies. In this regard, the thin veneer of democracy increasingly runs counter to the concentration and centralization of power in the hands of political and economic elites.

It is a cruel irony that Doug Ford has pushed through a singular vision of American-style "strong mayors," while US municipalities increasingly adopt Canadian style "council-rule." Whereas 53 percent of US municipalities used a so-called "strong mayor" system in 1981, this use had fallen to just 33 percent by 2011, with 59 percent utilizing a council-rule system.[31] In the US, strong mayor systems can feature a separate executive branch of government with unilateral appointment powers. Some cities use a council-manager form of government where an unelected city manager is the chief executive but still accountable to council. Neither of these forms of municipal government exists in Canada. Municipal government in Ontario's cities is completely different, with the mayor being elected separately through city-wide election, while council members are the winners of ward-based elections on the same ballot. The mayor sits as a member of the city council, wielding one vote like councillors. But mayors typically have far more political capital and media attention, allowing for more symbolic power and focus on their policy directives and campaign promises.

Before the Ford government's changes, Ontario mayors were neither weak nor strong, with both unilateral powers of appointment that were not total, and the mayor sat as an equal among council.[32] The council-rule system is noted for reducing corporate influence, ensuring departmental autonomy from political interference, enabling greater time to be spent on representing and servicing constituents, and providing more incentive to collaborate and constructively negotiate with other councillors, rather than incentivizing fealty to the mayor. Moreover, in no American city can bylaws be passed by less than a majority of councillors.[33] In grafting presidentialized veto power with parliamentarized notions of executive committee, Ford's government has centralized (or de-democratized) local municipal governments in unprecedented ways.

The push for strong mayors combined with a multiplicity of development-related legislation feigns the appearance of solving the housing crisis rather than actually solving it. The effect is to download responsibility onto municipalities without any of the tools to truly solve it. Affordable, subsidized and supportive housing cannot be resolved by municipalities on their own.[34] The housing crisis is the result of federal and provincial governments' withdrawal from social housing provision in the 1990s, which has left a void in all manner of housing supply for decades.[35] The deregulation of rent control and "vacancy decontrol," where low-paying tenants are removed in order to increase rents to "market" levels, and legislation allowing for rent increases above the cost of living have compounded the housing crisis further.[36] In short, while municipal policy can ameliorate or worsen these conditions, it cannot resolve them without multi-level fiscal arrangements and intergovernmental coordination. In this sense, stable and predictable commitments from federal governments vis-à-vis municipalities will be central to overcoming the long-standing tradition of ad hoc and conditional federal involvement in municipal affairs.[37]

There is a growing unevenness across municipalities in their ability to raise revenues, and in their dependencies on fiscal transfers and demands for services. Population growth or decline, economic composition, climate and local conditions all figure prominently. Despite this, one-time fiscal injections from federal and provincial governments will not fix the disconnect between revenue-raising capacities and spending requirements. Municipalities cannot resolve issues related to climate change, transportation, housing, wastewater and others on their own. These challenges require developing new coordinated intergovernmental planning capacities, dedicated funding, and locally specific development strategies, particularly in self-governing Northern and Indigenous communities.[38] In the absence of this support, pressures to contract-out municipal public services and sell-off assets will continue to grow. But the evidence from outsourcing and privatization across Canadian municipalities has corresponded with reduced public oversight, and more expensive yet lower-quality services.[39]

The Financial Accountability Office (FAO) of Ontario estimates that 45 percent of municipal infrastructure in the province — valued at nearly half a trillion dollars — is in a state of disrepair, which is estimated to cost roughly $52 billion. The FAO report also notes: "Postponing repairs raises the risk of service disruption and increases the costs associated with municipal infrastructure over time." In Toronto, the repair backlog is expected to rise to nearly $23 billion by 2033, due to a combination of higher interest rates, inflation and pressures from population growth. The Ford government's inaction to attend to the crisis of municipal infrastructure, like others before it, shifts the burden down the road while also providing a legitimating rationale for austerity-driven municipal privatizations.[40]

There is thus a pressing urgency to also expand dedicated fiscal transfers from federal and provincial governments, including more diverse revenue-raising capacities for municipalities with strong local economic foundations. Reversing the Ford government's policy of shifting the costs of development away from industry and onto local taxpayers to pay for growth will also be necessary.[41] It is worth the reminder that Canadian municipalities generally, and Ontario municipalities in particular, are among the most restricted in terms of local autonomy and revenue-raising powers. Whereas property taxes account for around one-third of municipal revenues across Organisation for Economic Co-operation and Development (OECD) countries, in Canada, they make up more than half of all local budgets. Municipalities in Germany, Switzerland, the Netherlands and the Nordic countries, for instance, are able to draw revenue from income taxes, while municipalities in France, Japan, Korea and the US also have access to sales taxes. In the case of Canadian municipalities, the asymmetric assignment of responsibility to provide services runs up against the means to actually pay for them.[42]

Of course, the size and corporate sophistication of municipalities, local fiscal conditions, tax administration capacity and efficiency considerations — such as the risk of leakage across jurisdictional boundaries — all play a role. In general, taxing powers make more sense for larger municipalities and regions that deliver a broader range of human services, have greater administrative capacity and could encourage the implementation of taxes across wider regions. Although the provinces wield constitutional power over municipalities, municipalities are not powerless, particularly since most people identify with the places they live and often work. An old proposal gaining new traction is the demand for "Charter Cities." A number of large Canadian cities like Calgary, Edmonton, Winnipeg and Vancouver already have such charters in place. In Ontario, the proposal would require provincial approval and perhaps even a Constitutional amendment, but would give the city full control over its governance makeup, exclusive or shared authority for key municipal functions, greater control of revenue and constitutionally protected political independence.[43] This movement is not without precedent in Toronto, as charter city proponents were very active in the late 1990s and early 2000s, led by public figures like Jane Jacobs, John Sewell and John Ralston Saul.[44] However, a major limitation of charter cities is that, in the absence of a constitutional change, municipalities will remain subject to provincial imperatives given their unwillingness to cede political and legal control. Additionally, it is only available to large cities with strong political and economic bases and may impede inter-municipal coordination. As well, in the absence of effective political vehicles to demand change, charter cities may languish as little more than paper tigers. Despite these challenges, movements for change most often begin "at home" — in our neighbourhoods, school districts, workplaces, wider networks and communities. From living wage mobilizations, urban environmental movements, migrant worker initiatives and affordable housing campaigns, to petitions, council demonstrations and neighbourhood rallies, linking these struggles in a coordinated and sustained way will be critical if an alternative political project to the Ford Agenda is to emerge.[45]

16

BUILDING TENANT POWER

Lily Xia

IN THE LAST FEW YEARS, tenant organizing in Ontario has become increasingly fraught and difficult, while nevertheless growing exponentially. More tenants than ever are realizing the precarious nature of renting in Ontario, as well as the lack of recourse, other than standing together and fighting for our right to our homes. The Ford government has followed an unabashed process of deregulating housing policy, a process that thinly veils the calculated policy of profit-driven development with a sheer shroud of affordable housing sympathy. This calculated deregulation is performed in support of private market logic that blames the troubles of society on those most marginalized, leaving them no room for survival. Tenants' organized struggles against this calculated deregulation pre-date Ford's government, but they have also been exacerbated by it. Recent tenant struggles against the deregulation of rent control and the weakening of tenant protections show us how tenants are coming together to fight deregulatory policies despite the difficulties.

Ford's Policies

Ford's government has enacted numerous, ironically named policies that profess to improve tenant rights and protections, but, in fact, they either do not address tenant concerns or they, in fact, further weaken tenant rights. In 2020, Bill 184, the *Protecting Tenants and Strengthening Community Housing Act*, strengthened landlords' power and did not consider the realities of tenants' lives. Organizations such as the Canadian Mental Health Association Ontario (CMHA Ontario) and Advocacy Centre for Tenants Ontario (ACTO), along with other tenant advocates, opposed the bill, with ACTO dubbing it an "Eviction Bill," and CMHA Ontario arguing that the bill "will ultimately end in weakening hard-won rights for tenants."[1] The bill proposed that any rent paid by the tenant for one year or more to be the legal rent, even if that rent was the result of an illegal rent increase. Previously, if a tenant discovered that they had been paying an illegal rent increase, they could legally recover all overpayments, indeterminant of time. Bill 184 legislated a new time limit for tenants to dispute the increase. The bill also introduced a clause (section 78) that allows landlords to evict tenants without a hearing — an ex parte order to evict — if the tenant fails to follow a repayment plan. If tenants are even a day late on their repayment plan, their landlord does not have to notify them before obtaining an eviction order. Practically, this means that some tenants first hear news of their enforced eviction when the sheriff shows up at their door and locks them out. Section 78 is now applied to almost all repayment plans at the Landlord and Tenant Board (LTB).

In 2023, the *Helping Homebuyers, Protecting Tenants Act* was also criticized by tenant organizations for not protecting tenants in any meaningful way. ACTO described the bill as "an initiative that only serves to delay the real opportunity to address the serious problems at hand."[2] The bill's proposals for protecting tenants centred around increasing fines for bad faith evictions and hiring more adjudicators at the LTB. However, the LTB is a dysfunctional body where the outcomes for tenants are often bleak and unjust.[3] For example, fines for bad faith evictions do not go to the tenants but to the LTB. As such, these increased fines have no material benefit to the tenant at the cost of a lot of energy spent working through the legal system. Moreover, the LTB often prioritizes the requests and profits of landlords over the needs of tenants, which can be seen in the relatively short turnaround time of landlords' applications for evictions (roughly six months), compared to the extremely long turnaround time for tenant applications for maintenance, harassment and other mistreatment (which is roughly two years). Rather than protecting tenants, hiring adjudicators for a more "effective" LTB only creates a more streamlined process for evicting tenants.

Rent Decontrol

The biggest blow to tenant rights was enacted shortly after Ford's government was elected, as a part of the *Restoring Trust, Transparency, and Accountability Act*. This bill removed rent control from all rentals first occupied for residential use after November 15, 2018, and has had devastating outcomes for tenants across Ontario. After the bill was tabled, the Ontario Federation of Labour (OFL) wrote a public letter that criticized the Ford government's priorities. As stated by OFL, "Once again, this government has prioritized big developers over Ontario families."[4]

Rent control in Ontario has had a complicated history. Rents were regulated in Ontario from 1975 to 1996, but rent control exemptions were introduced in 1997 for units built on or after November 1991.[5] In 2017, that exemption was removed in the *Rental Fairness Act*. Soon after, Ford's government was elected, and they moved to once again exempt new rental units from rent control. Ford justified rent decontrol by stating, "This will help create market-based incentives for supply growth that will encourage an increase in housing supply."[6] However, this "trickle-down," supply-side perspective shows a profound and purposeful misinterpretation of housing economics. It favours trusting the words and intent of developers and landlords while ignoring not only the lived realities of tenants living in increasingly precarious situations, but also in-depth research that shows the inaccurate presumptions embedded in supply-side solutions to the affordable housing crisis. Statistical analysis by CMHC of historical rent control policies in Canada "did not find evidence that rental starts were lower in rent control markets than in no rent control markets."[7] Most transparently, the Ford policy ignored the precedent set when Ontario implemented rent decontrol in 1996 for units built on or after November 1, 1991. In those 21 years, rent decontrol failed to build additional affordable rental units, averaging only 3,452 new rental housing units per year,[8] while rents and eviction rates skyrocketed.[9]

Incentivizing Development

If rent decontrol does not work to encourage rental construction, why is it being used again as a strategy by Ford's government? Ford's argument for his deregulatory policies focused on increasing profit and speeding up approvals for new builds, but approved and profitable developments are then still not being built. Ford's Building Faster Fund is a $1.2-billion fund that distributes funds to municipalities for infrastructure if they are able to meet a threshold of housing starts.[10] Many municipalities have sped up their development approval processes, in order to gain access to this fund, for needed sewer expansions and replacements, among other essential infrastructure. However, while many developments have been approved, many developers have not started building. In York Region, over 49,000 approved housing units have not started construction, while in Mississauga, there are 29,000 approved homes that have not broken ground.[11] In the meantime, condo developers are unable to find buyers, leaving many condos sitting empty as developers refuse to decrease their prices to affordable levels.[12] The irony of trusting private developers to fix the affordable housing problem while thousands of newly built, unsold condos sit empty and out of reach of those who would buy and live in them does not seem to bother Ford's government. They continue undaunted to appeal to the private market for housing solutions.

The narrative of supply-side solutions conceals the incentive that developers and landlords have to maintain their leverage over the housing market and housing as an attractive commodity. For housing to remain an attractive commodity, stable investment and source of profit, developers are incentivized to maintain a housing shortage, while arguing for looser regulations and supportive government funds that can allow them to maximize profit. Deregulation is really a calculated process for profiteering that hides behind an appeal to social benefit that doesn't actually result in any social benefit. While Ford's government treats deregulation as the main solution to the affordable housing problem, many housing and tenant advocates champion other solutions toward housing, such as increased tenant protections, support for tenant organizing and funding for non-market housing.

For governments such as Ford's to take developers and landlords at their word on their intent to "fix" the affordable housing problem requires them to ignore the words and experiences of countless tenants who have documented and reported their mistreatment at the hands of these developers and landlords. Ford's rent decontrol policy grants agency and profitability to developers and landlords, treating tenants as one of the "sacrifices without exception"[13] to fix the fiscal budget. Ironically, increasing tenant protections and expanding rent control are part of a regulatory policy that would have near zero impact on the government's fiscal position.

REITs, Squeezing Tenants and Renovictions

Overall, Ford's policies reveal a willingness to sacrifice tenants for the "economy." The need to sacrifice the profits of developers and landlords is never given a moment's consideration. Financialized landlords have a fiduciary duty to their investors and shareholders to extract the maximum amount of profit from tenants, and this duty is placed above the lives and well-being of tenants. All of Ford's policies strengthen the ability of developers and landlords to profit and exploit tenants while doing nothing to address the main concern of tenants — housing affordability and neglected maintenance. Facilitated by the lack of comprehensive tenant protections, the additional withdrawal of regulations for developers and landlords only facilitates further tenant exploitation. Ford's government attempts to absolve itself of all responsibility to tenants, seeking to offload the responsibility of affordable housing onto private developers and landlords, while ignoring the fact that the interests of private developers and landlords are fundamentally at odds with those of tenants.

Research into real estate investment trusts (REITs) revealed two common strategies for profit-centred exploitation of tenants: "squeezing" and "gentrification by upgrading."[14] Squeezing is when landlords ignore routine maintenance requests and reduce services while simultaneously investing in aesthetic enhancements and renovations that allow them to charge higher rent through Above Guideline Increases. The squeezing strategy was also often found to be associated with tenant harassment. Properties are often subject to squeezing when they are identified as part of an "undesirable" market. If that changes so the neighbourhood becomes seen as a "good market," the tenants there are then subject to gentrification through upgrading, or "renovictions." The goals of this strategy are eviction and replacement.

These strategies used by landlords to extract profit from tenants are no secret. Hazelview (formerly Timbercreek), a large, financialized landlord with a history of mass evictions,[15] have described strategies where they look to buy properties that they consider neglected and in good markets in order to renovate and resell in a few years. Hazelview and like companies are not incentivized to improve these properties to make them livable for the tenants that already live in them, but rather to evict, demolish and upgrade the property to be sold and rented to higher-income tenants. Using language such as "repositioning" and "value-add," developers and landlords signal this strategy to their investors, reassuring them of the stability and potential of their investments.[16] Dream Unlimited, a landlord and developer in Ontario who self-markets as a leader in "affordable housing" initiatives, outlines in its 2022 Sustainability Report how the expected benefits of investing in green net zero renovations include "increases in rents ... and attraction of certain tenants."[17] These landlords and developers see these exploitative strategies as a natural part of being a landlord, often seeing their right to profiteer as equal to or even above tenant rights to live well in their homes. Michael Brooks, the president of Realpac, an organization that represents landlords across Canada, justified these strategies in an interview with CBC. Brooks stated, "Of course, you're going to do that... If you don't, you're subsidizing the market and your investors are saying, 'Where's my return that I thought I was getting from this?'"[18] Despite these accounts and admissions from landlords, nowhere in any of Ford's policies are any of these common exploitative practices addressed.

Developer and landlord collusion to exploit tenants and extract maximum profit is common practice around the world. In 2021, more than 50 percent of unrented apartments were warehoused and held off market by New York City landlords.[19] The tendency of landlords to warehouse apartments when supply is greater than demand instead of lowering rents undermines the argument that an increase in the supply of housing will create more affordable housing. Instead of allowing rents to drop, landlords have the financial power to hoard housing until they are again able to leverage a housing shortage for higher rents. In 2022, ProPublica reported that US landlords were using YieldStar, an AI software that compiled data on local rents, allowing landlords to collude on rent prices and charge the highest rent possible.[20] YieldStar and similar software also operate in Canada, with companies such as Great West Life Realty Advisors Inc. using it to grow their profits by 182 percent in three years, even as vacancy rates in their buildings increase.[21] Given how developers and landlords game the system, it is no surprise that rent decontrol has had no effect on fixing the housing affordability problem.

Prioritizing Developer and Landlord Profit

Despite the extensive research and many accounts that depict how developers and landlords exploit tenants, Ford and his government have ignored the voices of tenants and tenant advocates. Rather, they enact policies that place the responsibility of fixing the affordable housing problem in the hands of developers and landlords who have no interest in solving it. In 2022, the *More Homes Built Faster Act* did exactly that. The act used the affordable housing problem to loosen regulations on developers and landlords, including environmental protections. In 2023, it was revealed that Ford had, in fact, colluded with developers and landlords, trying to gift Greenbelt land development to his developer friends and donors.[22] Ford's government ignored the call of tenants, removed tenants' agency and proposed that the solution to society's problems could only come at their sacrifice. Ford rationalized further disenfranchisement and displacement of the urban poor in service of offering developers and landlords more profit.

In 1996, geographer Neil Smith described this attitude among the wealthy as a "policy of revenge,"[23] where the wealthy blame the poor not only for being poor, but also for issues such as violence and pollution. This attitude can also be seen in the common strategies for exploiting tenants, including but not limited to squeezing, gentrification and warehousing. Language such as "repositioning," and "value-add" create positive connotations for the material reality of evicting poor people out of their homes and replacing them with wealthier tenants or new homeowners. The act of eviction is a violent revenge on the poor, seen as a necessary procedure to achieve a "cleaner" and more desirable neighbourhood. Ford's policy furthers this attitude, sacrificing the urban poor at the altar of profit.

Tenants Fighting Back

Recent tenant organizing reveals the true impact of these strategies and policies on tenants. Tenants are coming together with their neighbours to fight against neglected maintenance, against above-guideline rent increases, against evictions and against the devastating impact these exploitative strategies have on their daily lives.

Rent Strikes

In Ontario in 2024, three groups of tenants have been on rent strike since 2023 against three different landlords: Thorncliffe Park tenants against Starlight Investments, 33 King and 22 John Street tenants against Dream Unlimited, and 1440/1442 Lawrence Avenue West tenants against Barney River Investments. Going into their second year of rent striking, these groups of tenants have similar experiences and frustrations with their landlords, such as neglected maintenance and quickly rising rents. Many of these tenants have tried other avenues, but proper maintenance and affordable rents remained out of reach, leaving them to turn to more confrontational actions such as rent strikes.

At 33 King Street, the tenants' decision to go on rent strike came after years of above guideline increases (AGI) while needed maintenance in their homes was neglected. Landlords are often motivated to use AGIs not to do needed repairs but as opportunities to increase their revenues.[24] Dream Unlimited (Dream), the landlord for 33 King Street, portrays itself as a socially conscious company and a proponent of affordable housing. On their website and in their financial documents, Dream presents environmental, social and governance strategies that they proclaim benefit the communities they develop, including programs such as breakfast outreach.[25] It becomes clear when looking at their financial reports and presentations to investors that Dream uses this framing in order to access "government-affiliated debt."[26] Government-affiliated debts are attractive for developers because they often come with lower interest rates and longer terms. Jamie Cooper, son of CEO Michael Cooper and portfolio manager of Dream Impact Fund, as well as director of Development and Impact Investments, stated at 2023's Dream Investor Day that their affordable purpose-built rentals are "usually developed on lands sourced from the government, or with CMHC financing."[27] He went on to say that "generally, the cost of the land is reduced … and certain government fees and costs are also waived on these projects."

At the same time, Dream is pursuing "value add" initiatives, which Jamie Cooper described as:

> casual improvements on building systems including decarbonization, common area upgrades to lobbies and corridors, new unit creation where possible, and optimizing asset management operations, which includes renovating some turnover to achieve higher rents, leveraging our platform to manage costs more efficiently and optimizing parking, mono-graves, and other forms of non-rent income to maximize that as well. Today these assets are … we see them performing quite well.[28]

With these decreased costs and "value add" initiatives, Cooper stated, "we tend to target 12 to 15 percent return and we think these returns are sustainable and consistently achievable over a very long period of time and with relatively low risk." When listening to the narratives of tenants who rent from Dream, one learns where these stable 12 to

15 percent returns are coming from. Sharlene Henry, one of the tenant organizers at 33 King Street, describes "weeks of water coming out of our floors and our sinks" due to the ignored maintenance requests. [29]

Numerous confrontations with CEO Michael Cooper on these issues have resulted in Cooper doubling down on Dream's good work in affordable housing development, even in the face of tenants describing pest infestations, the impact of rising living costs and heartbreaking stories of losing their homes. In one meeting with Dream Community Foundation's executive director Runa Whitaker (who calls herself a "social impact leader" on LinkedIn), said that Dream had stopped the breakfast outreach at 33 King and 22 John because some tenants were taking too much food. Their attitudes are indicative of how many developers and landlords see tenants as people low on the "moral economy" hierarchy whose experiences and needs are easily dismissed and deemed unreasonable. [30]

At 22 John Street, Ford's rent decontrol policy was the main motivating factor for tenants to join the rent strike started by their neighbours and fellow tenants of Dream at 33 King Street. Originally public land, 22 John Street is one of Dream's targeted affordable purpose-built rentals funded by government-affiliated debt. Both 33 King Street and 22 John Street contain 189 affordable units in buildings that in total contain 841 units, and an unknown number are actually occupied. [31]

In April 2024, Alex, a tenant who moved into an "affordable unit" at 22 John Street, was violently evicted with his partner and their young daughter after their rent more than doubled to $3000 per month. Dream hired private security guards to prevent his neighbours from supporting him and along with the sheriff and police officers, they took a sledgehammer to his door to drag Alex out and evict him. Although on paper 22 John Street and 33 King Street are a part of Dream's affordable housing portfolio, in actuality, 22 John Street is marketed as West22, a "resort-style, purpose-built rental building" that "offers a lifestyle of convenience beyond compare."[32] Almost every tenant at 22 John Street faced rent increases of hundreds of dollars per month year after year. Tenants realized that their rents would eventually become unsustainable and began to worry about the precarity that they would all eventually face. When the landlord can increase rents as high as they can for no reason at all, tenants know they have little to no protection from eviction and displacement. In June of 2023, 100 tenants from 22 John Street signed strike cards, joining 200 of their neighbours at 33 King Street in a rent strike, protesting what they recognized as their purposefully deregulated and precarious housing status in the interest of Dream's profit.

As of the summer of 2024, tenants on rent strike have been served N4s — Notice of Evictions for Non-Payment of Rent. The outcome of these rent strikes is not yet certain, but their cases are currently being heard together at the LTB, despite the wishes of their landlords. Over the course of the LTB hearings, it became clear that the landlords were doing their best to divide the tenants into individual cases that they could more easily dismiss and evict. However, despite enormous pressure from the landlords to break them apart and weaken their collective power, tenants stuck together. As a result, 1440/1442 Lawrence Avenue West tenants on rent strike have received an interim order from the LTB regarding maintenance in their homes. Many tenants have finally received repairs for issues that have been neglected, sometimes for more than a decade. Repairs for massive holes in ceilings, missing closet doors and even completely new countertops were scheduled and completed within weeks of the interim order, showing that these maintenance problems were always resolvable. For the tenants, seeing the complete reversal in treatment from their landlord confirmed that they were always right to take action to stand together and mobilize to defend one another.

Fighting Evictions

Nowhere is the lack of tenant protections clearer than in eviction cases. In December 2023, shortly before the holidays, 1440/1442 Lawrence Avenue West faced a flurry of evictions. Tenants in these two buildings were already well organized, having fought against rent increases and poor maintenance for many years. In October of 2023, a group of tenants had gone on rent strike in protest of the poor conditions and above-guideline rent increases. Tenants were well prepared to support one another and knew of the aggressive tactics that Barney River used to intimidate and harass tenants. When one tenant alerted her neighbours that the sheriff was at her door looking to evict her, both buildings took action. Carmen, who had no idea she had an eviction order against her, had been paying her rent through automatic withdrawals from her bank for several months. However, a previous error in her rent had left her with just over $500 in arrears. Although Carmen was supposed to receive an eviction notice and hearing date information by mail, Canada Post had suspended mail delivery to her building at 1442 Lawrence Avenue West for three years due to unsafe working conditions. Canada Post reinstated service shortly after tenants went on rent strike in October, but the information that Carmen was supposed to receive months ago never reached her.

With her neighbours, the sheriff and police officers as witnesses, Carmen came to an agreement with the landlord that she would go downstairs to pay off her arrears at the property management office and her tenancy would be reinstated. One police officer promised that everything would be okay if she paid her arrears. However, when she reached the office with her wallet, staff told her that she had been evicted and they would no longer allow her access to her home. Suddenly, Carmen was locked out of her home with no access to her diabetes medications. At this turn of events, her neighbours began to occupy the property management office to pressure the landlord to keep their word and reinstate Carmen's tenancy.

While Lawrence Avenue tenants were holding the property management office, police officers escorted property management staff out of the building and tried numerous times to convince Carmen's neighbours to abandon her. Police officers argued that the best option for Carmen was to find space at a shelter. One police officer called the ambulance multiple times, claiming concern for Carmen's health, asking the paramedics to make Carmen go to the hospital and give up the fight for her home. Another police officer questioned why no one wanted to help Carmen find housing, but had no response when tenant supporters said that Carmen already had a home, right upstairs. Had police officers convinced Carmen's neighbours to abandon her, they would have enabled Carmen's violent eviction, displacement and dispossession. Carmen had no alternative form of housing, especially with such short notice. The shelter system that the police officers suggested was turning away hundreds of people every day, and with no place to move her belongings, Carmen would have had only 72 hours to find a new place to move her furniture and worldly possessions to before the landlord would have been legally allowed to go into her home to destroy them.

After 74 hours of tenants holding the property management office, Carmen was eventually allowed back into her home, and the landlord agreed to drop the eviction. However, while tenants were mobilizing to prevent Carmen's eviction, other tenants in the buildings were also being evicted. For reasons of their own, these tenants did not reach out and join the tenants mobilizing in the property management office. When their neighbours later learned of their eviction, it was with a sense of resignation, as at that point, there was little that could be done.

Unfortunately, stories like those of Carmen and her evicted neighbours are not uncommon. Tenant organizers regularly hear of fraudulent and illegal evictions — tenants left with nowhere to turn except for the streets. Developers and landlords prioritize profiteering over tenants' right to live in their homes. Evictions have become almost normalized, seen as a natural consequence of doing business, and many tenants face evictions year after year. Landlords have very little incentive to treat tenants well and provide tenants with basic information, such as accurate rent ledgers, and many of the ledgers seen by tenant organizers are rife with inaccuracies. For the most part, landlords get away with using these exploitative tactics, as often tenants will not have enough resources and energy to fight and win. On the off chance that a tenant is able to take their landlord to the LTB, wait two years for a hearing, argue their case and win, the fines are often less than the potential long-term profit from evicting the tenant. In a cost-benefit analysis, the outcome skews heavily in favour of further tenant exploitation. As seen in Carmen and her neighbours' cases, it is only through mobilizing together in confrontation with landlords that tenants can hope to stay in their homes.

Supporting Tenants' Rights

The outcomes of tenant organizing and tactics such as rent strikes are never clear-cut. As tenants continue to organize across Toronto and Ontario, it is clear that government policies claiming to "protect" tenants do no such thing, in actuality. What is also clear is that in a system built against tenant organizing — one that continues to throw up obstacles in front of tenants fighting displacement — the only option is for tenants to come together and support one another. This chapter shows a small slice of tenant organizing in Toronto over the last couple of years, and there are many more accounts of tenants supporting one another against their landlords, despite the odds. Policies coming from governments such as Doug Ford's, who do not respect tenant experiences or demands, only serve to distract from what tenants truly need — the ability to stay in their properly maintained homes.

17

FIGHTING FORD

John Clarke

THE REGIME THAT DOUG FORD HAS INFLICTED ON ONTARIO is not without its complexities and contradictions. This might seem a strange thing to suggest, since Ford himself is anything but a complex figure. He is a less-than-subtle right-wing Tory and, as he blusters and stumbles his way through the implementation of his regressive political agenda, very few would suggest that he is any kind of evil genius. His style of operating is crude and conniving, his political judgement is highly questionable and his performance in office is dangerously erratic.

Any assessment of Ford's period in power to date, along with the forms of social resistance that have emerged in response to it, must involve a comparison with the Mike Harris "Common Sense Revolution" that took Ontario by storm in the 1990s. I will consider the contexts in which they each carried out their grisly work and will explore the implementation of the Harris agenda, measuring it against Ford's performance. I will also evaluate the response of unions and social movements to each of these Conservative attack regimes so as to draw some conclusions with regard to the future that lies ahead.

It is, of course, worthwhile to note that Ford's austerity measures and attacks on workers follow in the footsteps of previous governments and he employs his cheap populism and reactionary instincts at a volatile and uncertain stage in the development of a political project that goes back several decades. In this context, the particular features of his government and his own qualities play out in some very curious ways.

Harris and Ford: Common Sense?

Harris's Common Sense Revolution took place at a much earlier stage in the long effort to tilt the balance more decisively in the interests of the wealthy at the expense of workers and communities. The Harris attack in Ontario followed on the heels of the decisive austerity measures that were taken at the federal level by Liberals Jean Chrétien and Paul Martin. Their austerity drive was one of the most severe around the world, and remains the foundation for the Conservatives' strategy of death by a thousand cuts.[1] The federal Liberals unquestionably opened up the pathway that Harris would follow in Ontario.

The Harris Tories, moreover, were able to follow examples that had been set on the international stage in the previous two decades by some outstanding right-wing vanguard regimes, particularly those of Ronald Reagan and Margaret Thatcher.[2] Harris was operating in a context where gutting the social infrastructure and undermining trade union power were proceeding at an uneven rate. The implementation of that agenda took an incremental form overall, but it was also marked by particular governments that adopted a more uncompromising approach and worked to intensify the rate and scale of the attack. The Harris Tories were very much of this second type. There is no need to provide here any detailed account of the damage done by Harris but the Ontario Federation of Labour (OFL) succinctly captured the sense of shock that was felt during that period with a statement issued in 1999, "'The Common Sense Revolution': 1,460 Days of Destruction."[3] The impacts of this shock are with us still.

The Ford Tories today are operating on the terrain of a significantly changed global capitalism. Harris was plying his trade in a period when Margaret Thatcher's confident assertion, that "There is no alternative," still held sway. At this time, class war policies could be implemented under relatively stable economic conditions, but things have changed considerably since the 2008 financial crisis and the Great Recession, and even more, since the shock of the global COVID-19 pandemic and the inflationary episode that followed it. As Alex Callinicos has pointed out, this is a period in which state power is still employed against workers with great enthusiasm, but it is also necessary for those in power to be far more attentive to the need to underwrite profit-making opportunities.[4]

In the present context, a leading enforcer of global capitalism like the International Monetary Fund (IMF) is ready to cheer on higher interest rates as a means of weakening the bargaining power of workers, and it is very anxious to ensure that fiscal policy is dominated by a complementary assault on social supports and programs. However, as robust as its appetite for class war policies may be, it has also had to accept that its approach must be "agile, integrated, and focused on its member countries."[5] This means that the austerity attack that has been a hallmark of the last forty years is still to be pursued, but in this period of "polycrisis," sudden abrupt tactical shifts to stimulatory spending may be necessary to stave off economic downturns or the failure of major businesses.[6]

Very strikingly in this regard, the Ford Conservatives had to weather the storm of the COVID-19 pandemic. They had to participate in the desperate effort to keep the world market functioning during an economic shutdown in ways that could hardly have been to their liking. Ford himself, wrestling with the dramatic situation, offered this remarkable advice to tenants, "If you have a choice between putting food on your table or paying rent, you're putting food on your table. The government of Ontario will make sure that no one gets evicted. We stand by that and we're gonna make sure we take care of those people."[7] As dubious and short-lived as that assurance was, devastating prevailing conditions generated by a global health emergency forced them out of Doug Ford.

It is worth noting that there is an obvious disparity in terms of the respective scale of the mobilized opposition between the Harris and Ford days. I say this neither to be dismissive of the struggles of the present period nor to set the challenge to the Common Sense Revolution on a romanticized pedestal that it doesn't deserve. However, it is beyond dispute that the Ford Conservatives have not yet had to contend with anything that could be remotely compared to the Ontario Days of Action. From 1995 to 1998, eleven Days of Action had city-wide strikes and gigantic rallies.[8] This is by no means a surrender to defeatism, since the Ford regime is still very much a work in progress, and the present period is marked internationally by unexpected upsurges. Still, we will have to address this deficit in social action and propose some means of addressing it.

If there was one quality that Mike Harris brought to his role, it was a remarkable intransigence. Certainly, he relied on a team of conservative ideologues and planners but he personally had the courage of his horrible convictions. He once infamously suggested that he would proceed with his agenda, though every blade of grass at the Ontario Legislature was trampled by protesters.[9] This is not to say that the sizeable struggles taken up during his period in office had no effect or failed to place some definite limits on the destruction he unleashed. Still, Harris was very much a warrior of austerity who was single-minded in gaining every inch of ground he could in the class war that he unleashed in Ontario. If Ford had to face an opposition comparable to that unleashed against Harris, it is highly unlikely that he would be able to muster the grit and defiance of his predecessor.

None of this is to suggest that the Ford government hasn't done a lot of damage because it most certainly has. As Greg Albo, Bryan Evans and Carlo Fanelli put it:

> There is a line of continuity extending back from the Ford government to the Common Sense Revolution of the Harris and Eves governments of 1995–2003. Their market-expanding and labour-disciplining agenda established Ontario as a low-tax, low-cost regional production zone. Despite the shift to a more "inclusionary" political discourse, the Liberal governments of McGuinty and Wynne from 2003–18 never departed from this fiscal legacy and, for the most part, consolidated a variation of the same strategy.[10]

I emphatically reject the idea that the Ford government can be regarded as a softer version of Harris. The present Tory regime is certainly not "austerity-lite" and it has aggressively amplified austerity logic, further undermining the fiscal capacity to fund program spending adequately. The pattern clearly emerges of a government that bases itself on the results of previous attacks on the social and public infrastructure that has advanced the assault considerably. Indeed, the Financial Accountability Office of Ontario has shown that Ontario's commitment to social provision is dramatically less than that of any other Canadian province. Despite this, my previous contention that Ford wouldn't have fared well in the face of any large and sustained social action is supported by the record of how he has responded to the challenges that have emerged since he became premier. Unlike Harris, Ford is a far more erratic and indecisive operator.

Fighting Back

Though the scale and intensity of the resistance to the Harris Conservatives have not been matched by the effort to date to contain Doug Ford's attacks, people in Ontario have nonetheless fought back on a wide front. Moreover, if we shouldn't dismiss the struggles being taken up at present, it would also be entirely wrong to exaggerate the fight that was taken up against Mike Harris and his cohorts. Major struggles were certainly unleashed that still offer us models of resistance, but the challenge to the Common Sense Revolution should not be presented as a golden age of social resistance that we have only to replicate in order to emerge victorious.

I was an organizer with the Ontario Coalition Against Poverty (OCAP) throughout the Harris years, and while it was certainly a time of major mobilizations and ubiquitous resistance, I felt then (and I still do) that the movement was operating well below its potential and failing to take an approach that could produce a decisive victory. When Harris took power, having signalled his brutal intentions at every turn as he campaigned for office, there was an initial phase of shocked passivity. The lead in confronting his government didn't come from the trade unions, with their far greater potential for power, but from relatively weak social movements and hastily assembled community-based coalitions.

There were a number of important and major strikes and a great variety of protests during the Harris years, but the defining form of generalized resistance was certainly the Ontario Days of Action. As someone who participated in every one of the city-wide actions that marked this campaign and helped to organize contingents to participate in most of them, I could clearly see a glaring contradiction within the whole initiative. On the one hand, the Days of Action were huge and powerful working-class mobilizations that filled us with hope and inspiration. At the same time, however, they fell considerably short of what they needed to be, and, in my view, what they could have been.

Doug Nesbitt has set out very effectively some of the political problems that beset the Days of Action. He charts the divisions inside the labour movement and the winding down of the campaign that ensued.[11] In my view, however, the problem was by no means confined to the outright reluctance to take to the streets that characterized the more conservative union leaders. Beyond providing a very loud oppositional voice that condemned the destructive Tory policies, the campaign's objectives were never clearly articulated. It was necessary to openly state and demonstrate in practice that the objective was to generate a level of disruptive social action that would make it impossible for the Tories to implement their program. In order to take such a path, a concrete plan to decisively escalate the struggle would have been essential.

The list of the centres that were chosen for the locations for the strikes and protests that took place is very revealing. In the order in which they occurred, Days of Action were held in London, Hamilton, Waterloo Region, Peterborough, Toronto, Sudbury, Thunder Bay, North Bay, Windsor, St. Catharines and Kingston. Assessing these locations from the standpoint of the size of their populations and their level of working-class strength, one recognizes that they were not selected with any objective of intensifying their economic and political impact, or preparing for something that would go beyond a city-by-city approach.

I raise this in the context of the struggle against Ford because, while unions and social movements are generally weaker today than they were in the 1990s, the challenge we face isn't simply to get back to the capacity for mobilization that existed in that earlier period. Indeed, if we are to build the kind of movement that is required, we will have to draw conclusions that were not reached, or at least didn't prevail, as the confrontation between working class movements and the architects of the Common Sense Revolution unfolded. In assessing the resistance to the Ford government in the present period, one needs to again stress that the struggle has unfolded in the face of some volatile and challenging factors that are unlike anything that was present at the time of Mike Harris. These include the impact of the COVID-19 pandemic and the rampant cost-of-living crisis that it helped to unleash. Lockdowns, galloping inflation and the huge uncertainties of the period have created a very different terrain on which to confront a provincial government.

Under Ford, we have seen workers and communities under attack, striving to find the means to fight back effectively. Grossly inadequate social assistance benefits, spending power gutted by rising prices and impossible rental costs have greatly exacerbated the problem of homelessness. In the major centres, especially in Toronto, encampments of unhoused people have mushroomed. When the authorities in Toronto decided that the pandemic was over and moved to disperse a number of these camps, there was fierce resistance. *CBC News* reported that the City of Toronto spent some $2 million on massive police operations to drive out the inhabitants of homeless camps in 2021 alone.[12] These actions were resisted, and, to this day, people who have been left without housing are establishing camps where they can survive in defiance of police and politicians. It remains an expression of resistance on the part of the poorest and most insecure part of the working-class population from whom we can all learn.

We have also seen an enormously hopeful wave of tenant struggles during the Ford years that contains enormous possibilities for the future. Patient forms of organizing, rent strikes and efforts to resist eviction have marked the last few years. Powerful corporate landlords, fully supported by the regime in Queen's Park, have faced an inspiring resistance from tenants. Low-paid and racialized working-class people have organized in their buildings to demand repairs, to challenge exorbitant rents and to counter the power of their landlords with a new sense of collective strength.[13]

Despite empty assurances that "hallway medicine" would become a thing of the past, Ontario's health care system has deteriorated disastrously under the Ford Tories.[14] We saw long-term care facilities become places of death and suffering during the pandemic, and today, hospital emergency room facilities are facing closures. The Ontario Health Coalition has sounded the alarm on these issues, major rallies have been held and an array of locally based initiatives are relentlessly challenging the Ford government. Still, even on such a critical issue that impacts so many lives, a mobilization that is as powerful and effective as the situation demands has most certainly not yet been achieved.

The OFL has attempted to fan the flames of discontent and lay the basis for a generalized resistance. However, its "Enough is Enough" initiative was not able to move beyond the tactic of rallying and speaking out.[15] A plan to challenge Ford and escalate disruptive forms of mobilization has not yet emerged. An effort to bring together the strands of working-class opposition to the Conservatives to take up a struggle that will do more than register outrage and issue calls for policy changes is still ahead of us.

A challenge to Ford that forced him to retreat and clearly exposed his glaring political weaknesses unfolded following his reckless and shameful decision to hand over a portion of the Greenbelt to his developer friends. This astounding episode has been documented exhaustively and there is no need to go into great detail here. Suffice it to say that with the highly questionable commitment to formal ethical standards that is his calling card, Ford imagined that he could hand over protected lands to profit-hungry developers and, in doing so, he ignited a firestorm of opposition. As the details of his dubious methods came out in the open, his wretched and panicked retreat drove home how ill-suited he would be in dealing with a determined and powerful social mobilization.

Class Compromise

The most important confrontation that Ford has generated, and the one that offers the most significant lesson, is the fight he blundered his way into with Ontario's education workers, members of Canadian Union of Public Employees (CUPE) and its Ontario School Board Council of Unions (OSBCU). Fifty-five thousand workers, with the most pressing grievances, faced down an attempt to crush their union rights and took up a challenge to the Tories that sent shock waves through the province. All talk that the kind of mobilization that marked the Ontario Days of Action was now a thing of the past was suddenly put on hold. It seemed that a defiant, "illegal" strike by the education workers might unleash solidarity actions on the part of other public sector and even private sector workers. Massive support for this struggle within the general population was seen in the opinion polls. It had become a rallying cry and it was being heard. Ford and his cohorts were shaken and confused and a decisive challenge to their agenda — that could have initiated a major and wide-ranging struggle — was entirely possible. In this regard, the conclusions we draw on the education workers' fight are important in terms of charting the way forward for any challenge to Ford in the days ahead.

As I have previously written:

> The education workers fully expressed the pent-up sense of grievance among working class people. The education workers at the heart of this struggle include education assistants, librarians and custodians who are disproportionately women and people of colour. Both their standard of living and working conditions have been under attack for a considerable time. Between 2011 and 2021, they faced an effective wage cut of 10% and the recent inflationary crisis has dramatically worsened their situation.[16]

As these workers prepared for strike action, Ford glaringly displayed his lack of both judgement and tactical ability. He had simply assumed that he could bully his way through, and he went ahead and imposed the infamous *Keeping Students in Class Act* to take away the right to strike and force a concessionary contract. When the response was defiant strike action and the very real prospect of sympathy actions by other unions, the Conservatives were temporarily in disarray. Their state of crisis was captured by one government official's admission to a reporter, "We didn't really think that they'll just say, 'We'll strike illegally.' We just didn't take that into account."[17]

With a dramatic escalation of the strike action impending, Ford offered to withdraw the legislation if picket lines came down and bargaining resumed. There has been disagreement whether the decision to take this offer was the correct thing to do and I'm certainly one who takes the view that it was a wrong turn. The momentum of the struggle and the level of support for it were formidable and the de-escalation that occurred certainly didn't lead to an agreement that reversed the losses of the education workers. As OSBCU president Laura Walton, in reluctantly accepting the compromise, said at the time:

> As a mom, I don't like this deal. As a worker, I don't like this deal. As the president of the OSBCU, I understand why this is the deal that's on the table. I think it falls short and I think it's terrible that we live in a world that doesn't see the need to provide services to kids that they need.[18]

I place such emphasis on the education workers' strike because, in my view, it points to an unresolved dilemma that plagued the struggle against Mike Harris in the 1990s and that remains before us in the present context: "Since the post-war years, union struggles have played out, for the most part, within the confines of state-enforced class compromise. In return for recognition and systems of bargaining, workers' struggles have been severely limited and compartmentalized inside collective agreements."[19]

The Days of Action, and decades later, the brief moment of defiance that marked the education workers' resistance, posed the possibility of breaking out of these confines. In both cases, however, the readiness to take the struggle where it needed to go was lacking. In the confrontation with Ford, he haplessly overplayed his hand and created a situation where defiance was the only alternative to a crushing defeat and deep humiliation. Once the offending legislation was withdrawn, however, a readiness to return to "the confines of state-enforced class compromise" took over. I believe that, as we consider the struggle against the Ford Tories that lies ahead, those confines are the key problem that must be grappled with.

The Struggle Ahead

The Ford regime seeks to advance a regressive agenda that is a long-standing work in progress, and it does so under social and economic conditions that are marked by uncertainty and volatility. A recent IMF blog post notes, "The world economy faces a sobering reality. The global growth rate — stripped of cyclical ups and downs — has slowed steadily since the 2008–09 global financial crisis." It suggests that a restoration of stability and robust growth rests on "policy intervention" and insists that "the key drivers of economic growth include labour, capital, and how efficiently these two resources are used, a concept known as total factor productivity."[20]

Though the IMF is far too circumspect to blurt out such a jarring truth, the measures it is proposing are a continuation and intensification of the goal of increasing the level of exploitation of working-class people that has been at work since the 1970s. We should fully understand by now what the "more efficient" use of labour is all about and, just as surely, appreciate the kind of "policy interventions" this entails on the part of governments. Doubtless, the Doug Ford Conservatives will continue to pursue these very goals relentlessly and the need to challenge and defeat their efforts is a pressing one.

There is copious evidence to support the conclusion that workers and communities in Ontario face a very dire threat to their living standards and to the social infrastructure they rely on. During the years I was involved in anti-poverty struggles, I frequently pointed out to trade union audiences that systems of income support were a key factor in determining the bargaining power of employed workers. If social assistance rates are driven down far below poverty levels, the ability of employers to resist wage demands or even to drive wages down is that much greater.

Today, the Ford government presides over a situation where social assistance rates have been reduced to levels of inadequacy that Mike Harris would never have dared to dream of. After the spending power of Ontario Disability Support Program benefits had already been devastated by the cost-of-living crisis, they were belatedly indexed to inflation, leaving those forced to try to survive on this program in deep poverty. The people on Ontario Works have had their benefits completely frozen since 2018, and are in an even more dreadful situation. A member of the

Toronto Underhoused and Homeless Union recently told the CBC, "It's like they're trying to wait you out until you give up, or you die on the street penniless."²¹ Such desperation among the poorest people is only the sharpest indication of how hard-pressed working-class people are at present.

In considering the factors that are intensifying the attacks we face, we most certainly can't leave out of our calculations the distinct possibility that the Conservatives might return to power at the federal level under the leadership of Pierre Poilievre. He is "an attack dog at the ready."²² He most assuredly represents the ascendency of the far-right elements within his party and, if he gains power, he will launch a major offensive against workers and communities that will also provide the Ontario Tories with very favourable conditions under which to take forward their own destructive agenda.

In the face of this situation, the mood of seething anger that is being generated cannot be underestimated. Indeed, the struggle of the education workers and the overwhelming support it drew behind it are indications that it is possible to go from a state of apparent demobilization to a powerful upsurge of social resistance very suddenly. As I write this chapter in the summer of 2024, the scale, momentum and determination of the resurgent Palestine solidarity movement have produced shock and dismay within the Canadian establishment. Yet, the establishment's efforts to intimidate it have not succeeded and major protests continue to take to the streets, week by week.²³ Obviously, the genocide unfolding in Gaza has generated a sense of crisis that has driven this movement, but the incremental pressure of austerity and social abandonment can also create breaking points that prompt people to act decisively. The question to consider is how to maximize the possibility of such developments.

Internationally, the present period is marked by upsurges of resistance that, as of yet, have failed to find the strategies and organizational forms that would enable them to prevail in the face of a higher level of intransigence on the part of those in power. We saw this with particular clarity during the struggle against French Prime Minister Emmanuel Macron's pension "reforms" in 2023. The largest social mobilization in that country since 1968 unfolded. However, though some union and social movement activists pressed for an escalation of the struggle, the movement remained at a level of massive shows of potential strength, rather than an attempt at taking indefinite strike action and unleashing a decisive confrontation. In this situation, Macron was able to proceed and his attack on the French pension system prevailed.[24]

Doug Ford is a far weaker and more erratic political player than Macron, but he also functions at a time when limited forms of struggle and efforts to obtain compromises are not likely to work. When the Days of Action came to Toronto, I recall well that a defiant Mike Harris registered his contempt by sneeringly characterizing the vast mobilization as a "good show." The question we face in 2024 is how do we move beyond forms of protest that indicate what we might be capable of to being able to fight back in a way that actually unleashes that potential strength? We have to bring together the unions, the social movements and the initiatives emerging within communities that are under attack and adopt the strategies and methods of resistance that are required in the present situation. We must break out of the rituals of class compromise and, as we used to say in OCAP, fight to win. The wretched and vicious government of Doug Ford provides both a pressing reason and a serious opportunity to take up such a struggle.

ENDNOTES

Chapter 1

1 See Stephen McBride and Bryan Evans (eds.), *The Austerity State* (Toronto: University of Toronto Press, 2017).
2 Murray Dobbin, *The Myth of the Good Corporate Citizen* (Toronto: Stoddart, 1998), 48.
3 Randall White, *Ontario 1610–1985: A Political and Economic History* (Toronto: Dundurn Press, 1985), 88.
4 Gerald Craig, *Upper Canada: The Formative Years, 1784–1841* (Toronto: McClelland and Stewart, 1963), 34.
5 White, *Ontario 1610–1985*, 93.
6 Aileen Durham, *Political Unrest in Upper Canada 1815–1836* (Toronto: McClelland and Stewart, 1963), 43.
7 For more information on this, see William Paul, Chapter 12, in this book.
8 See Mark Winfield's discussion of the Greenbelt in Chapter 13 of this book.
9 See Kathy Laird, Chapter 6, in this book.
10 Bryan Evans, "The Politics of Public Administration: Constructing the Neoliberal State," in *Canadian Political Economy*, ed. Heather Whiteside (Toronto: University of Toronto Press 2020).
11 Ministry of Treasury and Economics, *Ontario Budget* (Toronto: Queen's Printer, 1984).
12 Bryan Evans and Carlo Fanelli, "Ontario in an Age of Austerity: Common Sense Reloaded," in *The Public Sector in an Age of Austerity*, eds. Bryan Evans and Carlo Fanelli (Montreal and Kingston: McGill-Queen's University Press, 2018).
13 See Venai Raniga, Chapter 2, in this book.
14 For further discussion, see Tom McDowell, Chapter 14, in this book.
15 See Michael Hurley and Doug Allan, Chapter 7, in this book.
16 See Rachel Vickerson et al., Chapter 11, in this book.
17 See David Leadbeater, Chapter 5, in this book.
18 See Carlo Fanelli and Ryan Kelpin, Chapter 15, in this book.
19 See Carlo Fanelli and Kathy Nastovski, Chapter 8, in this book.
20 Keith Brooks, "Hot Air (and Other Gasses): A Review of the Past Four Years of Ontario's Climate Change (In)Action," *Environmental Defence*, May 2022. environmentaldefence.ca/report/ontario-climate-report-2022/.
21 FAO (Financial Accountability Office of Ontario), *2022–23 Interprovincial Budget Comparison: Comparing Ontario's Revenues, Spending, Budget Balance and Net Debt with Other Provinces* (King's Printer for Ontario, 2024). fao-on.org/web/default/files/publications/2022-23%20Interprovincial%20 Comparison/2022-23%20Interprovincial%20Comparison-EN.pdf.
22 Colin D'Mello and Isaac Callan, "'His Own Gravy Train': Cost of Staffing Doug Ford's Office More Than Double Kathleen Wynne's," *Global News*, April 2, 2024. globalnews.ca/news/10398355/ontario-premiers-office-salaries-doug-ford/.
23 See Lily Xia, Chapter 16, in this book.

24 See Leadbeater, Chapter 5.
25 Office of the Auditor General of Ontario, *2023 Annual Report* (Toronto: Office of the Auditor General of Ontario, 2023). auditor.on.ca/en/content/annualreports/arbyyear/ar2023.html?utm_source=sootoday.com&utm_campaign=sootoday.com%3A%20outbound&utm_medium=referral.
26 For more information, see Maria Rio, Chapter 9, in this book.
27 Angus Reid Institute, "Five-Year Decline: Canadians Growing More Critical of Their Provincial Governments as Unresolved Issues Linger," *Angus Reid Institute*, March 12, 2024. angusreid.org/provincial-government-performance-health-care-danielle-smith-eby-ford-legault/.
28 Sam Routley, "What Doug Ford's Shift to the Centre Says about the Longevity of Populism," *The Conversation*, May 10, 2022. theconversation.com/what-doug-fords-shift-to-the-centre-says-about-the-longevity-of-populism-182371; Steve Paikin, "Is Ontario's PC Party Too Moderate?" *TVO Today*, November 16, 2020. tvo.org/transcript/2635970; Andrew Coyne, "Neither a Conservative nor Quite a Populist, Doug Ford Isn't What Many Think," *National Post*, May 9, 2018. nationalpost.com/opinion/andrew-coyne-neither-a-conservative-nor-quite-a-populist-doug-ford-isnt-what-many-think; Jonathan Malloy, "Ontario Election: Doug Ford's Victory Shows He's Not the Polarizing Figure He Once Was," *The Conversation*, June 2, 2022. theconversation.com/ontario-election-doug-fords-victory-shows-hes-not-the-polarizing-figure-he-once-was-183885; Steve Paikin, "Here's How to Beat Doug Ford in the Next Election," *TVO Today*, July 29, 2024. tvo.org/article/heres-how-to-beat-doug-ford-in-the-next-election.
29 Mark P. Thomas, "For the People? Regulating Employment Standards in an Era of Right-Wing Populism." *Studies in Political Economy*, 101, 2 (2020):135–154. tandfonline.com/doi/full/10.1080/07078552.2020.1802834#d1e138; Peter Hillson and Mark Winfield, "Understanding the Political Durability of Doug Ford's Market Populism." *Studies in Political Economy* 105, 1 (2024): 69–93. tandfonline.com/doi/full/10.1080/07078552.2024.2325289.
30 John Richards, "Populism: A Qualified Defence." *Studies in Political Economy* 5, 1 (1981): 5–27. tandfonline.com/doi/abs/10.1080/19187033.1981.11675707.
31 R. Michael McGregor, Aaron A. Moore and Laura B. Stephenson, "Political Attitudes and Behaviour in a Non-Partisan Environment: Toronto 2014." *Canadian Journal of Political Science* 49, 2 (June 2016): 311–33. jstor.org/stable/24810785.
32 Simon Lewsen, "Populism Isn't Always Xenophobic. Just Ask Ontario's Premier," *Foreignpolicy.com*, July 14, 2020. foreignpolicy.com/2020/07/14/canada-ontario-populism-doug-ford/.
33 Quoted in Lewsen, "Populism Isn't Always Xenophobic."
34 Maura Forrest, "What Doug Ford's Blue-Collar Victory Means for Canada's Progressives," *Politico*, June 10, 2022. politico.com/news/2022/06/10/doug-ford-ontario-canada-progressives-00038502; Sabrina Nanji, "Why Doug Ford's Populist Politics are Resonating with Ontarians," *Toronto Star*, April 15, 2018. thestar.com/politics/provincial/why-doug-ford-s-populist-politics-are-resonating-with-ontarians/article_6616b5c2-cbd2-5e38-8508-7efdcc530e25.html.
35 Lewsen, "Populism Isn't Always Xenophobic."
36 Tamara Khandaker, "Why Doug Ford's Appeal Transcends Racial Lines" *Vice*,

May 28, 2018. vice.com/en/article/why-doug-fords-appeal-transcends-racial-lines/; Henry Olsen, "Doug Ford's Sweeping Win in Ontario Is a Model for Populist Republicans," *Washington Post*, June 3, 2022. washingtonpost.com/opinions/2022/06/03/doug-fords-sweeping-win-ontario-is-model-populist-republicans/.

37 See John Clarke, Chapter 17, in this book.

Chapter 2

1. United Nations Conference on Trade and Development, "Trade and Development Report 2023," *United Nations*, 2023. doi.org/10.18356/9789213584866c01.
2. Statistics Canada, "Gross Domestic Product, Expenditure-Based, Provincial and Territorial, Annual (x 1,000,000)," Table 36-10-0222-01. https://www150.statcan.gc.ca/t1/tbl1/en/tv.action?pid=3610022201.
3. International Monetary Fund (IMF), "World Economic Outlook Database," April 2024. imf.org/en/Publications/World-Economic-Outlook/Database/.
4. Finances of the Nation, "FON Macroeconomic Database," November 24, 2023. financesofthenation.ca/macro.
5. Vincent Hardy, "Defining and Measuring the Gig Economy Using Survey Data," *Statistics Canada*, March 4, 2024.
6. Mike Crawley, "Doug Ford's 'Red-Tape' Cuts Save Ontario Developers $400M a Year," *CBC News*, July 2, 2024. cbc.ca/news/canada/toronto/ontario-doug-ford-red-tape-reduction-savings-1.7249853.
7. For more information, see Mark Winfield, Chapter 13, in this book.
8. Ministry of Finance, "2023 Fall Statement: Taxation Transparency Report," Government of Ontario, November 2, 2023. budget.ontario.ca/2023/fallstatement/transparency.html.
9. Statistics Canada, "Gross Domestic Product (GDP) at Basic Prices, by Industry, Provinces and Territories (x 1,000,000)," Table 36-10-0402-01. doi.org/10.25318/3610040201-eng.
10. Organisation for Economic Co-operation and Development (OECD), *OECD Economic Surveys: Canada 2023* (Paris: OECD Publishing, 2023). doi.org/10.1787/7eb16f83-en.
11. OECD, *A Broken Social Elevator? How to Promote Social Mobility* (Paris: OECD Publishing, 2018). doi.org/10.1787/9789264301085-en.
12. Canada Mortgage and Housing Corporation, "Real Average Household Income (Before-Tax) by Tenure, 2006–2022," cmhc-schl.gc.ca/professionals/housing-markets-data-and-research/housing-data/data-tables/household-characteristics/real-average-total-household-income-before-taxes. Also, for more information, see William Paul, Chapter 12, in this book.
13. Statistics Canada, "Gini Coefficients of Adjusted Market, Total and After-Tax Income," Table 11-10-0134-01. doi.org/10.25318/1110013401-eng.
14. For further discussion of this matter, see Carlo Fanelli and Katherine Nastovski, Chapter 8, in this book.
15. Legislative Assembly of Ontario, *Bill 124: Protecting a Sustainable Public Sector for Future Generations Act*, 2019. www.ola.org/en/legislative-business/bills/parliament-42/session-1/bill-124. For further discussions on this matter, see Aylan Couchie, Chapter 3; Chris Chandler, Chapter 4; David Leadbeater,

Chapter 5; and Michael Hurley and Doug Allan, Chapter 7, in this book.
16 See Michael Hurley and Doug Allan, Chapter 7, in this book.
17 Allison Jones, "No Concern about 'Diminished Supply' of Doctors: Health Ministry," *CBC News,* May 8, 2024. cbc.ca/news/canada/toronto/doctors-ontario-medical-association-fees-1.7197475; Allison Jones, "Ontario Will Need Tens of Thousands of New Nurses, PSWs by 2032," *CBC News,* May 13, 2024. cbc.ca/news/canada/toronto/nurses-psws-ontario-foi-document-1.7202282.
18 Colin Craig, "Policy Brief: Died on a Waiting List," SecondStreet.org, December 2022. https://secondstreet.org/wp-content/uploads/2022/12/Policy-Brief-Died-on-a-Waiting-List-2022-Edition.pdf.
19 Statistics Canada, "Labour Force Characteristics by Sex and Detailed Age Group, Annual," Table 14-10-0327-01. doi.org/10.25318/1410032701-eng.
20 Tomoya Obokata, "Report of the Special Rapporteur on Contemporary Forms of Slavery, Including Its Causes and Consequences," *United Nations,* July 22, 2024. https://documents.un.org/doc/undoc/gen/g24/120/97/pdf/g2412097.pdf.
21 Ministry of Labour, "Employment Standards Enforcement Statistics," Government of Ontario. ontario.ca/document/your-guide-employment-standards-act-0/employment-standards-enforcement-statistics.
22 See Chris Chandler, Chapter 4, in this book.
23 See Collective Bargaining Ontario, Province of Ontario. lrs.labour.gov.on.ca/en/index.htm.
24 Angus Reid Institute, "Ontario Spotlight: Budget Deficit Adds to Ford Government's Challenges, as Criticism on Top Issues Mounts from All Sides," April 2, 2024, angusreid.org/ontario-spotlight-budget-deficit-april-2024/.
25 "Confederational Fairness: As Premiers Meet, Which Provinces Say They Get More, or Less, Out of Federation?" Angus Reid Institute, July 15, 2024. angusreid.org/confederational-fairness-premiers-meeting/.
26 See Lily Xia, Chapter 16, in this book.
27 Statistics Canada, "Consumer Price Index, Monthly, Not Seasonally Adjusted," Table 18-10-0004-01. doi.org/10.25318/1810000401-eng.
28 Bonnie Lysyk, "Special Report on Changes to the Greenbelt," *Auditor General of Ontario,* August 2023. auditor.on.ca/en/content/specialreports/specialreports/Greenbelt_en.pdf. Also, see William Paul, Chapter 12, in this book.
29 See Maria Rio, Chapter 9, in this book.
30 Statistics Canada, "Consumer Price Index."
31 Carolyn Stewart, "Ontarians Are Drowning Amid Surging Affordability Crisis," *Feed Ontario,* September 10, 2024. feedontario.ca/news/ontarians-are-drowning-amid-surging-affordability-crisis/.
32 Statistics Canada, "Canada's Labour Market: An Overview of Key Developments," (webinar), November 7, 2023. www.statcan.gc.ca/en/services/webinars/14220001.
33 Statistics Canada, "Employee Wages by Industry, Annual." doi.org/10.25318/1410006401-eng; Statistics Canada, "Consumer Price Index, Annual Average, Not Seasonally Adjusted." doi.org/10.25318/1810000501-eng.
34 Statistics Canada, "Income of Individuals by Age Group, Sex and Income Source, Canada, Provinces and Selected Census Metropolitan Areas," Table 11-10-0239-01. doi.org/10.25318/1110023901-eng; and author's calculation.
35 Advocacy Centre for Tenants Ontario, "A New Poll Shows the Majority of

Ontario Renters Are Having to Choose between Food and Paying Their Rents. When It Comes to Housing Affordability, This Province Is on Fire," May 30, 2022. acto.ca/a-new-poll-shows-the-majority-of-ontario-renters-are-having-to-choose-between-food-and-paying-their-rents-when-it-comes-to-housing-affordability-this-province-is-on-fire/.

36   Government of Ontario, "Building a Better Ontario 2024 Ontario Budget," *Ontario Budget*, March 26, 2024. https://budget.ontario.ca/2024/pdf/2024-ontario-budget-en.pdf.

37   Government of Ontario, "2024 Ontario Economic Outlook and Fiscal Review: Building Ontario for You," *Ontario Fall Economic Statement*, October 30, 2024. https://budget.ontario.ca/2024/fallstatement/pdf/2024-fall-statement-en.pdf.

38   Bonnie Lysyk, "Review of the Pre-Election 2022 Multi-Year Fiscal Plan," *Auditor General of Ontario*, May 2022. www.auditor.on.ca/en/content/specialreports/specialreports/Pre-Election-2022_EN.pdf.

39   Yefei Zhang and Nicolas Rhodes, "2022–23 Interprovincial Budget Comparison," *Financial Accountability Office*, April 10, 2024. fao-on.org/en/Blog/Publications/interprovincial-comparison-2024.

40   Sources for Figure 2-4 Sector Spending Table are: Statistics Canada Tables 18-10-0005-01, 17-10-0057-01, 17-10-0009-01, *2024 Ontario Budget*; and author's calculations.

41   Sabrina Afroz et al., "Provincial Infrastructure," Financial Accountability Office, November 26, 2020. fao-on.org/en/Blog/Publications/provincial-infrastructure-2020.

42   Matti Siemiatycki, "Public-Private Partnerships: Is a Reassessment Underway?" Ontario 360, November 2023. www.on360.ca/policy-papers/public-private-partnerships-is-a-reassessment-underway.

43   Government of Ontario, "Public Accounts of Ontario: Past Editions," September 28, 2015. ontario.ca/page/public-accounts-ontario-past-editions.

44   Colin D'Mello and Isaac Callan, "'His Own Gravy Train': Cost of Staffing Doug Ford's Office More Than Double Kathleen Wynne's," *CBC News*, April 02, 2024. globalnews.ca/news/10398355/ontario-premiers-office-salaries-doug-ford/; Colin D'Mello and Isaac Callan, "Cost of Doug Ford's Cabinet, Parliamentary Assistants Exceeds $10M," *CBC News*, June 10, 2024. globalnews.ca/news/10557934/doug-ford-cabinet-cost-increase-2024.

45   Trevor Tombe, "DeepDive: What a Pro-Growth Tax Reform Might Look Like," *The Hub*, June 24, 2024. thehub.ca/2024/06/24/deepdive-what-a-pro-growth-tax-reform-might-look-like/.

46   Tombe, "DeepDive."

47   Finances of the Nation, "Statutory Tax Rates," with Canadian Tax Federation (website). https://financesofthenation.ca/statutory-tax-rates/.

48   Government of Ontario, "2023 Fall Statement: Taxation Transparency Report," *Ontario Budget*, November 2, 2023. https://budget.ontario.ca/2023/fallstatement/transparency.html.

49   Government of Ontario, "Annex: Details of Tax Measures and Other Legislative Initiatives," *Ontario Budget*, March 26, 2024. https://budget.ontario.ca/2024/annex.html.

50   See John Clarke's discussion in Chapter 17 of this book.

Chapter 3

1. "OAC Celebrates Government's Increased Investment in Ontario's Professional Artists and Arts Organizations," Ontario Arts Council, September 8, 2017. arts.on.ca/news-resources/news/2017/oac-celebrates-government%E2%80%99s-increased-investment-i.
2. Codi Wilson, "MPP Calls on Ford Gov't to Reverse Cuts to After-School Program for At-Risk Youth," *CP24*, August 23, 2018. cp24.com/news/mpp-calls-on-ford-gov-t-to-reverse-cuts-to-after-school-program-for-at-risk-youth-1.4064919. Also, see Maria Rio, Chapter 9, for further discussion.
3. David Shum, "Ford Government Cuts Funding to Ontario Arts Council, Impacting Indigenous Culture Fund," *Global News*, December 14, 2018. globalnews.ca/news/4762100/ontario-arts-council-cuts/.
4. Steph Wechsler, "Ford Guts Grant to Help Further Truth and Reconciliation," *Canada's National Observer*, December 14, 2018. nationalobserver.com/2018/12/14/news/ford-guts-grant-help-further-truth-and-reconciliation.
5. See Venai Raniga, Chapter 2, for more discussion of this matter.
6. Jason Samilski, "2024 Ontario Budget Consultations," *CARFAC Ontario News* (blog), January 24, 2024. carfacontarionews.ca/2024/01/24/2024-ontario-budget-consultations/.
7. "Impact of the Arts in Ontario," Ontario Arts Council (website), accessed April 30, 2024. arts.on.ca/research-impact/impact-of-the-arts-in-ontario.
8. "Arts and Quality of Life for Ontarians," Ontario Arts Council, accessed October 10, 2023. arts.on.ca/research-impact/research-publications/arts-and-quality-of-life-for-ontarians.
9. "Indigenous Culture Fund," Ontario Arts Council, accessed April 30, 2024. arts.on.ca/grants/activity/discontinued/indigenous-culture-fund.
10. Allison Jones, "Ontario Government Eliminates Indigenous Culture Fund, Cuts Millions for the Arts," *Global News*, May 26, 2019. globalnews.ca/news/5318198/ontario-indigenous-culture-fund/.
11. Allison Jones, "Ontario Cuts Tourism Funding, Eliminates Money to Toronto and Ottawa," *CTV News*, May 7, 2019. ctvnews.ca/canada/ontario-cuts-tourism-funding-eliminates-money-to-toronto-and-ottawa-1.4412361.
12. Allison Jones, "Ford Government Cuts Music Fund by More than Half, Looks to Modernize It," *Global News*, April 28, 2019. globalnews.ca/news/5213750/ontario-cuts-music-fund-in-half/.
13. Music Canada, "Ontario Music Fund an Important Investment in Job Creation in Ontario's Music Industry," *Newswire*, May 1, 2013. newswire.ca/news-releases/ontario-music-fund-an-important-investment-in-job-creation-in-ontarios-music-industry-512355301.html.
14. "Making the Ontario Music Fund Permanent," Province of Ontario, June 17, 2015. news.ontario.ca/en/release/33241/making-the-ontario-music-fund-permanent.
15. Lisa Polewski, "Hamilton's Music Industry Braces for Impacts after Ontario Music Fund Cut in Half," *Global News*, May 1, 2019. globalnews.ca/news/5227851/hamiltons-music-industry-braces-for-impacts-after-ontario-music-fund-cut-in-half/.
16. "Celebrate Ontario," *MentorWorks* (website), accessed April 30, 2024. mentorworks.ca/government-funding/business-expansion/celebrate-ontario/.

17 "Experience Ontario 2024 Program," *MentorWorks* (website), accessed April 10, 2024. mentorworks.ca/government-funding/capital-investment/experience-ontario-2024/.
18 Adam Carter, "Province Slashing Millions in Celebrate Ontario Tourism Funding," *CBC News*, June 10, 2019. cbc.ca/news/canada/hamilton/celebrate-ontario-cuts-1.5169783.
19 Carter, "Province Slashing Millions."
20 CARFAC Ontario, "2024 Ontario Budget." https://carfacontarionews.ca.
21 Josh O'Kane, "Ford Government to Drop $5-Million One-Time Arts Grants but Maintain Ontario Arts Council Base Funding," *Globe and Mail*, March 17, 2023. theglobeandmail.com/arts/article-ford-government-to-drop-5-million-in-one-time-arts-grants-in-budget/.
22 Greg McGrath-Goudie, "'A Real Surprise': Province Slashes Over $100K in Orillia Mariposa Funding," *North Bay News*, July 31, 2023. baytoday.ca/local-news/a-real-surprise-province-slashes-over-100k-in-orillia-mariposa-funding-7348216.
23 Aya Dufour, "Sudbury's Up Here Festival Loses a Fifth of Its Anticipated Funding 3 Weeks Before the Event," *CBC News*, July 31, 2023. cbc.ca/news/canada/sudbury/province-ontario-downtown-mural-live-music-grant-northern-1.6923569.
24 Chelsea Papineau and Amanda Hicks, "Province Fires Back at Sudbury Festival, Says Funding Application Was 'Incomplete,'" *Northern Ontario*, August 1, 2023. northernontario.ctvnews.ca/province-fires-back-at-sudbury-festival-says-funding-application-was-incomplete-1.6501972.
25 Papineau and Hicks, "Province Fires Back."
26 Dufour, "Sudbury's Up Here Festival Loses."
27 Don Mitchell, "Ontario's Supercrawl to Absorb Shortfalls in Funding amid Increasing Demand for Government Grants," *Global News*, August 23, 2023. globalnews.ca/news/9913751/ontario-supercrawl-absorb-shortfalls-funding/.
28 Mitchell, "Ontario's Supercrawl to Absorb Shortfalls."
29 Joshua Chong, "What's Going on in Toronto's Arts Scene? Inside the Crisis Closing Festivals and Arts Organizations Left, Right and Centre," *Toronto Star*, April 13, 2024. thestar.com/entertainment/visual-arts/whats-going-on-in-torontos-arts-scene-inside-the-crisis-closing-festivals-and-arts-organizations/article_a328aaf8-f5aa-11ee-aad3-33ecca95b947.html
30 Joshua Chong, "Is Toronto's Theatre Sector on the Brink of a Crisis?" *Toronto Star*, January 28, 2024. thestar.com/entertainment/stage/two-years-after-reopening-from-the-pandemic-is-torontos-theatre-sector-on-the-brink-of/article_ddd67684-b96f-11ee-9b46-23fbacfbe665.html.
31 Isabel Teotonio, "Province Pulls $20M in Funding from OCAD University Expansion," *Toronto Star*, April 16, 2019. thestar.com/news/gta/province-pulls-20m-in-funding-from-ocad-university-expansion/article_dd636eaf-ec36-5688-bde7-04b6c63af36a.html. For further discussion, see David Leadbeater, Chapter 5, in this book.
32 Teotonio, "Province Pulls $20M."
33 Photograph taken by Aylan Couchie.
34 For instance, see discussions of Bill 124 in Chapters 2, 5 and 8 and of this book.

35 *Ontario English Catholic Teachers Assoc. v. His Majesty,* 2022, ONSC 6658, No. ONSC 6658 (Ontario Superior Court of Justice November 29, 2022). ona.org/wp-content/uploads/ontario-english-catholic-teachers-association-et-al.-v.-his-majesty-the-king-in-right-of-ontario-november-29-2022.pdf.

36 Allison Jones and Liam Casey, "Ontario to Repeal Wage-Cap Law," *CTV News,* February 12, 2024. toronto.ctvnews.ca/ontario-to-repeal-wage-cap-law-hours-after-loss-in-appeal-court-1.6764940. See also Carlo Fanelli and Kathy Nastovski's Chapter 8 in this book for more information regarding this matter.

37 Min Sook Lee and Julian Higuerey Nunez, "Bill 124 Has Been Ruled Unconstitutional, OCAD U Administration Needs to Pay Fair Wages," OCADFA, March 30, 2023. ocadfa.ca/blog/2023/03/30/bill-124-has-been-ruled-unconstitutional-ocad-u-administration-needs-to-pay-fair-wages/. Also, see Leadbeater, Chapter 5 in this book.

Chapter 4

1 Meagan Fitzpatrick, "Who is Tanya Granic Allen, The Kingmaker in the Ont. PC Leadership Race, and What's Next for Her?" *CBC News*, March 14, 2018. cbc.ca/news/canada/toronto/who-is-tanya-granic-allen-the-kingmaker-in-the-ont-pc-leadership-race-and-what-s-next-for-her-1.4574500.

2 Patrick Brown, "My Sex-Ed Letter Was a Mistake," *Toronto Star*, August 19, 2016. thestar.com/opinion/contributors/my-sex-ed-letter-was-a-mistake-patrick-brown/article_e17faddc-961d-51ab-9495-c423f6d8b1c4.html.

3 Joanne Laucius, "The New Ontario Sex Ed Curriculum Will Be Much like the Old," *Ottawa Citizen*, August 22, 2019. ottawacitizen.com/news/local-news/almost-all-sides-declare-ontarios-new-sex-ed-curriculum-a-victory.

4 Katherine DeClerq, "'Parents Must Be Fully Involved' in Student's Decision to Change Pronouns, Ontario Education Minister Says," *CTV News*, August 28, 2023. toronto.ctvnews.ca/parents-must-be-fully-involved-in-student-s-decision-to-change-pronouns-ontario-education-minister-says-1.6537959.

5 See Dayna Nadine Scott and Dania Ahmed, Chapter 10, in this book.

6 Shree Paradkar, "PCs Show Just What They Consider Essential by Cutting Indigenous Curriculum Writing Courses," *Toronto Star*, July 9, 2018. thestar.com/opinion/star-columnists/pcs-show-just-what-they-consider-essential-by-cutting-indigenous-curriculum-writing-courses/article_c315e990-17e2-51d8-b09d-fb969b0a4d55.html.

7 See Venai Raniga, Chapter 2, in this book.

8 Allison Jones, "Ontario Elementary Students' Math Scores Decline on EQAO Test," *The Canadian Press*, August 28, 2019. globalnews.ca/news/5824003/ontario-elementary-students-math-scores-eqao-test/.

9 Ontario Education Quality and Accountability Office, *Literature Review of the Empirical Evidence on the Connection Between Compulsory Teacher Competency Testing and Student Outcomes*, August 2019, 6–9. https://peopleforeducation.ca/wp-content/uploads/2021/05/EQAO-Literature-Review-Math-Qualifying-Test.pdf.

10 *Ontario Teacher Candidates' Council v. The Queen*, 2021 ONSC 7386 (CanLII), [24-35].

11 *Ontario Teacher Candidates' Council v. The Queen*, 2021 ONSC 7386 (CanLII), [5].
12 *Ontario Teacher Candidates' Council v. Ontario (Education)*, 2023 ONCA 788 (CanLII), [11].
13 Maham Abedi and Jessica Patton, "Doug Ford Says 'Discovery Math' is Hurting Ontario Students' Grades. Should It Be Scrapped?" *Global News*, May 10, 2018. globalnews.ca/news/4200010/doug-ford-discovery-math-ontario-election/.
14 Ontario Ministry of Education, "Statement by Education Minister on EQAO Results," Government of Ontario, August 29, 2018. news.ontario.ca/en/statement/49942/statement-by-education-minister-on-eqao-results.
15 Kristin Rushowy, "Ford Government Bans Cellphones from Classrooms for Noneducational Purposes," *Toronto Star*, March 12, 2019. thestar.com/politics/provincial/ford-government-bans-cellphones-from-classrooms-for-noneducational-purposes/article_38433187-e6f9-5255-a7f3-5c893038e876.html. Also, see Breanna Marcelo, "'Good Luck Enforcing That': Ontario Is Restricting Cell Phones and Vaping in Schools — Some Canadians are Doubtful It's Going to Work," *NOW Toronto*, April 29, 2024. nowtoronto.com/news/good-luck-enforcing-that-ontario-is-restricting-cell-phones-and-vaping-in-schools-some-canadians-are-doubtful-its-going-to-work/.
16 Office of the Premier of Ontario, "Ontario Introduces New Math Curriculum for Elementary Students," Government of Ontario, June 23, 2020. news.ontario.ca/en/release/57343/ontario-introduces-new-math-curriculum-for-elementary-students.
17 Jennifer Holm and Ann Kajander, "Ontario Math Has Always Covered 'The Basics,'" *The Conversation*, May 2, 2019. theconversation.com/ontario-math-has-always-covered-the-basics-115445.
18 Mike Crawley, "How Ontario's New Math Curriculum Goes Way Beyond Back-To-Basics," *CBC News*, June 27, 2020. cbc.ca/news/canada/toronto/ontario-elementary-math-curriculum-back-to-basics-1.5625289.
19 Ontario Ministry of Education, "Province Introduces New High School Graduation Requirements for a Stronger Ontario Diploma," Province of Ontario, May 30, 2024. news.ontario.ca/en/release/1004651/province-introduces-new-high-school-graduation-requirements-for-a-stronger-ontario-diploma.
20 See Carlo Fanelli and Katherine Nastovski, Chapter 8, in this book.
21 Organisation for Economic Co-operation and Development (OECD), *PISA 2015 Results (Volume IV): Students' Financial Literacy* (Paris: OECD Publishing, 2017), 30. oecd-ilibrary.org/education/pisa-2015-results-volume-iv_9789264270282-en. See also: OECD, *PISA 2022 Results (Volume IV): How Financially Smart Are Students?* (Paris: OECD Publishing, 2024), 20. oecd.org/en/publications/pisa-2022-results-volume-iv_5a849c2a-en.html.
22 Leora Klapper, Annamaria Lusardi and Peter van Oudheusden, *Financial Literacy Around the World: Insights from the Standard & Poor's Ratings Services Global Financial Literacy Survey* (Global Financial Literacy Excellence Center, 2015), 7. https://gflec.org/wp-content/uploads/2015/11/Finlit_paper_16_F2_singles.pdf.
23 See Lily Xia, Chapter 16, in this book.
24 Carolyn King, "The Cost of Credentials: The Shifting Burden of

Post-Secondary Education in Canada," Royal Bank of Canada (website), June 18, 2018. https://thoughtleadership.rbc.com/the-cost-of-credentials-the-shifting-burden-of-post-secondary-education-in-canada/.

25   Aloysius Wong, "How Student Loans Keep Some People Trapped in Debt," *CBC News,* June 18, 2023. cbc.ca/news/business/student-loans-debt-trap-1.6877888.
26   See David Leadbeater, Chapter 5, of this book.
27   Ontario Ministry of Education, "Province Introduces New High School Graduation Requirements for a Stronger Ontario Diploma," Province of Ontario, May 30, 2024. news.ontario.ca/en/release/1004651/province-introduces-new-high-school-graduation-requirements-for-a-stronger-ontario-diploma.
28   Yael Ginsler, "New Business Studies Courses: Building the Entrepreneurial Mindset, Grade 9, Open (BEM1O) and Launching and Leading a Business, Grade 10, Open (BEP2O)," Assistant Deputy Minister of Education, Memorandum to Directors of Education, July 2, 2024.
29   Jennifer Lewington, "Yes, You Will Get a Job with That Arts Degree," *Maclean's,* November 15, 2022. education.macleans.ca/getting-a-job/yes-you-will-get-a-job-with-that-arts-degree/.
30   Ricardo Tranjan, "Ontario's Core Education Funding Has Dropped by $1,500 per Student Since 2018," *The Monitor,* May 3, 2024. monitormag.ca/articles/ontarios-core-education-funding-has-dropped-by-1-500-per-student-since-2018/.
31   See Venai Raniga, Chapter 2, of this book.
32   Ricardo Tranjan, "Ontario Has Lost 5,000 Classroom Educators Since 2018," *The Monitor,* April 29, 2024. monitormag.ca/articles/ontario-has-lost-5-000-classroom-educators-since-2018/.
33   Colin D'Mello, "Ford Government Backs Down on High School Class Sizes, E-Learning Ahead of More Ont. Teacher Strikes," *CTV News,* March 3, 2020. toronto.ctvnews.ca/ford-government-backs-down-on-high-school-class-sizes-e-learning-ahead-of-more-ont-teacher-strikes-1.4837046.
34   "Ontario Government Cancels $100M School Repair Fund," *CBC News,* July 10, 2018. cbc.ca/news/canada/toronto/ontario-government-cancels-100m-school-repair-fund-1.4740271.
35   "End of Ontario Green School Repair Fund Costs Ottawa Board $5M," *CBC News,* July 11, 2018. cbc.ca/news/canada/ottawa/greenhouse-gas-reduction-fund-ottawa-schools-1.4741736.
36   Treasury Board Secretariat, *Public Accounts of Ontario: Annual Report and Consolidated Financial Statements 2018–2019* (Toronto: Queen's Printer for Ontario), 11. https://files.ontario.ca/tbs-annual-report-and-consolidated-financial-statements-2018-19-en.pdf.
37   "Ontario Government Cancels $100M."
38   Kristin Rushowy, "Repair Backlog in Ontario Schools Hits $16.3 Billion," *Toronto Star,* November 6, 2019. thestar.com/politics/provincial/repair-backlog-in-ontario-schools-hits-16-3-billion/article_29d2809a-470a-503e-aa79-9688795b11c2.html.
39   Vanessa Balintec, "Ontario Needs to Tackle $16.8B School Repair Backlog: Advocates," *CBC News,* May 29, 2024. cbc.ca/news/canada/toronto/school-repair-backlog-2024-1.7218105.

40 "End of Ontario Green School Repair Fund."
41 See the work, for example, of Hugh Mackenzie's *Education Funding in Ontario: How the Government Used Its New Funding Formula To Short-Change Our Children's Future* (Ontario Alternative Budget Working Group, 1998); and *Harris-Era Hangovers: Toronto School Trustees' Inherited Funding Shortfall* (Canadian Centre for Policy Alternatives, 2015). Also, see Dan Crow, "The Consequences of a Neoliberal Funding Formula: Time to Tear It Up and Start Again," *Our Schools/Our Selves* (Winter 2018): 21–25.
42 John Ibbitson, "Why Tories Backtracked on Private School Tax Credit," *Globe and Mail*, August 19, 2019. theglobeandmail.com/politics/article-why-tories-backtracked-on-private-school-tax-credit/.
43 Katherine DeClerq, "Ontario Gave Parents More Than $1B In Cash Over 2 Years. Here's Where the Money Went," *CTV News*, June 1, 2024. toronto.ctvnews.ca/ontario-gave-parents-more-than-1b-in-cash-over-2-years-here-s-where-the-money-went-1.6909148.
44 Ombudsman Ontario, "Ombudsman to Investigate Direct Education Payment Programs," December 11, 2023. ombudsman.on.ca/resources/news/press-releases/2023/ombudsman-to-investigate-direct-education-payment-programs.
45 Joanna Lavoie, "Decades of Neglect: Toronto MPP Calls out Education Minister over Flooding at West-End School," *CP24*, May 29, 2024. cp24.com/news/decades-of-neglect-toronto-mpp-calls-out-education-minister-over-flooding-at-west-end-school-1.6905554.
46 "Staff Shortages a Daily Issue for Many Ontario Schools," *People for Education*, March 24, 2024. peopleforeducation.ca/our-work/staff-shortages-a-daily-issue-for-many-ontario-schools/.
47 Caryn Ceolin, "Concerns over Classroom Violence Remain Top Issue for Ontario Teachers," CityNews, September 19, 2023. toronto.citynews.ca/2023/09/19/concerns-over-classroom-violence-remains-top-issue-for-ontario-teachers/.

Chapter 5

1 I was one of over two hundred Laurentian University faculty and staff who were terminated during the Laurentian University Board's CCAA process. Unless otherwise noted, the data in this chapter are from: David Leadbeater, "Laurentian University Insolvency Reflects a Structural Crisis in Ontario's Neoliberal University System," *The Monitor*, June 10, 2021; and David Leadbeater and Caitlin K. Kiernan, *Decline and Crisis in Ontario's Northern Universities and Arts Education* (Ottawa: Canadian Centre for Policy Alternatives, 2021).
2 Ministry of Training, Colleges, and Universities, "Government for the People to Lower Student Tuition Burden by 10 Per Cent," Government of Ontario, January 17, 2019. news.ontario.ca/en/release/50954/government-for-the-people-to-lower-student-tuition-burden-by-10-per-cent.
3 Moira MacDonald, "Niagara Falls Bets on a New Private University for Economic Growth," *University Affairs*, January 23, 2023.
4 See Chapter 3 of Ontario Ministry of Colleges and Universities, "Ensuring Financial Sustainability for Ontario's Postsecondary Sector," Blue-Ribbon Panel on Postsecondary Education Financial Sustainability, Province of Ontario, 2023.

5   Leadbeater and Kiernan, *Decline and Crisis*, 7.
6   Leadbeater and Kiernan, *Decline and Crisis*, 24–7; and 56–8.
7   It needs noting that not all tuition fees were frozen, nor were incidental fees and direct educational costs, such as textbooks. Generally, costs can vary by program and institution. Some students pay more or less in institutional costs, and for certain situations, such as for international students, students might pay more than the cost of provision. Further, cuts to the costs or quality of education services can also mean, given a fixed tuition, that the private share increases.
8   The chair of Ford's 2023 blue-ribbon panel, Dr. Alan Harrison, in an extended self-dissent to his report, openly proposed deregulation of fees for the University of Toronto.
9   Ron Srigley, "The Fix: Inside Laurentian University's Demise," *Canadian Dimension*, December 10, 2021; Reuben Roth, "The Shock Doctrine Comes to Canada: Laurentian University's Insolvency Claim and the Neoliberal Tide." *Critical Sociology* 47, 7/8 (2021): 1147–57. doi.org/10.1177/08969205211046.
10 Tricultural Committee for University Education at Sudbury, "N'Swakamok Reconciliation Declaration," September 7, 2021. https://1012sondages.qualtrics.com/CP/File.php?F=F_1NZWmtxU2TrWy8u
11 Alex Usher, "Laurentian (Really the Last This Time)," Higher Education Strategy Associates November 30, 2022. higheredstrategy.com/laurentian-really-the-last-this-time/.
12 The CCAA is corporate bankruptcy legislation dating from the Great Depression of the 1930s. No participant, including the Ontario Confederation of Faculty Associations (OCUFA), appealed the applying of the CCAA to a public university.
13 Auditor General of Ontario, "Special Report on Laurentian University," Office of the Auditor General of Ontario, November, 2022. auditor.on.ca/en/content/specialreports/specialreports/LaurentianUniversity_EN.pdf.
14 Auditor General, 9.
15 This statement was taken from Jill Dunlop's LinkedIn profile page. See: linkedin.com/in/jill-dunlop/.
16 Auditor General, See section 10.
17 Auditor General, 57.
18 Mike Crawley, "Ford Government Stopping University, College Profs from 'Double-Dipping.'" *CBC News*, April 16, 2019. cbc.ca/news/canada/toronto/doug-ford-university-college-faculty-pension-salary-1.5098929.
19 David Leadbeater, "Northern Ontario and the Crisis of Development and Democracy," in *Divided Province: Ontario Politics in the Age of Neoliberalism*, eds. Greg Albo and Bryan M. Evans (Montreal: McGill-Queen's University Press, 2018).
20 Srigley, "The Fix."
21 Under lower inflation assumptions than some would accept, Usher estimated the recommendation would make up for only the prior two years of losses. See Alex Usher, "What's in Ontario's Blue Ribbon Panel Report?" *Higher Education Strategy Associates*, November 20, 2023. higheredstrategy.com/whats-in-ontarios-blue-ribbon-panel-report/.
22 CBC News, "Ontario Boosts College and University Funding by More than $1.2B, Extends Freeze on Tuition Fees," February 26, 2024.

23 Council of Ontario Universities (COU), "Ontario's Response Falls Far Short of Blue-Ribbon Panel Recommendation." Ontario's Universities, February 26, 2024.
24 Ontario Federation of Labour (OFL), "The Time for Universal Post-Secondary Education Has Arrived: An Ontario Federation of Labour Toolkit," 2021. https://ofl.ca/ofl-toolkit-for-universal-post-secondary-education/.
25 Alex Usher, "Those Two New Laurentian Reports," *Higher Education Strategy Associates,* March 7, 2022. higheredstrategy.com/those-two-new-laurentian-reports/.
26 One insider on conditions of confidentiality characterized the process to me as a series of "gentlemen's agreements," "full of smoke and mirrors." However, the Ford Conservatives are proposing these agreements be weighted if not weaponized further with funding shifts.
27 Auditor General, 49.
28 Kristin Rushowy, "Almost Half of Ontario Universities Are Running Deficits, Putting Student Services at Risk, Council Says," *Toronto Star,* January 9, 2024. thestar.com/politics/provincial/almost-half-of-ontario-universities-are-running-deficits-putting-student-services-at-risk-council-says/article_639ebedc-af31-11ee-bdce-47e37d4e1808.html.
29 Rushowy, "Almost Half."
30 The COU in 2024 issued a statement noting the Ontario universities were "already at a breaking point." The COU was also at pains to claim concern for international students and that "Ontario's universities have been responsible players in the postsecondary sector, basing international student enrolment on the unique needs and labour market demands of institutions' communities." COU, "Response to Federal Announcement on International Student Cap," Ontario's Universities, January 22, 2024.

Chapter 6

1 See William Paul, Chapter 12, in this book.
2 Ontario Ombudsman, *Administrative Justice Delayed, Justice Denied,* May 2023, paragraphs 306–307. Also, see Lily Xia, Chapter 16.
3 *The Adjudicative Tribunals Accountability, Governance and Appointments Act, 2009.*
4 Tribunal Watch Ontario, *Statement of Concern about Tribunals Ontario,* May 14, 2020. https://tribunalwatch.ca/2020/statement-of-concern-about-tribunals-ontario/.
5 *Administrative Justice Delayed, Justice Denied,* paragraphs 306–309.
6 Legislative Assembly of Ontario, "Bill 179, Fewer Backlogs and Less Partisan Tribunals Act, 2024." ola.org/en/legislative-business/bills/parliament-43/session-1/bill-179.
7 Kate Schneider, "Ford under Fire as Opposition Condemns 'Political Meddling' in Tribunal Appointments Process," *Investigative Journalism Foundation,* October 12, 2023. theijf.org/ford-under-fire-as-opposition-condemns-political-meddling-in-tribunal-appointments-process.
8 See Tom McDowell, Chapter 14, in this book.
9 "No Turning Back: CBA Task Force Report on Justice Issues Arising from COVID-19," Canadian Bar Association, February 2021. cba.org/

Publications-Resources/Resources/2021/No-Turning-Back-CBA-Task-Force-Report-on-Justice

10 https://tribunalwatch.ca/2021/the-digital-transformation-at-tribunals-ontario-the-impact-on-access-to-justice/.
11 See Carlo Fanelli and Katherine Nastovski, Chapter 8, in this book.
12 Tribunals Ontario, "HRTO–Activity report: Decisions Issued," Open Data Inventory for 2022/23 and 2017/18. https://tribunalsontario.ca/en/open/data-inventory-reports/?x=0&n=5.
13 Frank Nasca, "Jurisdiction and Access to Justice: An Analysis of Human Rights Tribunal of Ontario-Issued Notices of Intent to Dismiss," *Canadian Journal of Administrative Law & Practice*, Vol. 35:3 (October 2022).
14 "1. An application that is within the jurisdiction of the Tribunal shall not be finally disposed of without affording the parties an opportunity to make oral submissions in accordance with the rules." See Human Rights Code, RSO 1990, s.43(2)1. ontario.ca/laws/statute/90h19/v11.
15 See Human Rights Tribunal of Ontario: https://www.canlii.org/en/on/onhrt/.
16 See Tribunals Ontario, "Governance Accountability Documents" at: tribunalsontario.ca/en/governance-accountability-documents/#annre.
17 See Tribunals Ontario, "Key Performance Indicators" at: tribunalsontario.ca/en/key-performance-indicators/hrto-key-performance-indicators/.
18 Tribunals Ontario, "HRTO–Activity report: Decisions Issued."
19 See Tribunals Ontario, *Annual Report 2022/23,* "Landlord and Tenant Board Operational Highlights." tribunalsontario.ca/documents/TO/Tribunals_Ontario_2022-2023_Annual_Report.html.
20 In January 2024, Tribunals Ontario told *CBC News* that the LTB now has 128 adjudicators — 70 full-time and 58 part-time. In 2018, there were approximately 53 adjudicators — 44 full-time and 9 part-time. www.cbc.ca/news/canada/toronto/landlord-tenant-cash-for-keys-1.7050393. For 2018 numbers, see Tribunal Watch Ontario: statement-of-concern-may-14.pdf (tribunalwatch.ca).
21 Isha Bhargava, "London, Ont., Landlord Fears Over $26K Lost Forever in Long Wait for Tenant Eviction Hearing," *CBC News*, March 6, 2024. cbc.ca/news/canada/london/london-landord-ltb-hearing-long-process-1.7133733.
22 See Tribunals Ontario Annual Reports and archived annual reports for the Social Justice Tribunal at: https://tribunalsontario.ca/en/governance-accountability-documents/#annre.
23 As of writing (August 2024), the most recent period for which Tribunals Ontario has published data on the time from application to order is the third quarter in 2022/23 — October 1, 2022 to December 31, 2022. See Tribunals Ontario Data Inventory - Open Data | Ontario's Open Data Directive at: https://tribunalsontario.ca/en/open/.
24 Ombudsman of Ontario, "Administrative Justice Delayed, Fairness Denied," Office of the Ombudsman of Ontario. May 4, 2023, para. 148. ombudsman.on.ca/resources/reports,-cases-and-submissions/reports-on-investigations/2023/administrative-justice-delayed,-fairness-denied.
25 Source for Figure 6.1: Annual Reports on the Tribunals Ontario website (note: the 2023/24 Annual Report was not published at time of writing). See: tribunalsontario.ca.

26 "Administrative Justice Delayed, Fairness Denied," para 306–307.
27 For further information, see "Administrative Justice Delayed, Justice Denied," paragraphs 108, 198, 214, 215–20, 225–28.
28 Tribunals Ontario, "Key Performance Indicators."
29 For a fuller discussion of these issues, see Paul Daly, "Virtual Hearings at Administrative Tribunals — Another Perspective (Lesli Bisgould & Daniel McCabe)," Administrative Law Matters (blog), July 29, 2024. administrativelawmatters.com/blog/2024/07/29/virtual-hearings-at-administrative-tribunals-another-perspective-lesli-bisgould-daniel-mccabe/.
30 Advocacy Centre for Tenants Ontario, "The Landlord and Tenant Board is Broken. Going Digital Hasn't Fixed It, and It's Time to End the Experiment," May 9, 2022. acto.ca/the-landlord-and-tenant-board-is-broken-going-digital-hasnt-fixed-it-and-its-time-to-end-the-experiment/?highlight=in-person.
31 See restrictions to public participation introduced in the Accelerating Access to Justice Act, 2021 and the Cutting Red Tape to Build More Homes Act, 2024. For a discussion of patronage appointments and access to justice at the Ontario Land Tribunal, se Charlie Pinkerton and Jack Hauen, "The OLT Decides What Gets Built in Ontario. Insiders Say It's Broken," The Trillium, February 1, 2024. thetrillium.ca/news/the-trillium-investigations/the-olt-decides-what-gets-built-in-ontario-insiders-say-its-broken-8183941.

Chapter 7

1 Canadian Institute for Health Information (CIHI), National Health Expenditure Trends, 2023, data tables. Table D.1.6.1 Total health expenditure by use of funds in millions of current dollars, Ontario, 1975 to 2023.
2 Hospital disclosure in collective bargaining.
3 Ontario Legislature, Standing Committee of Public Accounts, Long-Term Care Facilities Activity (section 4.04, 2004 Annual Report of the Provincial Auditor), 2nd Session, 38th Parliament 54 Elizabeth II, 2005. Statistics Canada, Table 17-10-0005-01 Population estimates on July 1, by age and gender. See also Financial Accountability Office, "Long-Term Care Homes Program, Review of the Plan to Create 15,000 New Long-Term Care Beds in Ontario," 2019.
4 CIHI, National Health Expenditure Database, 2023. Provincial government per capita health expenditure by use of funds in current dollars, Ontario, 1975 to 2023. Nbex Full data tables 2023.
5 See Venai Raniga, Chapter 2, in this book.
6 CIHI, National Health Expenditure Database, 2023. "Provincial government per capita health expenditure by use of funds in current dollars, Ontario, 1975 to 2023"; "Provincial/territorial government health expenditure per capita by use of funds in current dollars, Canada, 1975 to 2023."
7 Since the 2023 CIHI forecast, public sector workers forced the government to abandon Bill 124 that slashed real wages for three years. Hospital workers won significant retroactive wage increases as a result and the government was required at the very end of 2023–24 to increase hospital funding. Hospital funding often falls short of interim plans, but if this funding is fully implemented, Ontario per capita hospital funding may reach the levels of the second lowest province in Canada.

8   Calculated from CIHI data on hospital full-time equivalent employees (FTEs) by service area, province/territory and Canada (excluding Quebec and Nunavut) 2021/22 and from Statistics Canada, second quarter, 2021 provincial population reports.
9   CIHI, Trends in Hospital Spending, 2009–2010 to 2021–2022 — Data Tables — Series E: Hospital Calculated Full-Time Equivalents by Service Area.
10 Calculated from hospital 2023 bed data and 2023 Statistics Canada population report.
11 Statistics Canada. Table 17-10-0005-01 Population estimates on July 1, by age and gender.
12 The figures for the rest of Canada are based on the latest Canada-wide data from CIHI data tables, "Number of Hospital Beds Staffed and In Operation: Breakdown by Care Setting, 2021–2022."
13 OECD, Hospital Beds, https://www.oecd.org/en/data/indicators/hospital-beds.html.
14 Statistics Canada. Table 17-10-0009-01 Population estimates, quarterly.
15 Demand pressures are likely greater as the oldest part of the 65+ age group is growing more rapidly. The 75+ age group grew 21 percent over the five-year period — 3.9 percent annually since 2018. According to the Ontario Ministry of Finance, this more rapid growth of the oldest part of the elderly population will continue. The first baby boomers turn 80 in 2025.
16 CIHI, COVID-19 hospitalization and emergency department statistics, June 2024.
17 Trisha Greenhalgh, et al., "Long Covid: A Clinical Update," *The Lancet*, July 21, 2024.
18 Financial Accountability Office, Ontario Health Sector: Spending Plan Review, March 8, 2023.
19 OMA, "Ontario's Doctors Warn of Worsening Health-Care Crisis Family Doctor Shortage Is Not Addressed Immediately," January 29, 2024.
20 It is notable that LTC operators report only 76,000 available beds as of January 2024 based on government data — a *decline* in the number of operating beds (78,000 were reported by the government in 2019).
    See: oltca.com/about-long-term-care/the-data/#:~:text=There%20are%20just%20over%2076%2C000,spaces%20are%20at%20full%20capacity.&text=Ontario%20needs%20over%2030%2C000%20new,to%20meet%20the%20growing%20demand.
21 Ontario Legislature, Standing Committee of Public Accounts, Long-Term Care Facilities Activity (section 4.04, 2004 Annual Report of the Provincial Auditor), 2nd Session, 38th Parliament 54 Elizabeth II, 2005. See pages 2 and 11.
22 For more on this, see Doug Allan's website, "Defend Public Health Care: Notes from Left Words," specifically the blog post, "The Long Series of Failures of Private Clinics in Ontario." https://ochuleftwords.blogspot.com/2015/09/the-long-series-of-failures-of-private.html.
23 See: brantfordexpositor.ca/2013/05/30/physio-delivery-changes-will-expand-access-says-minister.
24 Allan, "The Long Series of Failures."
25 CIHI, National Health Expenditure Trends, 2023, Table D.1.6.1 Total health

expenditure by use of funds in millions of current dollars, Ontario, 1975 to 2023, and Table D.2.6.1 Private-sector health expenditure by use of funds in millions of current dollars, Ontario, 1975 to 2023.
26 Ontario Health Coalition, "The Ford government lied to the public re. their privatization of public hospital services," October 26, 2022.
27 Robert J. Campbell, et al., "Public Funding for Private For-Profit Centres and Access to Cataract Surgery by Patient Socioeconomic Status: An Ontario Population-Based Study." *Canadian Medical Association Journal* 196, 28 (August 2024): 965–72. doi.org/10.1503/cmaj.240414.
28 Mike Crawley, "Doug Ford Government Paying For-Profit Clinic More than Hospitals for OHIP-Covered Surgeries, Documents Show." *CBC News*, November 15, 2023. cbc.ca/news/canada/toronto/ontario-doug-ford-private-clinic-surgeries-fees-hospitals-1.7026926.
29 Benjamin Goodair and Aaron Reeves, "Outsourcing Health-Care Services to the Private Sector and Treatable Mortality Rates in England, 2013–20: An Observational Study of NHS Privatization." *The Lancet Public Health* 7, 7 (2022): 638–46. doi: 10.1016/S2468-2667(22)00133-5.
30 Benjamin Goodair and Aaron Reeves, "The Effect of Health-Care Privatisation on the Quality of Care." *The Lancet Public Health* 9, 3 (March 2024): 199–206. doi: 10.1016/S2468-2667(24)00003-3.
31 Calculations from CIHI data table, "Provincial Hospital Spending by Type of Expense in Millions of Current Dollars, Ontario, 2005–2006 to 2021–2022." Also, see Chris Chandler, Chapter 4, in this book.
32 Ontario Health, Annual Report 2022/23, page 40. The data refers to March 2023.
33 FAO, Ontario Health Sector: Spending Plan Review, March 2023.
34 As of August 16, 2024.
35 FAO, Ontario Health Sector, Spending Plan Review, March 8, 2023. fao-on.org/en/Blog/Publications/health-2023.
36 Ontario, Long-Term Care Staffing Study, July 30, 2020.

Chapter 8

1 See David Leadbeater, Chapter 5, in this book.
2 Mark P. Thomas, "For the People? Regulating Employment Standards in an Era of Right-Wing Populism." *Studies in Political Economy* 101, 2 (September 2020): 135–55. tandfonline.com/doi/abs/10.1080/07078552.2020.1802834.
3 Bob Wood, "Contracting Out Employment Services in Ford's Ontario" *Canadian Dimension*, March 5, 2020. canadiandimension.com/articles/view/contracting-out-employment-services-in-fords-ontario; Press Progress, "Doug Ford is Privatizing Low-Income Employment Services. An American Firm Linked to Trump's Welfare Cuts Wants the Contract," *Press Progress*, October 27, 2021. pressprogress.ca/doug-ford-is-privatizing-low-income-employment-services-an-american-firm-linked-to-trumps-welfare-cuts-wants-the-contract/.
4 Workers' Action Centre and Parkdale Community Legal Services, "Restoring Ontario's Competitiveness Act (Bill 66): Submission to the Standing Committee on General Government," *Workers Action Centre,* March 2019. workersactioncentre.org/wp-content/uploads/2019/03/Bill-66-submission-WAC_PCLS-March-2019.pdf.

5   Bryan Evans, Carlo Fanelli, Leo Panitch and Donald Swartz, *From Consent to Coercion: The Continuing Assault on Labour* (Toronto: University of Toronto Press, 2023).
6   Sheila Block, "The Ontario Government's Anti-Work Agenda Targets Women," *ETFO Voice*, Summer 2023. etfovoice.ca/feature/ontario-governments-anti-work-agenda-targets-women; Ontario Nurses Association (ONA) "About Bill 124 and Actions," *ONA.org*. n.d. www.ona.org/about-bill-124/.
7   See Chris Chandler, Chapter 4, in this book.
8   See Carlo Fanelli and Ryan Kelpin, Chapter 15, in this book.
9   See Tom McDowell, Chapter 14, in this book.
10 Hermes Azam et al., "Canada: CUPE Workers Presented with Deal that "Badly Sucks" — Vote No!" *In Defence of Marxism*, November 22, 2022. marxist.com/canada-cupe-workers-presented-with-deal-that-badly-sucks-vote-no.htm.
11 Martin Lukacs and Emma Paling, "The Inside Story of How Education Workers Beat Back Doug Ford," *The Breach*, December 14, 2022. breachmedia.ca/the-inside-story-of-how-education-workers-beat-back-doug-ford/; Sam Gindin, "Education Workers Lead but Come Up Short: What Lessons For Labour?" *Canadian Dimension*, December 15, 2022. canadiandimension.com/articles/view/education-workers-lead-but-come-up-short-what-lessons-for-labour; David Mastracci, "Should CUPE Have Kept Education Workers ON Strike?" *The Maple*, November 9, 2022. readthemaple.com/should-cupe-have-kept-education-workers-on-strike/.
12 *Ontario Catholic Teachers Assoc. v. His Majesty, 2022,* ONSC 6658. Ontario Nurses Association. ona.org/wp-content/uploads/ontario-english-catholic-teachers-association-et-al.-v.-his-majesty-the-king-in-right-of-ontario-november-29-2022.pdf.
13 Isaac Callan and Colin D'Mello, "Ford Government Documents Admit Low Wages, Bill 124 Worsening Health Staffing Issues," *Global News*, January 9, 2023. globalnews.ca/news/9340310/health-care-ontario-bill-124-ford-government-documents/.Also, see Michael Hurley and Doug Allan, Chapter 7, in this book.
14 Court of Appeal for Ontario, *Ontario English Catholic Teachers Association v. Ontario (Attorney General)*. February 12, 2024. coadecisions.ontariocourts.ca/coa/coa/en/item/22091/index.do#_Toc158212607.
15 Without a hint of irony, in his dissenting opinion, Justice Hourigan noted that "the Province's determination to come to grips with spiraling costs was fueled by the laudable desire to preserve and protect quality public services." He even went so far as to identify "good examples" of collective bargaining — as when Ontario Public Service Employees Union members at the LCBO, recognizing the "economic crisis," chose to focus on non-monetary issues — unlike the bad examples of unions, presumably restricted by Bill 124. By 2024, OPSEU members at the LCBO would be singing an entirely different tune going on strike for the first time in the 97-year history of the Crown retailer.
16 Allison Jones, "Ontario Has to Pay Public Sector Workers $6B and Counting in Bill 124 Compensation," *CBC News*, March 15, 2024. cbc.ca/news/canada/toronto/bill124-compensation-ford-government-1.7144793.
17 See Venai Raniga, Chapter 2, in this book.
18 See Bryan Evans and Carlo Fanelli, Chapter 1, in this book.

19 David MacDonald, "Canadian CEO Pay Breaks All Records, Reflecting a New Gilded Age for Canada's Rich: Report," *Canadian Centre for Policy Alternatives*, January 2, 2024. policyalternatives.ca/newsroom/news-releases/canadian-ceo-pay-breaks-all-records-reflecting-new-gilded-age-canada%E2%80%99s-rich.

20 Silas Xuereb, "Profits Rise as Investment Stalls in Canada's Affordability Crisis," *Canadians for Tax Fairness*, June 2024. taxfairness.ca/sites/default/files/2024-06/c4tf-corporate-profits-report.pdf; Jim Stanford, "Canadian Corporate Profits Remain Elevated Despite Economic Slowdown," *Centre for Future Work*, February 2024. centreforfuturework.ca/wp-content/uploads/2024/02/Resilience-of-Profits-Canada-end-2023.pdf.

21 David Milstead, "As COVID-19 Wanes and Recession Lurks, Corporate Profits Boom," *Globe and Mail*, January 18, 2023. theglobeandmail.com/business/article-company-profit-margins-economic-conditions/.

22 Keldon Bester, "How the Big Five Banks are Quietly Squeezing Billions out of Canadians," *Corporate Knights*, June 12, 2024. corporateknights.com/category-finance/canada-big-five-banks-squeezing-billions/.

23 Rachel Lee, "Shrinkflation in Ontario: A Study," *Community Researchers*, n.d. communityresearchers.org/_files/ugd/8a61e8_738f52aca6d94488acd-2637c180ef73f.pdf .

24 Scott Schieman, et al., "Has Canada Become the Land of Extreme Inequality? Some Believe It More than Others," *Financial Post*, June 30, 2024. financialpost.com/personal-finance/canada-extreme-inequality.

25 Andy Takagi, "Hourly Wages Have Been Fairly Stagnant for Most Workers—Except CEOs and Senior Management, StatCan Data Shows," *Toronto Star*, November 22, 2023. thestar.com/business/hourly-wages-have-been-fairly-stagnant-for-most-workers-except-ceos-and-senior-management-statcan/article_0af55173-eb20-5518-bd57-96ec021c7012.html.

26 Statistics Canada, "Distributions of Household Economic Accounts for Income Consumption, Saving and wealth of Canadian Households, Fourth Quarter 2023," April 17, 2024. www150.statcan.gc.ca/n1/daily-quotidien/240417/dq240417b-eng.htm; Daniel Skilleter, "Billionaire Blindspot: How Official Data Understates the Severity of Canadian Wealth Inequality," *Social Capital Partners*, April 2024. https://static1.squarespace.com/static/5edfe6ed-26bc3e59001d42d7/t/660d936553bb3e4b2d8bbded/1712165735599/2024.04.04-SCP-Billionaire+Blindspot+-+FINAL.pdf.

27 Andrew Sharpe and James Ashwell, "The Evolution of the Productivity-Median Wage Gap in Canada, 1976-2019," *International Productivity Monitor*, 41 (October 2021); Takagi, "Hourly Wages Have Been Fairly Stagnant for Most Workers."

28 Scott Schieman, et al., "Has Canada Become the Land of Extreme Inequality?" and Marc Ercolao, "Canadian Wages: Unionized Workers Bargaining for Their Fair Share," *TD Economics*, November 23, 2023. economics.td.com/domains/economics.td.com/documents/reports/me/Canadian_Wages_Unionized_Workers_Bargain.pdf.

29 Mike Crawley, "Noticing a Labour Shortage? Here's What's Really Going on in Ontario's Job Market," *CBC News*, January 30, 2023. cbc.ca/news/canada/toronto/ontario-workers-shortage-1.6727310; see Mostafa Henaway, *Essential Work, Disposable Workers: Migration, Capitalism and Class* (Halifax and

Winnipeg: Fernwood Publishing, 2023).
30. See Mario Rio, Chapter 8, in this book.
31. Sara Mojtehedzadeh, "The Ontario Government Says It's Recouped Tens of Millions in Unpaid Wages for Workers. Internal Data Raises Questions About the Provinces Math," *Toronto Star*, August 5, 2023. thestar.com/news/gta/the-ontario-government-says-it-s-recouped-tens-of-millions-in-unpaid-wages-for-workers/article_6d1798a8-19a1-58b3-9b01-bfc53f8b8a25.html.
32. David Parkinson, "Wage Increases Aren't Automatically an Inflation Problem, Former Bank of Canada Boss Poloz Cautions." *Globe and Mail*, October 12, 2023. theglobeandmail.com/business/commentary/article-wage-increases-arent-automatically-an-inflation-problem-former-bank-of/.
33. Douglas Porter and Priscilla Thiagamoorthy, "Will Wages Be the New Inflation Driver?" *BMO Economics*, May 13, 2023. economics.bmo.com/en/publications/detail/035a8954-2e3c-4049-baf6-9dc04dfb3596/; see also: Patrick Perrier and Laura Gu, "Wage Growth—Canadian Inflation's Last Leg?" *ScotiaBank Insights and Views* (website), August 21, 2023. scotiabank.com/content/dam/scotiabank/sub-brands/scotiabank-economics/english/documents/insights-views/insightsandviews_2023-08-21.pdf.
34. The Canadian Pres (staff), "More than Seven in 10 Canadian Workers Want to Leave Their Jobs: Report," March 14, 2024. ctvnews.ca/business/more-than-seven-in-10-canadian-workers-want-to-leave-their-jobs-report-1.6807574.
35. See Lily Xia, Chapter 16, in this book, for further discussion of this issue.
36. See John Clarke, Chapter 17, in this book.
37. Economic and Social Development Canada, "Work Stoppages in Canada, by Jurisdiction and Industry Based on the North American Industry Classification System (NAICS), Employment and Social Development Canada–Labour Program Occasional," Table: 14-10-0352-01 (formerly CANSIM 278-0015), July 15, 2024. www150.statcan.gc.ca/t1/tbl1/en/tv.action?pid=1410035201.
38. See Mostafa Henaway, *Essential Work, Disposable Workers: Migration, Capitalism and Class* (Halifax and Winnipeg: Fernwood Publishing, 2023); Aziz Choudry and Adrian A. Smith (eds.), *Unfree Labour? Struggles of Migrant and Immigrant Workers in Canada* (PM Press, 2016).
39. Marc Lee and DT Cochrane, "Canada's Shift to a More Regressive Tax System, 2004 to 2022," *The Monitor*, April 30, 2024. monitormag.ca/reports/canadas-shift-to-a-more-regressive-tax-system-2004-to-2022/#:~:text=Between%20 2004%20and%202022%20the,tax%20rate%20became%20less%20progressive.

Chapter 9

1. See Carlo Fanelli and Katherine Nastovski, Chapter 8, in this book.
2. "Who's Hungry Report 2023: A Call to Action from a City in Crisis," Daily Bread Food Bank and North York Harvest Food Bank, November 2023. dailybread.ca/wp-content/uploads/2023/11/DB-WhosHungryReport-2023-Digital.pdf.
3. "Beyond the Shelf: How Grocers Decide What Gets Donated and What Gets Dumped," *CP24*, February 16, 2024. cp24.com/news/beyond-the-shelf-how-grocers-decide-what-gets-donated-and-what-gets-dumped-1.6771533.
4. Agriculture and Agri-Food Canada, "Food Policy for Canada," Government

of Canada, 2019. Priority Outcome 3: "Improved food-related health outcomes: Improved health status of Canadians related to food consumption and reduced burden of diet-related disease, particularly among groups at higher risk of food insecurity. The food that Canadians eat is a key determinant of their health and wellbeing," 6. https://agriculture.canada.ca/sites/default/files/legacy/pack/pdf/fpc_20190614-en.pdf.

5   Calculated from Samir Djidel, et al., "Report on the Second Comprehensive Review of the Market Basket Measure," Statistics Canada, February 24, 2020. www150.statcan.gc.ca/n1/pub/75f0002m/75f0002m2020002-eng.htm; and "Market Basket Measure (MBM) Thresholds for the Reference Family by Market Basket Measure Region, Component and Base Year," Statistics Canada, April 26, 2024. www150.statcan.gc.ca/t1/tbl1/en/tv.action?pid=1110006601.

6   Padraig Moran, "This Woman is Considering Medical Assistance in Dying, Due to a Disability. But Poverty is also a Factor," *CBC Radio,* December 16, 2022. cbc.ca/radio/thecurrent/maid-poverty-disability-1.6687453.

7   Isabelle Docto, "Loblaw CEO Responds to Boycott Statement," *BlogTO,* May 2024. blogto.com/eat_drink/2024/05/loblaw-ceo-boycott-statement/.

8   "2022 State of the Sector in Uncertain Times," Ontario Nonprofit Network and *L'Assemblée de la francophonie de l'Ontario* (2022), 1. theonn.ca/wp-content/uploads/2022/08/Survey-2022-Policy-Report.pdf.

Chapter 10

1   See Dayna Nadine Scott, "Impact Assessment in the Ring of Fire: Contested Authorities, Competing Visions and a Clash of Legal Orders," in *Operationalizing Indigenous Impact Assessment,* eds. Jennifer Sankey et al. (Impact Agency Assessment of Canada, 2023), 89–113.

2   Liam Casey, "Inside the Battle over Ontario's Ring of Fire," *CBC News,* October 10, 2023. cbc.ca/news/canada/toronto/ont-ring-of-fire-1.6991468.

3   Far North Science Advisory Panel (Ontario Ministry of Natural Resources), *Science for a Changing Far North: The Report of the Far North Science Advisory Panel* (Toronto: Queen's Printer for Ontario, 2010), xi.

4   James Wilt, "The Battle for the 'Breathing Lands': Ontario's Ring of Fire and the Fate of Its Carbon-Rich Peatlands," *The Narwhal,* July 11, 2020. thenarwhal.ca/ring-of-fire-ontario-peatlands-carbon-climate.

5   Lucy Scholey, "Doug Ford Can't Bulldoze through First Nations to Ring of Fire, Say Indigenous Leaders." *APTN News,* June 15, 2018. aptnnews.ca/national-news/doug-ford-cant-bulldoze-through-first-nations-to-ring-of-fire-say-indigenous-leaders.

6   Matt Prokopchuk, "Ontario Government Ends Ring of Fire Regional Agreement with Matawa First Nations," *CBC News,* August 27, 2019. cbc.ca/news/canada/thunder-bay/regional-framework-ends-1.5261377.

7   Legislative Assembly of Ontario, "Ministry of Energy, Northern Development and Mines," June 16, 2021. ola.org/en/legislative-business/committees/estimates/parliament-42/transcripts/committee-transcript-2021-jun-16.

8   Prokopchuk, "Ontario Government Ends Ring of Fire."

9   A "remote" community, in this context, is one that is not connected by an all-season road to the provincial highway network.

10 Aroland First Nation, "Appendix A – Request for a Regional Assessment,"

Canadian Impact Assessment Registry, October 29, 2019. iaac-aeic.gc.ca/050/documents/p80468/133833E.pdf.

11. John S. Long, *Treaty No. 9: Making the Agreement to Share the Land in Far Northern Ontario in 1905* (Montreal: McGill Queen's University Press, 2010), 353; Andrew Costa, "Across the Great Divide: Anishinaabek Legal Traditions, Treaty 9, and Honourable Consent." *Lakehead Law Journal* 4, 1 (2020): 8.
12. Long, *Treaty No. 9*, 32.
13. Jacqueline Hookimaw-Witt, "Keenebonanoh Keemoshominook Kaeshe Peemishikhik Odaskiwakh – [We Stand on the Graves of Our Ancestors] Native Interpretations of Treaty #9 with Attawapiskat Elders" (Unpublished thesis, Trent University, 1997). www.collectionscanada.gc.ca/obj/s4/f2/dsk2/tape15/PQDD_0016/MQ30219.pdf.
14. Dawn Hoogeveen, "Sub-Surface Property, Free-Entry Mineral Staking and Settler Colonialism in Canada: Mineral Staking and Settler Colonialism in Canada." *Antipode* 47, 1 (2015): 121–138.
15. Northern Ontario Business Staff, "Greg Rickford Becomes Ontario's Natural Resources Czar," *Northern Ontario Business*, June 18, 2021. northernontariobusiness.com/industry-news/economic-development/greg-rickford-becomes-ontarios-natural-resources-czar-3888558.
16. Ian Pattison, "As the New 'Minister of Everything,' Rickford's Time Is Stretched Too Thin," *The Chronicle Journal*, July 18, 2021. www.chroniclejournal.com/opinion/as-the-new-minister-of-everything-rickford-s-time-is-stretched-too-thin/article_386e02ac-e7c6-11eb-b83c-378662d76321.html.
17. Pattison, "As the New 'Minister.'"
18. Ontario NDP, "Sol Mamakwa, Ontario NDP Critic for Indigenous and Treaty Relations, Calls for Indigenous Issues to be a Standalone Portfolio," July 12, 2021. ontariondp.ca/news/sol-mamakwa-ontario-ndp-critic-indigenous-and-treaty-relations-calls-indigenous-issues-be.
19. CBC News, "Caldwell First Nation Calls for Resignation of Provincial Indigenous Minister," September 22, 2023. cbc.ca/news/canada/windsor/caldwell-duckwroth-rickford-resignation-call-1.6975919.
20. Nick Dunne, "Ontario Mining Minister George Pirie Is about to Get a Lot More Powerful," *The Narwhal*, October 6, 2023. thenarwhal.ca/ontario-mining-act-george-pirie.
21. Len Gillis, "Mines Minister Calls for Economic Support for Critical Minerals," *Sudbury.com*, February 17, 2024. sudbury.com/local-news/mines-minister-calls-for-economic-support-for-critical-minerals-8320768.
22. Ian Ross, "Timmins' George Pirie Takes the Helm as Mines Minister," *Northern Ontario Business*, August 3, 2022. northernontariobusiness.com/industry-news/mining/timmins-george-pirie-takes-the-helm-as-mines-minister-5644772.
23. Len Gillis, "Ontario's New Mines Minister Has a Strong Pedigree in Mining," *Northern Ontario Business*, August 8, 2022. northernontariobusiness.com/industry-news/mining/ontarios-new-mines-minister-has-a-strong-pedigree-in-mining-5662102.
24. Mike Coyle, "Build More Mines — Minister of Mines of Ontario, Mr. George Pirie." *Insidexploration* (YouTube video), April 4, 2023. youtube.com/watch?v=m3QKxgK5MB8&t=65s&ab_channel=Insidexploration.

Endnotes 253

25 "Ontario Mining Minister Discusses Mining for a Greener Future," *CBC News* (video), September 6, 2022.
26 Anna Lowenhaupt Tsing, *Friction an Ethnography of Global Connection* (Princeton: Princeton University Press, 2005).
27 Paul Bradette, "A Message from MineConnect." *Canadian Mining Journal*, March 1, 2021. canadianminingjournal.com/featured-article/a-message-from-mineconnect.
28 NetNewsLedger News and Information, "Talking Ontario Mining with Minister George Pirie," YouTube (video), April 24, 2024. youtube.com/watch?v=CynB8CxEgys. 4:42.
29 Prime Minister of Canada Justin Trudeau, "Volkswagen's Electric Vehicle Battery Plant Will Create Thousands of New Jobs," Government of Canada, April 21, 2023. pm.gc.ca/en/videos/2023/04/21/volkswagens-electric-vehicle-battery-plant-will-create-thousands-new-jobs.
30 Logan Turner, "Ontario Mines Minister Says Ring of Fire Could Be Worth $1 Trillion, A Figure Critics Call Exaggerated," *CBC News*, March 17, 2023. cbc.ca/news/canada/thunder-bay/ring-of-fire-trillion-dollar-claim-1.6778551.
31 "Wyloo Metals Completes Acquisition of Noront Resources; Eagle's Nest to Set New Global Benchmark in Sustainable Mining," Wyloo (website), April 8, 2022. https://wyloo.com/media-release/wyloo-metals-completes-acquisition-of-noront-resources-eagles-nest-to-set-new-global-benchmark-in-sustainable-mining/.
32 "Wyloo Metals Completes."
33 Nick Dunne, "Ontario Mining Minister"; Ontario Legislative Assembly, "Bill 71, Building More Mines Act, 2023," 2023. ola.org/en/legislative-business/bills/parliament-43/session-1/bill-71.
34 Dunne, "Ontario Mining Minister."
35 Jamie Kneen, "More, Worse Mining: Ontario's Proposed Building More Mines Act," *MiningWatch Canada*, March 7, 2023. miningwatch.ca/blog/2023/3/7/more-worse-mining-ontarios-proposed-building-more-mines-act.
36 Kneen, "More, Worse Mining."
37 Dunne, "Ontario Mining Minister."
38 Coyle, "Build More Mines."
39 Dunne, "Ontario Mining Minister."
40 Matawa Chiefs Council, "Submission to Ontario's Proposed Bill 71 Building More Mines Act and Standing Committee Hearings," *Matawa First Nations*, April 3, 2023. matawa.on.ca/wp-content/uploads/2023/04/Matawa-CC-SC-Submission-Proposed-Bill-71-2.pdf.
41 It still may be the chromite that the miners are ultimately after.
42 Glen Coulthard, *Red Skin, White Masks: Rejecting the Colonial Politics of Recognition* (Minneapolis: University of Minnesota Press, 2014).
43 See, for example, *Platinex Inc v Kitchenuhmaykoosib Inninuwug First Nation*, 2006 CanLII 26171 (ON SC).
44 Attawapiskat, Fort Albany and Neskantaga First Nations, "First Nations Declare Moratorium on Ring of Fire Development," *Cision*, April 5, 2021. newswire.ca/news-releases/first-nations-declare-moratorium-on-ring-of-fire-development-854352559.
45 Mushkegowuk Council, "Mushkegowuk Chiefs Call for Moratorium on

Development Activities in the Ring of Fire to Ensure Sensitive Wetlands and Waters are Protected First," *WWF,* January 12, 2021. wwf.ca/wp-content/uploads/2021/01/Moratorium_.pdf.

46   Attawapiskat, Fort Albany, and Neskantaga First Nations, "First Nations Declare Moratorium."

47   Doug Diaczuk, "Neskantaga First Nation Demands a Halt to Assessment of Ring of Fire Road," *TBnewswatch,* May 10, 2021. tbnewswatch.com/local-news/neskantaga-first-nation-demands-a-halt-to-assessment-of-ring-of-fire-road-3766040.

48   Diaczuk, "Neskantaga First Nation Demands a Halt."

49   Scott, "Impact Assessment in the Ring of Fire," 98.

50   Bronson Carver, "Four First Nations Form Land Defence Alliance, Seek to Stop Encroachment on Their Territory," *Kenora Miner & News,* February 18, 2023. kenoraminerandnews.com/news/local-news/four-first-nations-form-land-defence-alliance-seek-to-stop-encroachment-on-their-territory; Mark Calzavara, "Ford Wants to Bulldoze His Way Through First Nations Land. The Land Alliance Won't Let Him," *The Council of Canadians,* September 21, 2023. canadians.org/analysis/ford-wants-to-bulldoze-his-way-through-first-nations-land-the-land-alliance-wont-let-him/.

51   Bronson Carver, "Four First Nations."

52   Mark Calzavara, "Ford Wants to Bulldoze."

53   Scott, "Impact Assessment in the Ring of Fire.

54   Aroland First Nation, "Appendix A–Request for Regional Assessment." See: https://iaac-aeic.gc.ca/050/documents/p80468/133833E.pdf.

55   Logan Turner, "First Nations Leaders Demand Equal Partnership in Ottawa's 'Broken' Regional Assessment for Ring of Fire," *CBC News,* January 28, 2022. cbc.ca/news/canada/thunder-bay/ring-of-fire-regional-assessment-broken-fn-leaders-1.6330328.

56   Matawa First Nations, "Matawa Chiefs Work Towards Solidifying Approach to Ring of Fire Regional Environmental Assessment," *Matawa First Nations,* June 23, 2022. matawa.on.ca/matawa-chiefs-council-work-towards-solidifying-approach-to-ring-of-fire-regional-environmental-assessment.

57   "Mushkegowuk Council Supports Matawa First Nations," *Mushkegowuk Council,* June 15, 2022. mushkegowuk.ca/posts/2022-06-15_mushkegowuk-council-supports-matawa-first-nations.

58   "Mushkegowuk Council Supports."

59   Supreme Court of Canada, "Reference re: Impact Assessment Act," October 13, 2023. scc-csc.ca/case-dossier/cb/2023/40195-eng.aspx.

60   Attawapiskat First Nation, et al., "Draft Statement of Claim," *APTN National News,* n.d. aptnnews.ca/wp-content/uploads/2023/04/2023-04-26-DRAFT-Statement-of-Claim-re-Treaty-9.pdf.

61   Attawapiskat First Nation, et al., "Draft Statement of Claim."

62   Attawapiskat First Nation, et al., "Draft Statement of Claim."

63   Emma McIntosh, "10 First Nations Sue Ontario and Canada over Resource Extraction and Broken Treaty 9 Promises," *The Narwhal,* April 26, 2023. thenarwhal.ca/ontario-treaty-9-lawsuit.

64   Logan Turner, "Can the Crown Make Land Decisions without First Nations

Consent? Treaty 9 Lawsuit Argues No," *CBC News*, April 26, 2023. cbc.ca/news/canada/thunder-bay/treaty-nine-lawsuit-1.6822266.
65 Sarah Hunt, "Settler Colonialism," in *The Routledge Handbook of Law and Society*, vol. 1, eds. Mariana Valverde, et al. (London: Routledge, 2021), 214.

Chapter 11

1 Ontario. Ministry of Education. *Ontario's Early Years and Child Care Annual Report 2023*. [Toronto], 2024. ontario.ca/page/ontarios-early-years-and-child-care-annual-report-2023.
2 Ontario. *Official Report of Debates (Hansard)*, 16 July 2018. (Mr. Doug Downey, PC). ola.org/en/legislative-business/house-documents/parliament-42/session-1/2018-07-16/hansard.
3 See Venai Raniga, Chapter 2, in this book.
4 Ontario. *Official Report of Debates (Hansard)*, 18 April 2019. (Mr. Stephen Lecce, PC). ola.org/en/legislative-business/house-documents/parliament-42/session-1/2019-04-18/hansard.
5 Financial Accountability Office (FAO). *Child Care in Ontario: A Review of Ontario's New Child care Tax Credit*. Province of Ontario, 2019. fao-on.org/en/Blog/Publications/child care-ontario-2019.
6 FAO, *Child Care in Ontario*.
7 City of Toronto. City Manager. *2019 Ontario Budget and Legislation Update* [Toronto], 2019. toronto.ca/legdocs/mmis/2019/mm/bgrd/backgroundfile-133070.pdf.
8 Ontario. *Official Report of Debates (Hansard)*, 6 May 2019. (Hon. Lisa M Thompson, PC). ola.org/en/legislative-business/house-documents/parliament-42/session-1/2019-05-06/hansard
9 Ontario. "Ontario Helping Parents Return to Work" Ontario Newsroom News Release, June 9 2020, news.ontario.ca/en/release/57142/ontario-helping-parents-return-to-work.
10 Canada. Department of Finance Canada. *Budget 2021*, [Ottawa] 2021. budget.canada.ca/2021/home-accueil-en.html
11 Ontario. *Official Report of Debates (Hansard)*, 3 June 2021. (Hon. Stephen Lecce, PC). ola.org/en/legislative-business/house-documents/parliament-42/session-1/2021-06-03/hansard.
12 Aisling Gallagher, *Childcare Provision in Neoliberal Times: The Marketization of Care* (Bristol: Bristol University Press, 2023), 77.
13 Armine Yalnizyan, "Private Equity is Embracing Child Care as Investors Look for Profit. Here are the Big Players in Canada," May 22 2024. thestar.com/business/opinion/the-problem-with-the-booming-business-of-child-care/article_139be45c-1785-11ef-a02d-ef2641193cf3.html.
14 Gordon Cleveland, "Giving Parents Money Doesn't Solve Child Care Problems," *The Prosperity Project*. canadianprosperityproject.ca/wp-content/uploads/TPP-Child-Care-Report_EN.pdf.
15 Rachel Mendleson and Brendan Kennedy, "How Intense Pressure from For-Profit Daycares Has Transformed Ontario's Rollout of $10-A-Day Child Care — and Sparked a Political Standoff," October 2 2022. thestar.com/news/investigations/how-intense-pressure-from-for-profit-daycares-has-transformed-ontario-s-rollout-of-10-a/article_87c85eb4-235d-5f03-8067-b75b24cfdab0.html.

16   Spokesperson for Minister Lecce quoted in "$10-a-Day Child-Care Program at Risk in Ontario Without More Funding, Toronto Operator Warns," *CBC News*, January 16 2024. cbc.ca/news/canada/toronto/child-day-care-funding-ontario-1.7085204.
17   Ontario Coalition for Better Child Care. "Who We Are." (website). www.child careontario.org/about.
18   Association of Early Childhood Educators Ontario, "About Us." (website). www.aeceo.ca/about.
19   Ontario. "Ontario Creating More Affordable Child Care Spaces Across the Province," Ontario Newsroom News Release, December 19 2022. news.ontario.ca/en/release/1002608/ontario-creating-more-affordable-child-care-spaces-across-the-province.

Chapter 12

1   See Kathy Laird's discussion in Chapter 6 of this book.
2   Rob Ferguson, "Ford Appoints Veteran Conservative Public Affairs Executive to Trade Envoy Post in Washington," *Toronto Star*, October 18, 2018. thestar.com/politics/provincial/ford-appoints-veteran-conservative-public-affairs-executive-to-trade-envoy-post-in-washington/article_072307a1-2be1-5b05-b3ab-982557be372b.html.
3   CBC News Online, "Ron Taverner, Friend of Doug Ford, Withdraws from Consideration for OPP Commissioner," March 7, 2019. cbc.ca/news/canada/toronto/ron-taverner-withdraws-from-consideration-for-opp-commissioner-1.5046120.
4   CBC News Online, "Ontario Reviewing Political Appointments After Latest Accusation of Nepotism," June 25, 2019. cbc.ca/news/canada/toronto/provincial-appointee-resigns-1.5189652.
5   Rob Ferguson, "The People in the Cronyism Scandal that has Rocked Premier Doug Ford's Government," *Toronto Star*, July 16, 2019. thestar.com/politics/provincial/the-people-in-the-cronyism-scandal-that-has-rocked-premier-doug-ford-s-government/article_f1c4f0c2-df5c-5b5c-af9b-b714aa970df4.html.
6   For more on this, see Venai Raniga's discussion in Chapter 2 of this book.
7   See Chris Chandler, Chapter 4, in this book.
8   See Tom McDowell's thoughts on this in Chapter 14; and Carlo Fanelli and Ryan Kelpin's response in Chapter 15, in this book.
9   For more on these matters, see Chris Chandler's Chapter 4 and Maria Rio's Chapter 9 in this book.
10 Martin Regg Cohn, "Doug Ford's Patronage Controversy Builds on a Pattern of Poor Decision-Making," *Toronto Star*, July 6, 2023. thestar.com/politics/political-opinion/doug-ford-s-patronage-controversy-builds-on-a-pattern-of-poor-decision-making/article_96cdcea9-9e7d-5f05-81d2-48065d7edd5e.html.
11 Michael Spratt, Interview with author, August 4, 2023.
12 Richard Lautens, "Why Doug Ford's Plan for 'Like-Minded' Judges is a Terrible Move," *Toronto Star*, February 27, 2024. thestar.com/opinion/editorials/why-doug-fords-plan-for-like-minded-judges-is-a-terrible-move/article_9090a562-d4da-11ee-8d7d-53e7a9d9c6c2.html.

13 Charlie Pinkerton, "Judges Selection Panel 'Concerned' About Low Number of Qualified Applicants," *The Trillium* March 7, 2024. thetrillium.ca/insider-news/justice/judges-selection-panel-concerned-about-low-number-of-qualified-applicants-8409534.
14 Steve Buist, Noor Javed, Emma McIntosh, "Friends with Benefits? An Inside Look at the Money, Power and Influence Behind the Ford Government's Push to Build Highway 413," *Toronto Star*, August 31, 2023. thestar.com/news/investigations/friends-with-benefits-an-inside-look-at-the-money-power-and-influence-behind-the-ford/article_9d6dcaf1-e00a-5360-a40f-8625ee6c77c5.html.
15 John Barber, "Key to $3-Million Land Profit: Luck," *Globe and Mail*, May 2, 2000. theglobeandmail.com/news/national/key-to-3-million-land-profit-luck/article1339974/.
16 Brady Deaton, "Ontario Farmland Value and Rental Value Survey," Ontario Agricultural College, University of Guelph, April 2024.
17 Steve Buist, Noor Javed, and Emma McIntosh, "Friends with Benefits? An Inside Look at the Money, Power and Influence Behind the Ford Government's Push to Build Highway 413," *Toronto Star*, August 31, 2023. .thestar.com/news/investigations/friends-with-benefits-an-inside-look-at-the-money-power-and-influence-behind-the-ford/article_9d6dcaf1-e00a-5360-a40f-8625ee6c77c5.html.
18 Buist, Javed, McIntosh, "Friends with Benefits?"
19 Tim Gray, Interview with author, October 27, 2023.
20 Emma McIntosh, Noor Javed, Brendan Kennedy, "Six Developers Bought Greenbelt Land After Ford Came to Power. Now, They Stand to Profit," *Narwhal*, November 17, 2022. thenarwhal.ca/ford-ontario-greenbelt-cuts-developers/.
21 CBC News Online, "Who Are the Developers Set to Benefit from Ford Government's Greenbelt Land Swap?" November 11, 2022. cbc.ca/news/canada/toronto/gta-developers-own-greenbelt-land-swap-1.6648273.
22 Sheila Wang, Noor Javed, "Developer Close to Ford Bought This Farmland and Got Special Permission to Build Desperately Needed Homes," *Toronto Star*, January 25, 2024. thestar.com/news/investigations/a-developer-close-to-doug-ford-bought-this-farmland-and-got-special-permission-to-build/article_ae3b97cc-a49c-5ed1-9a2b-fc2664080e43.html.
23 Office of the Auditor General of Ontario, *Special Report on Changes to the Greenbelt* (King's Printer Ontario, 2023), 8.
24 Auditor General, *Special Report*, 9.
25 Auditor General, *Special Report*, 9–10.
26 Robert Benzie, "Ford Government Defends Ontario Greenbelt Land Swap that Benefits PC donors," *Toronto Star*, November 28, 2022. thestar.com/politics/provincial/ford-government-defends-ontario-greenbelt-land-swap-that-benefits-pc-donors/article_b17739d8-982e-50a3-9e5b-e14f153c2302.html.
27 Elections Ontario, "Political Contributions." See: https://finances.elections.on.ca/en/contributions?fromYear=2014&toYear=2024. Please note: multiple attempts have been made to contact these people mentioned here, as well as other donors who are noted throughout this chapter, in order to verify their names as donors on the Election Ontario list. To date, only one has replied — to the affirmative.

28 Office of the Integrity Commissioner, *Report of J. David Wake, K.C. Integrity Commissioner* (King's Printer Ontario 2023) 6.
29 Integrity Commissioner, *Report,* 106
30 Charlie Pinkerton, "Texts Contradict Developer's Testimony about the Relationship with Ford Aide During the Greenbelt Investigation," *The Trillium,* April 24, 2024. thetrillium.ca/news/the-trillium-investigations/texts-contradict-developers-testimony-about-relationship-with-ford-aide-during-greenbelt-investigation-8643723.
31 Integrity Commissioner, *Report,* 78.
32 Integrity Commissioner, *Report,* 86
33 Integrity Commissioner, *Report,* 79–87.
34 Tim Gray, Interview, October 27, 2023.
35 Environmental Defence and Ecojustice, "Greenbelt FOI Release Documents," 2022-138 File 4, October 31, 2023, 439.
36 Freedom of Information Request, November 2023.
37 Charlie Pinkerton, Noor Javed, "Ontario Developers Who Benefitted from Ford Government Decisions on Greenbelt and MZOs Dined with the Premier at His Daughter's Wedding," *Toronto Star,* January 25, 2024. thestar.com/news/investigations/ontario-developers-who-benefitted-from-ford-government-decisions-on-greenbelt-and-mzos-dined-with-the/article_ca82e91b-63cc-50ba-8e26-eecd2e0441f5.html.
38 For more on this matter, see Hurley and Allan's discussion in Chapter 7 of this book.
39 Ontario Health Coalition, "Ontario Expands For-Profit Hospital in Violation of the Law," *The Bullet,* November 26, 2023. socialistproject.ca/2023/11/ontario-expands-for-profit-hospital-in-violation-of-law/.
40 CBC News Online, "Doug Ford Government Paying For-Profit Clinic More than Hospitals for OHIP-Covered Surgeries," November 14, 2023. cbc.ca/news/canada/toronto/ontario-doug-ford-private-clinic-surgeries-fees-hospitals-1.7026926.
41 CBC News Online, "Opposition Parties Critique PC Government Paying For-Profit Clinic More than Hospitals for Surgeries," November 15, 2023. cbc.ca/news/canada/toronto/opposition-react-clinic-hospital-funding-1.7029090. For more on this, see Laird, Chapter 6, in this book.
42 Natalie Mehra, Interview with author, January18, 2024.
43 Joint Task Force Central, *JTFC Observations in Long Term Care Facilities in Ontario,* May 14, 2020. www.documentcloud.org/documents/6928480-OPLASER-JTFC-Observations-in-LTCF-in-On.html.
44 David McLaren, "Remember Why our Seniors Died in Long-Term Care Homes," May 23, 2022. thespec.com/opinion/contributors/remember-why-our-seniors-died-in-long-term-care-homes/article_4947bd4d-6437-5511-b90d-fe0da80ee854.html.
45 CTV News Online, "Ontario Allocates Beds to Long-Term Care Company Accused of Ignoring Residents as they Cried for Help," October 27, 2021. ctvnews.ca/ontario-allocates-beds-to-long-term-care-company-accused-of-ignoring-residents-as-they-cried-hours-for-help-1.5640641.
46 CTV News Online, "Long-Term Care Company Accused of Leaving Residents 'Soiled in Diapers' Will Get Millions for New Beds," October 25,

2021. ctvnews.ca/ontario-long-term-care-company-accused-of-leaving-residents-soiled-in-diapers-will-get-millions-for-new-beds-1.5637018.
47 Office of the Integrity Commissioner, *Lobbyists Registration.* https://lobbyist.oico.on.ca/Pages/Public/PublicSearch.
48 Office of the Integrity Commissioner, *Lobbyists Registration.*
49 Laura Stone, "Former Doug Ford Aide Amin Massoudi Paid $237,000 by PC Caucus Services," *Globe and Mail,* September 27, 2023. theglobeandmail.com/canada/article-ford-advisor-amin-massoudi/?login=true.
50 Natalie Mehra, Interview, January 18, 2024.
51 Office of the Integrity Commissioner, *Lobbyists Registration.*
52 See Dayna Nadine Scott and Dania Ahmed's Chapter 10 on Ford's mining plans in this book.
53 Public Service of Ontario Act, *2006 Ontario Reg. 383/07,* August 20, 2007. ontario.ca/laws/regulation/070382#BK24.
54 Ian Stedman, Interview with author, January 2, 2024.
55 Office of the Commissioner of Lobbying Canada. "Lobbying at the Federal Level — At a Glance." https://lobbycanada.gc.ca/media/m4mohyjb/info-lobbying-at-a-glance-2023-11-en.pdf.
56 Elections Ontario, "Political Contributions." finances.elections.on.ca/en/contributions?fromYear=2014&toYear=2024.
57 Democracy Watch, "2021 Donations Show Ford PC Party Made Ontario Political Finance System More Undemocratic," May 31, 2022. democracywatch.ca/2021-donations-show-ford-pc-party-supported-most-by-wealthy-donors-ford-made-ontario-political-finance-system-more-undemocratic/.
58 Laura Stone, "Ford Government Looks to Rewrite Election Finance Rules," *Globe and Mail,* February 25, 2021. theglobeandmail.com/canada/article-ford-government-to-permit-higher-political-donations-restrict-third/.

Chapter 13

1 Ontario, *Ontario Provincial Climate Change Impact Assessment* (Toronto: Queen's Printer, January 2023). ontario.ca/files/2023-08/mecp-ontario-provincial-climate-change-impact-assessment-en-2023-08-17.pdf.
2 Mark Winfield, "Are Freeloading Premiers Undermining Canada's Climate Strategy?" *The Conversation,* November 19, 2023. theconversation.com/are-freeloading-premiers-undermining-canadas-climate-strategy-217638.
3 Mark Winfield, "Environmental Policy: Greening the Province from the Dynasty to Wynne," in *Government and Politics of Ontario,* sixth ed., eds. J. Malloy and C. Collier (Toronto: University of Toronto Press, 2016), 251–73.
4 Financial Accountability Office (FAO), *Cap and Trade: A Financial Review of the Decision to Cancel the Cap-and-Trade Program* (Toronto: FAO, 2018). fao-on.org/en/blog/publications/cap-and-trade-ending.
5 Mike Crawley, "Doug Ford Government Spent $231M to Scrap Green Energy Projects," *CBC News,* November 19, 2019. cbc.ca/news/canada/toronto/doug-ford-green-energy-wind-turbines-cancelled-230-million-1.5364815.
6 Mark Winfield, "Cleaning Up Ontario's Hydro Mess," *Policy Options,* January 15, 2021, policyoptions.irpp.org/magazines/january-2021/cleaning-up-ontarios-hydro-mess/.
7 Greg Gormick, "There Is Still Time to Stop the Ontario Line," *Toronto Star,*

August 25, 2021. thestar.com/opinion/contributors/there-is-still-time-to-stop-the-ontario-line/article_2eb08b43-84c1-5497-b539-dd33c09046b0.html. See also Matti Siemiatycki and Drew Fagan, *Transit in the Greater Toronto Area: How to Get Back on the Rails* (Toronto: University of Toronto, 2019). https://tspace.library.utoronto.ca/bitstream/1807/96710/1/Perspectives-26-Siemiatycki-Fagan-Transit-GTA-October-2019.pdf.

8   Ontario Nature, et al., "Letter Ministry of the Environment, Conservation and Parks, Re: ERO #013-5033 Review of the *Endangered Species Act, 2007*," May 18, 2019. ontarionature.org/wp-content/uploads/2019/05/ERO-013-5033-ESA-May-18-2019.pdf.

9   Mark Winfield, "Ford Government Endangers Gains on Water Quality," *The Hamilton Spectator*, June 28, 2021. thespec.com/opinion/contributors/2021/06/28/ford-government-endangers-gains-on-water-quality.html.

10 Marl Winfield, Faisal Moola, and Sheila Colla, "Scrapping Environmental Watchdog is Like Shooting the Messenger," *The Conversation*, November 22, 2018. theconversation.com/scrapping-environmental-watchdog-is-like-shooting-the-messenger-107345.

11 Mikaela Kyle, *COVID-19 in Ontario: An Opportunity to Degrade Environmental Law and Policy* (Toronto: MES/JD Major Paper, Sustainable Energy Initiative, York University, 2021). https://sei.info.yorku.ca/files/2021/06/Mikaela-Kyle-Major-Paper-Final-Version.pdf?x60126.

12 Auditor General of Ontario, *Follow-up on Value-for-Money Audit: Climate Change: Ontario's Plan to Reduce Greenhouse Gas Emissions* (Toronto: November 2021). auditor.on.ca/en/content/annualreports/arreports/en21/ENV_FU_ClimateChange_en21.pdf.

13 Peter Hillson and Mark Winfield, "Understanding the Political Durability of Doug Ford's Market Populism." *Studies in Political Economy* 105, 1 (2024): 69–93. doi.org/10.1080/07078552.2024.2325289.

14 Mark Winfield, "Ontario Election 2022: Summary of the PC, Liberal, NDP and Green Platforms on Climate and Energy Issues," York University (blog), May 19, 2022. https://marksw.blog.yorku.ca/2022/05/19/ontario-election-2022-summary-of-the-pc-liberal-ndp-and-green-platforms-on-climate-and-energy-issues/.

15 Mark Winfield, "Driving in the Wrong Direction," *The Toronto Star*, May 14, 2022.

16 For more on this issue, see Bryan Evans and Carlo Fanelli, Chapter 1, in this book.

17 Hillson and Winfield, "Understanding the Political Durability of Doug Ford's Market Populism."

18 For more on this, see Kathy Laird, Chapter 6, in this book.

19 Mark Winfield and M. Sterling, "The Environment, Megacity Growth and Ineffective Policy: Housing Policy Reform in Ontario," in *Ineffective Policies: Causes and Consequences of Bad Policy Choices*, eds. Ian Roberg, et al. (Bristol University Press, Forthcoming 2025).

20 Ontario Housing Affordability Task Force. *Report of the Ontario Housing Affordability Task Force* (Ottawa: King's Printer for Ontario, 2022), 10. ontario.ca/page/housing-affordability-task-force-report.

21 Kevin Eby, *Review of Existing Housing Unit Capacity Identify in Municipal Land Needs Assessments Prepared for Upper- and-Single Tier Municipalities in the Greater Golden Horseshoe* (Toronto: Alliance for a Liveable Ontario/ Environmental Defense Canada, 2023), 3. https://yourstoprotect.ca/wp-content/uploads/sites/3/2023/02/REVIEW-OF-EXISTING-HOUSING-UNIT-CAPACITY-IDENTIFIED-IN-MUNICIPAL-LAND-NEEDS-ASSESSMENTS-R.pdf.
22 Office of the Integrity Commissioner, *Report Re: The Honourable Steve Clark, Minister of Municipal Affairs and Housing and Member of Provincial Parliament for Leeds–Grenville–Thousand Islands and Rideau Lakes* (Toronto, Legislative Assembly of Ontario, 2023), 142. oico.on.ca/web/default/files/public/Commissioners%20Reports/Report%20Re%20Minister%20Clark%20-%20August%2030%2C%202023.pdf.
23 Office of the Auditor General of Ontario, *Special Report on Changes to the Greenbelt* (2023), 32. https://www.auditor.on.ca/en/content/specialreports/specialreports/Greenbelt_en.pdf. Also, see William Paul's chapter, "Riding the 'Gravy Train,'" in this book for a detailed discussion of this matter.
24 Ontario, "To Build More Homes, Ontario Launching Building Faster Fund and Expanding Strong Mayor Powers," *New Release,* August 21, 2023. news.ontario.ca/en/release/1003397/to-build-more-homes-ontario-launching-building-faster-fund-and-expanding-strong-mayor-powers.
25 Mark Winfield, and Joe Castrilli, "Has Ontario's Housing 'Plan' Been Built on a Foundation of Evidentiary Sand?" *The Conversation,* January 22, 2023. the-conversation.com/has-ontarios-housing-plan-been-built-on-a-foundation-of-evidentiary-sand-198133.
26 Emma McIntosh and Fatima Syed, "Documents Show Ontario May Move to Allow Expropriation of Land before Environmental Review," *The Narwhal,* February 2, 2024 https://thenarwhal.ca/ontario-expropriation-land-bill/.
27 See Tom McDowell's discussion in Chapter 14 in this book.
28 Ken Greenberg, "Ontario's Top-Down Approach to Urban Growth is Reversing Progress on Many Levels," *The Toronto Star,* April 20, 2022. thestar.com/opinion/contributors/ontario-s-top-down-approach-to-urban-growth-is-reversing-progress-on-many-levels/article_cf16c494-aa10-512b-b6a7-f9dc011a3672.html. Also, see Lily Xia's Chapter 16 in this book for more on this issue.
29 Crystal Fung, Sahil Parikh and Piotr Zulauf, "The Crisis of Affordable Rental Housing in Ontario," Ryerson (TMU) University, https://www.torontomu.ca/content/dam/social-innovation/Programs/Affordable_Housing_Visual_Systems_Map_Oxford.pdf.
30 Ontario, "Moving to a Project-List Approach under The Environmental Assessment Act," February 22, 2024. https://ero.ontario.ca/notice/019-4219.
31 Mark Winfield, "Ontario Back in the Business of Building Roads to Sprawl," *The Hamilton Spectator,* March 9, 2021. thespec.com/opinion/contributors/ontario-back-in-the-business-of-building-roads-to-sprawl/article_2b9d2772-668e-556a-b439-34c465c3e7d0.html.
32 Mark Winfield, "The Folly of Ontario's Nuclear Power Play," *Globe and Mail,* February 6, 2024. theglobeandmail.com/business/commentary/article-ontario-pickering-nuclear-power-plant-refurbishment/.
33 Mark Winfield, "Ontario Opts for High-Risk Nuclear over Low-Risk Energy

Sources," *Toronto Star*, July 21, 2023. thestar.com/opinion/contributors/ontario-opts-for-high-risk-nuclear-over-low-risk-energy-sources/article_49afb2a3-7cca-5dee-bc2b-5d57eef76a75.html.
34 Ralph Torrie, "Ford Government's Nuclear Push is a Costly Deja-Vu for Ontario's Power Sector," *Globe and Mail*, July 23, 2023. theglobeandmail.com/business/commentary/article-ford-governments-nuclear-push-is-a-costly-deja-vu-for-ontarios-power/.
35 Stephanie Levitz, "Doug Ford's First Term as Premier Was Upended by a Pandemic. Will His Response Earn Him an Encore?" *Toronto Star*, May 4, 2022. thestar.com/politics/provincial/2022/05/04/this-is-who-he-is-doug-ford-offers-ontario-another-four-years-of-what-he-promised.html.
36 Mark Winfield, "The Doug Ford Doctrine: Short-Term Gain for Long-Term Pain," *The Conversation*, April 28, 2019. https://theconversation.com/the-doug-ford-doctrine-short-term-gain-for-long-term-pain-116131.
37 See Michael Hurley and Doug Allan, Chapter 7; and Rachel Vickerson, et al., Chapter 11, in this book.
38 See John Clarke, Chapter 17, in this book.
39 Winfield and Sterling, "The Environment, Megacity Growth and Ineffective Policy."
40 Mark Winfield, "Ontario's Greenbelt is Safe for Now, But Will the Scandal Alter Doug Ford's Course?" *The Conversation*, September 23, 2023. theconversation.com/ontarios-greenbelt-is-safe-for-now-but-will-the-scandal-alter-doug-fords-course-214178.
41 Ontario, *Provincial Climate Change Impact Assessment*.
42 Auditor General of Ontario, "Conserving the Natural Environment with Protected Areas," (Toronto: Auditor General, 2020), https://www.auditor.on.ca/en/content/annualreports/arreports/en20/ENV_conservingthenaturalenvironment_en20.pdf.

Chapter 14

1 Tom McDowell, *Neoliberal Parliamentarism: The Decline of Parliament at the Ontario Legislature* (University of Toronto Press, 2021).
2 McDowell, *Neoliberal Parliamentarism*.
3 McDowell, *Neoliberal Parliamentarism*, 26.
4 Peter Russell, "The Notwithstanding Clause: The Charter's Homage to Parliamentary Democracy," *Policy Options* 28, 2 (2007): 65–68.
5 For more information on this matter, see Kathy Laird's discussion in Chapter 6 of this book.
6 Audrey O'Brien and Marc Bosc, *House of Commons Procedure and Practice* (Ottawa: House of Commons, 2009).
7 On this issue, also see Michael Hurley and Doug Allan's discussion in Chapter 7 of this book.
8 Bill 74, *The People's Health Care Act* (Legislative Assembly of Ontario, 2022).
9 Bill 74.
10 Bill 175, *Connecting People to Home and Community Care Act* (Legislative Assembly of Ontario, 2020).
11 Bill 60, *Your Health Act* (Legislative Assembly of Ontario, 2023).
12 See Carlo Fanelli and Ray Kelpin discussion in Chapter 15 of this book.

13 Bill 5, *Better Local Government Act* (Legislative Assembly of Ontario, 2018).
14 *City of Toronto et al., v. Attorney General of Ontario* (ONSC 5151, 2018).
15 Bill 31, *Efficient Local Government Ac.* (Legislative Assembly of Ontario, 2018).
16 Allison Jones, "Supreme Court to Hear Case on Ontario Election Advertising Rules," *CBC News,* November 9, 2023. cbc.ca/news/canada/toronto/supreme-court-ontario-election-law-appeal-1.7023381.
17 Bill 28, *Keeping Students in Class Act* (Legislative Assembly of Ontario, 2022).
18 For more on this, see Carlo Fanelli and Katherine Nastovski's discussion in Chapter 8 of this book.
19 Bill 35, *An Act to Repeal the Keeping Students in Class Act* (Legislative Assembly of Ontario, 2022).
20 Bill 3, *Strong Mayors, Building Homes Act.*
21 Edward Keenan, "'Good Luck, Toronto': Our New Minority-Rule Mayor Law Leaves Global Experts Baffled," *Toronto Star,* December 8, 2022. thestar.com/opinion/star-columnists/good-luck-toronto-our-new-minority-rule-mayor-law-leaves-global-experts-baffled/article_21461424-25f3-5439-a1e4-4a8a7d-b8efca.html.
22 McDowell, *Neoliberal Parliamentarism.*
23 McDowell, *Neoliberal Parliamentarism.*
24 Bill 57, *Restoring Trust, Transparency and Accountability Act* (Legislative Assembly of Ontario, 2018).
25 Andrea Migone, "The Ontario Executive," in *The Politics of Ontario,* second ed., eds. Cheryl Collier and Jonathan Malloy (Toronto: University of Toronto Press, 2024), 72–90.
26 McDowell, *Neoliberal Parliamentarism.*
27 McDowell, *Neoliberal Parliamentarism.*
28 McDowell, *Neoliberal Parliamentarism.*
29 McDowell, *Neoliberal Parliamentarism.*
30 Tom Yun, "Here's What Canadians Think about Privatization in Health-Care System." *CTV News,* February 27, 2023. ctvnews.ca/here-s-what-canadians-think-about-privatization-in-health-care-system-1.6288800.
31 Tom McDowell, "Javier Milei's 'Instant Democracy' and Neoliberalism," *CounterPunch,* February 15, 2024. counterpunch.org/2024/02/15/javier-mileis-instant-democracy-and-neoliberalism/.
32 Ian Bruff, "The Rise of Authoritarian Neoliberalism." *Rethinking Marxism,* 26, 1 (2014): 113–129. doi.org/10.1080/08935696.2013.843250.

Chapter 15

1 Carlo Fanelli, *Megacity Malaise* (Halifax: Fernwood Publishing, 2016); Ryan Kelpin, *The Creatures of the Province Doctrine and the Neoliberalization and De-democratization of Local Government in Toronto from 1996 to 2023,* [PhD Dissertation] York University, 2024; Marianna Valverde, "Games of Jurisdiction: How Local Governance Realities Challenge the 'Creatures of the Province' Doctrine." *Journal of Law and Social Policy* 34 (2021): 21–38.
2 Rob Ford and Doug Ford, *Ford Nation: Two Brothers, One Vision* (Toronto: Harper Collins, 2016).

3   Simon Archer and Erin Sobat, "The Better Local Government Act Versus Municipal Democracy," *Journal of Law and Social Policy* 34 (2021): 1–20; Prabha Khosla and Melissa Wong, "Bill 5: How the Better Local Government Act Silenced the Voices of Diverse Progressive Women Candidates in Toronto's 2018 Municipal Election," *Journal of Law and Social Policy* 34 (2021): 128–133.
4   David Shum, "Doug Ford to Invoke Notwithstanding Clause to Override Toronto Council Cut Ruling," *Global News*, September 10, 2018. globalnews.ca/news/4437313/toronto-council-legal-challenge-decision/.
5   Muriel Draaisma, "Activist Collect Signatures on Large Copy of Charter at Queen's Park Protest Picnic," *CBC News*, September 15, 2018. cbc.ca/news/canada/toronto/council-of-canadians-charter-ontario-government-1.4825407.
6   Supreme Court of Canada, *Toronto (City) v. Ontario (Attorney General)* [2021] SCC 34. decisions.scc-csc.ca/scc-csc/scc-csc/en/item/19011/index.do; see also, City of Toronto, "Supreme Court of Canada Rules Bill 5 is Constitutional," (Media Statement), October 1, 2021. toronto.ca/news/supreme-court-of-canada-rules-bill-5-is-constitutional/.
7   Alyshah Hasham, "Ontario Backtracks on Municipal Public Health Funding Cuts," *Toronto Star*, August 22, 2023. thestar.com/news/gta/ontario-backtracks-on-municipal-public-health-funding-cuts/article_d09b9322-b1ba-59d1-9700-4e7e54b582f4.html.
8   For more on this matter, see Mark Winfield's discussion in Chapter 13 of this book.
9   Steve Buist, "Ontario Land Tribunal Decisions Have Favoured Developers 97 Per Cent of the Time," *The Hamilton Spectator*, September 20, 2022. thespec.com/news/hamilton-region/ontario-land-tribunal-decisions-have-favoured-developers-97-per-cent-of-the-time/article_850b04e7-4fca-5b43-8473-9060bc024ce1.html.
10 For more on this, see William Paul's discussion in Chapter 12 of this book.
11 Charlie Pinkerton and Jack Hauen, "Land Tribunal Decides What Gets Built in Ontario, But Insiders Say It's Broken," *Newmarket Today*, February 4, 2024. newmarkettoday.ca/local-news/land-tribunal-decides-what-gets-built-in-ontario-but-insiders-say-its-broken-8198718.
12 Ryan Kelpin, "Right Populism or Neoliberalism? Understanding Austerity in Doug Ford's Ontario." *Alternate Routes: A Journal of Critical Social Research*, 34, 1 (2024): 64–79.
13 Doug Ford, *Municipal Elections*. Ontario Legislature. July 30, 2018. ola.org/en/legislative-business/house-documents/parliament-42/session-1/2018-07-30/hansard.
14 Ryan Kelpin, "Doug Ford's 'Strong Mayor' System is an Anti-Democratic Power Play," *Canadian Dimension*, August 8, 2022. canadiandimension.com/articles/view/doug-fords-strong-mayor-system-is-an-anti-democratic-power-play.
15 David Crombie, et al., "Former Toronto Mayors Warn 'Strong Mayors' Act Will Harm Local Democracy," *The Toronto Star*, August 15, 2022. thestar.com/opinion/contributors/former-toronto-mayors-warn-strong-mayors-act-will-harm-local-democracy/article_10c074c8-08a4-50bd-ad71-3cdfc7462140.html.

16 Marco Boffo, et al., "Neoliberal Capitalism: The Authoritarian Turn." *Socialist Register* 55,1 (2019): 24–70; Tom McDowell, *Neoliberal Parliamentarism: The Decline of Parliament at the Ontario Legislature* (Toronto: University of Toronto Press, 2021).
17 Kelpin, *Creatures of the Province Doctrine.*
18 Andrew Sancton, "Reassessing the Case for Development Charges in Canadian Municipalities." *Centre for Urban Policy and Local Governance* (London: Western University, 2021).
19 Association of Municipalities Ontario, "Unpacking Bill 23 — More Homes Built Faster Act, 2022," November 2, 2022. amo.on.ca/advocacy/health-human-services/unpacking-bill-23-more-homes-built-faster-act-2022.
20 Allison Jones, "Ontario Housing Bill to Short Municipalities by $5 Billion: AMO," *CTV Toronto*, November 17, 2022. toronto.ctvnews.ca/ontario-housing-bill-to-short-municipalities-by-5-billion-amo-1.6157777.
21 Open Council, "Strong Mayors Act Powers: Municipal Decision Tracker," April 25, 2024. opencouncil.ca/strong-mayor-powers-ontario.
22 Karen Martin-Robbins, "'Chilling': Caledon Mayor Using Ontario 'Strong-Mayor Powers' to Fast-Track 35,000 New Houses," *Caledon Enterprise*, March 27, 2024. caledonenterprise.com/news/chilling-caledon-mayor-using-ontario-strong-mayor-powers-to-fast-track-35-000-new-houses/article_9d82e412-9306-59ac-ab68-eae3c564b1b5.html.
23 Karen Martin-Robbins, "'My Guard Is Still Up': Caledon Mayor Removes 12 Developments for Fast-Tracked Rezoning from Council Agenda after Lengthy Public Meeting," *Caledon Enterprise,* April 29, 2024. caledonenterprise.com/news/council/my-guard-is-still-up-caledon-mayor-removes-12-developments-for-fast-tracked-rezoning-from/article_1e144983-46f8-5e39-b8ec-40b0cec082eb.html; Zachary Roman, "Province Unhappy with Caledon Mayor's Zoning Decision Due to Conflict with 413 Corridor," *The Hamilton Spectator,* May 9, 2024. thespec.com/news/canada/province-unhappy-with-caledon-mayor-s-zoning-decision-due-to-conflict-with-413-corridor/article_3bc3c052-d219-55a0-9a29-dd9b928bd824.html.
24 See Mark Winfield's discussion of this matter in Chapter 13 of this book.
25 City of Brampton, "Updated Data Confirms Dissolution Not in Best Interest of Region of Peel Taxpayers Across Brampton, Mississauga, and Caledon, Causing 38% Tax Increase." December 1, 2023. brampton.ca/EN/City-Hall/News/Pages/News-Release.aspx/1267. See also Region of Peel, "Region of Peel Financial Impact Analysis of Service Delivery Models, Final Report," May 21, 2019. peelregion.ca/government-review/pdf/;RegionofPeelFinancialImpactAnalysisofServiceDeliveryModelsFinalReportMay212019.pdf; Cynthia Mulligan, "Peel Dissolution Will Leave Brampton with $72 Million Deficit Every Year: New Report," *City News*, December 8, 2023. toronto.citynews.ca/2023/12/08/peel-dissolution-brampton-72-million-deficit-new-report/.
26 Saloni Bhugra, "Ontario Says Peel Region to Pay 'All Costs' for Transition Board," *CBC News*, April 22, 2024. cbc.ca/news/canada/toronto/peel-transition-board-bill-1.7181608; Isaac Callan and Collin D'Mello, "Peel Region Split Costs Grow to $4.4M as Council Demands Reimbursement," *Global News*, May 9, 2024. globalnews.ca/news/10485407/peel-region-transition-costs-increase-4-4/.
27 Issac Callan and Colin D'Mello, "Ontario Launched Audits to Find 'Waste' at

City Hall. No One Knows What They Say," *Global News*, May 9, 2024. globalnews.ca/news/10483920/ontario-bill-23-made-whole-audits/.
28 Desmond Brown, "Ontario Announces More Than $1.8B in New Funding to Help Municipalities Build Homes," *CBC News*, March 21, 2024. cbc.ca/news/canada/toronto/ontario-housing-funding-critical-infrastructure-1.7150799.
29 City Manager and Interim Chief Financial Officer and Treasurer, "Updated Long-Term Financial Plan," *City of Toronto*, August 14, 2023. toronto.ca/legdocs/mmis/2023/ex/bgrd/backgroundfile-238625.pdf. See also Fanelli's *Megacity Malaise*.
30 Robert Benzie and David Rider, "Auditor General to Probe Doug Ford's Controversial Scheme to Redevelop Ontario Place," *The Toronto Star*, November 3, 2023. thestar.com/politics/provincial/auditor-general-to-probe-doug-ford-s-controversial-scheme-to-redevelop-ontario-place/article_9026e1ed-47ff-5e3e-83c5-5fb477fd4ffb.html; Ian Darragh, "Ford's Legislation Fast-Tracking Ontario Place Mega-Spa Overrides Land-Use Protections," *Spacing: Canadian Urbanism Uncovered*, March 1, 2024. spacing.ca/toronto/2024/03/01/fords-legislation-fast-tracking-ontario-place-mega-spa-overrides-land-use-protections/.
31 International City-County Management Association (ICMA), *Municipal Form of Government 2011 — Full Dataset* (Mississippi State University: International City-County Management Association, 2011). https://scholarsjunction.msstate.edu/icma/2.
32 Kate Graham, "Leading Canada's Cities? A Study of Urban Mayors." (Unpublished doctoral dissertation, Western University, 2018). https://ir.lib.uwo.ca/etd/5745.
33 Zack Taylor, "Strong(er) Mayors in Ontario — What Difference Will They Make?" *Institute on Municipal Finance and Governance (IMFG)*, May 15, 2023. https://imfg.org/uploads/604/commentary_on_municipal_governance_changesdocx.pdf.
34 Taylor, "Strong(er) Mayors in Ontario."
35 For more on housing, see Lily Xia, Chapter 16, of this book.
36 Martine August, "The Financialization of Housing in Canada: A Summary Report for the Office of the Federal Housing Advocate," *The Office of the Federal Housing Advocate*, June 2022. publications.gc.ca/collections/collection_2023/ccdp-chrc/HR34-7-2022-eng.pdf.; see also, Andrew Crosby, *Resisting Eviction: Domicide and the Financialization of Rental Housing* (Halifax: Fernwood Publishing, 2023); Josh Brandon and Jim Silver, *Poor Housing: A Silent* Crisis (Halifax: Fernwood Publishing, 2015).
37 Neil Bradford, "A National Urban Policy for Canada? The Implicit Federal Agenda." Institute for Research on Public Policy, 24 (2018): 1–20. irpp.org/wp-content/uploads/2018/11/A-National-Urban-Policy-for-Canada-The-Implicit-Federal-Agenda.pdf.
38 See Dayna Nadine Scott and Dania Ahmed's discussion in Chapter 10 of this book.
39 John Loxley, *Ideology over Economics: P3s in an Age of Austerity* (Winnipeg: Fernwood Publishing, 2020).
40 Matt Elliot, "Toronto's Pricey and Ineffective New Plan for Snow Clearing is a Warning about Privatizing City Services," *The Toronto Star*, December 12, 2023. thestar.com/opinion/contributors/

toronto-s-pricey-and-ineffective-new-plan-for-snow-clearing-is-a-warning-about-privatizing/article_717ecaa2-9838-11ee-b528-638e145915ca.html; Allison Jones, "Ontario Seeks Municipal Daycare Audits, Raising Cost-Cutting Concerns," *CBC News*, January 31, 2024. cbc.ca/news/canada/toronto/municipal-daycare-audits-ontario-1.7100110.
41 See Carlo Fanelli and Katherine Nastovski, Chapter 8, in this book.
42 Gregory Albo and Carlo Fanelli, "Fiscal Distress and the Local State: Neoliberal Urbanism in Canada," in *Continuity and Change: Rethinking the New Canadian Political Economy*, eds. Mark Thomas, et al. (Montreal and Kingston: McGill-Queens University Press, 2019), 354–92.
43 John Sewell, "Toward City Charters in Canada." *Journal of Law and Social Policy* 34 (February 2021): 134–64. https://digitalcommons.osgoode.yorku.ca/jlsp/vol34/iss1/8/; see also: "A Proposal to Empower and Protect Toronto," Charter City Toronto, n.d. chartercitytoronto.ca/the-charter-city-proposal.html.
44 Mary Rowe (ed.), *Toronto: Considering Self-Government* (Toronto: Ginger Press, 2000).
45 See John Clarke, Chapter 17, in this book.

Chapter 16

1 Advocacy Centre for Tenant Ontario (ACTO), "Ontario is Dangerously Close to Enacting an Eviction Bill," July 2, 2020. acto.ca/ontario-eviction-bill. See also Camille Quenneville, "Bill 184: Protecting Tenants and Strengthening Community Housing Act, 2020," Canadian Mental Health Association Ontario, June 26, 2020. ontario.cmha.ca/wp-content/uploads/2020/07/CMHA-Ontario-submission-on-Bill-184-June-26-2020.pdf.
2 Douglas Kwan, "Submissions to the Standing Committee on Heritage, Infrastructure and Cultural Policy regarding Bill 97, Helping Homebuyers, Protecting Tenants Act, 2023," Advocacy Centre for Tenants Ontario, May 11, 2023. acto.ca/production/wp-content/uploads/2023/05/ACTO-Bill-97-Submissions-May-11-2023.pdf.
3 For more on this, see Kathy Laird, Chapter 6, in this book.
4 Chris Buckley, Patty Coates, and Ahmad Gaied, "The Simple Truth Behind Bill 57," Ontario Federation of Labour, December 2018. https://ofl.ca/wp-content/uploads/18-12-03-SM-Bill-57.pdf.
5 ACTO, "Tenant Protection and Rent Regulation in Ontario," Advocacy Centre for Tenants Ontario, March 2021. acto.ca/production/wp-content/uploads/2019/07/Factsheet_March2021.pdf.
6 Victor Fedeli (ed.), *A Plan for the People — Ontario Economic Outlook and Fiscal Review*. Ministry of Finance (Toronto: Queen's Printer, 2018).
7 Canada Mortgage and Housing Corporation. *Rent Controls, Rental Prices and Rental Supply: Empirical Evidence from Canadian Metropolitan Centres* (Ottawa: 2020).
8 ACTO, "Tenant Protections."
9 Elinor Mahoney, "The Ontario Tenant Protection Act: A Trust Betrayed." *Journal of Law and Social Policy* 16 (2001): 261–278. doi.org/10.60082/0829-3929.1059.
10 Ontario Newsroom, "To Build More Homes, Ontario Launching Building

Faster Fund and Expanding Strong Mayor Powers," August 21, 2023. news.ontario.ca/en/release/1003397/to-build-more-homes-ontario-launching-building-faster-fund-and-expanding-strong-mayor-powers.

11 Mike Crawley, "What Should Doug Ford's Government Do about Developers Who Go Years Without Building Homes?" *CBC News*, November 20, 2021. cbc.ca/news/canada/toronto/ontario-housing-doug-ford-developers-approvals-new-homes-1.7039776.

12 Ari Altstedter, "Toronto Condo Developers See Lowest New Unit Sales in 27 Years," *BNN Bloomberg*, July 18, 2024. www.bnnbloomberg.ca/business/real-estate/2024/07/18/toronto-condo-developers-see-lowest-new-unit-sales-in-27-years/.

13 Lucas Powers, "Ontario PCs Slash Spending and Oversight, Unveil Tax Cut and New LCBO Hours in 1st Economic Plan," *CBC News*, November 15, 2018. cbc.ca/news/canada/toronto/ontario-pc-fall-economic-outlook-cuts-tax-lcbo-1.4906718.

14 Martine August and Alan Walks, "Gentrification, Suburban Decline, and The Financialization of Multi-Family Rental Housing: The Case of Toronto." *Geoforum*, 89. (February 2018): 124-136.

15 Andrew Crosby, *Resisting Eviction: Domicide and the Financialization of Rental Housing*. (Halifax: Fernwood, 2023).

16 Cole Webber and Philip Zigman, "Renovictions: Displacement and Resistance in Toronto," *RenovictionsTO*, April 2023. https://renovictionsto.com/reports/RenovictionsTO-RenovictionsReport-Final.pdf.

17 Dream Unlimited, "Building Better Communities: 2022 Sustainability Report," (website). https://sustainability.dream.ca/wp-content/uploads/2023/05/DreamGroupofCompanies_SustainabilityReport_2022.pdf, p.159.

18 Angela Hennessy, "How 'Financialized' Landlords May Be Contributing to Rising Rents in Canada," *CBC News*, September 9, 2024. cbc.ca/news/financialized-landlord-higher-rents-canada-1.7307015.

19 Mac King, "'Warehousing': Why New York City Landlords Don't List All Their Empty Apartments," *Fox5 New York*, April 22, 2021. fox5ny.com/news/nyc-warehousing-empty-apartments.

20 Heather Vogell, "Rent Going Up? One Company's Algorithm Could Be Why," *Propublica*, October 15, 2022. propublica.org/article/yieldstar-rent-increase-realpage-rent.

21 Shane Dingman, "Tenant Groups Call for Scrutiny of American Software Company after U.S. Lawsuits Alleging Rent Collusion," *Globe and Mail*, July 24, 2024. theglobeandmail.com/real-estate/article-tenant-groups-call-for-scrutiny-of-american-software-company-after-us/.

22 For more on this, see William Paul, Chapter 12, in this book.

23 Neil Smith, *The New Urban Frontier: Gentrification and the Revanchist City* (London: Routledge, 1996).

24 Philip Zigman and Martine August, "Above Guideline Rent Increases in the Age of Financialization," *RenovictionsTO*, February 2021. renovictionsto.com/reports/RenovictionsTO-AGIReport-Final.pdf.

25 Dream Unlimited, "Bold Ideas for Better Communities," (website), n.d. https://dream.ca/.

26   Meaghan Peloso, "Dream Investor Day," (presentation), September 6, 2023.
27   Jamie Cooper, "Dream Investor Day," (presentation), September 6, 2023.
28   Cooper.
29   Lily Xia et. al., "Tenants' Experiences in Canada's Financialized Housing System: The Role and Responsibility of the Federal Government," Federation of Metro Tenants' Associations, August 2023. https://cms.nhc-cnl.ca/media/PDFs/RP1%20Written%20Hearing%20Record/Federation%20of%20Metro%20Tenants'%20Association%20-%20Tenant%20Action%20Committee.pdf.
30   Sunera Thobani, *Exalted Subjects: Studies in the Making of Race and Nation in Canada* (Toronto: University of Toronto Press, 2007).
31   See West 22 (website), n.d. https://www.west22.ca/.
32   West22 (website).

Chapter 17

1   Michal Rozworski, "Canada's Harsh 'Austerity' Policies Started with Liberals," *The Tyee,* August 25, 2015. thetyee.ca/Opinion/2015/08/25/Canadas-Harsh-Austerity/.
2   Kamran Mofid, "People's Tragedy: Neoliberal Legacy of Thatcher and Reagan," *Globalisation for the Common Good Initiative,* October 15, 2014. gcgi.info/index.php/blog/627-people-s-tragedy-neoliberal-legacy-of-thatcher-and-reagan. Also, see Bryan Evans and Carlo Fanelli's introduction in Chapter 1 of this book.
3   Ontario Federation of Labour (OFL), "'The Common Sense Revolution': 1,460 Days of Destruction," 1999 Election Edition. https://ofl.ca/wp-content/uploads/1999.01.01-Factsheets-Election-FightBack.pdf.
4   Alex Callinicos, "Neoliberalism is Alive and Useful to Rulers," *Socialist Worker,* May 4, 2021.
5   International Monetary Fund (IMF), "IMF Survey: IMF Work Agenda Stresses Agile, Integrated, Member-Focused Approach," *IMF News,* December 17, 2015. www.imf.org/en/News/Articles/2015/09/28/04/53/sopol121415a.
6   Michael Roberts, "Polycrisis Again," *Michael Roberts* (blog), October 8, 2023. https://thenextrecession.wordpress.com/2023/10/08/polycrisis-again/.
7   Mira Miller, "Doug Ford Just Told Tenants in Ontario They Don't Have to Pay Rent If They Can't Afford It," *BlogTO,* March 26, 2020. www.blogto.com/city/2020/03/doug-ford-tenants-toronto-dont-have-pay-rent-if-cant-afford-it/.
8   Dan La Botz, "Ontario's 'Days of Action' — A Citywide Political Strike Offers a Potential Example for Madison,' *Labor Notes,* March 9, 2011. labornotes.org/2011/03/ontarios-days-action-citywide-political-strike-offers-potential-example-madison.
9   Trevor Cole, "Tim Hudak Spent His Life Climbing the Tory Ladder and Now He Has a Shot at Taking Over Queen's Park — But Can He Convince Voters He's More than Just Mike Harris Lite?" *Toronto Life,* October 3, 2011.
10   Greg Albo, Bryan Evans and Carlo Fanelli, "So Much for 'Austerity-Light' in Ontario," *Policy Options,* May 15, 2019.
11   Dan Darrah, "Ontario's Days of Action Offer a Lesson for Canadian Workers Today," *Jacobin Magazine,* November 30, 2020. jacobin.com/2020/11/

ontario-days-of-action-canada-workers-unions-strike-mike-harris. Also, see Venai Raniga's Chapter 2 in this book.

12. Muriel Draaisma, "Nearly $2 Million Spent on Clearing Encampments Should Have Gone to Housing, Advocates Say," *CBC News,* September 18, 2021. Also, see Maria Rio's Chapter 9 for more discussion of this matter.

13. CBC News, "Hundreds Protest Ontario Bill They Say Gives Landlords More Ways to Evict Tenants," July 6, 2020. For more on this, see Lily Xia, Chapter 16, in this book.

14. See Michael Hurley and Doug Allan, Chapter 7, in this book.

15. OFL, "Ontarians Say 'Enough Is Enough' with Day of Action to Fight Cost-of-Living Crisis," June 3, 2023. https://ofl.ca/ontarians-say-enough-is-enough-with-day-of-action-to-fight-cost-of-living-crisis/. Also, see Mark Winfield, Chapter 13, and Carlo Fanelli and Ryan Kelpin, Chapter 15, in this book.

16. John Clarke, "Beyond Compromise and Constraint," *Spectre Journal,* January 10, 2023.

17. Allison Jones and Liam Casey, "'There Were No Other Options Left': Inside Ontario's Bid to End the Education Walkout," *Canadian Press,* November 10, 2022; Colin D'Mello and Isaac Callan, "CUPE Tells Education Support Workers in Ontario to Accept Tentative Contract Offer," *Global News,* November 23, 2022.

18. Jordan Fleguel, "'I Don't Like This Deal': Walton Says Tentative Agreement between CUPE and the Province Still Falls Short," *CP 24,* November 20, 2022.

19. Clarke, "Beyond Compromise."

20. Nan Li and Diaa Noureldin, "World Must Prioritize Productivity Reforms to Revive Medium-Term Growth," *IMF* (Blog), April 10, 2024.

21. Vanessa Balintec, "Advocates Decry Ontario Budget's Failure to Boost ODSP, OW," *CBCNews,* April 6, 2024. cbc.ca/news/canada/toronto/2024-budget-odsp-ow-1.7163436.

22. John Clarke, "Canada's Tories: An Attack Dog at the Ready," *Counterfire,* September 18, 2022.

23. "Heightened Police Repression against Palestinian Solidarity Protesters in Toronto," *Samidoun Network,* January 24, 2024. https://samidoun.net/2024/01/heightened-police-repression-against-palestinian-solidarity-protesters-in-toronto/.

24. Hugh Schofield and Paul Kirby, "France's Macron to Force through Pension Reform with No Vote," *BBC,* March 16, 2023. bbc.com/news/world-europe-64967516.

INDEX

accountability, 112, 208
    calls for, 120, 122–3, 130–1
    in education, 43, 68–9, 157
    for food insecurity/poverty, 122–3, 130–1
    lack of Ford government, 93, 127, 151–2, 181
    mayoral, 198–99, 203
    weakened legislative oversight for government, 182–6, 188, 191–3
    see also Financial Accountability Office reports
adjudicative tribunals,
    adjudicator replacement, 70–1, 73–5
    functions, 70, 72–6, 82–4
    see also Human Rights Tribunal; Landlord and Tenant Board; Ontario Land Tribunal
Advocacy Centre for Tenants Ontario (ACTO), 207–8
agricultural land, 122, 173
    real estate development on, 161, 177, 180–1
Alberta, 17, 50, 149, 172
Albo, Greg, 222
alcohol/beer, 5, 14, 115
Amato, Ryan, 162–4
Anishinaabe, 30–1, 132
Argo Developments, 159–60, 164
Art Gallery of Ontario (AGO) workers' strike, 28
artificial intelligence (AI), 212
    arts and culture impacts, 36, 38–40
arts and culture,
    COVID-19 pandemic struggles, 7, 34–6, 39–40
    economic impact of, 30, 34–5
    Francophone, 59, 62
    funding cuts, 28–9, 31–6, 39–40, 59, 63
    Indigenous, 28–32, 59, 134, 140
    postsecondary programs, 28–9, 36–40, 57–9, 62, 68–9

Association of Early Childhood Educators of Ontario (AECEO), 152–4
austerity policies,
    despite economic capacity, 13, 39
    Ford government, 4–10, 23, 29, 169, 219–22
    Harris government, 219–22
    Liberal government, 85, 219–20
    manipulating fiscal data and, 20–3
    populist, 8, 20, 219
    public service reductions and, 1–2, 20, 23, 26, 98, 204
    worker organizing amid, 112–13, 169–70, 229
Australia, 65, 137, 150–1
authoritarianism, 5, 106, 191–3, 195, 198

back-to-work legislation, 100–2, 104–5
Bank, Per, 128–9
banks, 1, 108, 110
basic income, 40, 158
Belobaba, Edward, 196
Better Local Government Act (BLGA; Bill 5): 187, 195–6
Better Municipal Government Act (BMGA, Bill 39): 191, 198
Bradford Bypass, 159–60, 173, 178
Brampton, 9, 159, 201
British Columbia,
    health care services in, 96–7, 100–1
    public service spending, 14, 21, 86, 149
Brown, Patrick, 41–2
budgets, 4, 18, 72, 118
    arts and culture cuts in, 29–30, 33, 35
    child care, 145–9, 155
    education cuts in, 36, 49, 68
    Ford austerity, 6, 13, 26–7, 155, 210
    manipulation of data for, 20–3, 26–7, 155
    municipal, 146–7, 188, 198, 205
    underspending in, 6–7, 49, 91–2

Building Faster Fund, 200, 209
business,
    curricular focus on, 43, 46–8, 55
    social services run as, 95, 151–2
    legislation to support, 15, 103–4, 150
    local/Indigenous, 36, 39, 133, 142
    privileging interests of, 2, 5–6, 10–11, 180
    reorganizing for profitability of, 4, 26–7, 102, 221
    taxation of, 14, 25
    worker/tenant interests versus, 108–10, 218
    see also corporations; developers

Caledon, 200–1
Canada-Wide Early Learning and Child Care (CWELCC) agreement, 143–4, 148–52, 155–6
Canadian Institute for Health Information (CIHI) data, 86, 90, 245n7
Canadian Union of Public Employees, see CUPE
cap-and-trade program termination, 6, 49, 158, 172
capitalism,
    accumulation in, 55, 68
    policies reinforcing, 4, 10, 118, 126–7, 220–1
carbon, 159
    pricing, 49, 171–2
    reduction schemes, 9, 52, 132, 214
    tax, 5, 172
Celebrate Ontario, 33–4
charter cities, 205
Charter of Rights and Freedoms,
    Ford government infringement of, 6, 17, 38, 44, 192
    legal challenges based on, 105–6, 107–8, 113–14
    notwithstanding clause, use against, 9, 17, 158, 184, 187–8, 196
child care,
    advocacy, 143, 147, 149–56
    CARE tax credit, 145–6
    federal support for, 143–4, 148–52, 155–6

Ford government impacts on, 143–4, 147–51, 153–6, 180
    funding, lack of, 97, 144–8, 156
    lack of accessible, 143–4, 149, 151, 156
    Liberal policies on, 144–5, 149, 153–4
    municipal coverage of, 146–8, 154–5, 194
    privatization, 6, 143–5, 147, 150, 156
    public, 143–5, 147–8, 151–3, 155–6
    workers, 143–8, 150, 153, 156
    see also Canada-Wide Early Learning and Child Care (CW-ELCC) agreement; early childhood educators
Chow, Olivia, 127
Clark, Steve, 162, 164
class,
    business/ruling, 2, 102
    compromise, 226–7, 230
    identity, 11–12, 112
    middle, 146, 153
    politics, 9, 220, 227
    struggles, 3–4, 11–12, 220–2
    working, see working class
Clearpoint (private hospital), 165–6
climate change, 12, 204
    Ford versus federal strategy on, 174–5, 177, 180–1
    lack of concern for, 9, 49–50, 171–2
clinics, private health, 93–7, 165, 169, 186
closure, legislative use of, 182–5, 191–2
collective bargaining, 60, 108, 113, 115, 248n15
    Conservative intervention into, 16, 98, 102–7, 187, 227–8
Common Sense Revolution, 3–6
    challenging, 219–24
Companies' Creditors Arrangement Act (CCAA), 69, 242n12
    Laurentian University debacle, 54, 58–64, 66–7
Connecting People to Home and Community Care Act (Bill 175): 185–6

Conservative governments,
  challenging, 219–24, 226–30
  discourse of, 1–8, 95, 148, 151–2, 174, 177–80
  Ford, see Ford Conservatives
constitutionality (lack of), 154
  challenging legislation for, 16, 19, 38, 46, 105–7, 172
  Crown-Indigenous relations and, 134, 141
  municipal-provincial relations and, 182, 186, 191–3, 205
  notwithstanding clause and, 9, 17, 158, 182–4, 187–8, 196
Convenient Care at Home Act (Bill 135), 185–6
Cooper, Michael and Jamie, 214–15
corporations, 198
  food insecurity and, 117–18, 120–1, 129–31
  lobbying by, 158, 160–5, 167–8, 225
  policies boosting profits of, 14–15, 59–61
  privileging involvement of, 65–6, 120–1, 179
  subsidies for, 5, 14, 115–16, 166
  tax cuts for, 1, 14, 24–6, 115
  worker wages versus, 102, 108–10, 115, 129–30
  see also business; developers
corporatization, 40, 126
  child care, 151, 156
  curricular reform and, 43, 46–8, 51–2
  health care, 92–3, 166
  municipal council, 198, 203, 205
  university, 53–8, 67–8
Cortellucci, Mario, 159, 165
cost of living, 174
  calculations of, 122–4, 128
  crisis, 18–20, 115, 224, 228
  housing and, 18, 39, 203, 215
  stagnant wages and, 14, 18, 122
COVID-19 pandemic, 51, 125
  arts and culture amid, 7, 34–6, 39–40
  child care in, 147–8, 154–6
  economic/housing impacts, 13–18, 26, 108, 220–1, 224

Ford government mishandling of, 21, 156, 166, 174, 180
  governance fast-tracking amid, 75, 190, 197
  hospitals/health care in, 85, 89–90, 94, 97–8, 139, 225
  Indigenous communities amid, 139–40
cronyism, 159, 168–9
CUPE (Canadian Union of Public Employees),
  education worker illegal strike, 17, 105–6, 187–8, 226–9
  Local 3903 York University strike, 102–3
curriculum, 51–2, 145
  financial literacy, 43, 45–8
  gender identity and consent, 41–2
  Indigenous Peoples' representation in, 42–3, 158
  mathematics, 43–5
Cree artists, 32, 37

Davis, Bill, 4, 183
Days of Action, 221–4, 226–30
De Gasperis family, 159–63
delegated legislation, use of, 182, 184–5, 189, 192
De Meneghi family, 159–60
democracy,
  cynicism about, 2, 11, 84, 181
  government infringement of, 9, 158, 167–9, 183–6, 192–3
  local, 169, 177, 180, 188–9, 195–200, 202–3
  parliamentary, 182–3
  university violations of, 54, 58, 61, 69
deregulation, 5, 14, 189, 203, 216
  legislation for, 14, 205–13
developers, 197
  Conservative connections with, 159–60, 164, 180–2, 218
  Greenbelt, 47, 50, 160, 173, 176–7, 225
  legislation for, 14, 173, 199–201
  privileging interests of, 6, 18, 84, 169, 178, 209–15
  "value add" initiatives, 211, 213–14

Diamond, Michael, 127, 158
Diamond, Sara, 36
Di Poce, John, 159
disabled people, 7, 104, 119, 144
   benefits support rates, 70, 108, 124–5
   see also Ontario Disability Support Program
doctors, family, 94
   lack of, 16, 91, 100
   performance of risky procedures, 93
Dream Unlimited (developer), 211–12
   rent strikes against, 213–18
Dubé, Paul, 51
Dunlop, Jill, 60, 64, 68

early childhood educators (ECEs), 144–5, 148, 150–5
economic performance, provincial, 3
   austerity and inequality amid strong, 13–14, 19–20, 115, 130, 204–5
   Conservative underfunding and, 6–7, 13–15, 110, 117, 148
   COVID-19 and, 13–18, 39–40, 220
   megaproject unsustainability and, 178–9
   neoliberal shaping of, 3–5, 46, 120, 172, 221, 228
education,
   Ford government policies on, 41–7, 105, 108, 158
   funding, lack of, 5–7, 21–2, 36, 48–51, 169
   job vacancies in, 17, 108
   postsecondary, see postsecondary education
   privatization of, 46, 48–51, 53–9, 66, 68
   STEM, 43, 63
   support for public, 3, 52, 54, 69
   university, see universities
   worker illegal strike, 17, 105–6, 187–8, 226–9
   see also schools; students; teachers
Education Quality and Accountability Office (EQAO), 43–4, 157–8
Efficient Local Government Act (Bill 31): 187, 196

elections, 158, 187
   abrupt decisions prior to/after, 19, 49–50, 60, 73–4, 153, 195
   campaign platforms, 1, 4–5, 49–50, 85, 144–5, 167, 178
   Conservative success in, 3, 8–10, 92
   cynicism about, 11, 181, 196
   donations amid, 162, 167–9, 171
   forcing legislative changes amid, 174–5, 183, 187–9, 192, 195–6
   gimmicks for, 8–9, 19–20, 64, 161–2
   municipal, 9, 187, 195–6, 203
electric vehicles (EVs), 49, 132–7, 142, 172
Elliott, Christine, 41, 165
employment, 40, 57
   health and safety, 14, 144
   hospital, 86–7
   Human Rights Tribunal and, 70, 74
   insurance, 115, 123
   poverty reduction and, 121–4
   precarious, 14–16, 26, 28–9, 38
   protections, 15–16, 103, 115, 117, 228
   standards, lack of, 15, 46, 102–4, 110, 112
   widespread lack of, 3–4, 199
environmental assessments, 133, 139–40, 174, 178–9
environmental regulations, 14, 138, 173
   breaching, 14, 135, 141–2, 174
equal pay, 15, 103, 115
Experience Ontario, 33–5
extraction, resource, 63, 171, 181
   "fast tracking," 137–8, 141
   (lack of) Indigenous consent for, 132–6, 140–2

Family Compact, 2, 11
far north, 75, 132–4, 136, 142
Feheley, Megan, 37–8
festivals, arts/music, 33–6, 38–9
Fidani-Diker, Nico, 164, 168
Fieldgate Homes, 159–60, 162, 164
Financial Accountability Office (FAO)
   reports, 6, 90, 99, 146, 204, 222
Flato Developments, 161, 164

food banks, 7, 18, 117–21, 125–30
food costs, inflation and, 17–18, 117, 120, 128
food insecurity,
  charity and, 117–20
  corporate influence on, 117, 120–1, 125
  government/corporate inaction on, 121, 123
  systemic inequities and, 119, 124–5, 129, 130
Ford Conservatives,
  accountability, lack of, 93, 127, 151–2, 181
  budgets, 6–7, 13, 20–3, 26–7, 155, 210
  COVID-19 mishandling, 21, 156, 166, 174, 180, 190, 197
  developer connections, 159–60, 164, 180–2, 218
  electoral success, 8–10, 70, 92
  fiscal policies, 4–10, 20–7, 29, 169, 219–22
  governance strategies, 2, 5–6, 43, 46–8, 55, 10–11, 180
  on hallway health care, 87–8, 97, 100, 225
  infringement of Charter, 6, 17, 38, 44, 192
  staff salaries, 23, 157, 164
  underspending by, 13–15, 49, 91–2, 97, 144–8, 156, 180
Ford, Doug, 219, 230
  antagonism toward progressive education, 41, 43–4, 48–52
  blaming-the-victim politics, 46–7, 221
  election of, 1, 29, 70, 121, 168
  as erratic, 219, 222, 230
  interference in municipal politics, 194–201
  labour movement versus, 102, 106–7
  patronage politics, 2–3, 10–11, 66, 157–60, 164
  populism of, 8–10, 19–20, 41, 115, 132
  slogans/gimmicks, 1, 8, 19–20, 64, 161–2
  see also gravy train

Ford, Rob, 157, 160, 164, 194
Ford Nation, 195
  malleable political imaginary, 8–9, 11, 133, 180–1
  as vehicle for market fundamentalism, 1–3, 5, 29
Fringe Festival (Toronto), 36
Fullerton, Merrilee, 54–5
funding, lack of,
  arts and culture, 28–9, 31–6, 39–40, 59, 63
  child care, 97, 144–8, 156
  education, 5–7, 21–2, 36, 48–51, 169
  health care, 85–6, 89–92, 100–1
  public services, 1–2, 20, 23, 26, 98, 204
  universities, 36–8, 55–9, 64–5, 68–9

gender identity/consent curriculum, 41–2
Granic Allen, Tanya, 41
Grassy Narrows First Nation, 140
gravy train, 8, 157, 167, 168–70
Gray, Tim, 161, 164
Greater Toronto Area, 111, 115, 123–4, 161, 173, 181
Greenbelt, 180–1
  environmental precarity of, 18, 160
  land-use challenges and, 176–7, 200
  Liberal protection of, 160–1
  Minister's Zoning Orders (MZOs) and, 160–1, 164–5, 173, 202
  opening to developers, 3, 18, 47, 50, 160–5, 213, 225
greenhouse gases (GHGs), 171–2, 179–80
Greenhouse Gas Reduction Fund (GGRF), 49–50
Greenlane Bathurst, 161–2
Guilbeault, Steven, 140–1

Harper, Stephen, 45, 157
Harris, Mike, 3, 173
  Doug Ford compared to, 5, 159, 173, 189, 219–24
  policies of, 50, 85, 92, 158, 188, 194; see also Common Sense Revolution

health care,
  aging population and, 25, 85, 88–92, 99–100
  clinics, *see* clinics, private health
  COVID-19 and, 85, 89–90, 94, 97–8, 139, 225
  funding, lack of, 85–6, 89–92, 100–1
  privatization, 92–4, 100–1, 165–6, 169, 185–6, 192
  staffing crisis, 13, 16, 97–101, 107–8, 147
  support for public, 3, 100–1
  see also hospitals
Highway 413: 159–61, 178, 200
home care,
  Conservative underfunding of, 7, 90–1, 100
  privatization of, 103, 185
homelessness, 167, 169, 224, 229
hospitals, 3, 96
  bed reductions, 85, 87–92
  COVID-19 and, 89–90
  emergency room back-ups/closures, 7, 86, 90, 97, 225
  hallway health care, 87–8, 97, 100, 225
  increasing demand for, 89–92
  private, 165–6
  underfunding of, 7, 85–6, 89–92, 245n7
  understaffing of, 86–7, 90, 92, 97–101
  see also health care
housing,
  adjudicative disputes about, 70, 72, 80, 83
  affordability crisis, 13, 18, 47, 110–11, 209–16
  deregulation, 205–13, 216
  Ford government planning for, 175–7, 198–203, 207–9
  Greenbelt land and, 18, 176–7, 200
  insecurity, 29, 37–9, 115, 130, 216, 224–5
  municipal provision of, 194–5, 198–204, 209–10
  private profits from, 23, 162–4, 169, 180, 199, 207
  rental, 70, 75, 177, 209–10
  supportive/non-profit, 7, 194, 201–3
  underspending on, 7, 110–11, 180, 202
Human Rights Code, 77, 105–6
Human Rights Tribunal (HRTO),
  adjudicator replacement, 70–1, 73–4
  backlog and case dismissal, 71–2, 76–80, 83
  functions of, 70, 79–80, 84
Hunt (Tłaliłila'ogwa), Sarah, 142

immigrants, 8–9, 119
Indigenous Culture Fund (ICF), 29–32
Indigenous people, 99, 119, 149
  arts and culture, support for, 28–32, 59, 134, 140
  COVID-19 pandemic impacts, 139–40
  culture/language revitalization, 30–2, 132
  curriculum representation of, 42–3, 158
  lack of consent for resource extraction, 132–8, 140–2
  postsecondary education, 59, 62–3, 66–9
  sovereignty, 138–42, 204
  Treaty No. 9: 132–4, 136–9, 141–2
industrialization, Ontario, 3, 140
industrial relations system, 111–14
inflation, 183, 204
  economic performance amid, 13–14, 18–23
  grocery/food price, 17–18, 117, 120, 128
  neoliberal policies and, 1, 16–17, 47, 110
  as pressing public issue, 7, 18, 47–8, 55, 220, 228
  public service spending versus, 14, 20, 22, 90, 155
  rising, 3, 16, 38, 98, 111, 224
  wages versus, 15–19, 38, 103–6, 109–10, 226
infrastructure,
  backlog/deteriorating, 23, 132–3, 204

building, 3, 5, 178–80, 194
Ford government approach to, 23, 92, 171–5, 201–2, 209–10
inadequate funding, 7, 23, 92, 176
megaprojects, 171, 178–80
municipal coverage of, 194, 199, 209–10
plans, 23, 92, 201
social, 20, 129, 220, 222, 228
International Monetary Fund (IMF), 220, 228

Jacobson, Kelsey, 35–6
judicial intervention, 2–3, 159, 196

Keeping Students in Class Act (Bill 28): 105, 187–8, 226–7
Koehnen, Markus, 38, 107

Land Defence Alliance, 140, 142
landlords,
dispute resolution, 70, 72, 80–4
policies favouring, 207–11, 225
"squeezing" tenants for profit, 210–13
tenant struggles against, 213–18, 225
see also Landlord and Tenant Board; tenants
Landlord and Tenant Board (LTB), 208
adjudicator replacement, 70–1, 74
backlog and wait times, 71–2, 80–3, 244n20
functions of, 70, 83–4
loss of in-person hearings, 75–6, 82–3
Laurentian University, 69, 241n1
blue-ribbon panel, 65–8
CCAA involvement, 54, 58–64, 66–7
faculty terminations, 58, 61–3
Ford government failure with, 58–61, 63
N'Swakamok Reconciliation Declaration, 58, 65
Lecce, Stephen, 47, 160
child care funding, 145–6, 149–52, 155–6

critiques of teachers, 44
curriculum reforms, 42–6
legislature, Ontario, 127, 221
Ford weakening capacity of, 182–5, 189–92
Standing Orders, 183, 189
Lewsen, Simon, 10
Liberal Party of Ontario, 157
Conservative governance versus, 44, 159–60, 166, 188–9, 222
dismantling prior initiatives of, 44, 49, 71, 73, 103, 172
Ford government critiques of, 42, 44, 81, 133
policies and programs of, 54, 85, 93, 122, 136, 153
see also Wynne, Kathleen
Liquor Control Board of Ontario (LCBO), 115, 158, 248n15
Loblaws, 121, 128–9
Local Health Integrated Networks (LHINs), 185
long-term care, 7
bed reductions, 85, 91, 246n20
Conservative privatizing of, 23, 50, 100, 165–7, 180
COVID-19 in, 85, 90, 98, 166, 225
staffing, 98–100
underfunding, 85, 88, 90–2, 169, 194
Loreto, Chris, 167–8
Lysyk, Bonnie, 162

Macron, Emmanuel, 229–30
Mamakwa, Sol, 32, 135
Massoudi, Amin, 163, 166
Matawa First Nations, 133, 138, 141
Math Proficiency Test (MPT), 43–4, 46
Matthews, Deb, 93–4
McGuinty, Dalton, 93, 189, 222
medical assistance in dying (MAID), 125
megaprojects, 63, 171, 178–80
Mehra, Natalie, 165–6
Metro grocery stores, 120–1
worker strikes, 111, 115
Miele, Tony, 159
minimum wage,
Ford cancellation of increased, 15, 46, 103, 158

inadequacy of, 47, 110, 115–18, 122–4, 129
living versus, 123–4, 127–30, 206
mining, 167, 180
    Ring of Fire negotiations, 132–8, 140–2
    see also extraction, resource
Ministry of Municipal Affairs and Housing (MMAH), 162–4, 166
Mississauga, 9, 126, 201, 210
Moonias, Wayne, 139–40
Mulroney, Caroline, 158, 160, 166
municipalities,
    budgets, 146–7, 188, 198, 205
    child care provision, 146–8, 154–5, 194
    corporatization of, 198, 203, 205
    elections, 195–6, 203
    Ford government interference in, 194–201
    housing/infrastructure provision, 194–5, 198–204, 209–10
Mushkegowuk First Nation, 138, 141
music programs/festivals, 29, 33–4, 39
Mutton, John, 163

NDP (New Democratic Party), 9, 32, 63, 81, 160
    government policies, 54, 85, 190
neoliberalism, 144
    anti-democratic governance and, 182–3, 198
    education sector changes and, 42–5, 48–50, 62, 68
    government policies reinforcing, 8, 53–4, 68, 159
    principles/emergence of, 1, 3–4, 14, 55, 170
Neskantaga First Nation, 134, 138–40
New Deal for Toronto Act (NDTA), 201–2
Niagara Region, 92, 159–60, 164, 195
Nigro, Carmine, 158, 165, 168
Nipissing First Nation, 28, 30–2
non-profit sector, 158, 194
    child care and, 143–4, 147, 150–1, 154
    food insecurity and, 117–22, 125–31
nuclear energy, 105, 173, 178–80

OCADU (Ontario College of Art & Design University),
    faculty association, 28, 38
    funding cut impacts, 36–40
    workers' strike, 28, 37–8
omnibus legislation, 102, 182, 184–6, 189, 199
Ontario Arts Council (OAC), 31
    arts funding (cuts), 28–30, 34
Ontario Coalition Against Poverty (OCAP), 223, 230
Ontario Coalition for Better Child Care (OCBCC), 152–4
Ontario Disability Support Program (ODSP), 104, 122–5, 228
Ontario Federation of Labour (OFL), 38, 65, 105, 209, 220, 225
Ontario Health Coalition (OHC), 85, 92–5
Ontario Hydro, 179–80
Ontario Integrity Commission (OIC), 61, 160, 162–3, 167–8, 176
Ontario Labour Relations Board (OLRB), 75, 103–5
Ontario Land Tribunal (OLT), 175, 177, 197, 199
    adjudicator replacement, 70–1, 73
Ontario Place, 167, 178
    privatization of, 3, 158, 201–2
Ontario Power Generation (OPG), 104, 179
Ontario Public Service Employees Union (OPSEU/SEFPO), 38, 65, 248n16
Ontario School Board Council of Unions (OSBCU), 17, 105–7, 112–13, 226–7
Ontario Science Centre, moving of, 3, 7, 178
Ontario Student Assistance Program (OSAP) cuts, 37–8, 54–5
Ontario Works (OW), 104, 124–5, 228
"open for business" policies, 15, 103–4, 150, 169
organized labour, 44, 107
    renewed militancy, 17, 111
    unions versus, 114–15

palliative care, 100, 129
patronage, 66, 74–5
    Ford government, 2–3, 10–11, 66, 157–60, 164
    historical, 2, 10
Peel Region, 147, 164, 195, 201
Pelletier, Christian, 35
per capita spending, 6, 34
    health care, 21–2, 86, 94, 245n4
    student/education, 48, 53–5, 64–5, 69
Pirie, George, 132, 135–8
Poilievre, Pierre, 10, 157, 229
police, 99, 194, 198
    Conservative privileging of, 105, 157, 201
    eviction involvement, 215, 217, 224
Poloz, Stephen, 110
populism, 189
    Ford-style, 8–10, 19–20, 50–1, 54, 63, 142
    functions of, 8–9, 57, 219
    market, 174, 181
postsecondary education,
    arts and culture, 28–9, 36–40, 57–9, 62, 68–9
    (de)stabilization of, 54, 57–8, 65, 68–9
    enrolment, 53–7, 61–2, 67–9
    Francophone, 59, 62–3, 67–9
    Indigenous, 59, 62–3, 66–9
    process/impacts of privatization, 53–9, 66, 68
    tuition costs, see tuition
    see also universities
post–World War II policy, 1, 3, 171–2
poverty,
    government perceptions/measures of, 117–19, 121–5
    (inadequate) measures to address, 122–5, 127, 129–30, 228
    inequitable program closures and, 29, 57, 76
    tax rates despite, 24
privatization, 104, 115, 204
    child care, 143–4, 150, 156
    education, 46, 48–51, 53–9, 66, 68
    government justification for, 3–5, 13, 21, 169

health care, *see* health care, 92–4, 100–1, 165–6, 169, 185–6, 192
public services/assets, 1, 6, 23–4, 26
Progressive Conservatives, 187
    early policies of, 4, 50, 85, 183, 188
    Ford government, *see* Ford Conservatives
    municipal interference by, 192, 194
    reinvention, 3–6, 50
    see also Common Sense Revolution
Protecting a Sustainable Public Sector for Future Generations Act (Bill 124): 38, 245n7
    impacts on workers, 15, 19, 98, 105–9, 248n15
    repeal/unconstitutionality of, 16, 28, 46, 65, 107
Protecting Tenants and Strengthening Community Housing Act (Bill 184): 207–8
public-private partnerships (P3s), 23, 93, 96
public schools, 194
    Conservative attacks on, 41, 45
    curriculum and testing in, 43–6, 48
    defunding and privatizing of, 49–52
public sector, 174
    Bill 124 impacts, *see Protecting a Sustainable Public Sector for Future Generations Act*
    decline in spending on, 4, 20–2, 158
    job vacancies, 4, 16–17, 26, 104
    workers, 19, 105, 111, 113, 187, 226
public services, 17, 115, 248n15
    business approach to, 95, 104, 151–2
    inflation versus spending on, 14, 20–2, 86, 90, 149, 155
    neoliberal policies and, 1–2, 20, 23, 26, 98, 204
    privatizing, 1–2, 6, 23–4, 26
    reliance on, 13–14, 108
    underspending on, 6, 21–3, 26, 104, 194

Quebec, 14, 21, 86, 111, 169

Rae, Bob, 85, 133
real estate investment, 18, 126, 211
Rehmatullah, Shakir, 161–3
Remtulla, Amir, 160, 168
rent control, 130–1, 203, 207–10
rent strikes, 213–18, 225
Restoring Trust, Transparency and Accountability Act (Bill 57): 189
Rice, Michael, 161–4
Rickford, Greg, 133, 135, 142
Ring of Fire, 63, 167
    Ford government approach to, 132, 135–8, 141, 171
    Indigenous resistance/lawsuit over, 133–5, 138–42

schools, 105, 194
    funding cuts for, 29, 49–52, 169
    public, *see* public schools
    repair backlog for, 49–50, 169
Simcoe, John Graves, 2
skilled trades, 45, 47, 109
social assistance, 3, 75, 201, 228
    inadequate rates, 7, 117–18, 121–4, 129–30, 224
Southbridge Homes, 166
Spratt, Michael, 158
strikes, worker, 28, 107, 111–12, 115
    Days of Action, 221–4, 226–30
    government denial of, 98, 102–5, 113, 226–7
    illegal, 17, 113, 226–7
strong mayor powers,
    anti-democratic reforms and, 188, 195–200, 202–3
    Ford government pushing, 169, 176, 192, 194–7
    legislation, *see* Strong Mayors, Building Homes Act
    US systems of, 202–3
    veto authority through, 188, 195, 198–9, 203
Strong Mayors, Building Homes Act (SMBHA, Bill 3): 188, 191, 197–8
Stryland, Krista, 93
students, 5, 42, 119
    financial literacy, 43, 45–8
    funding ratio for, 7, 48–9, 53–5, 64–5, 69
    protests by, 38–9, 102–3
Supercrawl (Hamilton), 33, 35

TACC (The Amazing Construction Company), 160–2, 164
Tanenbaum, Peter, 163–4
Taverner, Rod, 157
taxation, 19, 25
    breaks for wealthy, 1, 24, 26, 158, 222
    carbon, 5, 172
    Conservative policies on, 4–5, 120, 172, 180, 222
    corporate, 1, 14, 24–6, 115
    credits, 50, 145–7
    Ford weakening system of, 24–5, 115, 205
    gas, 19, 174
    lack of transparency on, 25–6, 199
    poverty rates and, 123–4, 127
    property, 201, 205
    revenue, 6, 24, 205
    subsidies, 5, 14, 26, 115–16, 166
    wealth, 14, 127, 130–1
teachers,
    ratios to children, 49, 144
    scapegoating of, 43, 46, 51–2
    strike actions by, 106, 115
    wages/working conditions, 44, 109, 147
tenants,
    dispute resolution, 70, 72, 80–4
    eviction of, 76, 207–13, 215–18
    exploiting for profit, 203, 210–13
    struggles for rights, 207–8, 213–18, 225
Teneycke, Kory, 9, 167
Thatcher, Margaret, 2, 220
The People's Health Care Act (Bill 74): 185–6
Therme Spa (Ontario Place), 158, 167, 178, 202
Thompson, Lisa, 42, 146–7
Tibollo, Michael, 32
time allocation, use of, 182–4, 189–92
Todd, Ian, 157
Toronto, 9, 230
    City Council ward boundaries, 187, 194–5

cost of living in, 123–4
COVID-19 impacts in, 36, 147–8
elections, 187, 195–6, 203
Ford as councillor in, 8, 41
government funding cuts in, 29, 32–3, 92, 146–7, 158
infrastructure backlogs, 173, 178, 204–5
provincial interference in, 194–202
strong mayor powers in, 188, 192, 195–200, 202–3
tenant organizing in, 207–8, 213–18, 224–5, 229
Toronto District School Board, 49, 155
tourism, 7, 30
funding cuts, 29, 32–3, 39
Tranjan, Ricardo, 48–9
Treaty No. 9: 132–4, 136–9
lawsuit over, 141–2
Tribunals Ontario,
case backlog, 77–8, 80–2
creation and Conservative involvement, 70–1, 74–5, 83–4
loss of in-person hearings, 75–6, 79
Trudeau, Justin, 127, 136
Trump, Donald, 8
Truth and Reconciliation Commission Calls to Action, 31, 42
tuition,
claims of reducing/freezing, 54–5, 57, 64–5, 242n7
increases, 47, 53, 61, 67–9
privatization and, 56–7
university dependence on, 54–5, 57, 68–9

unionization, 14, 17, 111–12, 115
unions, 229–30
government/corporate work against, 49, 61, 103–6, 121, 220, 226–7
legislation against, 16, 32, 38, 43, 103–5
organized labour versus, 11–12, 114–15, 223–4
public sector, 16
strikes by, *see* strikes, worker
worker perceptions of, 113–14, 122, 227–8

universities, 102–3
competition among, 54–7
corporatization of, 53–4, 57, 67–8
funding, lack of, 36–8, 55–9, 64–5, 68–9
Northern Ontario, 53–4 57, 59–61, 67, 69
privatization of, 53–9, 66, 68
public, 53–9, 61–3, 65–9, 242n12
"publicly supported," 53, 57–8
see also postsecondary education; tuition
University of Niagara Falls (UNF), 55–6
University of Toronto, 53, 57, 242n8
Up Here Festival, 35
Usher, Alex, 58, 66, 242n21

wages, 147, 228
caps/declines for, 15–19, 46, 98, 110, 158, 226
frozen/stagnant, 4, 14–15, 18–19, 38
grid for, 145, 150, 152–3
growth in, 15–16, 18, 27, 102, 109
inadequate, 18, 101, 104–6, 121–2
living, 123–4, 127–30, 206
minimum *see* minimum wage
union versus non-union, 109–10
wealthy versus average, 23, 108–9
Wake, David, 162–4
Walton, Laura, 106, 227
wealth, 136
concentration of, 8, 14–15, 102, 108–11, 130
inequality, 1, 43, 46, 102, 127
redistribution, 3, 12, 26, 130
upward transfer of, 11, 24, 120–1
wealthy,
earnings/profits of, 108–9, 130
government focus on, 15, 23–4, 26, 219–20
networking/connections of, 2–3
power/resources of, 5, 8, 11, 213
taxation of, 1, 14, 24, 127, 130–1
Weir, Sean, 74–5
workers,
gig, 11, 14, 122
health care, 13, 16, 86–7, 97–104, 107–8, 147

industrial relations system resistance, 112–14
migrant, 17, 26–7, 109–10, 114, 206
non-unionized, 11, 105, 109
part-time versus full-time, 15, 115, 123, 130
personal support (PSWs), 16, 99
public sector, 19, 105, 111, 113, 187, 226
unionized, 10, 17, 109, 115
wage caps/declines for, *see* wages
see also minimum wage; strikes, worker; unions

working class, 3, 59
Ford messaging to, 9–11
government policies versus, 2, 228–9
heterogeneity of, 11–12
mobilizing, 65, 223–6

workplaces, 102–4, 205–6
injuries/violence in, 11, 51, 70, 99, 197
inspections, decline in, 17, 110
union organizing in, 11, 112–13, 115

Wynne, Kathleen, 42, 153–4, 189, 222

Your Health Act (Bill 60): 165, 186, 191